Buddhist Philosophy

Buddhist Philosophy

A Comparative Approach

Edited by Steven M. Emmanuel

Virginia Wesleyan College
VA, USA

This edition first published 2018
© 2018 John Wiley & Sons, Inc.

We gratefully acknowledge the following for granting us permission to use their material in this book:

"From the Five Aggregates to Phenomenal Consciousness: Towards a Cross-Cultural Cognitive Science," by Jake Davis and Evan Thompson, reprinted in expanded and revised form from *A Companion to Buddhist Philosophy* ed. Steven Emmanuel, Copyright © 2013 John Wiley & Sons, Inc. Used with permission.

All rights reserved. No part of this publication may be reproduced, stored in a retrieval system, or transmitted, in any form or by any means, electronic, mechanical, photocopying, recording or otherwise, except as permitted by law. Advice on how to obtain permission to reuse material from this title is available at www.wiley.com/go/permissions.

The right of Steven M. Emmanuel to be identified as the author of the editorial material in this work has been asserted in accordance with law.

Registered Office
John Wiley & Sons, Inc., 111 River Street, Hoboken, NJ 07030, USA

Editorial Office
350 Main Street, Malden, MA 02148-5020, USA

For details of our global editorial offices, customer services, and more information about Wiley products visit us at www.wiley.com.

Wiley also publishes its books in a variety of electronic formats and by print-on-demand. Some content that appears in standard print versions of this book may not be available in other formats.

Limit of Liability/Disclaimer of Warranty
While the publisher and editor have used their best efforts in preparing this book, they make no representations or warranties with respect to the accuracy or completeness of the contents of this book and specifically disclaim any implied warranties of merchantability or fitness for a particular purpose. It is sold on the understanding that the publisher is not engaged in rendering professional services and neither the publisher nor the author shall be liable for damages arising herefrom. If professional advice or other expert assistance is required, the services of a competent professional should be sought.

Library of Congress Cataloging-in-Publication Data

Names: Emmanuel, Steven M., editor.
Title: Buddhist philosophy : a comparative approach / edited by Steven M. Emmanuel, Virginia Wesleyan College, VA, US.
Other titles: Buddhist philosophy (John Wiley & Sons)
Description: First edition. | Hoboken : Wiley, 2018. | Includes bibliographical references and index.
Identifiers: LCCN 2017017089 (print) | LCCN 2017017825 (ebook) |
  ISBN 9781119068259 (pdf) | ISBN 9781119068402 (epub) |
  ISBN 9781119068242   (cloth) | ISBN 9781119068419 (pbk.)
Subjects: LCSH: Buddhist philosophy.
Classification: LCC B162 (ebook) | LCC B162 .B848 2017 (print) | DDC 181/.043—dc23
LC record available at https://lccn.loc.gov/2017017089

Cover image: © Jonathan Fife/Gettyimages
Cover design: Wiley

Set in 10/12pt Warnock by SPi Global, Pondicherry, India
Printed and bound in Malaysia by Vivar Printing Sdn Bhd

10 9 8 7 6 5 4 3 2 1

Contents

Notes on Contributors *vii*
Acknowledgments *xi*
Abbreviations *xiii*

Editor's Introduction *1*
Steven M. Emmanuel

1 Buddhist Philosophy as a Way of Life: The Spiritual Exercises of Tsongkhapa *11*
   Christopher W. Gowans

2 The Other Side of Realism: Panpsychism and Yogācāra *29*
   Douglas Duckworth

3 Emergentist Naturalism in Early Buddhism and Deweyan Pragmatism *45*
   John J. Holder

4 Metaphysical Dependence, East and West *63*
   Ricki Bliss and Graham Priest

5 Metaphysics and Metametaphysics with Buddhism: The Lay of the Land *87*
   Tom J.F. Tillemans

6 Are Reasons Causally Relevant for Action? Dharmakīrti and the Embodied Cognition Paradigm *109*
   Christian Coseru

7 Zen's Nonegocentric Perspectivism *123*
   Bret W. Davis

8   **Rhetoric of Uncertainty in Zen Buddhism and Western Literary Modernism**   *145*
    Steven Heine

9   **From the Five Aggregates to Phenomenal Consciousness: Toward a Cross-Cultural Cognitive Science**   *165*
    Jake H. Davis and Evan Thompson

10 **Embodying Change: Buddhism and Feminist Philosophy**   *189*
    Erin A. McCarthy

11 **Buddhist Modernism and Kant on Enlightenment**   *205*
    David Cummiskey

12 **Compassion and Rebirth: Some Ethical Implications**   *221*
    John Powers

    Further Reading   *239*
    Index   *243*

Notes on Contributors

Ricki Bliss is Assistant Professor of Philosophy at Lehigh University. Her publications include "On Being Humean about the Emptiness of Causation," in *The Moon Points Back*, edited by Yasuo Deguchi, Jay Garfield, Graham Priest, and Koji Tanaka (Oxford University Press, 2015); "Viciousness and Circles of Ground," *Metaphilosophy* 45(2) (2014); and "Viciousness and the Structure of Reality," *Philosophical Studies* 166(2) (2013).

Christian Coseru is Associate Professor in the Department of Philosophy at the College of Charleston. He is the author of *Perceiving Reality: Consciousness, Intentionality, and Cognition in Buddhist Philosophy* (Oxford University Press, 2012), in addition to a number of articles that explore topics in Buddhist metaphysics and epistemology, including "Buddhism, Comparative Neurophilosophy, and Human Flourishing," *Zygon* 49(1); "Taking the Intentionality of Perception Seriously: Why Phenomenology is Inescapable," *Philosophy East and West* 65(3); "Dignāga and Dharmakīrti on Perception and Self-Awareness," in *The Buddhist World*, edited by John Powers (Routledge, 2013); and "Reason and Experience in Buddhist Epistemology," in *A Companion to Buddhist Philosophy*, edited by Steven M. Emmanuel (Wiley-Blackwell, 2013).

David Cummiskey is Professor and Chair of Philosophy at Bates College. His research focuses on contemporary issues in moral philosophy, political theory, and intercultural philosophy. He is the author of *Kantian Consequentialism* (Oxford University Press, 1996). Recent articles include "Comparative Reflections on Buddhist Political Thought: Asoka, Shambhala and the General Will," in *A Companion to Buddhist Philosophy*, edited by Steven M. Emmanuel (Wiley-Blackwell, 2013); "Competing Conceptions of the Self in Kantian and Buddhist Moral Theories," in *Cultivating Personhood: Kant and Asian Philosophy* (Walter de Gruyter, 2010); and "Dignity, Contractualism, and Consequentialism," *Utilitas* 20(4) (2008).

Bret W. Davis is Associate Professor of Philosophy at Loyola University Maryland. Among his books are *Heidegger and the Will: On the Way to Gelassenheit* (Northwestern University Press, 2007); co-edited with Brian Schroeder and Jason M. Wirth, *Japanese and Continental Philosophy: Conversations with the Kyoto School* (Indiana University Press, 2011); and co-edited with Fujita Masakatsu, *Sekai no naka no Nihon no tetsugaku* (Japanese Philosophy in the World) (Showado, 2005). He has also published numerous articles in English and in Japanese on continental and comparative philosophy, on the Kyoto School, and on Zen.

Jake H. Davis is Visiting Assistant Professor of Religious Studies at Brown University. He trained in Buddhist theory and meditative practice under the meditation master Sayadaw U Pandita of Burma and served for a decade as an interpreter between Burmese and English for meditation retreats in Burma and abroad. He has authored and co-authored articles at the intersection of Buddhist philosophy, moral philosophy, and cognitive science, and is editor of the forthcoming volume, '*A Mirror is For Reflection*': *Understanding Buddhist Ethics* (Oxford University Press).

Douglas Duckworth is Associate Professor of Philosophy at Temple University. He is the author of *Mipam on Buddha-Nature: The Ground of the Nyingma Tradition* (SUNY Press, 2008) and *Jamgön Mipam: His Life and Teachings* (Shambhala, 2011). He also translated Bötrül's *Distinguishing the Views and Philosophies: Illuminating Emptiness in a Twentieth-Century Tibetan Buddhist Classic* (SUNY Press, 2011).

Christopher W. Gowans is Professor of Philosophy at Fordham University. In addition to his numerous articles on topics in moral philosophy and Buddhist thought, he is the editor of *Moral Disagreements* (Routledge, 2000) and *Moral Dilemmas* (Oxford University Press, 1989), and author of *Buddhist Moral Philosophy: An Introduction* (Routledge, 2014) and *Philosophy of the Buddha* (Routledge, 2003).

Steven Heine is Professor of Religious Studies and History as well as Associate Director of the School of International and Public Affairs and Director of Asian Studies at Florida International University. His research specialty is the origins and development of Zen Buddhism, especially the life and teachings of Dōgen, founder of the Sōtō sect. He has published two dozen books, including *The Zen Poetry of Dōgen* (Tuttle, 1997) and, with Oxford University Press, *Opening a Mountain* (2002), *Did Dōgen Go to China?* (2006), *Zen Masters* (2010), and *Dōgen: Textual and Historical Studies* (2012).

John J. Holder is Associate Professor of Philosophy at St. Norbert College. He is the author of *Early Buddhist Discourses* (Hackett, 2006), a volume containing

English translations of Pāli discourses that are essential for the study of early Buddhist philosophy. He has also published articles on early Buddhist epistemology, ethics, and social theory, including "A Survey of Early Buddhist Epistemology," in *A Companion to Buddhist Philosophy*, edited by Steven M. Emmanuel (Wiley-Blackwell, 2013). His research focus is on comparative philosophy, specifically comparing early Buddhism and classical American pragmatism with the aim of developing a naturalistic theory of aesthetics and religious meaning.

Erin A. McCarthy is Professor of Philosophy at St. Lawrence University. Her research interests include Asian, feminist, continental, and comparative philosophy. She is the author of *Ethics Embodied: Rethinking Selfhood through Continental, Japanese and Feminist Philosophies* (Lexington, 2010).

John Powers is Research Professor at the Alfred Deakin Institute for Citizenship and Globalisation, Deakin University. A specialist in Tibetan Buddhism, he is the author of numerous articles and books, including *A Bull of a Man: Images of Masculinity, Sex and the Body in Indian Buddhism* (Harvard University Press, 2009), *A Concise Introduction to Tibetan Buddhism* (Snow Lion Publications, 2008), and *Introduction to Tibetan Buddhism* (Snow Lion Publications, 2007).

Graham Priest is Boyce Gibson Professor of Philosophy at the University of Melbourne, Distinguished Professor at the Graduate Center, City University of New York, and Arché Professorial Fellow at the University of St. Andrews. His books include *In Contradiction* (Nijhoff, 1987), *Beyond the Limits of Thought* (Clarendon Press, 2002), *Towards Non-Being* (Clarendon Press, 2005), *Doubt Truth to be a Liar* (Clarendon Press, 2006), and *Introduction to Non-Classical Logic* (Cambridge University Press, 2008).

Evan Thompson is Professor of Philosophy at the University of Toronto. He is the author of *Waking, Dreaming, Being: Self and Consciousness in Neuroscience, Meditation, and Philosophy* (Columbia University Press, 2014), and *Mind in Life: Biology, Phenomenology, and the Sciences of Mind* (Harvard University Press, 2007); co-author of *The Embodied Mind: Cognitive Science and Human Experience* (MIT Press, 1991); and co-editor of *Self, No Self? Perspectives from Analytical, Phenomenological, and Indian Traditions* (Oxford University Press, 2010).

Tom J.F. Tillemans is Emeritus Professor of Buddhist Studies at the University of Lausanne, Switzerland. He is the author of numerous books and articles on Buddhism and currently serves as editor in chief of the "84000" (see http://84000.co), a long-term project to translate Buddhist canonical literature.

Acknowledgments

Thanks to Wiley-Blackwell for permission to reprint an expanded version of Jake H. Davis and Evan Thompson's "From the Five Aggregates to Phenomenal Consciousness: Towards a Cross-Cultural Cognitive Science," which first appeared in *A Companion to Buddhist Philosophy* (Wiley-Blackwell, 2013).

Thanks also to the editorial team at Wiley-Blackwell for skillfully guiding this volume through every phase of its production.

Finally, I would like to express my deep gratitude to the contributors for generously lending their scholarly expertise to this project.

Abbreviations

Bibliographical

AN   *Aṅguttara Nikāya: The Book of the Gradual Sayings.* Trans. F.L. Woodward and E.M. Hare. 5 vols. London: Pali Text Society, 1932–36; *The Numerical Discourses of the Buddha.* Trans. Bhikkhu Bodhi. Boston: Wisdom, 2012.
DN   *Dīgha Nikāya: Dialogues of the Buddha.* Trans. T.W. Rhys Davids and C.A.F. Rhys Davids. 3 vols. London: Pali Text Society, 1899–1921; *Long Discourses of the Buddha.* Trans. M. Walshe. Second rev. edn. Boston: Wisdom, 1996.
MN   *Majjhima Nikāya: The Collection of the Middle Length Sayings.* Trans. I.B. Horner. 3 vols. London: Pali Text Society, 1954–59; *The Middle Length Discourses of the Buddha.* Trans. Bhikku Ñāṇamoli and Bhikku Bodhi. Boston: Wisdom, 1995.
MN-a   *Majjhima Nikāya Aṭṭhakathā (Papañcasūdani).* Commentary on MN.
SN   *Saṃyutta Nikāya: The Book of the Kindred Sayings.* Trans. C.A.F. Rhys Davids and F.L. Woodward. London: Pali Text Society, 1917–30; *The Connected Discourses of the Buddha.* Trans. Bhikkhu Bodhi. Boston: Wisdom, 2005.
Sn   *Sutta-nipāta: The Group of Discourses.* Trans. K.R. Norman. Second edn. London: Pali Text Society, 2001.

General

Ch.   Chinese
Eng.   English
Gk   Greek
Jp.   Japanese
K.   Korean
Skt   Sanskrit
Tb.   Tibetan

Editor's Introduction
Steven M. Emmanuel

In 1906, William DeWitt Hyde, then president of Bowdoin College, penned the words to "The Offer of the College," his inspiring statement of the value of a liberal education. Chief among the benefits he cited was the promise of becoming a citizen of the world – or as Hyde more elegantly put it, the ability to "be at home in all lands and all ages; …to carry the keys of the world's library in your pocket, and feel its resources behind you in whatever task you undertake" (Hyde 1906, 3). In retrospect, one would have to say that the claim to global literacy was something of an overstatement. For the students of Bowdoin's class of 1906, the world's library did not extend beyond the classics of the Western tradition. In the philosophy department, for instance, where Hyde served as a faculty member, the curriculum was comprised mainly of courses in psychology ("treated from the point of view of natural science"), introduction to philosophy (being a survey of the familiar "problems" and their proposed "solutions"), history of philosophy (focused on the formation of "the occidental mind"), and ethics (organized around the writings of Plato, Aristotle, Mill, and Spencer).[1]

While the curricula of American universities and colleges would, over the course of the twentieth century, gradually expand to include the study of non-Western civilizations, academic philosophy would remain notably resistant to recognizing the contributions made to its subject matter by other cultures. Indeed, the curriculum taught by Hyde in 1906 was not very different from what we would find in many philosophy departments today, especially in the way it approached the study of mind from "the point of view of natural science." The insularity of the profession is reflected in the "American Philosophical Association Statement on the Philosophy Major," which explicitly aligns the discipline with "an intellectual and historical tradition that began some 2,500 years ago in the Greek culture of the eastern Mediterranean region."[2] Although the statement does acknowledge the existence of "similar developments" in other cultures, it goes on to define the scope of the discipline by reference to

Buddhist Philosophy: A Comparative Approach, First Edition. Edited by Steven M. Emmanuel.
© 2018 John Wiley & Sons, Inc. Published 2018 by John Wiley & Sons, Inc.

the prominent figures and texts of the Western canon. Even in the association's statement regarding the "global character" of philosophy – where one might have expected to find a robust call for greater diversity in the curriculum – the reader is merely cautioned that "[t]erms such as 'History of Philosophy,' 'Ancient Philosophy,' and even 'the Classics' are ambiguous" and can easily give rise to confusion, "as when a specialist in the history of Chinese philosophy applies for a job advertised as 'history of philosophy,' in the expectation that his or her specialization is among those sought; usually such expectations will be disappointed."[3]

Despite the narrow Eurocentric focus of the profession, interest in Asian philosophy has risen steadily in recent decades. This research has been supported mainly by independent societies and a handful of peer-reviewed journals dedicated to publishing articles in area and comparative studies. We have also seen a noticeable increase in the number of titles on Asian philosophy coming from the most highly respected academic presses. Yet, philosophy departments have been slow to reflect these developments in their course offerings. Even at some of the nation's most prominent institutions, which have large, well-staffed philosophy programs,[4] students who wish to become acquainted with Eastern thought must look for opportunities in other departments. When Asian philosophy courses do appear, they are often limited to a single general survey. These courses vary in scope, from presentations of major themes in classical Chinese philosophy or Buddhist thought, to sweeping overviews of the philosophical traditions of South and East Asia. Needless to say, the sheer breadth of such courses does not allow for a very detailed treatment of the material, let alone a substantive engagement with the diversity it represents.

The tendency to treat Western philosophy as though it were coextensive with the history of the subject is not a harmless conceit. For one thing, it fails to appreciate the fact that philosophy is a universal human activity, and that the Western tradition is but one strand of thinking about questions that have preoccupied human beings for millennia. It suggests, moreover, an artificial and misleading picture of the history and transmission of ideas – one that fails to acknowledge the extent to which the philosophical traditions of every culture have been shaped by their interactions with others. As Justin E.H. Smith observed in a *New York Times* piece on "Philosophy's Western Bias," what we call the "Western" tradition of philosophy is "in the end only a historiographical artifact, a result of our habit of beginning our histories when and where we do, for there was always influence from neighboring civilizations" (Smith 2012). One pertinent example of this influence is the crucial role that scholars in the Islamic world played in preserving, interpreting, and transmitting the ideas of ancient Greek philosophers to medieval Europe.[5] Smith's observation is not intended to diminish the value of the Western tradition, but rather to remind us that its richness "has always been a result of its place as a node in a global network through which ideas and things are always flowing. This was true in 500 B.C. and is no less true today" (Smith 2012).

There is a certain irony in the fact that globalization was already creating vibrant and diverse intellectual cultures throughout the pre-modern world – not least among these the ancient Greco-Buddhist and medieval Islamic civilizations that flourished in Central Asia[6] – and yet, in the present age of unprecedented global interconnectedness, we manage to proceed as though the philosophical traditions of half the world did not exist. This irony is not lost on Smith, who concludes his editorial with an admonition:

> Western academic philosophy will likely come to appear utterly parochial in the coming years if it does not find a way to approach non-Western traditions that is much more rigorous and respectful than the tokenism that reigns at present.
>
> *(Smith 2012)*

Accomplishing this goal will not be easy. First and foremost, it will mean committing ourselves to a philosophical pluralism that not only welcomes non-Western voices into the conversation but also engages them on their own terms. Further, it will mean fostering the kind of intellectual humility exhibited in Philip L. Quinn's acknowledgment that we "have much to learn about and from the philosophical theology of medieval Islam, Indian logic and metaphysics, Buddhist philosophy of mind and language, Confucian and Taoist ethics and social philosophy, Zen spirituality and other non-Western traditions" (Quinn 1996, 172).[7]

Progress toward a globalized philosophical curriculum will undoubtedly be incremental at best. But shifting demographics, combined with a growing recognition that we must prepare our students to live and work in a world of increasing economic and political interdependence, will provide added impetus to change. As Quinn noted twenty years ago, "the waxing economic power of Asia provides an argument from prudence for the conclusion that Americans ought to be learning a lot more than they currently are about Asian cultures, including their philosophical traditions" (Quinn 1996, 172). The force of that argument has not diminished.

However, the pluralist faces other, more practical challenges, as decisions about which courses should be offered and the depth of coverage they should receive are invariably tied to programming constraints and the limitation of resources. The literature comprising the Western tradition is vast, and many departments already struggle with questions about how to provide adequate coverage of its history, seminal thinkers, texts, and problems. The prospect of adding the literatures of other cultural traditions complicates this task considerably. For smaller departments, faced with hard decisions about where to concentrate the talents and energies of their faculty, a truly globalized philosophy curriculum may seem virtually impossible to attain.

Even in departments that have the resources to expand, opponents of change may worry that pluralism threatens to undermine the integrity of the curriculum by promoting multiculturalism and inclusiveness at the expense of depth and specialization.[8] The preference for depth over breadth is stressed in the American Philosophical Association (APA) statement on the major, which notes that "[a] good understanding of a few important philosophers and central problems of philosophy is better than a mere acquaintance with many of them." Every philosophy major, we are told, should be introduced to the writings of figures "whose historical importance is beyond dispute, such as Plato, Aristotle, Descartes, Hume, and Kant," as well as "various problems central to the major areas of philosophical inquiry, pertaining to the world's and our own nature and existence (metaphysics), the knowledge we may have of them (epistemology), sound reasoning (logic), and human conduct (ethics)." These elements are said to constitute the "core" of a good philosophy program, which can then be filled out with a complement of courses that reflect the particular interests of a department. Here, however, the decision to cover non-Western traditions must compete with the potential value of exploring other periods of Western thought (e.g., Hellenistic or medieval philosophy) or other important subfields of philosophical inquiry, or adding courses in applied philosophy, or utilizing the research specializations of the faculty to engage in a deeper study of selected topics related to the core.

Let us be clear about the nature of the problem. The pluralist's goal is not, as some in the academy fear, to overturn the Western philosophical canon, but rather to broaden and enrich the curriculum by adding other cultural voices to the conversation.[9] As Jay L. Garfield and Bryan W. Van Norden explain,

> Clearly, there is nothing intrinsically wrong with philosophy written by males of European descent; but philosophy has always become richer as it becomes increasingly diverse and pluralistic. Thomas Aquinas (1225–1274) recognized this when he followed his Muslim colleagues in reading the work of the pagan philosopher Aristotle, thereby broadening the philosophical curriculum of universities in his own era. We hope that American philosophy departments will someday teach Confucius as routinely as they now teach Kant, that philosophy students will eventually have as many opportunities to study the "Bhagavad Gita" as they do the "Republic"....
>
> *(Garfield and Van Norden 2016)*

The question is whether, given the aforementioned constraints, we can realistically hope to accomplish this goal while honoring our commitment to preserve and transmit what is most valuable in the Western tradition. Can we do better than simply adding a perfunctory survey course on Asian philosophy?

Must we settle for what John J. Stuhr has called "a pluralism by partition," or a "mere plurality" (Stuhr 1997, 52) that amounts to the kind of tokenism decried by Smith?

It is the premise of this volume that we can do better. The goal of adding diversity to the philosophy curriculum does not require a proliferation of courses. A meaningful pluralism can be achieved simply by introducing a comparative element into the courses we already teach – that is, expanding our inquiry into the central problems of philosophy by incorporating the ideas and arguments of thinkers from other traditions. This comparative approach sidesteps concerns about watering down the curriculum, as it offers us a natural way of integrating different cultural perspectives into any course at any level, whether an introduction to philosophy, an advanced seminar in analytic epistemology, or a course on feminist thought.

The present volume demonstrates how a "more rigorous and respectful" engagement with the great thinkers and texts of the Buddhist tradition can expand and enrich our philosophical discourse. The contributors are all trained in the Western tradition but have a firm grounding in Buddhist philosophical literature. While the approach they take is comparative, their goal is not merely to provide descriptive accounts of what influential Buddhist thinkers have written. Nor is it simply to pose Western questions and look for Buddhist answers to them. Rather, the contributors have set up their discussions in a way that allows for a genuine cross-cultural dialogue by engaging Buddhist thinkers on their own terms, thereby allowing different questions and answers to be framed through the Buddhist texts.

The comparative approach modeled in this volume is informed by a deeper understanding of diversity – one that moves beyond the tokenism that *includes* but does not necessarily *value* different points of view. For what the pluralist seeks is not merely variety, but a richer sort of diversity that implies what Peter D. Hershock calls "a distinctive and achieved quality of interaction" (Hershock 2012, 49). Among other things, this means engaging culturally different perspectives in a way that allows for a process of rigorous critical assessment in both directions. As Julian Baggini commented in a recent piece,

> The point of cross-cultural inquiry is not to reach some kind of warm, ecumenical mutual understanding, rooted in profound respect for difference. Rather it is to see that our questions are not the only ones worth asking and that by considering others, we might not only open up new vistas but also see our familiar intellectual territory in a different light.
> *(Baggini 2016)*

A substantive engagement with Buddhist thought creates opportunities for us to gain insight into the nature of the philosophical process by reflecting on the kinds of questions we ask and the methods we use to arrive at answers to them.[10] It may even point to the limitations of certain questions that have been central to the Western tradition – questions that may not be as useful or meaningful today as they were in earlier times, and perhaps never were for thinkers in other traditions.

A key feature of this volume is the recognition that philosophical traditions are not monolithic. The history of Buddhist thought is long, culturally diverse, and informed by different textual traditions. One is always on thin ice when making blanket generalizations about what "Buddhists" think. The Western tradition is similarly heterogeneous, with a wide variety of methods and approaches having developed over the course of its rich history. For this reason, the chapters are organized around the writings of prominent thinkers and movements in Buddhist and Western thought, with a view to reflecting the diversity found within each tradition.

In the opening chapter Gowans compares Buddhist and Hellenistic conceptions of philosophy as a way of life. Focusing on a seminal text in Tibetan Buddhist literature, Tsongkhapa's *Great Treatise*, the discussion highlights the similarities between the two traditions, but also draws attention to some important differences between Tsongkhapa's approach, which emphasizes the importance of serenity meditation as a basis for sound philosophical reflection, and the various forms of "spiritual exercise" presented in Stoic and Epicurean writings.

Duckworth (Chapter 2) offers an illuminating discussion of the sixth-century philosopher Dignāga that draws important parallels between his Yogācāra theory and the panpsychism developed in the work of F.H. Bradley and others. The result is a nuanced reinterpretation of Dignāga's position that reveals it to be more complex than the version of subjective idealism commonly ascribed to him.

Holder (Chapter 3) explores the deep connections between Deweyan pragmatism and early Buddhist metaphysics. Borrowing philosophical ideas from each tradition, he constructs a strong ontological form of emergentist naturalism: a metaphysical view that represents a middle way between dualism and reductive physicalism.

Bliss and Priest (Chapter 4) investigate the concept of metaphysical dependence. They show that while Buddhist and Western philosophers put forward radically different accounts of the dependence relation (Buddhist accounts being largely anti-foundationalist, and Western accounts largely foundationalist), careful consideration of the arguments developed on each side provides rich opportunities for cross-cultural dialogue and critical reassessment.

Tillemans (Chapter 5) moves from metaphysical questions about the nature of reality to second-order questions about metaphysics itself. After sketching out the main types of metaphysical argumentation found in the Buddhist literature, he presents a comparative examination of various Buddhist meta-ontological stances, and considers the implications of these positions for traditional Buddhist teachings.

Coseru (Chapter 6) puts the seventh-century Indian Buddhist philosopher Dharmakīrti into conversation with contemporary epistemologists regarding the relation between reasons and causes. He shows that the causal model of embodied cognition implied in Dharmakīrti's theory of inference can be read as a version of "process externalism," according to which reasons depend on bodily processes that are embedded in the environment.

Davis (Chapter 7) discerns in Zen's nondualist approach a form of perspectivism that differs from egocentric versions of the theory developed in the West, most notably by Nietzsche. This nonegoistic perspectivism involves more than an awareness of the limits of any particular knowledge claim. In Zen Buddhism, meditation on the emptiness of the self cultivates one's ability to respond empathetically and compassionately to the world by alternately occupying the perspectives of "host" and "guest." Thus, like Nietzsche's theory, Zen offers a way of appreciating perspectival plurality, but it differs from Nietzsche's theory in offering a way of "engaging in perspectival delimitation in a manner that is neither willful nor egocentric."

Heine (Chapter 8) compares the view of enlightenment found in the kōan collection known as the *Blue Cliff Record* with the notion of epiphany developed in the writings of James Joyce. The discussion focuses on the rhetorical strategies of uncertainty, ambiguity, and incompleteness which, in the case of the Buddhist trainee, create the conditions for an instantaneous spiritual awakening, and in the case of Joyce's reader, a sudden and profound insight into a character whose deeper motives and reactions are not directly revealed in the story.

Davis and Thompson (Chapter 9) draw primarily on Pāli textual sources to develop a cross-cultural approach to cognitive science. In this expanded version of a chapter that was originally published in *A Companion to Buddhist Philosophy* (Emmanuel 2013), the authors combine a traditional Buddhist framework for understanding mind and the practice of mindfulness meditation with scientific methods currently used by clinical researchers to investigate the relation between attention and consciousness.

McCarthy (Chapter 10) employs the radical nondualism of Zen to develop a comparative feminist philosophical framework for the project of revalorizing women's bodies. Drawing on the writings of the thirteenth-century Zen master Dōgen, she demonstrates how the perspective of emptiness can help us transcend the limiting conceptualizations of "feminine" and "masculine" without discarding the difference of gender as the "lived experience of being in differently sexed bodies."

Cummiskey (Chapter 11) compares the concept of enlightenment developed in early modern European thought and Buddhist Modernism.[11] He shows that while both call for "a transformative reorientation of the self," socially engaged Buddhism presents a more complete account of the integration of personal moral development and social engagement, as well as of the challenges involved in achieving enlightenment.

In the concluding chapter, Powers reexamines the role of rebirth in Buddhist thought in light of the tendency among modernist Buddhists to downplay the importance of that teaching. Powers' discussion not only illuminates the deeper ethical implications of rebirth for understanding Buddhist compassion and social engagement, but also demonstrates some of the dangers involved in comparative studies that attempt to decontextualize Buddhist ideas.

Notes

1 *Catalogue of Bowdoin College & the Medical School of Maine for the Year 1906–1907* (Cambridge: The University Press, 1906), 62–64.
2 Published in *Proceedings and Addresses of the American Philosophical Association* 80(5): 76 (2007).
3 Published in *Proceedings and Addresses of the American Philosophical Association* 66(5): 38 (1992).
4 For example, as of this writing, the departments at Princeton and Yale offer no courses in Asian philosophy.
5 For a detailed account of this see Watt (1972).
6 See Beckwith (2011, 2015).
7 From an address presented at the Eastern Division Meeting of the APA on December 28, 1995. It was part of a symposium sponsored by the Metaphysical Society of America and the Society for the Advancement of American Philosophy and published the following year in *Proceedings and Addresses of the American Philosophical Association* 70(2): 167–187 (1996).
8 See Stuhr (1997, 82).
9 Even Smith (2012) concedes that the West has "an extremely rich philosophical tradition – one of the two or three richest, in fact – and it is eminently worthy of preservation and transmission to future generations."
10 J.B. Schneewind notes this role for comparative philosophy: "We find striking parallels in philosophies in different cultures at different times, and we can see how similar contexts shape problems in similar ways. If globalized history can produce more cases like this, it might help us to a better understanding of philosophy as a cultural form" (Schneewind 2005, 176).
11 For a comprehensive discussion of the development of Buddhism in the West, see McMahan (2008).

References

Baggini, Julian. 2016. "What Is the Self? It Depends." *New York Times*, February 8.
Beckwith, Christopher I. 2011. *Empires of the Silk Road: A History of Central Eurasia from the Bronze Age to the Present.* Princeton: Princeton University Press.

Beckwith, Christopher I. 2015. *Greek Buddha: Pyrrho's Encounter with Early Buddhism in Central Asia*. Princeton: Princeton University Press.
Emmanuel, Steven M. 2013. *A Companion to Buddhist Philosophy*. Malden: Wiley-Blackwell.
Garfield, Jay L. and Van Norden, Bryan W. 2016. "If Philosophy Won't Diversify, Let's Call It What It Really Is." *New York Times*, May 11.
Hershock, Peter D. 2012. *Valuing Diversity: Buddhist Reflection on Realizing a More Equitable Global Future*. Albany: SUNY Press.
Hyde, William DeWitt. 1906. *The College Man and the College Woman*. Boston and New York: Houghton Mifflin Company.
McMahan, David L. 2008. *The Making of Buddhist Modernism*. New York: Oxford University Press.
Quinn, Philip L. 1996. "Pluralism in Philosophy Departments." *Proceedings and Addresses of the American Philosophical Association* 70(2): 168–172.
Schneewind, J.B. 2005. "Globalization and the History of Philosophy." *Journal of the History of Ideas* 66(2): 169–178.
Smith, Justin E.H. 2012. "Philosophy's Western Bias." *New York Times*, June 3.
Stuhr, John J. 1997. *Genealogical Pragmatism: Philosophy, Experience, and Community*. Albany: SUNY Press.
Watt, M.W. 1972. *The Influence of Islam on Medieval Europe*. Edinburgh: Edinburgh University Press [reprinted 1987].

1

Buddhist Philosophy as a Way of Life: The Spiritual Exercises of Tsongkhapa

Christopher W. Gowans

Pierre Hadot's signature theme, that for which he is best known – indeed what made him rather well known – is his thesis that the ancient Greek and Roman philosophers regarded "philosophy as a way of life" devoted to bringing about a radical transformation of the self, so as to attain genuine well-being, through the practice of an ensemble of "spiritual exercises," of which the study of philosophical discourses is one part, but by no means the only or even most important part.[1] As an interpretation of ancient philosophy, Hadot's thesis is not without its critics.[2] But I suspect that, for many, the interest in Hadot has as much to do with the attraction of regarding philosophy as having such a practical aim as it does with the accuracy of his proposal as an interpretation of the early formative period of Western philosophy. In any case, that philosophy, with its propensity for rather abstract and often esoteric modes of rational reflection, could have "living well" as its primary rationale is certainly a thought worthy of consideration.

It has been suggested that Hadot's understanding of philosophy as a way of life might be valuable in interpreting Buddhist thought and practice.[3] From one perspective, this is a rather natural suggestion. Buddhist practice often involves spiritual exercises, and Buddhist philosophy is sometimes intimately related to these exercises. However, more inquiry is needed to see just how fruitful this interpretive proposal may be. The great diversity of Buddhist traditions should caution us against the temptation to make unqualified statements in this regard.

In this chapter I explore this proposal by reference to a single important text: Tsongkhapa's *The Great Treatise on the Stages of the Path to Enlightenment* (*Byang chub lam rim che ba*) (Tsongkhapa 2000–2004). The *Great Treatise* is a lengthy discourse on a form of Buddhist practice, and an understanding of Buddhist philosophy plays a crucial role in this practice. Hence, we have considerable reason to expect that Hadot's notion of philosophy as a way of life will be an illuminating interpretive strategy in reading this text. Though I hope to fulfill this expectation, I will also propose that the differences between Tsongkhapa and Hadot's philosophers are as important as the similarities.

Buddhist Philosophy: A Comparative Approach, First Edition. Edited by Steven M. Emmanuel.
© 2018 John Wiley & Sons, Inc. Published 2018 by John Wiley & Sons, Inc.

A central lesson is that Buddhist philosophy as a way of life, as understood by Tsongkhapa, takes us in directions that depart in important ways from the philosophical ways of life considered by Hadot.

I will begin with a brief elaboration of some central themes in Hadot based on a distinction between the concept of philosophy as a way of life and particular conceptions of this idea that he supposed were dominant in ancient Greek and Roman philosophy. I will then examine the *Great Treatise* in some detail and argue that it clearly exemplifies Hadot's concept of philosophy as a way of life. Finally I will highlight some of the main ways that Tsongkhapa's particular conception of this converged and diverged from the conceptions of the philosophers featured in Hadot's accounts.

Hadot on Philosophy as a Way of Life

Though Hadot believed that his account of philosophy as a way of life applied rather broadly to ancient Greek and Roman philosophers, he stressed that in some respects these philosophers developed it in divergent ways. For example, there are key differences in the manner in which the Stoics and the Epicureans envisioned philosophy as a way of life. In light of this, and in light of my interest in employing Hadot's account in interpreting Tsongkhapa, it will be helpful to distinguish the *concept* of philosophy as a way of life and particular *conceptions* of philosophy as a way of life. The concept is the basic idea, that which is largely shared by all proponents of philosophy as a way of life, and the conceptions are different ways the proponents fill out this idea by explaining, elaborating, and applying it in accordance with their distinctive philosophical visions.[4]

There are two interrelated aspects to Hadot's concept of philosophy as a way of life (sometimes referred to as an "art of living"). First, it is supposed that, in their ordinary condition, human beings are quite deficient in well-being in significant respects, but human beings have the capacity to undergo a radical transformation so as to achieve, or at least approach, an ideal state in which there is genuine well-being (the state of "the sage"). The deficiencies pertain primarily to beliefs, desires, passions, and actions. These deficiencies render our lives unsatisfactory in some fundamental ways: we are frustrated, anxious, fearful, angry, alienated, and so on. The ideal state is characterized by some kind of understanding or wisdom, a high level of contentment typically involving tranquility (*ataraxia*), and (at least often) some form of moral virtue.

Second, it is thought that the way to bring about this transformation is to practice a set of spiritual exercises (*askēsis* or *meletē*) in which philosophy plays an essential, but not exclusive, role. The exercises are wide-ranging: they involve cognitive, affective, sensory, imaginative, volitional, moral, and other aspects of a person's character. They are needed because the obstacles to our well-being are deep and diverse: only exercises that alleviate the totality of these obstacles can hope to liberate us from the suffering that is our usual condition. Though many religious ways of life involve spiritual exercises, what is distinctive about the idea of philosophy as a way of life is that philosophical reflection is regarded as one of the essential spiritual exercises.[5] Philosophy, in this view, is not a specialized theoretical or academic discipline: it is a way of living for all persons, practiced at each moment, and it has a practical goal. Philosophy as a way of life involves philosophical reflection. But this intellectual activity is not sufficient by itself to live in this way and attain the goal of well-being: philosophical reflection must be combined with the full range of spiritual exercises to be effective.

The concept of philosophy as a way of life is nicely captured in a well-known statement attributed to Epicurus: "Empty are the words of that philosopher who offers therapy for no human suffering. For just as there is no use for medical expertise if it does not give therapy for bodily diseases, so too there is no use in philosophy if it does not expel the suffering of the soul" (Long and Sedley 1987, 155 (25C)). The medical analogy – that philosophy cures the soul just as medicine cures the body – was a prominent theme in ancient philosophy.[6] According to Hadot, "philosophy presented itself as a therapeutic, intended to cure mankind's anguish" (Hadot 1995, 265–266). That philosophy must be understood by reference to a set of exercises with this practical goal is the key idea in the concept of philosophy as a way of life.

The different conceptions of philosophy as a way of life are distinguished in part by the different ancient schools of philosophy and their distinctive metaphysics (physics), epistemology (logic), and ethics – those of the Platonists, Aristotelians, Stoics, Epicureans, Skeptics, and the like (but especially the Stoics and Epicureans, the schools that are constantly at the center of attention in Hadot's analysis). However, though the philosophical doctrines associated with these schools are important, much of the substance of Hadot's account of the different conceptions emerges in his discussion of the various spiritual exercises that he thinks were important for the ancient philosophers.[7] He believes that these exercises were communicated primarily through "oral instruction" and, lacking a text that systematically outlines them, Hadot provides a reconstruction based on a variety of sources.[8] According to Hadot, some of the exercises were common to different schools, but some were practiced or at least emphasized only in certain schools. In any case, these exercises will provide a fertile field for comparison with Tsongkhapa's *Great Treatise*.

As noted above, some of the exercises are in the neighborhood of what nowadays would be regarded as philosophical inquiry. Hadot says that "philosophical discourse is one of the forms of exercise of the philosophical way of life" (Hadot 2002, 178). This discourse justifies the way of life, and it is important to learn the doctrines it articulates as well as to reflect on, question, and examine these doctrines. A related exercise is intellectual dialogue concerning these doctrines in the context of a community. Socratic dialogue is a "communal spiritual exercise"

(Hadot 1995, 90). Also important are dialogues with one's self (meditations). Hence, rational reflection on and discussion of philosophical ideas are important parts of the spiritual exercises. To this extent, there is some resemblance to what goes on in a typical graduate seminar in philosophy today. The difference, Hadot insists, is that for the ancient schools, philosophical thought and conversation was in the service of – in fact was one part of – living a philosophical way of life, such as the life of the Stoic or the life of the Epicurean. But it was only one part since other spiritual exercises were also necessary and perhaps even more important. Living a philosophical way of life required understanding some philosophy, but it did not require anything resembling an academic degree in philosophy, as may be seen in a figure such as Marcus Aurelius.

Some spiritual exercises directly focused on the practical application of philosophical ideas. We needed to meditate on (*meletē*), remember (*mneme*), and have readily available for everyday use basic doctrines, practical maxims, and even arguments of the favored philosophy. This is why it was important to assimilate brief résumés of the philosophy such as Epictetus's *Handbook* (*Enchiridion*) or Epicurus's *Principal Doctrines* – and also very brief formulae such as the Epicurean's "fourfold remedy": "the gods are not to be feared, death is not to be dreaded; what is good is easy to acquire, what is bad is easy to bear" (Hadot 2002, 123). Likewise, it was valuable to incorporate the philosophies into our daily life, not only by thinking, but by writing. Hadot interprets Marcus's *Meditations* as a spiritual exercise – "exhortations to himself" – intended to transform himself throughout his life so as to live in accord with Stoic doctrine (see Hadot 1995, ch. 6; 1998, ch. 3; 2002, 177).

Other spiritual exercises were more overtly practical in that they were designed to transform our habits. They focused on eliminating or at least limiting various troublesome desires and passions. For example, enduring forms of physical depravation was undertaken to learn how to become detached from external goods that are not necessary for well-being. That these goods are not necessary is something philosophical reasoning could teach us. For instance, the Stoics argued that all external goods are unnecessary for well-being while the Epicureans maintained that well-being requires fulfillment only of natural and necessary desires. But understanding the teaching and its rationale needed to be supplemented by practical training that would reshape our habits so that we would no longer want the goods we now understood we did not need. Since there were many troublesome desires and passions there were many exercises devoted to alleviating their various demands. Other practical exercises also contributed to these ends – for example, for the Epicureans, these included daily examination of one's conscience, public confession, and correction by other members of the community.

Many spiritual exercises centered on the theme of "philosophy as training for death" first articulated by Socrates in Plato's *Phaedo* (Plato 2002, 67e; see Hadot 1995, 94). These diverse exercises sometimes reinforced one another and sometimes pulled in opposite directions. They included: learning to appreciate the insignificance of human affairs; coming to accept whatever happens in life; learning to live each day as if it were one's last; realizing that death is nothing to fear (either on account of immortality or because the dead do not experience being dead); knowing how to separate one's true self, the soul, from what is foreign to it, the body with its partial senses, desires, and passions; focusing on the present moment and its value; and contemplating nature and the universal, objective character of the cosmos or whole.

The last two points relate to two sets of exercises Hadot believes were especially important for the ancient philosophers. According to Hadot, the most important spiritual exercises involve attention (*prosoche*) and concentration. It is this above all that gives rise to the detachment, tranquility, and freedom that is characteristic of genuine well-being. One form of attention centers on the present moment. Another form focuses on the cosmos as a whole. Both of these are sometimes described in terms of meditations regarding the self or "I," the first a concentration of the "I" and the second an expansion of the "I" (see Hadot 2002, 189–211).

Focusing attention on the present moment means realizing that, since happiness is to be found only in the present, we should not be preoccupied with regrets about the past or worries about the future. Rather, we should recognize that the present has "infinite value" and is the only thing that really matters. However, Hadot thinks that directing attention to the present meant quite different things for the Stoics and the Epicureans. For the Stoics, we are to focus on what we choose and do, and be constantly watchful of the moral quality of these, in light of the recognition that our well-being is up to us, up to our choices and actions, and does not depend on what happens to us. We are to purify our intentions so as to bring our will into accord with the will of universal nature (identified as reason). For the Epicureans, we are to focus on what happens and the pleasure of existing in each moment, free from unwarranted fears (of the gods and death) and unfulfilled desires (that are unnatural or unnecessary). We are to enjoy pleasant memories and the pleasures of friendship, and we are to take joy in and feel gratitude for our existence. Hadot says that "Stoicism and Epicureanism do seem to correspond to two opposite but inseparable poles of our inner life: tension and relaxation, duty and serenity, moral conscience and the joy of existence" (Hadot 1995, 108).

Attention to the present moment is said to relate to attention to the cosmos or the whole (the totality of nature, the universe, the infinite, the All). In this mode of attention, we realize that we are a part of the cosmos and feel unified and in harmony with it. This recognition enables us to transcend our individuality and humanity. According to Hadot, "the sage never ceases to have the whole constantly present to mind. He thinks and acts within a cosmic perspective. He has the feeling of belonging to a whole which goes beyond the limits of his individuality" (Hadot 1995, 273). Another aspect of this mode of attention is that it allows us to look down on earth from above so as to situate ordinary human affairs in the cosmic perspective and realize their insignificance. This is said to impart a measure of objectivity, impartiality, and detachment to our outlook. According to Hadot, physics was meant to be a reasonable explanation of nature, but was always understood within this moral orientation (at least for the Hellenistic philosophers). Hence, for the Stoics physics allows us to accept our fate while for the Epicureans it enables us to overcome our fear of death and the gods.

There is tremendous richness in Hadot's account of the spiritual exercises. The diverse practices just outlined are interconnected in a variety of ways, and there are many details and differences between the various schools that I have not discussed. But this summary should be sufficient to bring his account into conversation with Tsongkhapa.

Tsongkhapa on Philosophy as a Way of Life

Tsongkhapa was a Buddhist monk who lived in Tibet in the fourteenth and fifteenth centuries (1357–1419). He is often considered Tibet's most important and influential Buddhist philosopher, and his *Great Treatise* of 1402 is commonly regarded as his best-known and most significant work. The Dalai Lama says that Tsongkhapa "is one of the very best Tibetan scholars," and that he carried a copy of the *Great Treatise* with him when he fled Tibet for India in 1959 (Dalai Lama 2013, 1–2). As we will see, this work clearly exemplifies Hadot's concept of philosophy as a way of life. To this extent it provides powerful support for the contention that Hadot's concept is useful for understanding Buddhist thought. Nonetheless, it is only one example, and a central theme in the book is a critique of an alternative understanding of Buddhism, represented by Ha-shang (Hva-shang Mohoyen), that appears *not* to exemplify Hadot's concept. In the background is a famous debate that according to Tibetan tradition took place near the end of the eighth century at the Samyé monastery between Ha-shang, representing the "Chinese" simultaneous (or sudden) enlightenment approach (an outlook associated with Chan), and Kamalaśīla, representing the "Indian" gradual enlightenment approach.[9] According to the simultaneous approach, enlightenment is an instantaneous, non-conceptual experience that does not require, and in fact is inhibited by, any prior discursive analysis. By contrast, for the gradualist approach, enlightenment can only be achieved through long practice, centering on the six perfections, in which discursive analysis is crucial (as essential to the perfection of wisdom). Discursive analysis is a form of rational philosophical reflection on topics such as no-self and emptiness. Hence, a central issue in the debate was to a significant extent the role of philosophy, so-understood, in attaining Buddhist enlightenment. Tibetan tradition maintains that the "winner" of the debate was Kamalaśīla and the gradualist approach, and this is the position that Tsongkhapa defends. But his defense draws attention to the fact that not all Buddhist approaches regard philosophy in this sense as an important spiritual exercise.[10]

Tsongkhapa had a Buddhist monastic education centered on study of, and debate about, Indian and Tibetan Buddhist texts. Various phases of his life were devoted to meditation, ritual practices, monastic reform, and philosophical reflection. His mature philosophical works were composed in the last two decades of his life, beginning with the *Great Treatise*. Tsongkhapa developed his own distinctive interpretation of the Prāsaṅgika-Mādhyamika philosophy rooted in Nāgārjuna and subsequently developed by later Mādhyamika thinkers such as Āryadeva, Buddhapālita, Bhāvaviveka, and especially Candrakīrti. However, his version of the Middle Way perspective, aiming to avoid both over-negation (to preserve conventional truth) and over-reification (to preserve emptiness), involved using reasoning to establish the absence of intrinsic existence. It is for this synthesis of different Indian Buddhist traditions that he is best known as a philosopher.[11] He also wrote on the ethical codes of different levels of Buddhist practitioners and the "deity yoga" of tantric practice (and the relationship between these).[12] In addition, he played an important role in the development of the Geluk order that has had such importance in Tibetan Buddhism through its relationship with the position of the Dalai Lama. Tsongkhapa was obviously well positioned to speak authoritatively about Buddhist spiritual practices and Buddhist philosophy as they had developed in a key phase of Tibetan history.

The *Great Treatise* is plausibly and informatively read as presupposing a concept of philosophy as a way of life as understood by Hadot. First, Tsongkhapa supposes that human life is ordinarily problematic insofar as it is permeated by suffering, but human beings have the capacity to radically transform themselves so as to attain genuine well-being by achieving enlightenment. The ways in which our lives are problematic have much to do with our beliefs, desires, passions, and actions: our lives are full of misunderstandings, cravings, emotions such as anger, and vicious actions. By contrast, enlightenment involves wisdom, tranquility, and virtue. Second, it is possible to bring this transformation about by a set of diverse spiritual exercises, and one of these exercises is necessary but not sufficient, namely philosophy – specifically for Tsongkhapa the perfection of wisdom on the basis of insight. This requires reasoning, analysis, and examination, all employing conceptual thought, in order to understand the ultimate truths of selflessness and emptiness. Insight is a recognizable kind of philosophy, and as a crucial spiritual exercise in Tsongkhapa's program we evidently have a form of Hadot's philosophy as a way of life.

The primary purpose of Tsongkhapa's text is to provide a guide to an extensive set of Buddhist spiritual exercises. It is implicitly divided into four parts: after several preliminary chapters, there are three groups of chapters devoted to persons of small, medium, and great capacity, respectively. These categories represent increasing levels of understanding, well-being, and virtue. The last, the exercises for persons of great capacity, receives the most attention and includes a long, detailed discussion of Prāsaṅgika-Mādhyamika philosophy (over 200 pages, nearly a quarter of the entire text). This is the main place in which philosophy is discussed, though the importance of philosophy is insisted upon throughout.

Tsongkhapa opens the book with praise for the qualifications of Atisha and the greatness of his teaching in the *Lamp for the Path to Enlightenment* (*Bodhipathapradīpa*; see Atisha 1997). Atisha (982–1054) is regarded by Tibetan Buddhists as the leading figure in the "second dissemination" of Buddhism from India to Tibet in the eleventh century. His *Lamp* is a brief sixty-eight verse summary of Buddhist gradualist practice from a Mahāyāna – and ultimately Vajrayāna – perspective. It became the basis for the "stages of the path" (*lam rim*) literature in Tibet of which Tsongkhapa's *Great Treatise* is a prominent example.[13] Tsongkhapa says that the *Lamp* is his "root text" (11/1:45).[14] It is a key source of his organizing principle of the three persons with different capacities as well as his Mādhyamika philosophy and his insistence on the importance of both reasoning and non-conceptual meditation (the *Lamp* includes a brief but explicit discussion of Nāgārjuna's emptiness philosophy).

Before distinguishing the three persons, Tsongkhapa emphasizes several concerns that are important for anyone undertaking the Buddhist path: finding and learning from a good teacher, having faith in your teacher, making confession, engaging in prayer, undertaking meditation, having appropriate diet and sleep, studying, reasoning, and the like. The language of exhortation is the dominant mode of expressing these concerns. In the course of this preliminary discussion, there is extensive development of a medical analogy: you are to "think of yourself as a sick person," your "instructor as a doctor," your "instructor's explications as medicine," and your "earnest practice as the way to cure your disease" (23–24/1:58–59). Forms of medical analogies are common in Buddhist texts from the Pāli Canon on; for example, the Buddha is sometimes depicted as a doctor and his teaching as a medicine to cure us of the disease of suffering. Tsongkhapa draws on Śāntideva and several other Buddhist sources to develop his version of the analogy. In this respect, there is a striking similarity to the passage from Epicurus cited earlier in which we were told that the goal of philosophy is to dispel suffering from the soul just as the goal of medicine is to eliminate bodily diseases.[15] The importance of the medical analogy for Tsongkhapa is a key indication of the practical orientation of his teaching.

The three types of persons are distinguished as follows. Persons of small capacity "diligently strive for the excellent high states of human or divine rebirth in future lifetimes" (87/1:130). Persons of medium capacity "develop disenchantment with all of cyclic existence, and then make their goal their own liberation from cyclic existence" (87/1:130). Persons of great capacity "under the influence of great compassion, make buddhahood their goal in order to extinguish all the sufferings of all living beings" (87/1:131). This trichotomy expresses a familiar Mahāyāna perspective. All persons are caught in a cycle of rebirth governed by karma: a morally good (bad) life now brings about greater (lesser) well-being in a future life. Persons of small capacity are simply trying to live a morally good life so as to attain greater well-being in future lifetimes. However, in the Buddhist view, no matter what level of well-being is attained, all lives in the cycle of rebirth are permeated by suffering (*duḥkha* in the Sanskrit). This motivates the desire to escape the cycle of rebirth entirely and attain the state of liberation or enlightenment that is *nirvāṇa* – the highest form of well-being. From the Mahāyāna perspective, a follower of the Hinayāna vehicle is striving to attain *nirvāṇa* only for him or herself. These are persons of medium capacity. However, the characteristic feature of a person who follows the Mahāyāna vehicle is to promote enlightenment not simply for oneself but for all beings. From the start, the Mahāyāna practitioner is committed to enabling all beings to overcome suffering. This is what persons of great capacity do.

From Tsongkhapa's point of view, the commitments of all three kinds of person are sanctioned by the Buddha, but they involve increasingly higher commitments. A person of medium capacity has a higher aspiration than a person of small capacity, and a person of great capacity has the highest aspiration of all. The "three types of person" terminology is misleading if it suggests that each person by nature has exactly one of these capacities. To the contrary, the Buddhist view is that at different stages in the cycle of rebirth a person may instantiate different categories. Hence, I may be a person of small capacity in this lifetime, but advance to a person of medium capacity in my next lifetime. In fact, Tsongkhapa's text may be read as depicting the journey of one person through three stages of spiritual practice. He makes it clear that the training of the lower stages is presupposed in the training of the higher stages. For example, persons of great capacity share the moral convictions of persons of small capacity, but they have other moral commitments that go beyond these (in particular, to alleviate the suffering of all beings). Tsongkhapa says that we are to "strive to maintain the fundamental trainings completely, gradually assuming the higher vows while using the lower ones as supports" (205/1:263).

Becoming a person of small capacity is itself an achievement. Many persons focus on the immediate concerns of this life and do not consider the karmic effects of their actions in their future rebirths. Hence, Tsongkhapa outlines a series of spiritual exercises to overcome this attitude. We are urged to contemplate the certainty of death and the uncertainty of the time of death. We are enjoined to reflect on the miserable rebirths that await us if we live a life of wrongdoing. And we are instructed to live an ethical life and to take refuge in the three jewels (the Buddha, his teaching, and his community) so as to have a happier rebirth. Much of the discussion in these chapters explains Buddhist doctrine pertaining to karma and rebirth. For example, we are told about different kinds of non-virtuous actions, what makes them weighty, different kinds of karmic effects, how we can weaken these effects (for instance, through contrition and confession), and so on. These instructions in doctrine are put forward to convince us to live morally better lives. The practical aim is paramount. In passing Tsongkhapa warns persons of small capacity against "befriending non-Buddhist philosophers" (144/1:194), urges them to recollect impermanence and selflessness and to admire emptiness (150/1:199), and enjoins them to acquire knowledge of dependent arising so as to better understand karma (192/1:248). But he does not propose that they be given any real philosophical instruction or training. This is reserved for the higher stages. Insofar as many Buddhists in this life strive only for a better rebirth, philosophy is not really part of their way of life as Tsongkhapa understands it.

Persons of medium capacity strive to bring about their own liberation from the cycle of rebirth by attaining *nirvāṇa*. For this Tsongkhapa says they need to develop an attitude of "disgust with all of cyclic existence" (206/1:266). Many of the spiritual exercises proposed for these persons involve meditation on the suffering that attends any rebirth no matter how "happy" it may be. A wide array of kinds of suffering are catalogued in detail to motivate escape from cyclic existence. Moreover, in the course of these considerations, persons of medium capacity are urged to reflect on various features of the Buddha's teaching: the Four Noble Truths, no-self, dependent arising (and its twelve factors culminating in suffering), afflictions that give rise to suffering, and so on. In this respect, these persons require greater understanding of Buddhist doctrines than persons of small capacity. In fact, at the end of this discussion, Tsongkhapa urges these persons to renounce household life in favor of the more ascetic life of a renunciate and to undertake the "three trainings" in ethical discipline, concentration, and wisdom. Though some attention is devoted to ethical discipline at this stage, he foregoes giving an account of the trainings in concentration and wisdom because, he says, these will be considered in the discussion of meditative serenity and insight in connection with persons of great capacity (see 269/1:342). Since insight requires philosophical reflection, the implication is that persons of medium capacity need to undertake some philosophical reflection as well. Though there is no explanation of what this involves that distinguishes it from the activity of persons with great capacity, it is evident that Tsongkhapa believes that persons of medium capacity, seeking only their own enlightenment, need to engage in philosophical analysis.[16] This spiritual exercise is essential to one of the three trainings. For this reason, Hadot's concept of philosophy as a way of life applies to persons of medium capacity.

About two-thirds of the *Great Treatise* is devoted to persons of great capacity. Their commitment and the spiritual exercises required to fulfill it are clearly Tsongkhapa's preeminent concern. These persons seek not simply to end their own suffering, but to enable all beings to overcome suffering. "The fundamental orientation of a great person is to focus solely on achieving the happiness and benefit of others" (282/2:14). The "spirit of enlightenment," the aspiration and dedication to attain buddhahood for the sake of all beings, is the centerpiece of Mahāyāna Buddhism and of Tsongkhapa's understanding of the culmination of Buddhist practice. The chapters on persons of great capacity first explain how to develop and maintain the spirit of enlightenment, then analyze the six perfections that are at the heart of Mahāyāna practice, and finally elaborate in detail the serenity and insight associated with the last two of these perfections.

The key to developing the spirit of enlightenment is to generate universal and impartial compassion for all beings. Two techniques for doing this are emphasized. According to the "seven cause-and-effect method," we first endeavor to recognize all beings as our mother, remember their kindness, and wish to repay their kindness. Then, on this basis, we cultivate love for all beings, compassion for all beings, wholehearted resolve to liberate all beings and, finally, the spirit of enlightenment. The second technique is Śāntideva's meditation on "exchanging self and other": you are to view yourself as you do others, and others as you do yourself. Tsongkhapa also discusses various rituals for undertaking the spirit of enlightenment and diverse techniques for maintaining it (such as eliminating "four dark practices" involving deception and disrespect that tend to weaken it).

Once the spirit of enlightenment is in place, it is necessary to fulfill it through practice. Tsongkhapa maintains that the only way to do this is by developing the six perfections. These are generosity, ethical discipline, patience, joyous perseverance, meditative stabilization, and wisdom. He says that these encompass all other ways of categorizing Mahāyāna practice, and he insists on the importance of developing each perfection in the order just given. They constitute a fixed sequence of development, each superior to its predecessor, but also easier to develop. Part of Tsongkhapa's concern here is to defend the crucial role of moral virtues against what he represents as the position of Ha-shang that they are detrimental because they involve conceptual thought. A central theme in Tsongkhapa's outlook is that ethical training is essential to the Buddhist path.

The key to generosity is a generous attitude: it is "the intention to give away to others all your possessions" (365/2:115). Tsongkhapa elaborates in considerable detail various aspects of this virtue: ways to overcome hindrances and develop it, various divisions of generosity (e.g., gifts of material goods, protection from harm, and Buddhist teaching), and appropriate motivations, purposes, ways of giving, recipients, times, and so on. The second perfection, ethical discipline, is the "attitude of abstention that turns your mind away from harming others and from the sources of such harm" (390/2:143). Tsongkhapa's account of this is rather brief (though it refers to other parts of the text and to another text of his). The three divisions of ethical discipline are restraint, gathering virtue, and promoting the welfare of all beings. Restraint means "abstaining from deeds that are wrong by nature" (396/2:149). These are the ten non-virtues: killing, stealing, sexual misconduct, lying, divisive speech, offensive speech, senseless speech, covetousness, malice, and wrong views (discussed earlier in the section on persons of small capacity at 165–174/1:218–227). Patience is primarily "disregarding harm done to you" and "accepting the suffering arising in your mind-stream" (397/2:152). With respect to harms done to us by others who prevent our happiness or increase our suffering, the primary opponent of patience is anger, and a great deal of Tsongkhapa's discussion focuses on why anger is unjustified and harmful. For harms done to us by the attitudes of others (e.g., those who fail to praise us or who have contempt for us), he recommends that we not be attached to these attitudes. As for accepting suffering, Tsongkhapa urges courage and recognition that it has some good qualities such as encouraging us to seek liberation.

Cultivating the first three perfections involves forms of ethical training that are supposed to develop universal compassion directly. The remaining three perfections have different relationships to this goal. Joyous perseverance, Tsongkhapa says, is being "enthusiastic about accumulating virtue and working for the welfare of beings, together with the physical, verbal, and mental activity such a state of mind motivates" (424/2:182). The path to full buddhahood is difficult and long, requiring numerous lifetimes to complete. In view of this, frustration and discouragement are serious dangers, and we need joyous perseverance to overcome them. For this reason, Tsongkhapa says it is "armor-like." It creates the steadfast and joyful energy needed to defeat these obstacles.

Tsongkhapa introduces the last two perfections in a single chapter, indicating that he sees a deep connection between them. The first, meditative stabilization, "is a virtuous, one-pointed state of mind that stays fixed on its object of meditation without distraction to other things" (448/2:210). The second, wisdom, "is what thoroughly discerns the ontological status of an object under analysis" (449/2:211). Each of these is necessary to fulfill the other perfections, including one another, so as to bring about complete buddhahood. But Tsongkhapa is primarily interested in specific forms of these perfections. The form of meditative stabilization that concerns him is serenity. This concentration involves "mindfulness and vigilance" so as to "produce the delight and bliss of physical and mental pliancy" (471/3:16). He also says that "serenity entails no discursive thought whatsoever" (549/3:89). Undistracted, continuous, non-discursive awareness of an object is the hallmark of serenity meditation. The form of wisdom that concerns him is insight. This involves reflection, examination, differentiation, analysis, conceptual thought, and reasoning (for these characterizations, see especially 769–795/3:327–350). Only these philosophical tools can provide the proper understanding of selflessness and emptiness, specifically that everything lacks an intrinsic existence (contrary to what is usually thought); that things and persons nonetheless exist conventionally; that absence of intrinsic existence is compatible with dependent arising and other Buddhist teachings pertaining to cyclic existence and *nirvāṇa*; that there are rational criteria for determining what does and does not exist conventionally; and a host of additional themes in Tsongkhapa's distinctive Prāsaṅgika-Mādhyamika philosophical outlook – as he argues in considerable detail in the latter part of the book.

Tsongkhapa insists, repeatedly, that both serenity and insight are required for enlightenment. If we have serenity without insight, we will not have the eyes to see reality, but if we have insight without serenity, we will not see the meaning of reality. Though we must attain serenity before we attain insight, once we have attained both, we must alternate between them and ultimately unify them. Only when analysis itself induces pliancy and one-pointed focus do we have "genuine insight" (798/3:354). This means that "in a continuous process" we "experience both serenity which observes a non-discursive image and insight which observes a discursive image" (804/3:358–359). It is his insistence on the necessity of insight, motivated by his conviction that Ha-shang failed to see the importance of discursive, philosophical reasoning, that makes it appropriate to attribute to Tsongkhapa the view that philosophical reflection is an essential spiritual discipline – the distinctive contention in Hadot's interpretation of the Greek and Roman philosophers.

Convergences and Divergences

There is no question that Tsongkhapa's program in the *Great Treatise* exemplifies Hadot's concept of philosophy as a way of life. As we have seen, Tsongkhapa supposes that human lives are deeply problematic, but that we have a capacity to bring about a radical transformation so as to achieve an extraordinary kind of well-being. And he thinks that the way to do this is by practicing a diverse array of spiritual exercises that crucially includes philosophy. The key feature of Hadot's understanding of philosophy as a way of life is that philosophical reflection is important as part of a practical program of personal transformation that addresses our most fundamental concerns. Tsongkhapa shares this outlook. In fact, from one perspective, Tsongkhapa may exemplify philosophy as a way of life better than any of the philosophers referred to by Hadot. The *Great Treatise* provides a much more extensive, detailed, systematic, and regimented set of spiritual exercises than we find in any of Hadot's extant sources (though perhaps works of similar scope and character were produced in the ancient Mediterranean world).

In addition, there are several more specific concerns and practices that Tsongkhapa holds in common with many of Hadot's Greek and Roman philosophers. For both there is a focus on human suffering as manifested in disruptive desires and unruly passions, unease pertaining to our mortality, and misunderstandings of human nature and the world of which we are a part. And for both there is the promise of liberation into a state of wisdom, virtue, and contentment. In addition, there are similarities in many of the practices prescribed to bring about this transformation. There is an explicit emphasis on the development of moral virtues and associated activities such as confession. In some cases, the nature of moral development is strikingly similar. For example, overcoming anger is a common theme among many Hellenistic philosophers as well as in Tsongkhapa and other Buddhist advocates (see Vernezze 2008; Gowans 2010). There are also, in both, similar exercises involving bodily deprivation and reflections on our mortality. In addition, for both there is recognition of the importance of engaging in spiritual exercises in a communal context. And finally, of course, there is the common emphasis on the importance of philosophical reflection as well as, in connection with this, appreciation of the value of brief summaries to help us put the philosophical outlook into practice – as in Atisha's *Lamp* and Epictetus's *Handbook*.

At the same time, however, as substantial as these similarities are, there are also deep differences between Tsongkhapa and the philosophers featured by Hadot. First, though the ethical aspirations of persons of small capacity are modest, those of persons of medium and especially great capacity are quite extraordinary. The culmination of moral development in Tsongkhapa's program is, as we saw, to attain buddhahood "in order to extinguish all the sufferings of all living beings" (87/1:131). The "spirit of enlightenment" – the commitment to universal and impartial compassion, to seek enlightenment for the sake of all beings, and to remain in the cycle of rebirth until this goal is fulfilled – is the most fundamental feature of Tsongkhapa's ethical outlook, and of Mahāyāna Buddhism as a whole, and this has no counterpart in the Greek and Roman philosophers that concerned Hadot. Though the ethical standpoints of some of them, especially the Stoics, involved an appreciation of impartiality and could be quite demanding in their own way, they were still very different than the bodhisattva ideal in Tsongkhapa. There are some common ethical themes, such as the critique of anger, but in the end the ethical framework of Tsongkhapa sharply contrasts with the ethical perspectives that concerned Hadot's philosophers.

The second major area of difference pertains to cosmology and metaphysics. Tsongkhapa presupposes that sentient beings have long been, and will continue to be, born and reborn in a series of lives governed by the principle of karma, but always permeated by a measure of suffering – until enlightenment brings about liberation from this cycle. The cosmology of karma and rebirth is a basic feature of his understanding of the world. The idea of rebirth is by no means unheard of in ancient Greek and Roman philosophy; for example, both Pythagoras and Plato embraced a form of this. Nonetheless, for the most part the spiritual exercises of the philosophers explicated by Hadot did not presuppose and gain their purpose from an ethical cosmology similar to that of Tsongkhapa. The difference with respect to metaphysics is even more striking. The fundamental metaphysical insight for Tsongkhapa, that which brings about liberation, is the realization of the selflessness and emptiness of all things. That in ultimate truth persons are not selves, and nothing has an intrinsic nature, is the heart of Tsongkhapa's Mahāyāna Buddhist metaphysics. None of the ancient philosophers practicing Hadot's philosophy as a way of life believed this. However, there is a theme in Hadot's discussion that mitigates this difference to some extent. One form of attention he stressed is attention to the cosmos in which the sage feels unified with the whole and thereby "goes beyond the limits of his individuality" (Hadot 1995, 273). This sense of connection with the world as a whole bears some resemblance to what a Buddhist sage might be expected to feel upon grasping selflessness, emptiness, and – what is at the root of both these notions – the dependent arising of all things. However, for Tsongkhapa this insight was thought to fulfill the aspiration to universal compassion, and Hadot's attention to the cosmos was not thought to have this ethical implication.

The final area of important difference pertains to epistemology. What is common here, and what is essential to the concept of philosophy as a way of life, is recognition of the importance of rational philosophical reflection. Tsongkhapa and the ancient Greek and Roman philosophers share an appreciation of the crucial role of reason in the personal transformations they envision. The difference is that Tsongkhapa believes this primarily because he thinks that philosophical analysis in the form of insight is required to properly comprehend what serenity meditation can reveal, and because enlightenment ultimately requires a unity of serenity and insight. Hence, Tsongkhapa has a quite specific reason for valuing philosophical reflection. Contrary to the position attributed to Ha-shang, serenity is not enough. It must be complemented with insight. This is the main reason why Tsongkhapa's program exemplifies the concept of philosophy as a way of life. For the philosophers featured by Hadot, however, this is not why philosophical reflection is valued. Though some of their activities might have an affinity with some forms of Buddhist meditation, they did not practice serenity meditation (or more broadly any form of Buddhist tranquility meditation), with its emphasis on long, continuous, mindful attention to a single object. The "attention to the present moment" emphasized by Hadot might appear to have some kinship with serenity meditation, but the purpose of this attention is to increase our appreciation of the value of each moment; it is not to develop our powers of concentration so as to properly comprehend what we experience. Hadot's ancient philosophers thought philosophical reason enabled us to understand reality (except for the Skeptics). However, they did not think that anything resembling serenity meditation was required as a supplement.[17] Hence, their understanding of the value of philosophy was quite different than that of Tsongkhapa. For him, serenity meditation was a distinctive and fundamental spiritual exercise. Hence, even as he supposed that Ha-shang was mistaken in not recognizing the importance of insight, he would have supposed that Western philosophers were mistaken in not recognizing the importance of serenity. The value of this form of meditation for any viable philosophy as a way of life is a primary challenge to the Western philosophical tradition from Tsongkhapa – and more broadly from the many ancient Indian traditions that stress the importance of related meditative practices – a challenge that is still barely recognized in the West today.

Notes

1. See Hadot (1995, 1998, 2002, 2011). Others who have emphasized the practical dimension of ancient Greek and Roman philosophy include Foucault (1986), Nussbaum (1994), Sorabji (2000), Long (2006), and Sellars (2009).
2. For example, see Cooper (2012, ch. 1). For a response to Cooper, see Sharpe (2014).
3. See Dreyfus (1995), Kapstein (2001, 7–20; 2013), Gowans (2003; 2014, 202–203), and Ganeri (2013). Hadot himself has acknowledged some similarity with Buddhism (see Hadot 2002, 232–233, 278–279).
4. For the distinction between concept and conception, see Rawls (1971, 5–6).
5. Hadot thought that the sixteenth-century *Spiritual Exercises* of Saint Ignatius were based on the Greco-Roman tradition, but divorced from philosophy (see Hadot 1995, 82, 269–270). For discussion of the relationship between Christianity and the ancient spiritual exercises of the philosophers, see Hadot (1995, ch. 4). Hadot was aware that his use of the phrase "spiritual exercises" might be misleading (see Hadot 1995, 81–82; 2011, ch. 6). A prominent theme in criticism of Hadot is that his emphasis on spiritual exercises wrongly downplays the role of reason (*logos*) in ancient philosophy (see Nussbaum 1994, 353; Sellars 2009, 116–118; Cooper 2012, 18–19).
6. A different analogy, also pertaining to the body, is athletic training (see Hadot 2002, 189).
7. He discusses these exercises in many places. Two of the most important sources are Hadot (1995, chs. 3 and 11) and Hadot (2002, ch. 9). Also important are Hadot (1995, ch. 4), Hadot (1998, ch. 3), and Hadot (2011, ch. 6).
8. See Hadot (1995, 83–84) and Hadot (2002, 188). He relies partly on two lists from Philo of Alexandria, and he notes that there is a brief text on the exercises by the Stoic Musonius Rufus.
9. For an account of the debate and its importance in Tibetan philosophy, see Ruegg (1989).
10. Of course, this raises the question (which I do not pursue here) of to what extent and in what way a form of philosophy might have a role to play in the Chan and Zen traditions. They are certainly sometimes represented as anti-philosophical, but important thinkers associated with them, such as Dōgen, are often regarded as philosophers in some sense.
11. For an analysis of Tsongkhapa's philosophy, see Jinpa (2002). The philosophy of the *Great Treatise* is examined in Napper (1989); an accessible introduction may be found in Newland (2009). For an introduction to the *Great Treatise* as a whole, addressed to a broad audience, see the Dalai Lama (2013).
12. Tsongkhapa is committed to the importance of tantric practice and refers to it at the very end of the *Great Treatise*, but consideration of it is beyond the scope of that work and of this chapter.
13. Dreyfus (1995, 30) was the first, to my knowledge, to suggest kinship between the *lam rim* literature rooted in Atisha's *Lamp* and Hadot's spiritual exercises.

14 References to the *Great Treatise* will first give page numbers in the Bya-khyung edition published in Qinghai in 1985 and then page numbers in the three-volume English translation cited earlier (the volume number followed by the page number).
15 For a discussion of the medical analogy in Buddhist thought and practice, see Burton (2010), and for a comparison of this analogy in Buddhist and Hellenistic thought, see Gowans (2010).
16 Later Tsongkhapa says that we should differentiate the Hinayāna and Mahāyāna vehicles, corresponding to the persons of medium and great capacity, "not by philosophical view, but by deeds." They share in "the wisdom that knows emptiness," but differ in that only the Mahāyāna practitioner is motivated by compassion for all beings (286/2:18).
17 On rare occasions Hadot refers to something that might suggest a practice akin to serenity meditation (e.g., Hadot 2002, 179), but the theme is not explored.

References

Atisha. 1997. *Lamp for the Path to Enlightenment, with Commentary by Geshe Sonam Rinchen*. Translated by Ruth Sonam. Boston: Snow Lion.

Burton, David. 2010. "Curing Diseases of Belief and Desire: Buddhist Philosophical Therapy." In *Philosophy as Therapeia*, edited by Clare Carlisle and Jonardon Ganeri, 187–217. Royal Institute of Philosophy Supplement 66. Cambridge: Cambridge University Press.

Cooper, John M. 2012. *Pursuits of Wisdom: Six Ways of Life in Ancient Philosophy from Socrates to Plotinus*. Princeton: Princeton University Press.

Dalai Lama. 2013. *From Here to Enlightenment: An Introduction to Tsong-kha-pa's Classic Text The Great Treatise on the Stages of the Path to Enlightenment*, edited and translated by Guy Newland. Boston: Snow Lion.

Dreyfus, Georges. 1995. "Meditation as Ethical Activity." *Journal of Buddhist Ethics* 2: 28–54.

Foucault, Michel. 1986. *The Care of the Self, Volume 3 of The History of Sexuality*, translated by Robert Hurley. New York: Vintage Books.

Ganeri, Jonardon. 2013. "Philosophy as a Way of Life: Spiritual Exercises from the Buddha to Tagore." In *Philosophy as a Way of Life: Ancients and Moderns – Essays in Honor of Pierre Hadot*, edited by Michael Chase, Stephen R.L. Clark, and Michael McGhee, 116–131. Hoboken: John Wiley & Sons.

Gowans, Christopher W. 2003. *Philosophy of the Buddha*. London: Routledge.

Gowans, Christopher W. 2010. "Medical Analogies in Buddhist and Hellenistic Thought: Tranquility and Anger." In *Philosophy as Therapeia*, edited by Clare Carlisle and Jonardon Ganeri, 11–33. Royal Institute of Philosophy Supplement 66. Cambridge: Cambridge University Press.

Gowans, Christopher W. 2014. *Buddhist Moral Philosophy: An Introduction*. New York: Routledge.

Hadot, Pierre. 1995. *Philosophy as a Way of Life: Spiritual Exercises from Socrates to Foucault*, translated by Michael Chase. Cambridge, MA: Blackwell.

Hadot, Pierre. 1998. *The Inner Citadel: The Meditations of Marcus Aurelius*, translated by Michael Chase. Cambridge, MA: Harvard University Press.

Hadot, Pierre. 2002. *What is Ancient Philosophy?*, translated by Michael Chase. Cambridge, MA: Harvard University Press.

Hadot, Pierre. 2011. *The Present Alone is Our Happiness: Conversions with Jeannie Carlier and Arnold I. Davidson*, 2nd edition, translated by Marc Djaballah and Michael Chase. Stanford: Stanford University Press.

Jinpa, Thupten. 2002. *Self, Reality and Reason in Tibetan Philosophy: Tsongkhapa's Quest for the Middle Way*. London: RoutledgeCurzon.

Kapstein, Matthew T. 2001. *Reason's Traces: Identity and Interpretation in Indian and Tibetan Buddhist Thought*. Boston: Wisdom Publications.

Kapstein, Matthew T. 2013. "Stoics and Bodhisattvas: Spiritual Exercises and Faith in Two Philosophical Traditions." In *Philosophy as a Way of Life: Ancients and Moderns – Essays in Honor of Pierre Hadot*, edited by Michael Chase, Stephen R.L. Clark, and Michael McGhee, 99–115. Hoboken: John Wiley & Sons.

Long, A.A. 2006. "Hellenistic Ethics as the Art of Life." In *Studies in Hellenistic and Roman Philosophy*, 23–39. Oxford: Clarendon Press.

Long, A.A. and Sedley, D.N., eds. 1987. *The Hellenistic Philosophers, vol. 1: Translations of the Principal Sources, with Philosophical Commentary*. Cambridge: Cambridge University Press.

Napper, Elizabeth. 1989. *Dependent-Arising and Emptiness: A Tibetan Buddhist Interpretation of Mādhyamika Philosophy*. Boston: Wisdom Publications.

Newland, Guy. 2009. *Introduction to Emptiness as Taught in Tsong-kha-pa's Great Treatise on the Stages of the Path*, revised edition. Boston: Snow Lion.

Nussbaum, Martha. 1994. *The Therapy of Desire: Theory and Practice in Hellenistic Ethics*. Princeton: Princeton University Press.

Plato. 2002. *Five Dialogues: Euthyphro, Apology, Crito, Meno, Phaedo*, 2nd edition, translated by G.M.A. Grube. Indianapolis: Hackett Publishing Company.

Rawls, John. 1971. *A Theory of Justice*. Cambridge, MA: Harvard University Press.

Ruegg, David Seyfort. 1989. *Buddha-Nature, Mind and the Problem of Gradualism in a Comparative Perspective: On the Transmission and Reception of Buddhism in India and Tibet*. London: School of Oriental and African Studies.

Sellars, John. 2009. *The Art of Living: The Stoics on the Nature and Function of Philosophy*, 2nd edition. London: Bristol Classical Press.

Sharpe, Matthew. 2014. "How It's Not the Chrisippus You Read: On Cooper, Hadot, Epictetus, and Stoicism as a Way of Life." *Philosophy Today* 58: 367–392.

Sorabji, Richard. 2000. *Emotion and Peace of Mind: From Stoic Agitation to Christian Temptation*. New York: Oxford University Press.

Tsongkhapa. 2000–2004. *The Great Treatise on the Stages of the Path to Enlightenment*, three volumes, translated by the Lamrim Chenmo Translation Committee. Ithaca: Snow Lion Publications.

Vernezze, Peter J. 2008. "Moderation or the Middle Way: Two Approaches to Anger." *Philosophy East and West* 58: 2–16.

2

The Other Side of Realism: Panpsychism and Yogācāra
Douglas Duckworth

Yogācāra, "the yogic practice school" – from *yoga* and *ācāra* (practice) – came to be one of two main lines of interpretation of Mahāyāna Buddhism. There is a good deal of internal diversity within this "school," and this chapter will make some distinctions among its interpretative strands, including an important one between *subjective* idealism and *absolute* idealism. Subjective idealism is the claim that only mind exists (as Berkeley said, "existence is perception"), and absolute idealism is the claim that everything is unitary and thus that all relations are internal. The latter does not necessarily entail the former.

The place of mind in Yogācāra texts remains an open question. Namely, are external objects reducible to mind (subjective idealism)? Or are objects co-dependent with minds (in a relational network), or in some sense nondual (absolute idealism)? I wish to argue that Yogācāra is not necessarily a form of subjective idealism, although it can be. Yet when read as subjective idealism (as in the philosophy of "mind only"), it is not so interesting. Other readings, such as absolute idealism or relational pluralism, are more promising. Absolute idealist and pluralist readings are clearly distinct from subjective idealism, for subjective idealism collapses objects into a subject. In contrast, in absolute idealism, external relations (like those between subject and object) are unreal as they are subsumed by the whole. Alternatively, neither mind nor matter need have a privileged place in a relational ontology where the world is constituted by relations.

Just as is the case with Yogācāra, there are a number of different interpretations of panpsychism. "Panpsychism," from the Greek *pan* (all) and *psyche* (mind or soul), has been defined as "the view that all things have mind or a mind-like quality" (Skrbina 2005, 2). Like Yogācāra, there are parallel distinctions to be made in terms of how panpsychism has been conceived: in a relational, pluralistic, or singular (or nondual) way. In its strong form, panpsychism can mean that everything, including electrons, has a mental dimension along with a physical one. I will refer to this strong form of panpsychism as

Buddhist Philosophy: A Comparative Approach, First Edition. Edited by Steven M. Emmanuel.
© 2018 John Wiley & Sons, Inc. Published 2018 by John Wiley & Sons, Inc.

"animistic panpsychism"[1] (but since this is not a form directly relevant to Yogācāra, I will not discuss it further here). Panpsychism also can be taken in a singular form as absolute idealism, where everything takes place within a unified structural whole. Yet a panpsychist position need not be so extreme; a weak form of "relational panpsychism" can simply refer to observer-dependence, whereby mind is affirmed to be everywhere simply because any actual reality is always an experienced one.

A singular (or nondual) form of panpsychism presents a necessary unity of the whole, while deeming relations to be unreal. F.H. Bradley articulates this absolute idealism by stating that "Everywhere in the end a relation appears as a necessary but a self-contradictory translation of a non-relational or super-relational unity" (Bradley 2012 [1914], 209 n.1). The "non-relational or super-relational unity" is the supermind of absolute idealism.[2] On the other hand, a relational form of panpsychism (as the one put forward by William James, who critiqued the "block universe" (James 1977, 140) of Bradley's idealism as a static singularity) does not presume a singular whole, but only acknowledges a relational structure. Like the singular (or nondual) account of absolute idealism, relational panpsychism is not subjective idealism, either. It need not be an assertion that mind is only internal, nor that the world is only mental, but expresses a dynamic process of interactions.

For example, consider the case for this kind of panpsychism with the appearance of something like a rainbow. For a rainbow to appear we need at least three things in place: white light (e.g., the sun), a refracting medium (e.g., water), and a receptor of light (e.g., eyes). Of course the eyes have to be looking in the right direction, and the light coming to the eyes at the right angle (between 40 and 42 degrees) to be visibly refracted, too. Without any of these things (light, water, eyes) properly configured, no rainbow appears. It is not that the rainbow is "out there" in the world, nor is the rainbow only "in here" in our eyes or minds. Rather, the appearing rainbow is the result of an intricate relational structure in which the perceiving eye is intertwined. Just as the eyes are integral to the perception of a rainbow, we need not be subjective idealists to affirm that the mind is constitutive to the world. In other words, "beauty is in the eye of the beholder" does not necessarily mean that beauty is totally subjective, as if it were "all in our heads," but it can simply mean that the subject is an integral part of the dynamic process by which beauty takes place.

Buddhism and Panpsychism

Buddhists describe an irreducibly complex matrix of interrelation: a causal process that denies singularity and difference to cause and effect (temporal entanglement), and likewise posit a spatial entanglement that denies real singularities (and real differences, too). Buddhists like Nāgārjuna have claimed that there is nothing really singular because nothing exists independently; there is only ever a relational presentation of the world – nothing can be found that is truly singular because everything is dependent on something else.[3] A.N. Whitehead made this point in the twentieth century:

> The misconception which has haunted philosophic literature throughout the centuries is the notion of "independent existence." There is no such mode of existence; every entity is only to be understood in terms of the way in which it is interwoven with the rest of the Universe.
> *(Whitehead 1941, 687)*

A relation entails at least two things, but there is not a single thing that is outside the relational matrix (and if there were, we could not know it, because knowledge implies the relation of knower and known). The only viable candidate for "one" is the whole itself, the uni-verse – the unified structure of the multiplicity – yet the "one" of the universe cannot be a determinate, static one, for it is constituted by interpenetrating relations.[4]

Panpsychism can be understood as a theoretic articulation of the relational structure of existence – the matrix of dependent arising as the Buddhists call it. The mind is clearly implicated in this structure, as a dependent component, and a necessary condition for the arising of anything. Whereas the mind is a *necessary* condition for a world, it is not necessarily a *sufficient* condition for a world because the mind alone – as if floating in a vacuum in space – cannot know or be known without being immersed in a field of interaction – stimuli, the phenomena of a world. This does not mean that phenomena are simply reducible to mind (as in subjective idealism), it just means that they do not exist – and cannot exist – as they do without mind.

We can take a lesson straight out of modern physics: observers always affect a phenomenon. It is not that what we observe is totally controlled by our observing, but it is just that being there as an observer plays a part, an inextricable part, of the phenomenon that is observed. Reality is a participatory affair. This is not just true on the quantum level; this is true everywhere. When the truth of this fact *everywhere* is taken seriously, writ large, we come to panpsychism, at least in its weak form (i.e., mind-dependence).

Importantly, panpsychism does not treat the substance of the world as a mysterious thing called "matter," the working assumption of materialism, nor does it posit a non-material spirit or "ghost in the machine," as in dualism. Rather, for a panpsychist, the mind inhabits the world fundamentally – whether relationally ("weak panpsychism"), constitutively ("animistic panpsychism"), or comprehensively ("absolute idealism"). In any case, the takeaway from panpsychism is that mental life is the one experiential reality of which we have certainty – not as the grammatical subject of Descartes' *cogito*, but the sheer facticity of cognitively inhabiting a lived world. To claim anything more (or less) than the experiential world is to delve into the realm of metaphysical speculation.

Panpsychism is not only a claim in the realm of metaphysics, it can be an empirical claim, too. A motion to take seriously the *matter of experience* was put forward by William James in his *radical empiricism*: "To be radical, an empiricism must neither admit into its constructions any element that is not directly experienced, nor exclude from them any element that is directly experienced" (James 1912, 42). James sought to overcome abstract metaphysics, which rely on "faith" in notions like "matter" to build knowledge. In doing so, panpsychists like James clarify the implications of empirical knowledge and their foundations, all the way to their counter-intuitive and uncomfortable conclusions.

F.H. Bradley, despite being criticized by James, formulated a logical foundation for this kind of experiential metaphysics in his *Appearance and Reality*:

> Find any piece of existence, take up anything that any one could possibly call a fact, or could in any sense assert to have being, and then judge if it does not consist in sentient experience. Try to discover any sense in which you can still continue to speak of it, when all perception and feeling have been removed; or point out any fragment of its matter, any aspect of its being, which is not derived from and is not still relative to this source. When the experiment is made strictly, I can myself conceive of nothing else than the experienced.
>
> *(Bradley 1930, 127–128)*

This kind of analysis is the starting point of panpsychism.

While the notion of panpsychism may strike a casual reader of philosophy as strange, the strangeness of the notion "materialism" is too often casually overlooked, as Galen Strawson starkly observes:

> If one hasn't felt a kind of vertigo of astonishment, when facing the thought, obligatory for all materialists, that consciousness is a wholly physical phenomenon in every respect, including every Experiential respect – a sense of having been precipitated into a completely new confrontation with the utter strangeness of the physical (the real) relative to all existing commonsense and scientific conceptions of it – then one hasn't begun to be a thoughtful materialist. One hasn't got to the starting line.
>
> *(Strawson 2008, 36)*

Whether or not panpsychism is true, it is no stranger than materialism (and arguably less so).

Contemporary philosophers like Timothy Sprigge have argued that panpsychism offers a more coherent account of the world than the alternatives of physicalism (a.k.a. materialism) and dualism (Sprigge 1983). David Ray Griffin also makes this case, citing his mentor, Charles Hartshorne, who argued that materialism is "dualism in disguise" because materialists implicitly acknowledge a difference between experiencing and non-experiencing things (Griffin 1998, 77). Materialists reduce mind to matter, yet idealists do just the opposite: they reduce matter to mind. In this way, idealists, too, are crypto-dualists. The environmental philosopher Freya Matthews articulates how panpsychism offers a way around the crypto-dualisms of materialism and idealism:

> Dualistic theories are typically contrasted with materialist theories, on the one hand, which explain mentality or ideality reductively in physicalist terms, and idealist theories, on the other hand, that posit forms of mentality or ideality that cannot be thus theoretically reduced to physics and in which indeed matter is often written off altogether as a mere mirage of appearances. But materialism and idealism are in fact just flip sides of dualism itself… The true converse of mind-matter dualism is neither materialism nor idealism but a position that posits some form of nonduality of mind-matter unity, implicating mentality in the definition of matter and materiality in the definition of mind.
>
> *(Matthews 2003, 26–27)*

Contrary to idealists (who describe a matter-independent world) and materialists (who describe a mind-independent world), panpsychism can be understood as a relational philosophy of mind-matter, a philosophy of nonduality. Matthews continues to formulate this alternative:

> A theory that posits mind-matter unity should be described as panphysicalist as well as panpsychist, since psychic or ideal phenomena will be as physically based, from the unified point of view, as physical phenomena will be psychically based.
>
> *(Matthews 2003, 27)*

Matthews argues that panpsychism is not only compatible with "panphysicalism,"[5] she furthermore contends that panpsychism, in contrast to materialism and idealism, offers a sound basis for ethics:

> Materialism – the deanimation of the world – has always been in a relation of philosophical codependency with idealism. Materialism tends to front up as the commonsense version of dualism, idealism as the esoteric, philosophical version. Idealist philosophies are thus always current in materialist cultures. (Poststructural relativism is the

prevalent form of idealism in Western societies today: poststructuralism disallows inference from cultural constructions of reality to any postulate concerning an "objective" dimension of things, such as that which was traditionally regarded as the province of physics.) Materialism and idealism are equally retrograde from an environmental point of view: the materialist regards the world as an inert lump of putty for his own designs; for the idealist it is an inconsequential mirage of appearances, unknowable and hence for practical purposes nonexistent in its own right.

(Matthews 2003, 27)

Clearly, not every panpsychism is a metaphysical idealism. As is the case among Buddhist (and Yogācāra) philosophies, we find a range of meanings for panpsychism.

One of the takeaways from panpsychism, besides the fact that non-experiential matter is incoherent, is that the notion of mental-matter can serve pragmatic purposes, just like mindless-matter. Nothing need be lost by including mind in matter, and there is much to gain, particularly when we recognize the important difference between (methodological) objectivity and (ontological) objectivity: the former serves to remove biases of prejudice (interests that color subjective orientations such as wish-fulfillment or fear), while the latter presumes to remove the subjective component of experience *in toto*. The former is an important component in a pragmatic, scientific method, yet the latter is an impossibility for the simple fact that everything known is necessarily experienced. A common mistake in modern notions of the world is the presumption that materialism is a predetermined fact – the realm of hardnosed scientists – whereas panpsychism is a flakey, metaphysical notion. Yet as the contemporary analytic philosopher Galen Strawson pointed out, "We really don't know enough to say that there is any non-mental being" (Strawson 2008, 44).

In his influential article subtitled "Why Physicalism Entails Panpsychism," Strawson makes a distinction between *physicalism*, "the view that every real phenomena in the universe is…physical," and *physicSism*, "the view – the faith – that the nature or essence of all concrete reality can in principle be fully captured in the term *physics*" (Strawson 2006, 3–4). A problem inherent in the position Strawson outlines as physicSism (a.k.a. physicalism) has been dubbed "Hempel's dilemma." Hempel's dilemma (named after the philosopher Carl Hempel) points to a major problem with the tenet of physicalism, namely, that it cannot account for phenomenal experience within the current model of physics, so it must appeal to a future physics that supposedly will be able to do so. Yet the idea of what constitutes "physical" in the future may be quite different from what is held to constitute the physical in present-day physics, and if history has taught us anything, the future physics will conceive the world in a much different way than the physics of today. So that leaves us with the dilemma: will the future "physical" include the mental?[6]

Panpsychism is not so easily dismissed just because it is counter-intuitive or "weird," a common complaint about it (if it is taken seriously at all and not just ignored). Thankfully, simply being counter-intuitive is not enough to exclude a topic from intelligent inquiry, for where would science be if any claim that was counter-intuitive were *a priori* taken off the table of reasonable truth?

Subjective and Absolute Idealisms in Yogācāra

Buddhist Yogācāra traditions do not postulate a metaphysical notion of matter independent of experiential reality. Since the "stuff" of the world is cognitive, the primary material of the world is not completely opaque to cognition, unlike a physicalist's mysterious notion of "matter." The eighth- and ninth-century Indian Buddhist Prajñākaragupta conveyed the problem with the claim to an external world concisely as follows: "If blue is perceived, then how can it be called 'external'? And, if it is not perceived, how can it be called 'external'?"[7]

In Yogācāra texts we find a number of arguments that deny a mind-independent world, such as the dream argument (that our perceptions of external objects are as mistaken in waking perception as they are in dreams), arguments that objects are observer-dependent (e.g., water appears differently to fish and humans), and arguments that objects are always accompanied by cognitions (objects are always *known* objects).[8]

Other arguments found in Yogācāra texts attack the very notion of materiality, such as Vasubandhu's arguments against partless particles constituting extended phenomena (*Viṃśatikā* v. 11–14; Vasubandhu 1957), Dignāga's argument that neither external particles nor their combinations can provide an account of the perception of phenomena (*Ālambanaparīkṣā* v. 1–5; Dignāga 1957a), and Dharmakīrti's argument that perceived objects are not real because they are neither unitary nor singular: "That form in which entities are perceived does not exist in reality, for these (things) have neither a unitary nor a multiple form" (*Pramāṇavārttika* III.359; Dharmakīrti 1957a).[9] It is needless to say that these Buddhists, famous for proclaiming the absence of a self, were not afraid to follow logic to its counter-intuitive consequences, including the denial of an external world.

Vasubandhu is the godfather of arguments against external realism. In the fifth century, he clearly pointed out a central problem of emergence: that we cannot get extended objects from what is not extended. His successor, Dignāga, pointed out a further problem with a dualistic metaphysic, namely, dualism's inability to provide a coherent account of the phenomenal world. Both of these influential figures raised philosophical problems in terms of a coherent account that can relate the (indivisibly) small with the (macroscopically) large.

Dignāga's arguments shed light on a problem in terms of (i) the relation between extended things and what is not extended, and (ii) the relationship between mind and matter. For the first problem, Dignāga echoes Vasubandhu's argument in the *Twenty Stanzas* that extended objects cannot be constituted by indivisible particles that lack extension. The second problem – the relationship not between macro-objects and micro-objects, but between cognition and matter – is known as the "hard problem" of consciousness. It is a version of the mind–body problem that addresses the question: how can experience arise from matter, which does not share its nature? This problem is set up by the presumptions of a mental–physical dualism, but can be answered with monism. Dignāga's answer is not, however, a physicalist monism (which is left with an explanatory gap that fails to address experiential reality), but rather the monism of panpsychism.

A distinctive feature of Dignāga's panpsychism is that he makes external realism compatible with idealism – the same principles that guide a coherent causal process in terms of external entities can function without those entities as well. That is, we might call something "matter" or a "configuration of energy" and presume a causal story around the kind of entity we designate. We can presume that matter is external and separate from mind, or we can presume that matter (or energy) is the same kind of stuff as the mind and still have the same regularity of causal processes that external realism demands.

Furthermore, with panpsychism the causal process need not be initiated by mind (as in the "top-down" mental causation of subjective idealism) or by matter (the "bottom-up" causation of physicalism) but by means of a third entity, which is neither external nor internal but the cause of both. In fact, this third alternative, as a form of neutral monism (that is neither mental nor physical but shares properties of, or is the cause of, both), is another possibility available to describe a Yogācāra metaphysic. In fact, the status of the world, as either subjective idealism or absolute idealism (or neutral monism), is another level of ambiguity at play in Dignāga's philosophy (in addition to the one between external realism and subjective idealism). We can say that the ambiguity here is one between *subjective* idealism (everything that exists is perceived) and *absolute* idealism (nothing is outside the unitary structure within which there are only internal relations). In the former case, mind is constitutive of the world; in the latter case, mind is intertwined with the world. In both cases, there is nothing outside mind.

An important feature of Dignāga's Yogācāra is his notion of self-awareness, which is not simply a subjective feature, but the unity of the subject–object structure of the world. In Dignāga's self-awareness, as in absolute idealism, the subjective and the objective components constitute two facets of a larger whole. With this kind of account, the content of mental perception need not be a mental projection, as in the fictional objects of (subjective) idealism, for the subjective mental image along with the objective mental image form the structure of self-awareness (*Pramāṇasamuccaya* 1.8–10; Dignāga 1957b).

The dual-aspected nature of self-awareness resembles the substance of Spinoza's dual-aspect monism. Like Spinoza, who used thought and extension as examples of *attributes* of substance, Dignāga and his commentator, Dharmakīrti, outlined subjective and objective features of self-awareness. In his *Pramāṇaviniścaya*, Dharmakīrti claimed that "What is experienced by cognition is not different [from it]"[10] (Dharmakīrti 1957b). Self-awareness in this case is thus both the means and content of knowledge, similar to Spinoza's notion of substance, which he defined as "what is in itself and is conceived through itself" (Spinoza 2002, 217 definition 3). Spinoza also supported the case that subjects and objects only appear to be distinct but in fact are not by following the principle that unlike things cannot be causally related,[11] like Dharmakīrti.[12]

While a supermind of absolute idealism is not explicated by Dignāga or Dharmakīrti, such a form of self-awareness, as the ultimate substance or truth, is found in the works of the Tibetan scholar Śākya Chokden (*shākya mchog ldan*, 1428–1507). Self-awareness for Śākya Chokden is *sui generis*, like Spinoza's substance (a.k.a. God). In the way that for Spinoza, mind and matter are nothing but attributes of the one (infinite) substance of God,[13] Śākya Chokden claims that the only thing that is real is self-awareness, and that this self-awareness is the ultimate reality – the real ground for the unreal subject–object presentation of duality. Yet the self-awareness that Śākya Chokden claims to be real is exclusively a nondual awareness, not ordinary (conventional) self-awareness, for he denies the reality of any awareness that perceives duality (Śākya Chokden 1975, 477–478). Real self-awareness for him is of another order than ordinary cognitions. Śākya Chokden creates a third category for self-awareness, beyond dualistic subjectivity and objectivity. This self-awareness is thus a kind of supermind, or gnosis (*ye shes*), as opposed to ordinary consciousness (*rnam shes*).

Although Dignāga may not necessarily follow Śākya Chokden down the road to absolute idealism, his explanation does not simply reduce cognition to the *subject*, as in a simplistic model of subjective idealism (a.k.a. "mind-only") in which objective percepts are simply the products of a *subjective* mind. Rather, there is a more complex and arguably more nuanced causal story.

Dignāga's account of perception entails a temporal, self-generating, and self-regulating process of conscious experience, which is driven by a feedback loop of predisposition and habituation to predispositions. That is, he says that the capacities for perception reside in cognition, and cognition arises from these capacities. In this way, his account of the cognitive process exemplifies the cognitive coupling of agent and environment, which mutually cooperate to create a life-world. In this system, moreover, both the dualist's and physicalist's problem of emergence – how mind arises from matter – is skirted, because the transcendental structure of the world is not spatially located *in here* or *out there*, and so is not bound by the temporality that it shapes.

The status of the external world is clear in Yogācāra: there is none. Yet what constitutes reality is ambiguous: is it all mind or not? This question is reflected in the status of the *dependent nature* in the Yogācāra theory of three natures: the *imagined nature*, the *dependent nature*, and the *consummate nature*. Conceptual construction is the *imagined nature* – what we impute as the reality of things like trees, selves, and tables, and the concepts we use to capture these entities. We hold these things to be real and a natural part of reality, when they are in fact cultural artifacts; that is to say, they are not separate from our conceptual constructions. The real world is not the way we construct it to be; reality's emptiness of constructions is the *consummate nature*. Reality is the *dependent nature*, the basis of our false conceptions, which is the inexpressible field of reality and an indeterminate matrix of relations.

The dependent nature is structured by dependent arising, a structure that implicates the mind, too. The dependent nature is thus entangled with cognition; it constitutes a panpsychist world. The dependent nature has been identified with the distorted mind,[14] like the foundational consciousness, and we can see how both these notions play pivotal roles in Yogācāra, as the causal story of the world. Like the dependent nature, the foundational consciousness is a structure that is not only internal, nor only mental, but a causal process that is the source and content of the attribution of subjects and objects.

While the foundational consciousness, being nominally a "consciousness" (*vijñāna*), may be identified with the subjective pole of perception, it is the source not only of the subjective representations of mind, but also of objective representations of bodies, environments, and materials as well. Thus, the function of the foundational consciousness supports a form of *panpsychism* – that all is mind or mind-like (or at least a weak form of panpsychism, that all is mind-dependent). Alternatively, the foundational consciousness can be seen as a form of neutral monism: a causal matrix that is neither mind nor matter, but the ground of both. This is because rather than simply being a form of subjective idealism, the foundational consciousness constitutes the content of *subjects* as well as objects.

At the end of the day, Yogācāra may better be described in the more neutral terms of panpsychism rather than the subjective idealism of "mind-only" because panpsychism not only captures the fact that the foundational consciousness is a consciousness and the content of object presentation, but also conveys that the foundational consciousness is the content of the presentation of subjectivity, too. In this way, the reality of the *subject* along with its subject–object presentation can be denied while affirming a conscious process (like the dependent nature), just as when the mere flow of consciousness is affirmed in a causal story that denies any enduring entity like a unified self. This process comes from something that is not itself a *subjective* consciousness, but from what is said to be an "internal" consciousness nonetheless (simply because it is not "out there").

We can discern a tension in Yogācāra, namely, a tension between subjective idealism and panpsychism, as seen in the respective meanings ascribed to subjectivity, internality, and cognition. Given that the foundational consciousness is said to be "internal," the meaning of *internality* – retained as something distinct from ordinary subjectivity, and particularly in the absence of external objects – leaves the ambiguity of Yogācāra in place.

Conclusion

Yogācāra is often harnessed with the unspecified label "idealism," and thus saddled with the problems associated with *subjective* idealism – such as those of solipsism, there being an asymmetry between a (real) mind and an (unreal) object, and there being no way to drive a wedge between an "internal" mind and an "external" object (the wedge upon which subjective idealism depends, since there is no place to stand outside of a subject–object relation to split those up and privilege the former). Yet the importance of Yogācāra analyses is often overlooked in one-sided caricatures of this tradition.

While subjective idealism is logically problematic, absolute idealism (or panpsychism) is not. In fact, A.K. Chatterjee puts forward Yogācāra as a philosophy of idealism that cannot simply be replaced by another constructive philosophy, but one that can only be challenged by deconstruction or silence:

> Yogācāra philosophy is…a perfect example of coherent construction. It is not to be challenged by other constructive philosophies; one dogmatism is not refuted by another dogmatism. If one refuses to accept idealism, one can do so, not by embracing another speculative philosophy, but only by ceasing to have any speculation at all.
>
> *(Chatterjee 1975, 229)*

The logical coherency of absolute idealism is quite different from the critical or skeptical modes of thought that simply unmask the shaky foundations of any system of thought. Like panpsychism, Yogācāra is a formidable philosophy, even while it is often represented in the form of a straw man, and criticized as simply subjective idealism. Panpsychism, however, cannot be dismissed simply because it is counter-intuitive, for it remains a coherent model of the universe, and a metaphysic with empirical and logical support.

Notes

1 With "animistic panpsychism" I mean to express a view that distinct minds inhabit discrete entities, as opposed to a view that the mind is intertwined with the world in a relational structure.

2 Reflecting the "implicative negation" (*ma yin dgag*) of a Yogācāra interpretation of emptiness, which leaves a ground that remains in emptiness, Bradley says, "Every negation must have a ground, and this ground is positive" (Bradley 1922, 117).
3 Throughout his *Mūlamadhyamakakārikā*, Nāgārjuna consistently showed the contingent nature of entities, that nothing has intrinsic nature. He furthermore stated: "Without intrinsic nature, how could there be extrinsic nature?" (*Mūlamadhyamakakārikā* XV.3; Nāgārjuna 1957).
4 Perhaps the organization can be articulated with Arthur Koestler's notion of *holons*. A holon is composed of parts, is a whole itself, and is part of a larger whole. As Koestler said, "A 'part,' as we generally use the word, means something fragmentary and incomplete, which by itself would have no legitimate existence. On the other hand, a 'whole' is considered as something complete in itself which needs no further explanation. But *'wholes' and 'parts' in this absolute sense just do not exist anywhere*, either in the domain of living organisms or of social organizations. What we find are intermediary structures on a series of levels in an ascending order of complexity: sub-wholes which display, according to the way you look at them, some of the characteristics commonly attributed to wholes and some of the characteristics commonly attributed to parts… It seems preferable to coin a new term to designate these nodes on the hierarchic tree which behave partly as wholes or wholly as parts, according to the way you look at them. The term I would propose is 'holon'" (Koestler 1967, 48). A panpsychist takes account of the *psychically* configured structure of multiple and hierarchical layers of the universe.
5 "Psychicism" might be a better alternative to the term *panpsychism*, because physicalists do not use the prefix *pan-* as in "*pan*physicalism," but simply use physicalism.
6 This physicalist's dilemma is exasperated by Buddhist philosophers who kowtow to the popular notion of a "scientific establishment" – as Amber Carpenter, in her otherwise excellent book, echoes the voice of a (real or imagined?) natural scientist when she claimed that "philosophers are best off taking the natural world to be as the natural scientists describe it" (Carpenter 2014, 112). Socrates would roll over in his grave if he were to hear that a philosopher is best off transmitting "truths" from *de jour* scientific consensus (unless by "best off," what is meant is survival – that is, it is dangerous to stand up for truth and deadly to swallow the hemlock)!
7 Prajñākaragupta in PVBh 366, 17 (III.718). Cited in Kajiyama (1966, 140): *yadi saṃvedyate nīlaṃ kathaṃ bāhyaṃ tad ucyate/na cet saṃvedyate nīlaṃ kathaṃ bāhyaṃ tad ucyate*.
8 Sakya Paṇḍita states two main reasons for the view that the world has a cognitive nature: (i) all objects of cognitions are cognitive because it is impossible for an object of cognition to lack clarity and awareness; and (ii) objects are always necessarily observed together with cognitions (*lhan cig dmigs nges*) (Sakya Paṇḍita 1989, 55).

9 *Pramāṇavārttika* III.359: *bhāvā yena nirūpyante tad rūpaṃ nāsti tattvataḥ/ yasmād ekam anekaṃ vā rūpaṃ teṣāṃ na vidyate.* Citation and translation from Steinkellner (1990, 78).
10 *Pramāṇaviniścaya* 1.38a: *nānyo 'nubhāvyo buddhyāsti.* See Keira (2004, 40 n.75).
11 Spinoza claims that "If things have nothing in common with one another, one of them cannot be the cause of the other" (Spinoza 2002, 218 Proposition 3); also, he adds that "although two attributes may be conceived to be really distinct (i.e., one may be conceived without the aid of the other), we still cannot infer from that that they constitute two beings, *or* two different substances" (Spinoza 2002, 221 Scholium to Proposition 10).
12 See Dharmakīrti on self-awareness, in *Pramāṇavārttika* III.326–327; and on causes "of the same type" (*sajāti*), in *Pramāṇavārttika* II.36. See also Arnold (2012, 33).
13 Spinoza states in Proposition 15 of the *Ethics*: "Whatever is, is in God, and nothing can be or be conceived without God" (Spinoza 2002, 224).
14 For instance, Asaṅga characterized the dependent nature as follows in the *Mahāyānasaṃgraha* I.21: "What is the characteristic of the dependent nature? It is a cognition comprised by unreal imagination concerning the basic consciousness potentiality" (Asaṅga 1977). In Tibet, Mipam also described the dependent nature in cognitive terms. See Duckworth (2008, 48).

References

Arnold, Dan. 2012. *Brains, Buddhas, and Belief.* New York: Columbia University Press.
Asaṅga. 1977. *Mahāyānasaṃgraha* (*theg pa chen po'i bsdus pa*). In *sde dge mtshal par bka' 'gyur: a facsimile edition of the 18th century redaction of Situ chos kyi 'byung gnas prepared under the direction of H.H. the 16th rgyal dbang karma pa*, text no. 4048, 13a. Delhi: Delhi Karmapae Chodhey Gyalwae Sungrab Partun Khang.
Bradley, F.H. 1922. *The Principles of Logic*, vol. 1. Oxford: Oxford University Press.
Bradley, F.H. 1930. *Appearance and Reality.* Oxford: Clarendon Press.
Bradley, F.H. 2012 [1914]. *Essays on Truth and Reality.* Cambridge: Cambridge University Press.
Carpenter, Amber D. 2014. *Indian Buddhist Philosophy: Metaphysics as Ethics.* Abingdon: Routledge.
Chatterjee, A.K. 1975. *The Yogācāra Idealism*, 2nd edition. Delhi: Motilal Banarsidass.
Dharmakīrti. 1957a. *Pramāṇavārttika* (*tshad ma rnam 'grel*). In *The Tibetan Tripitika, Peking Edition*, edited by D.T. Suzuki (P. 5709). Tokyo: Tibetan Tripitika Research Institute.

Dharmakīrti. 1957b. *Pramāṇaviniścaya* (*tshad ma rnam par nges pa*). In *The Tibetan Tripitika, Peking Edition*, edited by D.T. Suzuki (P. 5710). Tokyo: Tibetan Tripitika Research Institute.

Dignāga. 1957a. *Ālambanaparīkṣā* (*dmigs pa brtag pa*). In *The Tibetan Tripitika, Peking Edition*, edited by D.T. Suzuki (P. 5703). Tokyo: Tibetan Tripitika Research Institute.

Dignāga. 1957b. *Pramāṇasamuccaya* (*tshad ma kun btus*). In *The Tibetan Tripitika, Peking Edition*, edited by D.T. Suzuki (P. 5700). Tokyo: Tibetan Tripitika Research Institute.

Duckworth, Douglas. 2008. *Mipam on Buddha-Nature*. Albany: SUNY Press.

Griffin, David Ray. 1998. *Unsnarling the World Knot*. Berkeley: University of California Press.

James, William. 1912. *Essays in Radical Empiricism*. London: Longmans, Green, and Co.

James, William. 1977. *A Pluralistic Universe*. Cambridge, MA: Harvard University Press.

Kajiyama, Yuichi. 1966. *An Introduction to Buddhist Philosophy: An Annotated Translation of the Tarkabhāṣa of Mokṣākaragupta*. Kyoto: Kyoto University.

Keira, Ryusei. 2004. *Mādhyamika and Epistemology: A Study of Kamalaśīla's Method for Proving the Voidness of All Dharmas*. Vienna: Arbeitskreis für Tibetische und Buddhistische Studien Wien.

Koestler, Arthur. 1967. *The Ghost in the Machine*. New York: The Macmillan Co.

Matthews, Freya. 2003. *For Love of Matter: A Contemporary Panpsychism*. Albany: SUNY Press.

Nāgārjuna. 1957. *Mūlamadhyamakakārikā* (*dbu ma rtsa ba*). In *The Tibetan Tripitika, Peking Edition*, edited by D.T. Suzuki (P. 5224). Tokyo: Tibetan Tripitika Research Institute.

Śākya Chokden (*shākya mchog ldan*, 1428–1507). 1975. *Commentary on Pramāṇavārttika* (*rgyas pa'i bstan bcos tshad ma rnam 'grel gyi rnam bshad pa sde bdun ngag gi rol mtsho*). Collected Works, vol. 18, 189–693. Thimphu, Bhutan: Kunzang Tobgey.

Sakya Paṇḍita (*sa skya paṇḍita*, 1182–1251). 1989. *Treasury of Epistemology* (*tshad ma'i rigs gter*). Beijing: Nationalities Press.

Skrbina, David. 2005. *Panpsychism in the West*. Cambridge, MA: MIT Press.

Spinoza, B. 2002. *Ethics*. In *Spinoza: The Complete Works*, edited by M. Morgan, translated by Samuel Shirley. Indianapolis: Hackett Publishing.

Sprigge, Timothy. 1983. *The Vindication of Absolute Idealism*. Edinburgh: Edinburgh University Press.

Steinkellner, Ernst. 1990. "Is Dharmakīrti a Mādhyamika?" In *Earliest Buddhism and Madhyamaka*, edited by David Seyfort Ruegg and Lambert Schmithhausen, 72–90. Leiden: E.J. Brill.

Strawson, Galen. 2006. "Realistic Monism: Why Physicalism Entails Panpsychism."
In *Consciousness and Its Place in Nature*, edited by Anthony Freeman, 3–31.
Exeter: Imprint Academic.
Strawson, Galen. 2008. *Real Materialism and Other Essays*. Oxford:
Oxford University Press.
Vasubandhu. 1957. *Viṃśatikā* (*nyi shu pa*). In *The Tibetan Tripitika, Peking Edition*, edited by D.T. Suzuki (P. 5557). Tokyo: Tibetan Tripitika Research Institute.
Whitehead, A.N. 1941. "Immortality." In *The Philosophy of Alfred North Whitehead*, vol. 3, edited by Paul Schilpp. Evanston: Northwestern University Press.

3

Emergentist Naturalism in Early Buddhism and Deweyan Pragmatism
John J. Holder

A Middle Way Between Dualism and Reductive Physicalism

The field of contemporary metaphysics remains largely polarized into two camps. One camp defends a dualistic position that proposes that reality is a combination of the natural (physical) and the non-natural (mind, soul, consciousness). The dualist position has a long history in philosophy that goes back to Aristotle and was most famously defended in early modern philosophy by Descartes. The second camp defends reductive physicalism. This position has become increasingly popular in the last century. Physicalism proposes that reality is coincident with the world as described by the natural sciences, that is, everything that exists is some configuration of matter or energy alone. Physicalist metaphysics claims that all supposedly non-natural phenomena, such as human minds, are really just the complexities of matter and energy. In other words, physicalists hold that minds as a non-physical entity do not exist in what is an exhaustively physical world.

Each of these metaphysical positions has significant philosophical problems. Dualists have yet to explain how the natural and non-natural can interact. For example, how can an immaterial mind have any interaction with a physical body (or vice versa), whereas there are myriad examples that suggest they must interact (e.g., any volition that is carried out by the body). Dualists are also fighting upstream against the discoveries of modern science that have made belief in non-natural entities appear superfluous. Knowledge in the neural sciences, for example, has grown exponentially in recent decades and the strong correlations that neuroscience has found between brain processes and consciousness make it almost undeniable that mental phenomena are at least partially dependent on physical brain processes.

Buddhist Philosophy: A Comparative Approach, First Edition. Edited by Steven M. Emmanuel.
© 2018 John Wiley & Sons, Inc. Published 2018 by John Wiley & Sons, Inc.

In short, to be a dualist in the contemporary metaphysical debate means holding a position that is fundamentally unscientific.

And yet physicalism has its own significant philosophical problems. Physicalism seems unable to account for the subjective, first-hand, properties of mental phenomena. The subjective feeling of pain, for example, appears to be categorically different from complex brain chemistry. Humans do not experience themselves as complex neural events and it may well be impossible *in principle* that there could ever be a reduction of the phenomenological aspects of human experience to an account that uses only terms like matter and energy (regardless how closely correlated observed brain events and mental phenomena might become). Even more troubling is the fact that if physicalism is true, it is hard to see how the human values that form the core of ethics and religious systems could be retained. There is just no way to capture values using terms like molecules and energy, thus it is extremely difficult to account for normative ethical principles in a physicalist metaphysics. Moral responsibility is an illusion if normative ethical principles do not exist.

Into this metaphysical debate a third position has been proposed, namely, *emergentist naturalism*. This is a promising position that has the benefits of remaining naturalistic like the sciences, avoiding talk of a distinct non-natural substance or reality, and at the same time it avoids the reductive extremes of physicalism that cannot account for the subjective aspects of experience. Most importantly, emergentist naturalism avoids the attempt to explain away human consciousness and ethical values in terms of the concepts of the natural sciences. Thus, a metaphysical position that is attuned to the natural sciences but also recognizes the genuine existence of moral, aesthetic, and perhaps religious values is a highly attractive metaphysical position.

Although emergentist naturalism has recently gained some traction as a popular alternative to dualism and physicalism in contemporary metaphysical discussions, it is not a completely new development in metaphysics.[1] Emergentist naturalism has been the central metaphysical philosophy of two important philosophical traditions, Deweyan pragmatism and early Buddhism.[2] The aim of this chapter is to show how a consistent emergentist naturalism position can be crafted by drawing on elements of Deweyan and Buddhist metaphysics. In particular, this chapter argues that both traditions defend a "strong ontological emergentism" that recognizes the human person and human values (moral agency) as levels of reality that have their own integrity. The chapter proceeds by first laying down a comparative framework for understanding Deweyan pragmatism and early Buddhism – most importantly, that both philosophical traditions understand *causality* as the key to existence. The following sections discuss the radically different purpose of metaphysics in these traditions, followed by an articulation of naturalistic emergentism at various levels (from lower order to higher order): biological emergence, the emergence of consciousness, moral agency (karma), and the prospects of religious meaning in emergentist naturalism.

Comparing Deweyan Pragmatism and Early Buddhism

There are quite a number of important philosophical similarities between Dewey's pragmatism and early Buddhism that serve as a basis for comparative study of these two traditions.[3] A very brief survey of some of these similarities sets the stage for the more detailed exploration of their naturalistic metaphysics that follows.

In conceiving their general philosophical orientations, both Dewey and the Buddha each regarded his philosophical approach as a "middle way" (*via media* or *majjhimāpaṭipadā*) between the ethical, metaphysical, and epistemological extremes prevalent among their contemporaries. Interestingly, the extreme positions between which Dewey and the Buddha tried to steer a middle course were not all that different. The Buddha, for example, rejected the essentialist and absolutist metaphysics in the Brahmanical tradition, on the one extreme, and the annihilationist metaphysics of the materialists, on the other extreme. Similarly, Dewey was trying to carve out a position between the extremes of idealism and the reductive physicalism that takes its cue from the natural sciences.

In regard to metaphysics, both Dewey and the Buddha held forms of *naturalism*, by which it is meant that everything that exists is a causally interdependent order of phenomena; that is to say, everything that exists is a *natural process*. More specifically, both held "emergentist" or non-reductive forms of naturalism in which higher order processes emerge from, but are not reducible to, lower order processes. In accord with their naturalism, both rejected the idea that behind this world of change stands a permanent, transcendent reality. Unlike traditional forms of metaphysics, neither the Buddha nor Dewey was attempting to describe an Ultimate Reality. In both pragmatism and Buddhism, metaphysics is not an inquiry that discovers truths that are independent of human existence. Instead, metaphysical inquiry gives us the contours of reality insofar as existing things and events are evident in the broadest conceptions of human experience of a natural world. For this reason, Dewey referred to metaphysics as the study of the "generic traits of existence" (Dewey 1958, 51). In the case of Buddhism, the Buddha articulated a view of reality within the context of his psycho-ethical therapy for the removal of suffering (*dukkha*). This came by way of his most fundamental insight into the causes and elimination of suffering, the very catalyst of his enlightenment, namely, the doctrine of dependent arising (*paṭiccasamuppāda*). Metaphysics, so conceived, is not an attempt to escape the human condition because metaphysical commitments are contextualized by the human problematic – namely, how to achieve a meaningful life in a precarious world. No doubt, the philosophies of Dewey and the Buddha differed in important ways, but at a certain level of generality both philosophers can be interpreted as working on a similar naturalistic project framed as a question: without reaching beyond the natural world, the world of experience, how can a human life be reorganized to create the transformation of experience that achieves the highest levels of human meaning?

Defining Emergentist Naturalism

It is extremely important to understand the special meaning of "naturalism" as it applies to Dewey's pragmatism and early Buddhism, because this concept has many different meanings within contemporary philosophy. Crucially, "*emergentist*" naturalism must be differentiated from *reductive* or *eliminative* kinds of naturalism. The fact that many philosophers assume that all naturalisms are reductive has led to much misunderstanding. Reductive naturalism equates naturalism with physicalism. Physicalism holds that everything in the universe, even consciousness, art, and morality, can be explained *in toto* by physical substances operating mechanically. The mantra of physicalism is that everything ultimately is physics.

Emergentist naturalism, however, stands apart from reductive forms of naturalism, holding that higher order processes (such as mental phenomena or aesthetic meanings) emerge from, but are not reducible to, lower order processes. Emergentism asserts that novel properties arise as a product of a system taken as a whole. These new properties subsume the properties of the parts but, as a genuinely novel set of properties, remain distinct from those parts. For example, a painting conveys meanings that emerge from, but are not reducible to, the molecules of paint adhering to canvas. If one wants to understand a painting as an art object that conveys aesthetic meaning, one should approach an art historian, not a physicist. It is impossible, even in principle, to explain aesthetic meaning in terms of molecules and energy. This position does not deny that a painting is also an aggregation of molecules. Thus emergentism asserts that the painting exists on a number of qualitatively different levels and that the higher ones have an irreducible integrity.

As Philip Clayton helpfully defines it, "emergence" is the view that novel and unpredictable phenomena are naturally produced by interactions in nature; that these new structures, organisms, and ideas are not reducible to the subsystems on which they depend; and that the newly evolved realities in turn exercise a causal influence on the parts out of which they arose (Clayton 2004, vi). Emergentist naturalism makes an *ontological* claim that what emerges is a genuinely new type of reality in the world, but the novel properties do not replace the lower level phenomena from which they emerge – the natural world can operate simultaneously on a number of discrete levels. For example, sounds do not cease to be physical events when they become articulate speech; but by conveying linguistic meaning, they take on new distinctions and arrangements and thus new qualities emerge. The novelty of an emergent level lies in the way in which the lower level phenomena behave in a qualitatively different way when considered *as a whole*. This fact is illustrated clearly in the painting example given earlier. This position is called *strong ontological emergence* because it maintains there are ontologically distinct levels of phenomena in the world, each of which plays its own causal role in conjunction with its *own* set of laws or patterns that are irreducible *in principle* to phenomena at lower levels.[4] In other words, in strong ontological emergentism, novel entities and properties emerge that become causal agents in their own right, not merely as aggregates of underlying components. In an emergentist ontology, nature itself expands. No longer is nature ontologically coincident with what is physical; rather, nature includes also many of the higher order levels (biological, mental, social, and aesthetic) that make up our world. In the parlance of contemporary philosophy, higher order phenomena *supervene* on the lower level processes.[5] In this way, emergentist naturalism coheres with the findings of modern science and yet maintains that higher order phenomena (such as consciousness and human values) are genuine, irreducible, features of reality.

As the remainder of the chapter argues, Dewey and the Buddha each held a *strong ontological* form of emergentist naturalism. And by drawing on the relative strengths of these two philosophic traditions, a compelling form of emergentist naturalism takes shape that contributes a new perspective in contemporary metaphysical debates.

A Metaphysics of Causality and Emergent Levels of Reality

Dewey and the Buddha focused on *causality* and *change* as the most fundamental traits of existence. According to both philosophies, change so dominates reality that what we think of as "things" should be viewed as events, or processes, not as substances or entities. In remarkably similar ways, both early Buddhism and Deweyan pragmatism describe reality as a *causally* interdependent order of phenomena. "All phenomena are dependently arisen," said the Buddha; all phenomena are a nexus of causal factors that exhibit both stasis and change, identity and difference (SN.II.25). Importantly, all phenomena are *impermanent* processes; they arise at some point and cease to be at another point. On this basis, both pragmatism and early Buddhism deny the existence of a transcendental or unchanging realm beyond the world of change. In other words, for the Buddha as for Dewey, causality in the natural world should be the basis for our ontology – reality is comprised of nothing other than causal relationships or networks. A metaphysics of change implies that the world is incomplete, precarious, and perilous. This fact constitutes the fundamental challenge to the achievement of meaning in human lives.

Some scholars of Buddhism might object to calling early Buddhism a form of naturalism because the Pāli Canon is filled with references to gods (*devas*), demons, and the like. But, as A.K. Warder argues, references to such beings are consistent with naturalism because, in the Buddha's cosmology, gods and demons "fall within the realm of change and are subject to the laws of causality" (Warder 1980, 155). Furthermore, such beings play no essential role in the Buddha's teachings regarding the path to religious liberation. Thus, to consider early Buddhist metaphysics as "naturalistic" requires only the stretching of the term naturalism to include beings and forces that co-inhabit the natural world.

More importantly, the Buddha's teaching is naturalistic because causality – dependent arising – plays a central role in his account of suffering and the path that leads to religious transformation. This, in fact, was his greatest insight and revolutionary idea. The doctrine of dependent arising shows that the Buddha held an *emergentist* form of naturalism. The Buddha called dependent arising the essence of his teaching and explained the doctrine in a concise formula:

> When this exists, that comes to be; from the arising of this, that arises. When this is absent, that does not come to be; on the cessation of this, that ceases.
>
> *(SN.II.28)*

The Buddha elaborated further on this concise formula for dependent arising by applying it to the arising of suffering; this application is widely known as the "twelvefold formula of dependent arising."[6] Whereas some scholars think that dependent arising was meant to apply only to the arising and elimination of suffering and not the world at large, the concise formula itself and the Buddha's analysis of many different phenomena (such as the emergence of consciousness) suggest otherwise. To sum up, then, the changing, natural world is reality – it is the "all" and there is no other, as the Buddha put it in the "Discourse on the All" (SN.IV.15) – and so whatever way human striving might create meaning, it must do so in this changing natural world.

Causation is typically conceived as the mechanical, deterministic, operations of physical phenomena described in the hard sciences. But the natural world has produced life, consciousness, communities, and artistic meanings, all of which seem to operate causally, but not in mechanical ways. This begs for a richer conception of causality along the lines of emergentist naturalism. As explained earlier, in emergentist naturalism nature has potentialities that operate on distinct levels, and phenomena on these levels exhibit completely novel sets of properties. And yet the phenomena on higher levels only become actualized when certain conditions obtain on a lower level; they are not completely unrelated to the lower order phenomena. For such reasons, both

Dewey and the Buddha argued for a genuinely pluralistic metaphysics that they described in terms of distinct emergent levels of reality. A pluralistic metaphysics denies that there is ultimately only one type of causal reality (physico-chemical reality) to which all the other levels are to be reduced. The descriptions of the emergent levels of reality in each tradition are strikingly similar. Dewey recognized three levels or plateaus in his emergentist naturalism: (i) the physico-chemical level; (ii) the organic/psycho-physical level; and (iii) the social/aesthetic level that includes the mind (Dewey 1958, 272). According to the early Buddhist commentaries, the Buddha held that there are five levels in which causation (dependent arising) functions: (i) the physical inorganic world (*utuniyāma*); (ii) the organic world (*bījaniyāma*); (iii) the psycho-physical world (*cittaniyāma*); (iv) the social and moral world (*kammaniyāma*); and (v) the higher spiritual sphere (*dhammaniyāma*) (Kalupahana 1976, 30). Given the historical and cultural distances between early Buddhism and pragmatism, the parallel between these descriptions of the levels of emergence is truly remarkable.

The Principle of Continuity and Biological Emergence

The "principle of continuity" is the central concept in Dewey's emergentist naturalism. Change happens within nature. Phenomena *naturally* grow together to form wholes and these wholes sometimes exhibit qualitatively different properties that allow us to distinguish between "higher" and "lower" order operations. "Continuity" both means that higher order operations grow out of lower order operations without being identical with that from which they emerge, and it denies that explanations must appeal to non-natural realities. Dewey's clearest statement of the principle of continuity occurs in his discussion of logic as a kind of inquiry that is prefigured by the complex transactions between an organism and its environment:

> The term "naturalistic" has many meanings. As it is here employed it means, on one side, that there is no breach of continuity between operations of inquiry and biological operations and physical operations. "Continuity," on the other side, means that rational operations *grow out of* organic activities from which they emerge... The primary postulate of a naturalistic theory of logic is continuity of the lower (less complex) and the higher (more complex) activities and forms... [Continuity] excludes complete rupture on one side and mere repetition of identities on the other; it precludes the reduction of the "higher" to the "lower" just as it precludes complete breaks and gaps. The growth of any living organism from seed to maturity illustrates the meaning of continuity.
> *(Dewey 1938, 18–19, 23)*

Continuity, for Dewey, refers to the realization of newer, more inclusive types of order. Continuity thus involves more than sheer identity or repetition; there must be some novelty that grows out of prior conditions. The emergence of a higher level is thus continuous in the sense that the higher level is founded on a lower one and in a sense contains it, but at the same time integrates it into new structures which cannot be explained by the lower phenomena on which it supervenes. In this way, the higher level phenomena are *not fully determined* by the lower level phenomena.

Continuity does not eliminate novelty, but, as Dewey insisted, "what *is* excluded by the postulate of continuity is the appearance upon the scene of a totally new outside force as a cause of changes that occur" (Dewey 1938, 24). Emergence is a process fully grounded *in* nature, so there is no reason to appeal to an essence that exists outside of nature to account for the novel properties of the phenomena that emerge from phenomena on lower levels. The temptation in philosophy has typically been to treat higher order properties as transcendental/supernatural realities (e.g., Plato's Forms or Hegel's Spirit). In modern philosophy, this is represented by dualistic metaphysics. On the other extreme, the temptation in the natural sciences has been to explain higher order phenomena away by referring only to matter and energy. Emergentist naturalism represents a middle way, explaining higher order phenomena without either reduction to physics or invoking supernatural metaphysics.

Continuity is most clearly evident in biological emergence, as the emergence of organic life from inorganic components illustrates perfectly how properties of a whole (the organism) cannot be explained in terms of the properties of the lower level (physico-chemical) component parts. What distinguishes organic life from inorganic entities is that living organisms exhibit purposeful behavior and attempt to maintain themselves as wholes, whereas inorganic things (like rocks) do not. Dewey held that at each upward step in the hierarchy of biological order, unique properties emerge that were not present at the lower levels of organization. In the context of strong emergentism, organisms are not merely shorthand for lower level forces; they have their own integrity and act as causal forces in their own right. As the quotation on a naturalistic conception of logic clearly shows, Dewey went much further than biological emergence by arguing that the higher cognitive functions in humans have their basis in the patterns that are evident in the life of every organism.

As it has developed in contemporary philosophy, emergentist naturalism derives much of its support from evolutionary biology. Whereas Dewey fully recognized the importance of Darwinian evolutionary theory for all modes of philosophical inquiry, it would be highly anachronistic to suggest that the Buddha was a Darwinian evolutionist more than two millennia before Darwin. Thus it is reasonable to rely mainly on Dewey's discussion of evolutionary biology as a basis for emergentist naturalism because his work on biological modes of emergence advances emergentist naturalism in ways that early Buddhism cannot. But that is not the same as saying that the Buddha's ideas are incompatible with Darwinian evolution. The Buddha's conception of change in the natural world does not rule out biological evolution and the Buddha even sometimes referred to biological patterns – for example, the growth of plants – to explain change and emergence.[7]

Dewey appealed to emergentist naturalism to explain the emergence of phenomena at the social level, the level of human meanings and communication. As we saw earlier, emergence occurs on the biological level as the realization of possibilities that derive from the complex integration of an organism with its environment. But for human beings, our environment is far richer than mere physics and biology. Humans do not interact with other things mainly on the physical or biological level. Rather, our human environment is mainly populated by things having *social* meanings. A book, for example, is not for us primarily an aggregation of wood fibers and ink, but a social mode of communication. Dewey's work on language and communication offers a clear statement of emergentist naturalism at these higher levels:

> Of all affairs, communication is the most wonderful. That things should be able to pass from the plane of external pushing and pulling to that of revealing themselves to man, and thereby to themselves…is a wonder by the side of which transubstantiation pales. When communication occurs… [mere physical] events turn into objects, things with a meaning. … Events when once they are named lead an independent and double life.
> *(Dewey 1958, 166)*

The things that carry linguistic meanings (sound, for example) certainly exist also on the level of brute physical realities; they are vibrations in the air or ink and paper. But when a sound has linguistic significance, the physical level is not primary; rather, linguistic meaning operates primarily at the level of social reality. The existence of linguistic meaning is a sure sign that nature is capable of creating new levels of reality with novel properties. As Dewey went on to argue in *Art as Experience* (Dewey 1934a), nature includes the heights of aesthetic meaning just as much as the pushing and pulling of material forces. Indeed, humans are highly cultured, social, and artistic, beings, and yet humans do not cease to be biological and physico-chemical beings by the mere fact that such higher levels of existence emerge.

The Human Person: The Emergence of Mind and Consciousness

For both Dewey and the Buddha, emergentist naturalism applies to human nature itself. Human beings are an emergent feature of the natural world; we are not a being standing outside of nature. "This human situation falls wholly within nature," wrote Dewey (1958, 421). And "man is within nature, not a little god outside, and is within as a mode of energy inseparably connected with other modes" (Dewey 1958, 434). The Buddha likewise rejected supernatural accounts of human nature. He famously denied that the human person has a permanent self or essence (*ātman*). But neither Dewey nor the Buddha was thereby saying that human beings and human agency do not exist at all. For the Buddha, as for Dewey, there *is* no self or agent apart from the processes of acting, experiencing, or willing. Human beings, as conceived in emergentist naturalism, are an aggregation of natural processes. To use Dewey's mode of expression, personhood "emerge[s] with complexly organized interactions organic and social" (Dewey 1958, 208). Such a view is a middle way between mind–body dualism and physicalism that reduces mental phenomena to brain states.

The Buddha's emergentist naturalism is evident in his explanation of a human person as a *dependently arisen* process comprised of the five aggregates (*khandhas*): processes of the body (*rūpa*), processes of feeling (*vedanā*), processes of apperception (*saññā*), processes of volition (*sankhāra*), and processes of consciousness (*viññāṇa*). The five aggregates are not substances or entities, but processes having certain qualities. Although the Buddha saw the body as a necessary component of a person, he did not try to reduce the other four aggregates to the physical body. This fact clearly establishes that the Buddha was not a reductive physicalist in regard to the human being. But neither was he a metaphysical dualist. The texts make it clear that non-bodily functions have their basis in the physical body and, even more importantly, that there is an integration of the physical and psychical that is denoted by the compound term "*nāma-rūpa*." *Nāma* refers to the psychological or mental aspects of a person and *rūpa* refers to physical/bodily aspects of a person. Thus, a human person is an *integration* of the mind and body, a *psycho-physical* being. In this way, the Buddha held that humans are truly a "body-mind" in the sense that we manifest both physiological and mental features in an integrated way. Dewey came to the same position on human nature:

> In the hyphenated phrase body-mind, "body" designates...the registered and cumulative operation of factors continuous with the rest of nature, inanimate as well as animate; while "mind" designates...the features which emerge when "body" is engaged in a wider more complex and interdependent situation... [Such] external or environmental affairs, primarily implicated in living processes...undergo modifications in acquiring meanings and become objects of mind, and yet are as "physical" as ever they were.
>
> *(Dewey 1958, 285)*

So the difference between the body and the mind is not that the mind is something *other than* the physico-chemical body; rather, "it lies in the *way* in which physico-chemical energies are interconnected and operate, whence different *consequences* mark inanimate and animate activity respectively" (Dewey 1958, 254). Mental phenomena depend on the physical in a manner analogous to the dependency relations of other emergent phenomena. The mind emerges as part of the natural world, as a manifestation of the evolutionary process. What we call "mind" is not a substance, not a metaphysical entity, but a functionally developed, changing process that accounts for habits, volitions, and dispositions. The mind exhibits novel properties that emerge from human bodily functions and social interactions which though qualitatively different from bodily functions remain continually dependent on their subvenient base. To sum up, for the Buddha and Dewey, the best explanatory ontology regarding the human person has to include multiple levels of really existing properties, since the body, mental properties, and interpersonal structures all have their own irreducible integrity.

For some philosophers, the distinctive qualities of subjective mental phenomena are compelling evidence for a non-naturalist dualism. In the dualistic account of experience, the mind and the body are taken to be metaphysically distinct entities involving distinct substances. But dualist theories fail because "the idea that matter, life and mind represent separate *kinds* of Being is a doctrine that springs, as so many philosophic errors have sprung, from a *substantiation* of eventual *functions*" (Dewey 1958, 261). All mental phenomena should be treated as natural *processes* (not as entities) that emerge from the complex relationship organisms have with their environments. For emergentist naturalism, the challenge is maintaining the ontological integrity of mental phenomena like consciousness without the overemphasis on novel properties that leads to full-fledged dualism. Emergentist naturalism, however, is not dualism because mental phenomena exist *within* nature, that is, the mind is not a supernatural interloper in a natural world, and mental phenomena have a continuing dependence/emergence relationship with the physical body. In sum, dualists have overemphasized cognitive operations by setting up the mind as a distinct, non-natural, entity and physicalists have simply failed to recognize the existence of mental phenomena as such. Emergentist naturalism avoids these problems.

The Buddha offered a clear rejection of dualism when he gave an emergentist analysis of consciousness as a natural process that arises from the complexities of sense experience. In the "Discourse of the Honeyball" (*Madhupiṇḍika sutta*), the Buddha described the conditioned arising of consciousness as a coordination of functional factors including the physical sense organs, a sensory object, and a sensory mode of consciousness. The key passage from the "Discourse of the Honeyball" reads as follows:

> Visual consciousness arises dependent on the eye and visible objects. The meeting of the three is contact. Dependent on contact, there is feeling... Auditory consciousness arises dependent on the ear and sounds;

the meeting of the three is contact... Olfactory consciousness arises dependent on the nose and smells; the meeting of the three is contact... Gustatory consciousness arises dependent on tongue and tastes; the meeting of the three is contact... Bodily consciousness arises dependent on body and tangible objects; the meeting of the three is contact... Mental consciousness arises dependent on mind and mental objects. The meeting of the three is contact.

(MN.I.112)

According to this discourse, experience at the most basic level involves three necessary components: a sense faculty, a sense object, and a particular mode of sensory consciousness (e.g., visual consciousness) that arises dependent on the sense faculty and sense object. Consciousness is thus not a prior metaphysical entity (as dualists see it), but an emergent, natural, process that arises under certain complex conditions. And yet these three components (sense faculty, object, and mode of consciousness) are not sufficient by themselves to be "experience." There must be the meeting of these three in just the right way; this is called "contact" (*phassa*). Experience, the passage suggests, should be conceived holistically and functionally, that is, as a complex *whole* phenomenon wherein the subject and object are *mutually interdependent* (not separate entities) and all distinctions between subject and object are *functional* (rather than "metaphysical") distinctions. The text quoted above goes on to claim that consciousness leads to feelings and other mental phenomena that causally condition the future states of the psycho-physical person. As discussed in the following section, this causal process unfolds according to the doctrine of karma. Here the Buddha uniquely offered the moral implications of treating consciousness as a network of processes that are rooted in, and emergent from, the complex relationship between a human person and his or her environment.

Karma and Moral Agency in Emergentist Naturalism

Early Buddhism distinguishes between physical and psychological kinds of causation (Jayatilleke 1963, 453–454). Unlike physical causation that involves mechanical necessity or determinism, psychological causality involves strong tendencies or probabilities. This pattern of causation is best described as "conditionality." The early Buddhist conception of karma is a theory about how psychological phenomena operate causally in the sense of conditionality, rather than deterministically or mechanically. To many Western philosophers, the doctrine of karma is considered to be one of the least defensible parts of the Buddhist tradition. But interpreted in the context of emergentist naturalism, the doctrine of karma gains some plausibility. In essence, the doctrine of karma amounts to accepting the idea that human beings are moral agents in the world and that there is causal regularity between human action and moral consequences. But, importantly, karma works *within nature*; it is one way that psychological phenomena behave causally, even though it does not partake of the same type of causality that applies to the physical realm.

The word "karma" (Pāli *kamma*) literally means "action." In Brahmanical tradition, karma was specifically used in the sense of "ritual action" that takes place in the physical world (Gombrich 2009, 7). But the Buddha revolutionized the meaning of the word when he said, "by karma, I mean *intention*" (AN.III.415). Karma thus refers to psychological operations, rather than bodily processes. The Buddha invoked the doctrine of karma because it makes sense of moral responsibility. An action derives its moral value (good or bad) from the intention involved. According to the doctrine of karma, intentions get reinforced by actions, such that actions motivated by good intentions develop into moral habits that guide further deeds. As in traditional virtue ethics, the moral habits that are regularly enacted in deeds establish the moral basis of one's personality or character. For example, a person who gives generously to others in need, and does so regularly, develops a generous personality. Karma, as a Buddhist doctrine, explains the causal relationship between actions/intentions and the quality of life a person enjoys. As such, the doctrine of karma supports the ethical or normative principles that we need to live meaningfully. The idea that karma refers to fatalism – as the term is often used by many Westerners – is mistaken; in fact, that's the very opposite of the meaning given to the term by the Buddha. If karma is interpreted as fatalism, it could be used as an excuse to avoid moral responsibility for one's actions. The Buddha used the concept of karma for exactly the opposite purpose, to emphasize that each person has the moral freedom to control their quality of life.

Karma does not operate randomly, because it connects a person's moral status to prior volitions, and yet it does not operate deterministically either. Were karma to operate deterministically, as the *Ājīvaka* sage Makkhali Gosāla held, moral responsibility would be undermined. A moral agent should not be held responsible for actions that could not have been avoided. Richard Gombrich astutely comments that "for karma to work as an ethical doctrine, it must steer between the extremes of determinism and randomness. If we have no free will, if our actions are rigidly determined, we are not ethical agents and the rest of the Buddha's teaching makes no sense at all" (Gombrich 2009, 18). The Buddha was at great pains to preserve moral responsibility in a world which operates according to causal processes and to do that he realized that the causal processes that apply to mental events – or at least those psychological phenomena involved in making moral choices – must operate differently from the causal processes that shape the physical world. Importantly, this implies that karma operates on an emergent level within the natural world. As we have already seen, the crux of the argument for strong emergence is the notion of distinct levels within the natural world, with each level being defined by the existence of distinct types of causal activity at that level.

In an important passage in the *Saṃyutta Nikāya*, the Buddha was asked by a renunciate, Moliya Sīvaka, whether a person's experiences (pleasurable, painful, or neutral) are the direct result of some prior action – the Buddha rejected such a deterministic explanation of personal experience (SN.IV.230–231). One could never verify such a view in experience, he says. The Buddha goes on to say that the quality of a person's experience is due to eight causes, and karma is but one of those causes. In fact, karma is the last among the eight causes. The first five causes of the quality of a person's experience depend on the disposition of the body (explained in terms of the understanding of physiology at that time). Gombrich takes this to mean that one should only appeal to karma as an explanation of one's experiences when an alternative physiological explanation is not available. The fact that karma is a proper explanation for the pleasures or pains in one's present experience only *after* other possible explanations have been exhausted shows that the Buddha considered karma to operate on a *different level* from the physical (physiological) causes (Gombrich 2009, 21). Therefore the Buddhist conception of karma refers to an emergent level of moral causation that preserves moral responsibility, but it does not compete with (or replace) physical explanations of human action. To sum up, the doctrine of karma is the Buddha's way of demonstrating a clear commitment to the reality of human ethical values and moral responsibility as a distinct level of reality within a metaphysical naturalism. Compared with physicalism, emergentist naturalism has an important advantage because it treats moral agency as real. And compared with dualism, emergentist naturalism has the advantage of avoiding the mysterious metaphysics that posits supernatural realities to account for the moral values that physics cannot explain.

Emergentist Naturalism and Religious Meaning

John Dewey wrote only one small book, *A Common Faith*, that attempted a naturalistic approach to religious meaning (Dewey 1934b). This is disappointing because Dewey's work on art as transformative experience provides a blueprint for the emergence of radically new modes of human meaning that could well have been applied to the emergence of religious levels of meaning. Dewey saw nature as full of potential meanings. To achieve even the highest (artistic and religious) meanings one need not reach beyond nature because nature "supplies potential material for embodiment of ideals. Nature, if I may use the locution, is idealizable. It lends itself to operations by which it is perfected" (Dewey 1960, 302). But Dewey never fully developed his naturalistic view on religious meaning; so, unsurprisingly, it is Buddhism that has a great deal more to offer regarding a theory of religious meaning that is consistent with emergentist naturalism.

In *A Common Faith*, Dewey did, however, offer a strongly worded criticism of the supernatural foundations of traditional forms of religion. To rely on the supernatural (e.g., God, or a transcendent reality) for achieving meaning is to abandon our human responsibilities; it represents a pessimistic "surrender of human endeavor" (Dewey 1934b, 46). The Buddha agreed with Dewey's sentiment about supernaturalism, as he regularly criticized Brahmanical reliance on gods and transcendent reality. In the Pāli Canon, the Buddha is portrayed as making every attempt to demystify the religious life by eliminating reliance on supernaturalism and replacing it with a transformative moral psychology.

Many naturalistic philosophers today reject supernaturalism, but they are often skeptical that naturalism can include *religious* kinds of meaning because the concept of religious meaning seems to *require* a commitment to supernatural realities. Granted, if it is taken as axiomatic that religious meaning requires supernaturalist metaphysical commitments (e.g., belief in God), then, of course, a naturalistic account of religious meaning would be impossible. But Dewey and the Buddha attempted to map out a richer form of naturalism that *is consistent* with the development of religious levels of meaning. Religious meaning in emergentist naturalism is achieved through psychological and moral transformation that each person must accomplish for themselves without assistance from any external force, not even God (or gods). Emergentist naturalism thus offers a middle way between traditional religions that have supernatural foundations on the one hand, and reductive forms of physicalism that dismiss everything religious on the other.

The religious life, as the Buddha conceived it, is a response to the fact that normal human life is fraught with suffering, anxiety, and despair. The Buddha taught that human beings try foolishly to cling on to things in a changing world and that, therefore, rather than happiness, we experience various modes of suffering that permeate our normal experience. The Buddha claimed that he understood the causes and elimination of suffering. He located the primary causes of suffering in the corruptions of the human mind and thus the elimination of suffering must focus on retraining the mind. The Buddha's insight into dependent arising is the key here because it explains specifically how suffering arises through causes and also explains that the prescription for achieving religious liberation is a matter of taking control of those same causal factors. More specifically, the causal factors in question are corrupting psychological defilements (*asavas*) like greed, hatred, and delusion. The goal is to replace the defilements with mentally healthy or skillful (*kusala*) volitional factors that lead to freedom and happiness. The fundamental point of the Buddha's teaching (*dhamma*), therefore, is ethical transformation through a gradual retraining of the mind, not knowledge of (or escape to) a transcendent reality.

The Buddha's commitment to emergentist naturalism is evident in the details of his psycho-ethical therapy. This therapy is the gradual cultivation of the human personality based on the threefold training, namely, moral conduct (*sīla*), meditation (*samādhi*), and wisdom/insight (*paññā*). This training suggests not only naturalism, but also emergentism in the sense that the three stages delineate a *continuous* (using Dewey's term) development of the person. The texts relate that the "fruit" or "benefit" of moral conduct is mental culture and that the "fruit" of mental culture is wisdom (or insight). In other words, each of the stages of training constitutes a level that is taken up and transformed in the subsequent mode of training, not abandoned or replaced. The practical recommendation for achieving a moral life commences with the practice of moral actions, which lead to the development of moral habits. Moral habits develop into a morally transformed personality that is achieved by reshaping deep psychological structures through meditation and insight.

The highest level of religious meaning in Buddhism, its final goal, is referred to as *nibbāna* (Skt *nirvāṇa*). *Nibbāna* is described in the Pāli texts as a state of moral purification that is achieved by eliminating the defiling characteristics of the mind; it is synonymous with "liberation," "peace," "calm," and "tranquility." *Nibbāna* is a radical transformation of lived experience; it is a kind of empowerment that transforms one's existence in *this natural world*. *Nibbāna* is not a transcendent reality or "other-worldly" reality like heaven in the Christian theology. Neither is it knowledge of a transcendent Reality like Brahman in the Hindu tradition. It is "transcendent" (*lokuttara*) only in the *ethical sense* that it is beyond the corrupting conditions that are compounded (*saṅkhata*) in experience. *Nibbāna* conforms to dependent arising, because it is part of the natural/causal functioning of the world. Even an enlightened person lives in *this* world of dynamic change, explained the Buddha:

> In this case, monks, a monk is a worthy one who has destroyed the defiling impulses, lived the [higher] life, done what has to be done, laid aside the burden, achieved the noble goal, destroyed the fetters of existence, and is freed through wisdom. He retains his five senses, through which, as they are not yet destroyed, he experiences pleasant and unpleasant sensations and feels pleasure and pain. His cessation of craving, hatred, and confusion is *nibbāna in this life*.
>
> *(Itivuttaka 38)*

In short, *nibbāna* is an ideal way of *living*; it connotes the emergence of perfected human possibilities in this natural world. In this way, *nibbāna* is fully consistent with the emergentist naturalism that has been attributed to the Buddha in this essay. There are, of course, other very different interpretations of *nibbāna* and the textual evidence is far from unambiguous on this matter. But as emergentist naturalism offers a highly coherent interpretation of the Buddha's teaching, the reconstruction of *nibbāna* along such lines provides a unique opportunity to account for religious meaning in a contemporary world that is dominated by modern science.

Notes

1 For an example of recent work on emergentist naturalism see Clayton (2004). Clayton provides an excellent bibliography of recent work in this area.
2 "Early Buddhism" here refers to the philosophy of the Pāli Canon, the earliest source for the Buddha's teaching.
3 Despite the remarkable similarities between the two traditions, it would be a mistake to think of Dewey as a crypto-Buddhist or the Buddha as a proto-pragmatist – in historical and cultural terms Buddhism and pragmatism are quite distinct traditions.
4 "Weak" emergentism (as opposed to "strong" emergentism) claims that the emergence of new levels of phenomena is due only to our ignorance of the way the underlying physical phenomena can produce novel effects. This position is often called "epistemological" emergentism. Regarding ontology, weak emergentism asserts that physics is all that is really going on.
5 The concept of "supervenience" indicates both the dependence of mental phenomena on brain states (as established by the discovery of neural correlates of consciousness) and the irreducibility of the mental to the physical.
6 The full twelvefold formula of dependent arising: "Dependent on ignorance, there are dispositions to action; dependent on dispositions to action, there is consciousness; dependent on consciousness, there is psycho-physicality; dependent on psycho-physicality, there are the six bases of sense; dependent on the six bases of sense, there is contact; dependent on contact, there is feeling; dependent on feeling, there is craving; dependent on craving, there is attachment; dependent on attachment, there is becoming; dependent on becoming, there is birth; dependent on birth, there is ageing-and-death, sorrow, lamentation, pain, despair and distress. Thus there is the arising of this whole mass of suffering" (SN.II.17).
7 For examples of the Buddha's use of biological change as an illustration of changing phenomena in general, see SN.I.134, III.54; AN.I.135, I.223, III.404.

References

Clayton, Philip. 2004. *Mind and Emergence: From Quantum to Consciousness*. Oxford: Oxford University Press.
Dewey, John. 1934a. *Art as Experience*. New York: Minton, Balch & Co.
Dewey, John. 1934b. *A Common Faith*. New Haven: Yale University Press.
Dewey, John. 1938. *Logic: The Theory of Inquiry*. New York: Henry Holt and Company.
Dewey, John. 1958. *Experience and Nature*. New York: Dover Publications.
Dewey, John. 1960. *The Quest for Certainty*. New York: Capricorn Books.
Gombrich, Richard. 2009. *What the Buddha Thought*. London: Equinox Publishing.

Jayatilleke, K.N. 1963. *Early Buddhist Theory of Knowledge*. London: George Allen and Unwin.

Kalupahana, David. 1976. *Buddhist Philosophy: A Historical Analysis*. Honolulu: University of Hawaii Press.

Warder, A.K. 1980. *Indian Buddhism,* 2nd revised edition. Delhi: Motilal Banarsidass.

4

Metaphysical Dependence, East and West
Ricki Bliss and Graham Priest

Introduction

It is a natural thought that many things have whatever form of being they have because they depend on other things: the shadow depends on the object which casts it, the beauty of a work of art depends on its line and balance, the goodness of a cricket team depends on the goodness of each player, and so on. Although it is often not put in these terms, discussions of metaphysical dependence are common in both Eastern and Western philosophy; and of recent years the topic itself has come in for some intense scrutiny in Western philosophy. However, the Eastern and Western traditions have evolved largely independently of each other. We feel that there can be mutual benefit by bringing them into contact. This is what this chapter aims to do.

In Section 4.3, we will look at some of the ways in which metaphysical dependence occurs in Eastern traditions, and in Section 4.4 we will look at its occurrence in Western traditions. In Section 4.5 we will spell out some of the ways each tradition can benefit by being informed of the other.

Before we do this, however, there is a necessary preliminary. The views on metaphysical dependence are many, and there is a great variety of answers to central questions such as "What sorts of things is it which are dependent or independent?", "What is the nature of metaphysical dependence?", and "What is the reality like that metaphysical dependence structures?" To get some order into the chaos we need a framework in which to fit views. We do this by providing a taxonomy, the subject of Section 4.2.

Buddhist Philosophy: A Comparative Approach, First Edition. Edited by Steven M. Emmanuel.
© 2018 John Wiley & Sons, Inc. Published 2018 by John Wiley & Sons, Inc.

A Taxonomy

Properties of Dependence Relations

How many different kinds of metaphysical dependence relationships there are, and what the connections are between them, are somewhat contentious questions. However, we ignore this point for the moment, and produce a taxonomy by abstracting away from the *nature* of such dependence relations and focusing on *structural features*. For those who do not wish to work through the following in detail we give a brief summary at the end of the subsection, which will provide most of what is necessary to understand what follows.

First, some notation. We write "x depends on y" as $x \to y$.[1] (We may write $x \to x$ as $\hat{x}$.) Next, four structural properties.

Antireflexivity, AR

- $\forall x \neg x \to x$

[Nothing depends on itself.]

- So $\neg AR : \exists x\, x \to x$

[Something depends on itself.]

Antisymmetry, AS

- $\forall x \forall y (x \to y \supset \neg y \to x)$

[No things depend on each other.]

- So $\neg AS : \exists x \exists y (x \to y \wedge y \to x)$

[Some things depend on each other.]

Transitivity, T

- $\forall x \forall y \forall z ((x \to y \wedge y \to z) \supset x \to z)$

[Everything depends on anything a dependent depends on.]

- So $\neg T : \exists x \exists y \exists z (x \to y \wedge y \to z \wedge \neg x \to z)$

[Something does not depend on what some dependent depends on.]

Extendability, E

- $\forall x \exists y (y \neq x \wedge x \to y)$

[Everything depends on something else.]

- So $\neg E : \exists x \forall y (x \to y \supset y = x)$

  [Something does not depend on anything else.]

There are certainly other properties of $\to$ that we may consider, as we shall see. However, considerations of combinatorial explosion require us to select a relatively small number of conditions to frame the taxonomy. We select *AR*, *AS*, and *T*, since in contemporary discussions these are often taken to be features of metaphysical dependence. We select *E* since it is fundamental to the issue of whether there is a "fundamental level" of dependence.

The Taxonomy

We can now give the taxonomy, which is as follows. After the enumeration column, the next four columns list the 16 possibilities of our four conditions. We take up the next two columns in the next subsection.

	AR	AS	T	E	Comments	Special cases
1	Y	Y	Y	Y	Infinite partial order	*I*
2	Y	Y	Y	N	Partial order	*A, F, G*
3	Y	Y	N	Y	Loops	*I*
4	Y	Y	N	N	Loops	*F, G*
5	Y	N	Y	Y	×	
6	Y	N	Y	N	×	
7	Y	N	N	Y	Loops of length >0	*I*
8	Y	N	N	N	Loops of length >0	*F, G*
9	N	Y	Y	Y	×	
10	N	Y	Y	N	×	
11	N	Y	N	Y	×	
12	N	Y	N	N	×	
13	N	N	Y	Y	Preorder	*C, I*
14	N	N	Y	N	Preorder	*C, F, F′, G*
15	N	N	N	Y	Loops of any length	*I*
16	N	N	N	N	Loops of any length	*F, F′, G*

Discussion

Consider, next, the Comments column. Here's what it means.

- There is nothing in categories 5 and, 6, since if there are x, y, such that $x \leftrightarrows y$, then by T, $\widehat{x \leftrightarrows y}$, contradicting *AR*. (¬*AS* and *T* imply ¬*AR*.)
- There is nothing in categories 9–12, since if for some x, $x \to x$, then for some x and y, $x \leftrightarrows y$, contradicting *AS*. (¬*AR* implies ¬*AS*.)
- All the other categories are possible, as simple examples (left to the reader) will demonstrate.

- In categories 13–16, since $\neg AR$ implies $\neg AS$, the second column (AS) is redundant.
- In categories 1 and 2, $\rightarrow$ is a (strict) partial order; and in category 1, the objects involved must be infinite because of E.
- In categories 13 and 14, $\rightarrow$ is a (strict) preorder, so loops are possible. (A loop is a collection of elements, $x_1, x_2, ..., x_{n-1}, x_n$, for some $n \geqslant 1$, such that $x_1 \rightarrow x_2 \rightarrow ... \rightarrow x_{n-1} \rightarrow x_n \rightarrow x_1$.)
- In categories 3, 4, 7, 8, 15, and 16, transitivity fails, and there can also be loops. In categories 7 and 8, there are no loops of length zero, $\widehat{x}$, since AR holds.

Turning to the final column, this records some important special cases.

- The discrete case is when nothing relates to anything. Call this *atomism*, A. In this case, we have AR, AS, T, $\neg E$. So we are in category 2 (though this is not the only thing in category 2).
- If $\rightarrow$ is an equivalence relation (reflexive, symmetric, transitive), we have $\neg AR$, $\neg AS$, T, so we are in categories 13 or 14 (though this is not the only thing in these two categories). In category 13, there must be more than one thing in each equivalence class, because of E. A limit case of this is when all things relate to each other: $\forall x \forall y x \rightarrow y$. Call this *coherentism*, C.
- Call x a *foundational element* (FEx) if there is no y on which x depends, except perhaps itself: $\forall y(x \rightarrow y \supset x = y)$. *Foundationalism*, F, is the view that everything grounds out in foundational elements. One way to cash out the idea is as follows.[2] Let $X_0 = \{x : FEx\}$, and for any natural number, $n \in \omega$: $x \in X_{n+1}$ iff $x \in X_n$ or $\forall y(x \rightarrow y \supset y \in X_n)$. $X = \bigcup_{n \in \omega} X_n$. F is the view that everything is in X, $\forall x\, x \in X$.[3] Intuitively, this means that everything is a foundational element, or depends on just the foundational elements, or depends on just those and the foundational elements, and so on. E entails that there are no foundational elements. Hence, this is incompatible with F. So, given F, we must be in an even-numbered case — except those that are already ruled out by other considerations. (All are possible. Merely consider $x \rightarrow y \rightarrow z$. z is foundational; add in arrows as required to deliver the other conditions.)
- A special case of foundationalism is when the foundational objects, and only those, depend on themselves: $\forall x(FEx \equiv x \rightarrow x)$. Call this view F'. Since AR must fail in this case, we must be in categories 14 or 16 of the taxonomy.
- Another special case of foundationalism is when there is a unique foundational object on which everything else depends: $\exists x(FEx \wedge \forall y(y \neq x \supset y \rightarrow x))$. [Something is a foundational element, and everything else depends on it.] The x in question does not depend on anything, except perhaps itself, and it must be unique, or it would depend on something else. Call this case G (since the x could be a God which depends on nothing, or only itself). This is a special case of F, and could be in any of the cases in which F holds.
- Write $x \xrightarrow{*} y$ to mean that y is in the transitive closure of $\rightarrow$ from x. That is, one can get from x to y by going down a finite sequence of arrows.

An element, x, is *ultimately ungrounded*, UGx, if, going down a sequence of arrows, one never comes to a foundational element: $\forall y(x \stackrel{*}{\to} y \supset \neg FEy)$. Infinitism, I, is the view that every element is ultimately ungrounded: $\forall x UGx$.[4] We note that infinitism allows for the possibility of loops, that is, repetitions in the regress. Thus, we have the following possibility: $x \to y \to z \to x \to y \to z \to \ldots$. However, if $\to$ is transitive and antisymmetric (T and AS), such loops are ruled out. Infinitism entails extendability, E. So if I holds we must be in an odd-numbered category of our taxonomy (which is not ruled out by other considerations). All such are possible, as simple examples demonstrate. (Merely consider $x_0 \to x_1 \to x_2 \to x_3 \to \ldots$, where these are all distinct. Add in other arrows as required.) Note that if there are at least two elements, then C is a special case of I.

- A final special case. Let $x \rightleftarrows y$ iff $x \to y \lor y \to x$. Then x and y are connected along the dependence relation, xCy, iff for some $n \geqslant 1$:

$$x \rightleftarrows y \lor \exists z_1 z_2 \ldots z_n (x \rightleftarrows z_1 \land z_1 \rightleftarrows z_2 \land \ldots \land z_n \rightleftarrows y)$$

[Everything relates to everything else along some sequence of dependence relations.] $\to$ itself is connected iff $\forall x \forall y\, xCy$. In all of the ten possible cases, $\to$ may be connected or not connected. G is a special case of connectedness; C is an extreme case of connectedness; and A is an extreme case of disconnectedness.

Let us finish this section with an informal summary. The taxonomy is built on four conditions: (i) *antireflexivity*, AR: nothing depends on itself; (ii) *antisymmetry*, AS: no things depend on each other; (iii) *transitivity*, T: everything depends on whatever a dependent depends on; and (iv) *extendability*, E: everything depends on something else. This gives us 16 ($=2^4$) possibilities. Six of these are ruled out by logical considerations, leaving ten live possibilities. Within these, some special cases may be noted: *atomism*, A: nothing depends on anything; *foundationalism*, F: everything is a fundamental element or depends, ultimately, on such; F': foundationalism, where the fundamental elements and only those depend on themselves; G: foundationalism where the fundamental element is unique; *infinitism*, I: there are no fundamental elements; *coherentism*, C: everything depends on everything else.

Metaphysical Dependence in the Buddhist Traditions

Orientation

We will now turn to discussions of metaphysical dependence in Eastern traditions, specifically the Buddhist tradition. We do not wish to suggest that there are no interesting discussions to be found in other Eastern traditions, such as

Vedic and Daoist traditions; but only so much can be done in one article, and the Buddhist tradition is the one we know best. (We would encourage those who know more about these other traditions to engage in the discussions.) Moreover, the Buddhist tradition, itself, is not homogeneous, as we shall see. We will talk of three parts of it. Again, we do not wish to suggest there are no interesting elements in other parts of the tradition; we choose the three we do because they provide particularly interesting and contrasting views concerning metaphysical dependence.

For those unfamiliar with Buddhist philosophy, let us start with a brief description of its historical development. Buddhist thought started with the historical Buddha, Siddhārtha Gautama. His dates are uncertain, but he flourished around 450 BCE, and his ideas were developed in a canonical way for the next 500 years or so. The philosophical part of this development was called *Abhidharma* (higher teachings). There were many Abhidharma schools. The only one to survive to this day is *Theravāda* (Way of the Elders).

Around the turn of the Common Era, novel ideas emerged which were critical of the older tradition. This generated a new kind of Buddhism: *Mahāyāna*. The foundational philosopher of this kind of Buddhism was Nāgārjuna. Dates are, again, uncertain, but he flourished around 200 CE. He founded the version of Mahāyāna Buddhism called *Madhyamaka* (Middle Way).

Buddhist thought died out in India around the twelfth century, but by that time it had spread to the rest of Asia, Theravada going south-east, and Mahāyāna going north-west into central Asia, and thence across the Silk Route into East Asia. It entered China around the turn of the Common Era, where it met the indigenous philosophical traditions Confucianism and Daoism. Daoism, in particular, exerted a crucial influence on Buddhist thought.[5] This resulted in the emergence of distinctively Chinese forms of Mahāyāna Buddhism, around the sixth century. Some of these, such as *Chan* (Jp. *Zen*) are still extant. But perhaps the most philosophically sophisticated of these flourished in China for only a few hundred years (though it still has a presence in Korea and Japan). This was *Huayan* (Skt *Avataṃsaka*; K. *Hwaeom*; Jp. *Kegon*; Eng. *Flower Garland*) Buddhism, named after the *sūtra* it took to be most important. Many Huayan ideas were incorporated into other forms of Buddhism (and indeed into Neo-Confucianism). The most influential philosopher in this tradition was Fazang, traditionally dated as 643–712.[6]

With this background, let us turn to our three views concerning ontological dependence: those of Abhidharma, Madhyamaka, and Huayan.

Well-Founded Buddhism

It is common to all types of Buddhism that the world of our common experience is a world of dependent origination, *pratītyasamutpāda*. Nothing is permanent: things come into existence when causes and conditions are ripe, and go out of existence in the same way. Now, how should one think of a person in this context?

The understanding of a person that developed in the Abhidharma literature was as follows. Consider a car.[7] This comes into existence when its parts are put together. The parts interact with each other and the environment; they wear out and are replaced; and they finally fall apart entirely. Persons are just like that. True, their parts (*skandhas*), unlike the car's, are both physical (*rūpa*) and mental. But otherwise the story is the same. Of course we can think of this dynamically evolving bunch of parts as a single thing, a person; we can even give it a name, say "Bertrand Russell"; but this is just a matter of convenience.

The Abhidharma philosophers could see nothing special about people in this way. Anything with parts, like our friend the car, is exactly the same. Indeed, what *anything* in our common world of experience is, depends on what its parts are and how we think about them.

So take the car again. This depends on its wheels, engine, chassis, and so on. The engine depends on its combustion chambers, fuel-injection system, and so on. If we keep deconstructing in this way, do we come to things where no further deconstruction is possible? The Abhidharma philosophers thought that the answer was obviously "yes." If something is a conceptual construction, there must be something, *dharmas*, out of which it is constructed. You can't make something out of nothing. This would seem to be the point when Asaṅga (fl. ca. fourth century CE), in a late Abhidharma text, says:

> Denying the mere thing with respect to dharmas such as rūpa and the like, neither reality nor conceptual fiction is possible. For instance, where there are the skandhas of rūpa etc., there is the conceptual fiction of the person. And where they are not, the conceptual fiction of the person is unreal. Likewise if there is a mere thing with respect to dharmas like rūpa etc., then the use of convenient designators concerning dharmas such as rūpa and the like is appropriate. If not then the use of convenient designators is unreal. Where the thing referred to by the concept does not exist, the groundless conceptual fiction likewise does not exist.[8]

There was some dispute about the nature of the dharmas (a common view was that they are tropes of some kind). But, as all agreed, they are just as impermanent as anything else; what distinguishes them is the fact that they are what they are independently of anything else (parts, concepts, each other). They have *svabhāva* (self-being).[9]

The Abhidharma philosophers described the picture as one of two realities.[10] There is the fundamental reality composed of dharmas – ultimate reality (*paramārtha-satya*); then there is the conceptual reality constructed out of this – conventional reality (*saṃvṛti-satya*).

Clearly, the whole picture paints a story concerning metaphysical dependence. Where does it lie in our taxonomy of Section 4.2.2? It is obviously some kind of foundationalism, where *Fx* is "*x* is a dharma." Does it endorse *AR*, *AS*, and *T*? We know of no explicit discussion of these matters in the texts, but let us extrapolate. The Abhidharma philosophers would probably have endorsed transitivity. If the car depends on its engine, and the engine depends on its fuel-injector, the car depends on its fuel-injector. Moreover, a whole would appear to depend on its parts, in a way that the parts do not depend on the whole.[11] So the dependence relation would seem to be antisymmetric. Since antisymmetry entails antireflexivity, we have that as well. So this puts us in category 2 of the taxonomy.

Non-Well-Founded Buddhism

We now turn to Madhyamaka. Madhyamaka entirely rejected the notion of the dharmas. *Nothing* has *svabhāva*. Everything is what it is by relating to other things. The Madhyamaka philosophers accepted the Abhidharma view that the relations in question could be mereological and conceptual, but also added an important third dimension: causal (e.g., a person is what they are because of their relations to their parents, their genetic structure, etc.). Everything depends on other things in some or all of these ways. That is, all things are empty (*śūnya*) of self-being.[12]

In much of his enormously influential text the *Mūlamadhyamakakārikā* (MMK, Fundamental Verses of the Middle Way) Nāgārjuna mounts the case that nothing has *svabhāva*.[13] He does this by running through all the things one might suppose to have it (causation, consciousness, space, etc.), and rejecting each one. Many of the arguments are *reductio* ones. We assume that something has *svabhāva* and show that this cannot be.[14] We will not consider the arguments in any detail here.

More to the point in this context, one might expect Nāgārjuna to have rejected the distinction between the two realities. But he does not (MMK XXIV.8–10):

> The Buddha's teaching of the Dharma
> Is based on two truths:
> A truth of worldly convention
> And an ultimate truth.
>
> Those who do not understand
> The distinction between these two truths
> Do not understand
> The Buddha's profound truth.[15]

Conventional reality is the world of our familiar experience. But if there are no things with *svabhāva*, what is ultimate reality?

Though hardly explicit in the MMK, the view that emerged in Madhyamaka was that ultimate reality is what is left if one takes the things of conventional reality and strips off all conceptual overlays: emptiness (Skt *śūnyatā*; Ch. *kong*) itself. One might well think that this ultimate reality provides some foundational bedrock.[16] It does not. According to Madhyamaka, *everything* is empty, including emptiness itself. In perhaps the most famous verse of the MMK (XXIV.18), Nāgārjuna says:

> Whatever is dependently co-arisen
> That is explained to be emptiness.
> That, being a dependent designation,
> Is itself the middle way.

Emptiness, as the verse says, is a dependent designation. That is, emptiness depends on something. Conventional reality clearly depends on ultimate reality. But what does ultimate reality depend on? It is hard to extract a clear answer to this question from the MMK; let us set it aside for the moment.

We are now in a position to see how the Madhyamaka view fits into our taxonomy. In general it takes over the Abhidharma view, but simply rejects its foundationalism. That is, it endorses *E*. We have infinitism, *I*, and we are in category 1.

Buddhist Coherentism

Let us now turn to Huayan.[17] This, like all Chinese Buddhisms, is Mahāyāna, and so inherited Madhyamaka thought. But whilst Madhyamaka held that all things depend on *some* other things, the Huayan universalized: all things depend on *all* other things. How did they get there? We come back to the question of what ultimate reality depends on.[18]

As we have noted, Chinese Buddhism was indebted to Daoism. According to a standard interpretation of this, behind the flux of phenomenal events there is a fundamental principle, *dao*, which manifests itself in the flux. To Chinese Buddhist eyes, it was all too natural to identify the flux with conventional reality, and the *dao* with ultimate reality. That is exactly what happened. Moreover, just as one cannot have manifestations without whatever it is of which they *are* a manifestation, one cannot have something whose nature it is to manifest, without the manifestations. So conventional reality depends on ultimate reality, and ultimate reality depends on conventional reality: they are two sides of the same coin. In his *Treatise on the Golden Lion*, Fazang explains the point in this way. Imagine a statue of a golden lion. The gold is like ultimate reality; the shape is like conventional reality. One cannot have the one without the other.

By this time in the development of Buddhist thought, the objects of phenomenal reality are called *shi* and ultimate reality is referred to as *li*, principle. Hence we have the Huayan principle of the mutual dependence of li and shi: *lishi wuai*. The matter is put this way by the Huayan thinker Dushun (557–640):

> Shi, the matter that embraces, has boundaries and limitations, and li, the truth that is embraced [by things], has no boundaries or limitations. Yet this limited shi is completely identical, not partially identical, with li. Why? Because shi has no substance [*svabhāva*] – it is the selfsame li. Therefore, without causing the slightest damage to itself, an atom can embrace the whole universe. If one atom is so, all other dharmas should also be so. Contemplate on this.[19]

But if every shi depends on li, then by the transitivity of dependence, every shi depends on every other shi. Hence we have the Huayan thesis of the dependence (interpenetration) of every shi on every other shi: *shishi wuai*. Chengguan (738–839?), another Huayan thinker, puts the matter thus:

> Because they have no self-being [*svabhāva*], the large and the small can mutually contain each other... Since the very small is very large Mount Sumeru is contained in a mustard seed; and since the very large is the very small, the ocean is included in a hair.[20]

We therefore arrive at this: all things, whether li or shi, depend on each other.

The situation is depicted in what is arguably the most famous image in Huayan: the Net of Indra. A god has spread out a net through space. At each node of the net there is a brightly polished jewel. Each jewel reflects each other jewel, reflecting each other jewel, reflecting... to infinity. Fazang puts the metaphor thus:

> It is like the net of Indra which is entirely made up of jewels. Due to their brightness and transparency, they reflect each other. In each of the jewels, the images of all the other jewels are [completely] reflected... Thus, the images multiply infinitely, and all these multiple infinite images are bright and clear inside this single jewel.[21]

Each jewel represents an object. And it is the nature of each jewel to encode every other jewel, including that jewel encoding every other jewel, and so on.

So where is the Huayan picture in our taxonomy? Clearly, this is coherentism, *C*, and we are in category 13 (since there is more than one object).

Metaphysical Dependence in Western Traditions

The General Picture

Now let us turn to discussions of metaphysical dependence in the Western traditions. In contrast to the Eastern literature, two aspects are immediately striking. The first is that, unlike in the Eastern traditions, there is an absolute orthodoxy on how reality is structured: some kind of foundationalism.[22] The second is that the contemporary period, at least, in the West has seen concerted attempts to theorize about the dependence relation itself – in terms both of its nature and its structure. Discussions of metaphysical dependence in the West are, then, richer than those in the East in one sense, and poorer in another. We will see both of these in what follows. But, again, first some general background.

The idea that reality has a particular kind of structure is as old as the Western tradition itself. An example of this is the *great chain of being* of the Neo-Platonists.[23] First and foremost, there is the One, or God, who grounds successive layers of reality – hypostates – in a hierarchy of dependence.

Whilst it is certainly not the case that the Western literature is a long history of philosophers speaking in the idioms of metaphysical dependence, the ideas that, on the one hand, reality is hierarchically structured, and, on the other, there is something fundamental have cast a very long shadow over the tradition.[24]

In the footsteps of the ancient Greeks, the Medievals and the Moderns were also concerned with what was independent – substances and God, commonly – and the dependence ordering in relation to them. The works of Aquinas, Scotus, Kant, and Leibniz, amongst many others, are, in places at least, wholly focused upon arguing for a distinctively foundationalist picture. Empiricists such as Hume arguably also have foundationalist leanings, with the atomisms of Russell, Wittgenstein and, more recently, Armstrong continuing the tradition.

In Sections 4.4.2 and 4.4.3 we review some material from the history of Western philosophy. As it is clearly impossible to do justice to the whole of it here, we select two important figures: Aristotle and Leibniz. Indeed, we can hardly hope to do justice to the richness of their thoughts either, but we hope we can say enough to indicate the general lay of the land. In Sections 4.4.4 and 4.4.5 we turn to a consideration of some of the contemporary proponents of foundationalism and their reasons for holding the view, along with some reasons for rejecting it.

We end these preliminary comments by noting that there is a distinction drawn in the contemporary literature between two kinds of metaphysical dependence: ontological dependence and grounding. What exactly these are, and the relationship between them, are contentious matters; indeed, the terminology is not itself well defined.²⁵ However, a few points can be stated with a relative degree of confidence. First, grounding is generally taken to be a relation between facts,²⁶ whereas ontological dependence can obtain between relata of all ontological categories. Next, many hold that there is some kind of necessity involved in a relationship of metaphysical dependence. If so, it is often taken to run in different directions in the two cases. Where A ontologically depends on B, A necessitates B, whereas if A is grounded in B, B necessitates A. Finally, ontological dependence *might* involve explanatory connections, whereas grounding *always* does.

Some Historical Views I: Aristotle

So to Aristotle. It has become something of a common – if mistaken – assumption that Aristotle was not particularly concerned with what exists. Instead, it is said, Aristotle was concerned with what depends on what.²⁷ He was, indeed, very much concerned with a particular kind of dependence ordering in nature.

To discuss dependence in Aristotle we must first begin by introducing some basic features of his account, and we choose here to focus upon the account offered in the *Categories*.²⁸ For Aristotle, the categories of existents include substance, quantity, quality, and relation, with each category containing both individuals and universals. This means that we can distinguish individual substances from both universal substances and, say, individual relations, for example. An example of an individual substance for the Aristotle of the *Categories* is a horse; and an example of a universal substance is HUMAN. COLOR, on the other hand, is an example of a quality, a non-substance. Henceforth, we refer to everything that is neither an individual nor a universal substance as a non-substance.

One of Aristotle's great concerns in the *Categories* is securing a certain ontological status for the individual substances. The distinction between individual substances and everything else is drawn by him in terms of a distinction between *being in* and being *said of* something else: individual substances are that of which things are said, or in which things are. What this means is that the subjects of predications are individual substances with predicates being in, or said of, them. So, for example, to say that Sam is human is to say of an individual substance, Sam, that he is human. Color, on the other hand, we say is *in* Sam.

On the relationship between individual substances (primary substances) and universal substances (secondary substances), Aristotle says:

> A substance – that which is called a substance most strictly, primarily, and most of all – is that which is neither said of a subject nor in a subject, e.g. the individual man or the individual horse. The species in which the things primarily called substances are, are called secondary substances,

as also are the genera of those species. For example, the individual man belongs in a species, man, and animal is a genus of the species; so these – both man and animal – are called secondary substances.[29]

The use of the expressions "primary" and "secondary" should give us our first clue as to what Aristotle is up to, for they convey the idea of one thing's being more or less basic in an ordering than another. Metaphysical dependence is widely thought to be framed in the language of *separation* and *priority* in Aristotle.[30] One thing is metaphysically dependent on something else just in case it is not separate from that thing; where that something else is prior to it. For Aristotle, non-substances and universal substances are inseparable from that in which they are, or that of which they are said; where individual substances are said to be prior. Importantly, on the Aristotelian picture, the individual substances are that which, and only that which, are separate from all else: so only they can be without the non-substances.[31] The primary substances are said to play a particularly important role:

> All the other things are either said of the primary [i.e. individual] substances as subjects or present in them as subjects… [C]olor is present in body and therefore also present in an individual body; for were it not present in some individual body it would not be present in body at all… So if the primary substances did not exist it would be impossible for any of the other things to exist.[32]

But what are we to make of all this talk of separability, priority, and substance? It seems very natural to understand them in terms of some kind of metaphysical dependence. What we might understand Aristotle as saying, then, is that where *A* is prior to and separate from *B*, *B* depends on *A*, in the sense of being metaphysically explained by it.[33] Consider universal substances, for example, HUMAN. These appear to have their being in virtue of being said of individual substances. There would be no universal substance HUMAN were there no humans at all. So universal substances are posterior to and not separable from individual substances because they have their being explained in terms of them. However, individual substances do not appear to have anything in virtue of which they have their being explained. So individual substances are prior and separate because there is nothing in virtue of which they have their being.[34]

So where in our taxonomy should we place Aristotle? It seems clear that Aristotle was at pains to establish a priority ordering in which dependence was not symmetric, so we can take him as embracing *AS*. As Aristotle assumes that without the primary substances nothing else would exist, he seems to be committed to *T*. For this same reason, it seems safe to say that he denied *E*. This would put Aristotle firmly in category 2. As Aristotle is often cited as the grandfather of the foundationalist view that currently dominates Western traditions, this hardly comes as a surprise.

Some Historical Views II: Leibniz

Next, we turn to some aspects of Leibniz' thought relating to metaphysical dependence. What is striking here is that although Leibniz' picture of the world offers a radical departure from the standard view at the time, the picture presented is nonetheless a thoroughgoing foundationalism. Again, we can hardly do justice to all aspects of his thought, and we choose to focus on the grounding of modal facts as a special case of the grounding of everything in God. Although Leibniz certainly believed that everything within the created world was dependent upon the monads, we do not venture into the thorny issue of how the monads fit into Leibniz' big picture.[35]

The idea that everything depends on God is a cornerstone of Leibniz' thought (and, of course, of theistic philosophy in general). But what exactly does it mean? Is it enough that God exists to explain everything else, or is there something that God needs to do beyond merely existing to explain the world? As we will see, for Leibniz, God's mere existence is necessary to explain the existence of everything else, but it is not sufficient: God's intellect forms a crucial part of the story.

Let us first consider Leibniz' cosmological argument for the existence of God. In the *Monadology*, Leibniz states:

> [B]ut all this detail only brings in other contingencies…and each of these further contingencies also needs to be explained through a similar analysis. So when we give explanations of this sort we move no nearer to the goal of completely explaining contingencies. Infinite though it may be, the train of detailed facts about contingencies…doesn't contain the sufficient reason, the *ultimate* reason for any contingent fact. For *that* we must look outside the sequence of contingencies.[36]

Invoking contingencies to explain contingencies leaves us in the unfortunate position, thinks Leibniz, of not having completely explained the contingencies at all. If what we want is a *complete explanation* of the contingencies – as Leibniz thinks we do – then we need something beyond the collection of contingent things in order to do that: what is needed to explain the existence of the contingent things is a necessary being. And this necessary being, thinks Leibniz, is God.

There is much that can be said about this argument, but for our purposes what is interesting is that, unlike many of the other arguments in the literature, this one makes appeal to a distinctive kind of metaphysical explanation. Leibniz is not concerned with efficient causation: he is not worried that if there were no first cause in time, nothing would exist whatsoever, for example. Instead, Leibniz is concerned with how the world can be *fully* accounted for – what sufficient reason we can uncover for its existence.

The story of how God explains the world is much more complex than this, however. After all, if it's simply that we need a necessary being in order to explain the contingencies, there are plenty more mundane necessities around that would be available for the task.

Amongst the set of truths to be explained by God are the modal truths: truths such as that $2+2$ is necessarily 4, and that Leibniz could have traveled to Kyoto. Let us narrow our focus to these for a moment. How might such truths depend on God? In broad strokes, according to Leibniz, modal truths express facts about essences which, in turn, are grounded in God's intellect. The grounding of modal truths, then, is the story of how essences depend on the mind of God.[37]

But what kind of relation does God bear to all these essences for Leibniz? Does God thinking about the nature of something *cause* that nature to exist? No. God's ruminations on essences are to those essences as substances are to modes.[38] It is not that my apple causes its redness to exist but, rather, that my apple *qua* substance grounds its redness *qua* mode. The apple is ontologically prior to its redness, just as the redness depends on the apple. So too for essences and their dependence on the mind of God. Being thought of by God lends reality to and grounds the existence of essences.

So where in our taxonomy might we place Leibniz? Leibniz was certainly a foundationalist, which has him in categories 2, 4, 8, 14, or 16. As everything for Leibniz depended ultimately on God, we can assume that he accepted *T*. This rules out categories 4, 8, and 16. Leibniz denied, though, that dependence was antireflexive: God, for Leibniz, depended on Himself. This leaves us, then, in category 14 and with Leibniz, according to our characterization, endorsing *G*.

Contemporary Orthodoxy

We now turn to contemporary Western discussions of metaphysical dependence. First, we discuss the dominant contemporary picture. Then we consider some of the contemporary challenges that have been made to it, and relate these back to our taxonomy of possible positions. In the process we will see, as promised, how dependence itself has become an object of philosophical scrutiny.

Although contemporary philosophers tend not to concern themselves with the existence of God, and our understanding of the natural world has evolved considerably, without question the prevailing view amongst contemporary metaphysicians is that reality is hierarchically structured with chains of entities ordered by ontological dependence relations that terminate in something fundamental. This is obviously a species of metaphysical foundationalism, and it is not, in many important, abstract senses, a wildly different view of reality than that which has held sway for thousands of years in the West.

A quick look at our taxonomy reveals, however, that there are five different ways in which one can be a foundationalist. Is one of these views more common than the others? As the reader may have guessed, it most certainly is, and that is category 2: *AR*, *AS*, *T*, and ¬*E*. But why? Why suppose that reality is hierarchically arranged by metaphysical dependence relations that are antisymmetric, antireflexive, and transitive, where those dependence chains terminate in something fundamental? Let us first consider the idea that our relations induce a partial order.

One quick justification for committing to the view is that it just seems plain obvious. Take the flagpole and its shadow. Common sense tells us that the shadow depends on the flagpole in a way that the flagpole does not depend on its shadow (antisymmetry). Similarly it seems right to suppose that where I depend on my vital organs and they on their cellular components, I also depend on those cellular components (transitivity).[39] And the idea that anything depends on itself, some say, is plain ridiculous (antireflexivity).[40]

Why suppose there must be something fundamental? There is a host of sometimes not very well-articulated arguments. Kit Fine considers that it is at least a plausible demand on the ground that chains ordered by the relation yield "completely satisfactory" explanations.[41] Ross Cameron thinks that a theory that posits fundamentalia is *ceteris paribus* better than one that does not.[42]

Perhaps the most compelling argument available in defense of fundamentalia, however, is one from vicious infinite regress. According to such an argument, where one thing depends upon something else and that thing upon still something else, and so on *ad infinitum*, nothing within the chain has any being or reality whatsoever. As Jonathan Schaffer puts it: if there is nothing fundamental, being would be "infinitely deferred, never achieved."[43]

Challenges to Contemporary Orthodoxy

Although category 2 of our taxonomy is the standard orthodoxy, it has not gone without challenge. Consider, first, the idea that we might accept extendability, and therewith reject the idea that there is something fundamental. A reality in which there is nothing fundamental would be a reality in which there are infinitely descending dependence chains: there is no fundamental level (infinitism). Both Tahko (2014) and Morganti (2014) have defended the possibility of species of infinitism. Other authors (e.g., Paseau 2010) have suggested it is at least advisable to remain neutral as to whether there is anything fundamental.

What would be so bad about such a picture, if anything at all, is more difficult to establish than commonly realized.[44] One thought might be that there would just be too much stuff – a violation of quantitative parsimony. But this doesn't seem like a legitimate worry: not only is parsimony normally understood qualitatively and not quantitatively, but the foundationalist is generally happy to admit that there may be an infinite number of fundamentalia.[45]

The worry might be that there is something special about our dependence chains that means that it is necessary that they terminate downwards. It might seem obvious that where our explanatory chains do not terminate, we don't really have *complete* explanations of everything we have encountered along the way. Whatever the intuitive pull of this concern, it is very difficult to formulate it in a way that would actually allow us to motivate foundationalism. On the face of it, this concern just looks like the demand that we terminate our explanatory chains. As explanatory chains are not defective simply by dint of being incomplete, it is not entirely clear what the problem is supposed to be. Is there perhaps some appeal to an appropriate version of the Principle of Sufficient Reason?[46] A closer examination of the arguments reveals that not much at all may be lost if we abandon our commitment to fundamentality.

Let us now turn to a consideration of the possibility of reflexive instances of dependence. Why suppose that ontological dependence relations are necessarily antireflexive? One way to respond to this question is with "They're not!" Some philosophers consider that there is no *in principle* problem with the thought that ontological dependence can be reflexive.[47] In fact, Jenkins has even argued that there appear to be instances of dependence that *are* reflexive.[48] Many philosophers, however, are of the view that grounding cannot be reflexive. This seems to be due to the intimate connection between grounding and explanation: reflexive explanations are trivial and uninformative.

Similar reasoning would appear to be in operation in defense of the view that dependence is necessarily antisymmetric: symmetric explanations are epistemically undesirable. But what, if any, might be the *metaphysical reasons* to suppose that ontological dependence relations must be antisymmetric? One thought might be that where A depends on B and B depends on A, whilst we can account for A, and we can account for B, we haven't really accounted for how A and B came to be in the first place. This worry, we suppose, is also what might drive the thought that loops of any size would be unacceptable. How to respond to such an objection might begin by noting that such explanatory loops are not altogether bereft of explanation – after all, we've explained both A and B. What we haven't explained, though, is how the whole lot got going in the first place. But note that this is a different issue, and there are at least two ways that we can respond to it. The first involves claiming that the loop itself just doesn't need an explanation. The second involves embedding the loop in a larger structure: what explains the fact that A grounds B and B grounds A is some further fact, C.

Some authors have also suggested that there are relatively clear-cut cases of failures of transitivity. Consider the following. It seems reasonable to suppose that the fact that a ball has a dent in it grounds the fact that it has a certain shape, *S*. It also seems reasonable to suppose that the fact that that thing has shape *S* grounds the fact that it is more or less spherical. What does not seem acceptable, however, is the claim that the fact that some thing has a dent in it grounds the fact that it is more or less spherical.[49] We appear to have a failure of transitivity.

Let us end this discussion by locating some of the unorthodox contemporary positions mooted or espoused with respect to our taxonomy as given in the table in Section 4.2.2. Let us begin by considering the view at line 1. We can think of this as a kind of *metaphysical infinitism*. It is like the standard view in the sense that reality retains its hierarchical structure, but unlike the standard view in that it denies that there is anything fundamental. Bliss (2013), Bohn (2009), Morganti (2014), Tahko (2014), and Schaffer (2003) (before he changed his mind) have all defended the possibility of this view. The views at both lines 3 and 4 are unique in that they allow the possibility of loops in which chains of phenomena ordered by an antireflexive, antisymmetric relation double back on themselves. Fine (1994) has expressed that the view at line 4 is at least a possibility.

Elizabeth Barnes (forthcoming) has argued that we have good reasons to question the dogged commitment to antisymmetry. Line 8, then, is also occupied. And the possibility of line 7 has been defended by Bliss (2012). Priest (2014, chs. 11 and 12) has defended the view that ontological dependence relations are reflexive, symmetric, and non-well-founded: a radical kind of metaphysical coherentism. So line 13 also has an occupant. And both Dasgupta (2014) and Lowe (2012) believe that whatever serve as our fundamentalia can be and are, respectively, self-dependent, so line 14 also has takers. And the possibility of lines 15 and 16 has also been defended by Bliss (2012).

The Fruits of Dialogue

As we have seen, the literatures of the East and West involving ontological dependence and grounding look quite different. We believe that when brought into contact, these two literatures can mutually benefit one another and extract some of the possible fruits below.

First, Western traditions have been largely foundationalist and contain important arguments for foundationalism, whilst Buddhist traditions have been largely anti-foundationalist and have no well-developed arguments for this view. The Eastern anti-foundationalist positions need to take the arguments from the Western traditions into account.

Second, an understanding of the view that there are major philosophical traditions that are not foundationalist can remove the myopia of the Western foundationalist view. Moreover, the Buddhist views are a rich source of anti-foundationalist arguments, which Western views need to take into account.

Third, recent discussions of dependence in the West have cast a critical eye on the nature of dependence as such. What sorts of thing are they which are so related: objects? properties? facts? Or can *all* such things enter into dependence relations? Does this mean that there is more than one kind of dependence relation? And what are the structural properties of the dependence relation or relations? Is it (are they) transitive, antisymmetric, antireflexive? And what exactly is the connection, if there is one, between dependence and modal notions, or dependence and explanation?[50] Debates in the West may certainly be inconclusive at the moment; but never mind. A closer philosophical scrutiny of dependence as such can only deepen an understanding of notions of dependence in the Buddhist tradition, making them more sophisticated.

Conversely, of course, the sorts of dependence relations present in the Buddhist traditions can only help to hone our understanding of dependence in general.

Much is therefore to be gained on both sides.

Conclusion

In this chapter we have looked at the relation (or relations) of metaphysical dependence as they feature in philosophy – both historical and contemporary. In an essay of this nature we have been able to do little more than sketch briefly some of the terrain; neither have we attempted to resolve any substantial philosophical issues. Our main aim has been to show that the notion of metaphysical dependence is an important feature of both Western and Eastern traditions, and to alert philosophers who are aware of only one side of this divide to the existence of the other. If it serves to bring the two traditions into dialogue, and so advance this central area of metaphysics, we will feel it has achieved its goal.[51]

Notes

1 One may distinguish between full dependence and partial dependence (see, e.g., Dixon 2016, sect. 1). Just to be clear: the notion of dependence we are concerned with here is partial dependence.
2 We note that how exactly to cash out the idea of foundationalism is contentious. For some discussion, see Dixon (2016). We suspect that the notion may be vague, and so susceptible to different precisifications. The definition we give here is strong, simple, and very natural.
3 One may, if one wishes, iterate the construction into the transfinite, collecting up at limit ordinals in the obvious way.
4 We note that infinitism is certainly susceptible to various precisifications. For example, one might require that only *some* element is ungrounded. Again, the definition we give here is strong, simple, and natural.

5 Buddhism (Mahāyāna) entered Tibet relatively late in the piece, in the eighth century. The indigenous Tibetan views did not have an impact of such magnitude.
6 For good introductions to the history of Buddhist thought, see Mitchell (2002), Siderits (2007), and Williams (2009).
7 The standard Buddhist example is a chariot, but we take the liberty of updating a bit.
8 *Bodhisattvabhumi* 30–32. Translation by Mark Siderits.
9 For all this, and what follows, see Siderits (2007, chs. 3 and 6).
10 The Sanskrit word is *satya*. This can mean either *truth* or *reality*. It is standard to translate the word as *truth*. Of course if there are two realities, there are also two (sets of) truths: one about each of the realities. But in the present context, and others that we will come to soon, the best translation is "reality."
11 By "part" here, we mean *proper part*, i.e., a part distinct from the whole.
12 For a discussion of this and what follows, see Siderits (2007, ch. 9) and Williams (2009, ch. 3).
13 It must be said that this is a highly cryptic text, and there can be significant differences as to how to understand its claims. In what follows we try not to go beyond a general consensus.
14 The arguments themselves are often by cases, though the cases are not the ones familiar to Western philosophy – *true* and *false* – but the four delivered by the *catuṣkoṭi* (Eng. four corners) – *true*, *false*, *both*, and *neither*.
15 Translations from the MMK are from Garfield (1995). In this context, "Dharma" means *correct doctrine*.
16 In which case, we are still in category 2 of our taxonomy, but G is true. Ultimate reality is the unique foundation.
17 For the following, see Williams (2009, ch. 6).
18 It must be said that these thoughts were available, in principle, to Madhyamaka philosophers, but no one ever articulated them.
19 Quoted in Chang (1972, 144–145). The character translated as "identical" is better translated in this context as "interpenetrating."
20 Quoted in Chang (1972, 165).
21 Quoted in Liu (1982, 65).
22 This is not to say that foundationalism is universally endorsed, rather, that it is the only view that is taken seriously.
23 See Lovejoy (1936) for an extended discussion.
24 Though one can also find complaints about deploying such a dark notion as metaphysical dependence.
25 Indeed, some people use the term "ontological dependence" as we are using "metaphysical dependence." See Tahko and Lowe (2015).
26 One notable exception to this view is Jonathan Schaffer (2009).
27 Schaffer (2009, 347).
28 What follows draws largely from Corkum (2013, 2016).

29 As quoted by Corkum (2013, 71), who takes the translation from Barnes (1984).
30 See Corkum (2013, 2016). Corkum cites Gail Fine as responsible for first introducing this understanding.
31 *Met.* 1029a27–28.
32 *Cat.* 2a34b-7, as quoted by Corkum (2016, 2), taking the translation from Ackrill (1963).
33 See Corkum (2013, 2016) for extended discussions of cashing out dependence in Aristotle in terms of grounding.
34 Note, however, that on this approach to independence we are not forced to deny there are things that substances cannot be without: things to which they are necessarily yoked.
35 On which, see Levey (2007).
36 Bennett (2007, 6).
37 See Newlands (2013, sect. 2.2).
38 Newlands (2013, 171–172).
39 Indeed, transitivity of dependence relations would seem to be part and parcel of views such as physicalism.
40 See Fine (2010, 98).
41 Fine (2010, 105).
42 Cameron (2008).
43 Schaffer (2010, 62).
44 See, e.g., Bliss (2013).
45 It is not uncommon to suppose that what matters for considerations of theoretical virtue is a sparsity of *kinds* of things and not the number of things themselves.
46 See Dasgupta (2014).
47 E.J. Lowe (2012) thinks that there *must be* some things that are self-dependent.
48 Jenkins (2011).
49 Schaffer (2012, 126–127).
50 See Bliss and Trogdon (2014).
51 Part of the paper was written while Ricki Bliss was a Humboldt Fellow, and she gratefully acknowledges the support of the Alexander Humboldt Foundation.

References

Ackrill, J.L., trans. 1963. *Aristotle's Categories and De Interpretatione*. Oxford: Clarendon Press.

Barnes, E. (forthcoming). "Symmetric Dependence." In *Reality and Its Structure*, edited by Ricki Bliss and Graham Priest. Oxford University Press. http://elizabethbarnesphilosophy.weebly.com/uploads/3/8/1/0/38105685/symmetric_dependence.pdf

Barnes, J., ed. 1984. *The Complete Works of Aristotle: The Revised Oxford Translation*. Princeton: Princeton University Press.
Bennett, J., trans. 2007. *The Principles of Philosophy Known as Monadology*. www.earlymoderntexts.com
Bliss, R.L. 2012. *Against Metaphysical Foundationalism*. Doctoral dissertation, University of Melbourne.
Bliss, R.L. 2013. "Viciousness and the Structure of Reality." *Philosophical Studies* 166: 399–418.
Bliss, R.L. and Trogdon, K. 2014. "Metaphysical Grounding." In *Stanford Encyclopedia of Philosophy*, edited by E. Zalta. http://plato.stanford.edu/entries/grounding/
Bohn, E.D. 2009. "Must There be a Top Level?" *The Philosophical Quarterly* 59: 193–201.
Cameron, R. 2008. "Turtles All the Way Down: Regress, Priority and Fundamentality." *The Philosophical Quarterly* 58: 1–14.
Chang, G.C.C. 1972. *The Buddhist Teaching of Totality: The Philosophy of Hwa Yen Buddhism*. London: George Allen & Unwin Ltd.
Corkum, P. 2013. "Substance and Independence in Aristotle." In *Varieties of Dependence: Ontological Dependence, Supervenience, and Response-Dependence*, edited by B. Schnieder, A. Steinberg, and M. Hoeltje, 65–96. Basic Philosophical Concepts Series. Munich: Philosophia Verlag.
Corkum, P. 2016. "Ontological Dependence and Grounding in Aristotle." *Oxford Handbooks Online – Philosophy*. doi:10.1093/oxfordhb/9780199935314.013.31
Dasgupta, S. 2014. "Metaphysical Rationalism." *Noûs* 48: 1–40.
Dixon, T.S. 2016. "What is the Well-Foundedness of Grounding?" *Mind* 125(498): 439–468.
Fine, K. 1994. "Essence and Modality." *Philosophical Perspectives* 8: 1–16.
Fine, K. 2010. "Some Puzzles of Ground." *Notre Dame Journal of Formal Logic* 51: 97–118.
Garfield, J. 1995. *The Fundamental Wisdom of the Middle Way*. New York: Oxford University Press.
Jenkins, C.S. 2011. "Is Metaphysical Dependence Irreflexive?" *The Monist* 94: 267–276.
Levey, S. 2007. "On Unity and Simple Substance in Leibniz." *The Leibniz Review* 17: 61–106.
Liu, M.W. 1982. "The Harmonious Universe of Fazang and Leibniz." *Philosophy East and West* 32: 61–76.
Lovejoy, A.O. 1936. *The Great Chain of Being: A Study of the History of an Idea*. Cambridge, MA: Harvard University Press.
Lowe, E.J. 2012. "Asymmetrical Dependence Individuation." In *Metaphysical Grounding: Understanding the Structure of Reality*, edited by F. Correia and B. Schnieder, 214–233. Cambridge: Cambridge University Press.

Mitchell, D. 2002. *Buddhism: Introducing the Buddhist Experience*. Oxford: Oxford University Press.
Morganti, M. 2014. "Dependence, Justification and Explanation: Must Reality be Well-founded?" *Erkenntnis* 80: 555–572.
Newlands, S. 2013. "Leibniz and the Ground of Possibility." *Philosophical Review* 122: 155–187.
Paseau, A. 2010. "Defining Ultimate Ontological Basis and the Fundamental Layer." *Philosophical Quarterly* 60: 169–175.
Priest, G. 2014. *One*. Oxford: Oxford University Press.
Schaffer, J. 2003. "Is there a Fundamental Level?" *Noûs* 37: 498–517.
Schaffer, J. 2009. "On What Grounds What." In *Metaphysics: New Essays in the Foundations of Ontology*, edited by D. Manley, D. Chalmers, and R. Wasserman, 347–383. Oxford: Oxford University Press.
Schaffer, J. 2010. "Monism: The Priority of the Whole." *Philosophical Review* 119: 31–76.
Schaffer, J. 2012. "Grounding, Transitivity and Contrastivity." In *Metaphysical Grounding: Understanding the Structure of Reality*, edited by F. Correia and B. Schnieder, 122–138. Cambridge: Cambridge University Press.
Siderits, M. 2007. *Buddhism as Philosophy*. Aldershot: Ashgate.
Tahko, T.E. 2014. "Boring Infinite Descent." *Metaphilosophy* 45: 257–269.
Tahko, T.E. and Lowe, E.J. 2015. "Ontological Dependence." In *The Stanford Encyclopedia of Philosophy*, edited by E. Zalta. http://plato.stanford.edu/entries/dependence-ontological/
Williams, P. 2009. *Mahāyāna Buddhism: The Doctrinal Foundations*, 2nd edition. London: Routledge.

5

Metaphysics and Metametaphysics with Buddhism: The Lay of the Land[1]

Tom J.F. Tillemans

Metaphysics is ontology, the attempt to find the widest ranging and most fundamental description of what exists and how it exists. Of course, argumentation about that description has a very large place in contemporary analytic philosophy; in Buddhism it does too. And in both the argumentation quite easily moves to the second order matter of whether it is intellectually legitimate to search for such a description and how one should do so if it is. One's answers to those second order questions *about* metaphysics, then, constitute one's metaontological stance, or "metametaphysics."[2] If metaphysics is concerned with the foundations of reality, metametaphysics deals with the foundations of metaphysics as a whole.

Engagement and cross-cultural collaboration are the watchwords of this volume. What, then, would a cross-cultural metaphysics look like when significantly engaged with Buddhism? Presenting baldly the Buddhists' own abundant, and often obscure, arguments on specific issues of what there is, alas, often clouds the picture with detail. To begin to see the lay of the land we need to discern the broad recurring styles of Buddhist metaphysical argumentation. We can then move on to a critical look at Buddhist metaontology, its various stances on metaphysics as a whole, and the promise of those stances for cross-cultural thinking.

Buddhist Metaphysical Argumentation: Unqualified and Qualified

Indian and Tibetan Buddhist authors, whatever the school to which they belong, accord a large role to negative metaphysical argumentation, using much ingenuity to show that there *are no* entities of the sort F, or that things *do not* have F-properties. I see two recurring and quite different versions of this negative argumentation. I shall frame them initially in terms of the "neither one nor many" arguments (Skt *ekānekaviyogahetu*; Tb. *gcig du bral gyi gtan tshigs*), the part–whole dialectic that one finds throughout Buddhist philosophy. In fact, however, the two styles need not be formulated in terms of part–whole issues: they are generalizable *mutatis mutandis* to a variety of Buddhist first order arguments, including those about the external world, the self, God, mind, time, causality, and relations.

For example, consider the difference between an argument like "There is no self because it is/would be neither one with the psycho-physical aggregates nor different from them" and "There is not REALLY a self because it is/would be neither REALLY one with the psycho-physical aggregates nor REALLY different from them." Call the first an "unqualified argument," in that it does not involve the qualifier REALLY. Generalize it as follows:

1 An *F* does not exist (or a thing does not have property *F*), because it is not *A* nor *B*..., etc.

The second sort of argument – for example, "The self does not REALLY exist because it is neither REALLY one..., etc." – is thus a "qualified argument," generalizable along the following lines:

2 An *F* does not REALLY exist (or a thing does not REALLY have property *F*), because it is not REALLY *A* nor REALLY *B*..., etc.

A typical example of that unqualified sort of metaphysical argumentation is found in the third chapter of the *Pramāṇaviniścaya* of the sixth/seventh-century writer Dharmakīrti and in the commentator Manorathanandin's *Pramāṇavārttikavṛtti* (eleventh century). There we find a classic Buddhist argument against real universals: "a universal is not many different things and therefore not present in many different things" – *nānekaṃ sāmānyaṃ tasmān nānekavṛtti*.[3] The point is that a universal, if it were to be existent, would have to be present in its numerous instances, which in turn would imply that the universal was not one thing but many different things, like its instances. However, a universal is not many different things; therefore it cannot be present in its many instances. The conclusion: "There are no universals (*sāmānya*)." There is no use of a qualifier here; the argument is a simple refutation of existence. As Dharmakīrti elsewhere categorically states, *na vai kiṃcit sāmānyaṃ nāmāsti*, "there is no so-called universal whatsoever."[4]

One can find numerous other such examples of unqualified nonexistence proofs in the Epistemological school, in the Abhidharma, or in the Idealist Yogācāra school. They regularly show that various sorts of *F*'s do not exist, but are only fictions (*asadartha*) or appearances (*ābhāsa/pratibhāsa*) that people commonly and mistakenly (*bhrānta*) believe to exist.[5] The Epistemologists, Ābhidharmikas, and Idealists are however metaphysical realists (*dngos smra ba*) and thus maintain that, if we are to avoid nihilism, there must exist some *G*'s that underlie at least some of the commonly accepted fictitious *F*'s. The Buddhist follower of the Abhidharma, for example, will say that partite, complex, things are nonexistent fictions but that impartite simples are fully real – they are the *G*'s for the fictional *F*'s (tables, chairs, people, etc.). Idealist Buddhists of the Yogācāra school hold that external objects (*bāhyārtha*) are the *F*'s and mental states (*citta*) are the *G*'s. Nominalist Buddhists, following Dignāga (480–540 CE) and Dharmakīrti (late sixth–early seventh century), hold that universals (*sāmānyalakṣaṇa*) are the *F*'s and particulars (*svalakṣaṇa*) are the *G*'s.

Now jump to fifteenth-century Tibet for one of the clearest examples of the second sort. Sera Chökyi gyaltsan (Se ra Chos kyi rgyal mtshan, 1469–1544), a monastic textbook writer, gives the following example of a *qualified* argument, where "REALLY" plays a prominent and indispensable role at every stage:

> Take the bases, paths and aspects as the topic of debate; they are not REALLY (*bden par*) established, because they are not REALLY established individual things nor REALLY established different things.[6]

Once again we have an argument turning on oneness and manyness, but this time with the conspicuous addition of the qualifier, "REALLY." It should not, however, be thought that the use of qualified argumentation was only a late Tibetan development. In fact, such qualifiers are found quite frequently in Indian, Tibetan, and Chinese Buddhist literature. Take the "neither one nor many" argument as it figures in verse 1 of Śāntarakṣita's *Madhyamakālaṃkāra*:

> [All] those entities asserted by ourselves and others are in reality (*tattvatas*) without any intrinsic natures (*svabhāva*), as they lack the intrinsic natures of oneness or manyness – like a reflection.[7]

In Chökyi gyaltsan's argument the qualifier is the Tibetan term *bden par* (truly); in the passage from Śāntarakṣita it is the Sanskrit term *tattvatas* (in reality). Other expressions figure in other contexts. The Indian thinker Bhāviveka (sixth century), for example, regularly used *paramārthatas* (absolutely, ultimately) and explicitly called it "a qualifier" (*viśeṣaṇa*).[8] We can go further: traditional Buddhist contexts regularly use several well-attested terms that can, and often are, used equivalently: for example the Sanskrit *satyatas* (really, truly), the Sanskrit *dravyatas* (substantially), *svabhāvena* (by its intrinsic nature), Chinese *zhen* 真, *shi* 實, or *shi you* 實有 (truly, substantially) and others. In Tibetan we also have very important and suggestive terms that, to my knowledge, do not come from Sanskrit and do not have equivalents in Chinese texts: "from its own side" (*rang ngos nas*), and "in terms of its own specific mode of being" (*rang gi thun mon ma yin pa'i sdod lugs gyi ngos nas*).

All of these terms form a kind of semantic circle of interlocking and mutually explaining concepts. For our purposes, we shall disregard the terminological differences; we are deliberately and, I think, harmlessly simplifying things by using the word "REALLY."

This much will have to do as philological evidence that there is indeed a very important distinction to be made between qualified and unqualified metaphysical arguments in Buddhism. Of course, there are several Buddhist texts in which we cannot clearly determine whether the arguments were intended to be qualified or not. But the broad outlines of the distinction are attested often enough, sometimes even very clearly and explicitly. Let us now move on to the various Buddhist second order stances about metaphysics. As we shall see, a metaphysics relying on unqualified argumentation has some major drawbacks; the stance that seems the most promising is a type of quietism using qualified reasonings, involving the REALLY operator, to show that no metaphysical thesis can be established.

The Majority View: Metaphysics is Both Legitimate and Necessary

Uncontestably the majority of Buddhist philosophers see metaphysics and argumentation about it as an intellectually legitimate and religiously necessary pursuit. For them it is integral to the path to liberation that we have the right account of what exists and what does not; we need to know what is real and what is no more than a fiction that people commonly and mistakenly believe to be real. How promising is such a Buddhist metametaphysics when the widescale, fundamental description of all is to be framed in terms of a dichotomy between existent things and commonly accepted fictions, or mere erroneous appearances, that do not exist at all? What consequences ensue when Buddhists use – as they regularly do – a form of *unqualified* argumentation to show that most things in which we believe are just purely fictitious? Let's skip the thorny issues as to whether individual metaphysical arguments are good or not and see whether the general picture is acceptable.

Nowadays, some of the most sophisticated reflection on what good metaphysics has been and should be comes from Australia, largely following the philosophy of David Lewis and the Canberra school. Frank Jackson calls this metaphysics "serious metaphysics" and others talk about "ontological seriousness" and the like. Here is how Jackson formulated things:

> Metaphysics is about what there is and what it is like. But it is not concerned with any old shopping list of what there is and what it is like. Metaphysicians seek a comprehensive account of some subject matter – the mind, the semantic, or, most ambitiously everything – in terms of a limited

number of more or less basic notions... In sum, serious metaphysics is discriminatory at the same time as claiming to be complete, or complete with respect to some subject matter, and the combination of these two features of serious metaphysics means that there are inevitably a host of putative features of our world which we must either eliminate or locate.[9]

So, is Buddhist metaphysics *serious* in this way? The short answer: typical Buddhist accounts do seem to fulfill the requirements of being discriminating and complete, but, seductive as that might be, seriousness involves more.[10]

To get a feeling for why metaphysics in Buddhist garb might be *thought to be* in keeping with Jackson's program, consider what the nominalist Dharmakīrti says in the *Pramāṇavārttika* about universals failing the requirements for inclusion in a proper ontology:

> It [i.e., the universal] does not come there [from somewhere else], it was not there already, nor does it exist subsequently, nor does it have any parts. [And even when in other places] it does not leave the previous locus. Oh my! It is just one disaster after another.[11]

Paṇḍita Aśoka (eleventh century), in turn, in his "Refutation of Universals" (*Sāmānyadūṣaṇa*), ridicules them as follows: "One can clearly see five fingers in one's own hand. One who commits himself to a sixth general entity fingerhood, side by side with the five fingers, might as well postulate horns on top of his head."[12] The *F*'s in question, that is, universals, cannot belong in a *discriminating* account of what there is. They are just too weird, ineffectual, and generally problematic to exist – the *G*'s are only particulars.

The second major requirement for seriousness would unpack as follows: besides being discriminating and parsimonious about what there is, a would-be nominalism needs to provide *completely* for the role and importance universals have for us in our thought and language. Now, some Western analytic philosophers have thought that the Buddhist position might just be able to fulfill this very requirement: it was once called by Hans Herzberger a "resourceful nominalism" and, in his view, presented marked advantages over "happy nominalism," as he dubbed the versions of the medieval *flatus vocis* account of universals, which take talk of common properties as not due to any entities, universals, but just the brute linguistic fact that people regularly use general terms.[13] The Buddhist keeps a place for universals themselves, qua fictions, in his account of concepts and properties by analyzing them as exclusions – the notion of fingerhood is analyzed as actually being a notion of non non fingers. The ingenious twist for the Buddhist is that because absences and negative facts are unreal, an analysis in terms of non non *F* is less ontologically committing than would be acceptance of *F*-ness – we can continue to say that *a*, *b*, and *c* are fingers (i.e., non non fingers) and the grand nominalist theory in which there are only particulars would remain: universals, qua exclusions, are simply fictions created by language and thought.

Now, I am not convinced that the Buddhist nominalist succeeds in replacing universals like *blue* with quasi-universals like *non non blue*. Indeed many Brahmanical thinkers, like the Mīmāṃsaka Kumārila Bhaṭṭa (sixth century), do have powerful replies to this move, accusing it of circularity – one cannot understand non non *F* without understanding *F*; understanding the exclusion (*apoha*) of *non blue* presupposes that one has understood *blue*. The jury is still out whether *apoha* and Buddhist nominalism *can* be a complete account or whether the circularity is fatal.[14] We leave that issue open. At the very least, it has to be said that the theory is some of the best metaphysics we will find in Buddhist texts. It is subtle and ingenious.

Let's grant, then, for the sake of argument, that *apoha*-style nominalism may well satisfy two significant requirements of a modern program about how to do metaphysics. But, if we look deeper, is it actually serious metaphysics in Frank Jackson's sense? Where it would seem to fall down and where, I would maintain, Buddhist metaphysical theories regularly fall down – particularly those that proceed along the lines of the first style of argumentation – is that they leave the *F*'s as fictions, commonly accepted because of a causal story about the longstanding psychic baggage of habits and tendencies (*vāsanā*) we have accumulated, but nonetheless nonexistent and thoroughly erroneous. Here, for example, is how Dharmakīrti argues that universals are just fictions (*asadartha*) and appearances (*pratibhāsa*). It's a very typical case of argumentation of the first sort to prove that *F*'s are no more than ingrained erroneous appearances.

> [Objection:] Now, how is it that the exclusion of what is other (*anyavyāvṛtti*) could be a universal (*sāmānya*), since one excluded thing cannot be present in any others? [Reply:] It is [a universal] because it appears to be that way to the cognition [we have] of it (*tadbuddhau tathāpratibhāsanāt*). But indeed there is no so-called universal whatsoever (*na vai kiṃcit sāmānyaṃ nāmāsti*). A cognition based on words ends up combining elements, even though they are not [actually] combined, because of the power of beginningless tendencies [to make cognition do so] (*anādivāsanāsāmarthyād*). It is on account of how things appear to be (*pratibhāsavaśena*) to that [word-based cognition] that universals and co-reference (*sāmānādhikaraṇya*) are established, though they are fictions (*asadartha*), for [actual particular] things are neither combined [to be a universal] nor differentiated [into the various qualities we think they have].[15]

Jackson's program requires much more than *that* if we wish to conserve and not eliminate things: serious metaphysics requires that entities be "located" in the grand theory, that is, that statements about an acceptable entity, if it is not itself one of the basic entities, must at least be entailed by the theory one espouses. If one is, for example, a physicalist, then the theory of everything is told in physical terms; nothing is acceptable unless its existence is demanded by the physical theory. Being yellow, for example, might be something described in the non-preferred, non-basic, vocabulary of a folk theory that uses color language, but there would be an entailment between the non-preferred vocabulary of colors and the preferred language of physical properties. Typically, non-basic F's would exist as supervenient upon the basic G's.[16]

Now, there is nothing like location, inter-vocabulary entailment, or supervenience in the *apoha* theory, nor for that matter elsewhere in Buddhist metaphysics. Elsewhere I have gone into the "theory of unconscious error" that Buddhists repeatedly rely upon.[17] And indeed an error theory and talk of long-standing habits and mindsets is never very far off in Buddhist metaphysics, especially when pursued via the first sort of argumentation. Things like selves, partite objects, and universals are explicable qua common ingrained mistakes, appearances, and fictions, but there is no inter-vocabulary entailment between talk of selves and talk of impersonal psycho-physical elements, partite and impartite objects, or universals and particulars.

Does it matter much that Buddhist metaphysics would not address the location problem? Yes, I think it does. The danger is that much of it collapses into a thinly veiled eliminativism. Instead of some non-basic F's being located in the grand theory and hence existent, they are explained as commonly accepted and more or less tenacious errors; they are things that simply do not exist, and that people who know better might even do without at some time, for example when they attain *nirvāṇa*, arthatship, or when they have their first realizations on the "path of seeing" (*darśanamārga*) as "noble beings" (*ārya*). Recall that Frank Jackson spoke of a "host of putative features of our world that we must either eliminate or locate." These are the F's we have been speaking about so far. Serious metaphysics is one of the most sophisticated programs on the market precisely because it attempts to *locate* the problematic entities that one wishes to keep and doesn't treat them as fictions or tenacious errors. Eliminativism is much less so.

Are there ways to counter the specter of thinly veiled eliminativism and still arrive at a grand hierarchical theory of everything using Buddhist arguments? One approach is to explain our acceptance of fictions as due to their usefulness to us, and not just due to our ingrained and wrong mindsets. Mark Siderits (2003) has promoted this as a Buddhist approach that avoids eliminations of the fictional F's; instead of casting them out, we have Buddhist-style *reduction* of F's to the appropriate G's. Does it get us any further? I rather doubt it. First, pragmatism is not what Buddhist texts explicitly promote, nor, for that matter, do they seem to make a clear distinction between elimination and reduction, at least as far as I can see. But, what is probably more telling, it is not easy to imagine pragmatism on the wide scale that would seem to be required to make that distinction stick. I'll take up the issue in more detail in the next section.

A More Promising Metametaphysical Stance: Quietism

What if one is not optimistic about the prospects for a grand hierarchical theory of everything? There are, after all, important contemporary philosophers who do not think there is, or could be, a legitimate discipline of ontology and who think that we should thus stay lucidly out of the fray as quietists whenever it appears on the scene.[18] And many important Buddhists *were* indeed quietists. They were typically followers of the school coming from Nāgārjuna (second century CE), Candrakīrti (sixth century), Bhāviveka (sixth century) *et alii*, in other words, Mādhyamikas or followers of the "Middle Way" school (*madhyamaka*). The passages in Buddhist texts that are generally cited in these discussions are well known. Two will suffice, namely, Nāgārjuna's famous pronouncement in *Vigrahavyāvartanī* that "I don't have any thesis and thus I don't have that fault [of which you metaphysical realists accuse me]"[19] and the oft-cited verse 50 in his *Yuktiṣaṣṭikā*: "Superior individuals have no theses (*pakṣa, phyogs*) and no philosophical debates; how could there be any opposing theses for those who have no theses [themselves]?"[20]

What connection is there between quietism and the use of one or another of the two types of argumentation? I think it's clear that at least a significant number of Mādhyamikas – perhaps even Nāgārjuna himself – *did* use the unqualified style of argumentation in the service of quietism. They, in effect, agreed that *F*'s do not exist and are only fictions that are commonly (but mistakenly) accepted. On the other hand, and in sharp contrast to Dharmakīrti, Ābhidharmikas, Yogācāras, and other metaphysical realists, they said that there are no *G*'s that are more basic. Thus they argued instead for a kind of panfictionalism: no *F*'s exist, whatever *F* one might take, and there are no basic *G*'s anywhere, just more of the same old fictions.[21] This does lead to a kind of quietism. But the general picture is not attractive at all.

Here is how a Buddhist panfictionalist gets to quietism and here is what I think goes badly wrong when she does. The point that the Mādhyamika adept of the first style of reasoning is seeking to prove is that under analysis everything supposedly turns out to be nothing but "false and deceptive" (*mṛṣāmoṣadharmaka*), to use a cliché term in Madhyamaka writings that is often taken pretty much literally. Things don't exist, they just appear to, and people erroneously think and talk as if they did. There are no right answers (because there are no *pramāṇas*, "sources of knowledge") about anything; at most there is just what people ignorantly think to be right, or in the phrase of the Tibetan Jo nang pa Mādhyamikas, "things that seem to exist to mistaken minds" (*blo 'khrul ba'i ngor yod pa*). From here we might rather easily go to a certain type of quietism about metaphysics. If it were to be accepted that *everything* just *seemed* to be thus and so but wasn't at all, one could then say that deeper ontological inquiry was always pointless, as it could never be about anything but erroneous appearances.[22]

The price to be paid for a cocktail of quietism and panfictionalism is potentially very high. It's hard to see how the panfictionalist could account for the complex and evolving rational discriminations between truths and falsities that we do make, if all were just completely false and deceptive. Of course, at some point the global fictionalist or error theorist may well say that the world's *thinking* some propositions to be true and others false is based on the brute fact of some erroneous beliefs turning out to be *useful* to us as white lies and others remaining relatively *useless*. But while we might perhaps (like an ethical irrealist) be able to take as "true" *certain sorts* of shared white lies, like beliefs in there being good or bad actions because such erroneous beliefs make people more respectful, gentle, and so on, it would be hard to see why many beliefs and statements – in ethics, physics, geography, car mechanics, or what have you – would be so useful on a wide and complex scale if one stripped them all of any truth.[23]

Not only that, but the pragmatic account of why things "exist" *could not* easily be given on the scale demanded. Indeed very large-scale or exclusive appeals to usefulness and human ends to explain the "existence" of everything would seem to involve a vicious circularity: in order to determine usefulness in human enterprises, one already needs to have a world largely in place, with people and many macroscopic objects too. In short, usefulness of carts, tables, and the like to people *presupposes* a context in which there are people, their environments, and complex interactions with a lot of quite different sorts of objects. If strategies to further human ends were themselves responsible for the genesis of all these entities, their genesis would seem to become unintelligible.[24]

Finally, while an unqualified approach might enable a Mādhyamika to show that some specific items don't exist, generalized quietism would remain elusive, at most a tentative stance. The reason is that an unqualified approach lacks an overarching diagnosis to show that ontology *always* goes wrong and that metaphysical positions/theses, or ontological claims, are therefore somehow *all* false or meaningless. Instead of a clearly articulated "master argument" to this effect, we would have a number of *ad hoc* Mādhyamika counterarguments against some specific metaphysical positions on the existence of specific things. This procedure is inconclusive. Even if the Mādhyamika were to be right in rejecting the going metaphysical arguments of the third century, or the major positions held historically in Classical Indian philosophy, that is no assurance that better ontologies will not be found later by more sophisticated thinkers, somewhere in the East or West, and that they will not, at some point, carry the day.

Qualified Argumentation and Quietism

Enter the qualified approach in the service of quietism. Let us be clear that for us, and I think for Buddhists too, a genuine qualifier affects the truth value of the statement to which it is added. It is not simply used for emphasis or rhetorical force, as if one merely said "Actually..." or "In fact..." out of mere insistence; rhetorical force does not generally affect truth of the original statement. What is important on this qualified approach to Madhyamaka is that P may be true while REALLY P is not.

Now suppose you argued, "It is not REALLY so that P, because it is not REALLY so that Q and R, etc." This leaves you able to say that P, Q, and R are true/so but not REALLY true/so. That's precisely what the great Tibetan thinker Tsongkhapa (Tsong kha pa Blo bzang grags pa, 1357–1419) did by adding *bden par* (truly, really) and its equivalent operators to the arguments in Indian Madhyamaka texts, and it had a number of interesting consequences for him and for us. First, it allowed him to say that the truth of P, Q, and R was not just a matter of them *seeming* to be true to all or most worldlings who mistakenly believed in them, but that they *were* true – in his jargon, they are established by means of knowledge (*pramāṇa, tshad ma*). Secondly, it allowed him to say that the culprit was the "REALLY" operator, as thinking that things are REALLY so is a very seductive but pernicious superimposition (*samāropa, sgro 'dogs*) on the otherwise innocent truths P, Q, R. The consequence is that one should reject all theses and positions that implicitly or explicitly involve "REALLY." Thirdly, we could have something like an overarching diagnosis of where metaphysics goes wrong and why we should be quietistic about it. The diagnosis would be like this: philosophical/metaphysical claims that F's exist, as contrasted with innocent common sense claims, or even scientific claims, involve the "REALLY" operator; statements that may or may not be true taken innocently are false with the REALLY operator added.

We have left "REALLY" as a term of art. Graham Priest, Mark Siderits, and I used it in that way in a chapter in *Moonshadows* to try to make sense of the contrast between ultimate and customary truths in Buddhism.[25] One could also proffer the somewhat comforting assurance that it is not just modern writers on Buddhism who use it; philosophers like Paul Horwich (e.g., Horwich 2006) and Kit Fine do too in their discussions of ontology, or they use an equivalent term like "ROBUSTLY." The catch, of course, is that we want to know better at some point what that REALLY operator involves and what difference it makes from just asserting a common variety proposition< P>, or "< P> is true." That, indeed, is not an easy task. Tsongkhapa himself was acutely aware that the difference was subtle and he devoted a large section of the last chapter of his *Lam rim chen mo* to what he called the problem of "recognizing what is to be rejected" (*dgag bya ngos 'dzin*), trying to find a kind of middle way between refuting too much (*khyab che ba*) – i.e., just saying that P, Q, R are false – and too little (*khyab chung ba*) – i.e., construing what is to be refuted in a way that is just speculative and implausible, a straw man which nobody but a few extreme philosophers would worry about.

So, how could we thread that needle with Buddhists? A start would be to recognize that in many respects a similar issue arises when modern philosophers seek to distinguish neutral, even banal, discussions of what there is from discussions committed to ontology and metaphysical realism. So, let's look at some possibilities for collaboration offered by analytic philosophy. Kit Fine made a particularly useful distinction in his 2009 article "The Question of Ontology" between quantificational and ontological questions, a distinction that is not far from (though not completely identical with) Rudolf Carnap's famous contrast between internal and external questions (Carnap 1950). Thus, we often ask things, like, for example, Are there trees in Switzerland, in Antarctica? Are there properties in common that define the races? Is there a prime number greater than seventeen that satisfies such and such an equation? Is there a Higgs boson? More generally, is there an x such that x is an F? All these are what Fine would term *quantificational questions*: if one asserts that an item a is an F, it is a simple logical inference of no metaphysical import whatsoever to assert "There is an x such that x is an F." The move is a banal application of existential generalization, as you might find in first order predicate calculus, one which allows you to go from an atomic formula Fa to the existentially quantified statement $(\exists x)\ Fx$.

Many quantificational questions are of course important, subtle, and even technically abstruse, such as when, for example, one is asking a scientific question about whether there are certain types of subatomic particles. It is however striking that when one asks a quantificational question about the typical matters treated by metaphysics – for example, Are there any numbers? Are there any common properties? Are there absences? Are there thoughts, minds? Are there good or bad actions? – the answer will be a trivial "Yes, of course." That thin answer will be forthcoming whatever one might also say in a discussion on ontology.

Quantificational questions are thus to be contrasted with *ontological* questions, like "Does the x that is F exist?" Here "exist" is used in some deeper, thicker, sense, one where "exists" means something like "is fully real" or is a constituent of a bedrock set of real entities. Interestingly, Fine himself sees no adequate way to define that thick sense of "exists" or the concept of a "constituent of reality" in any way other than by a circle of ideas to which they themselves belong. He takes it as primitive and says that we have a good intuitive grasp of the notions at stake and how to apply them. That, for him, is enough to ensure the bona fides of ontology. Arguably he is profoundly right about an inescapable circle; key normative concepts seem to be like that. He may not be right, however, in saying that our seeming "grasp" of this circle of concepts about the real and genuinely existent indicates their bona fides and the legitimacy of ontology.[26]

Indeed, it is important to stress that Kit Fine *himself* is not pursuing a quietist anti-ontology line. He makes his distinction in order to better *pursue* ontology and logic without an encumbering prescriptive baggage about what existential quantification should be and without the distortions that come when one uses formal logical structures or criteria borrowed from science to specify what ontology is in terms *other* than those of ontology itself. He is thus arguing *against* the Quinean program in "On What There Is" according to which there should be just one clear unambiguous sense of "there is" – the ontological should be the same as the quantificational – and deviations from the clear, univocal use that we supposedly find in the existential quantifier are just cases, for Quine, of sloppy thinking, loose uses of language, or worse, detestable double-talk. Kit Fine and many others reject that Quinean program; but Kit Fine, at least, certainly does not reject ontology.

What the Mādhyamika would be doing, however, is much more radical, as it is a refusal of ontology across the board. Indeed, the semantic circle of which Fine speaks is not far from the circle of interlocking Buddhist concepts and terms we mentioned earlier and grouped under the term of art "REALLY." It is an *absolute* conception, or in Buddhist terms, the notion that some things must exist *paramārthatas* (absolutely, ultimately) and that others are nothing more than them. Fine states: "This account of our method for settling ontological dispute requires that we have a grasp not only of an absolute conception of reality, of there *being nothing more than* ..., but also of a relative conception, of *there being nothing more to ... than* ...., ..."[27] I think we are on East–West common ground here. When an atomist like Democritus says that there is nothing more to the universe than atoms and that there is therefore nothing more, or really more, to a chair than the constituent atoms, the Buddhist Ābhidharmika metaphysician – indeed almost all classical Indian philosophers – would feel they grasp the issue perfectly. They would typically proceed to argue that chairs are *nothing but* their impartite constituents or, if they accept chairs as genuine entities, that they are wholes (*avayavin*) distinct from their constituents but linked to them by some kind of inherence (*samavāya*) relation. The Mādhyamika quietist, however, is a unique case: he would be out of step with his East–West colleagues. He recognizes that we do intuitively *feel* we grasp the interlocking notions involved in an *absolute* conception of reality. But, contrary to Fine and the Buddhist metaphysician, the Mādhyamika Buddhist says that *this* is a seductive trap: it is a commitment to the idea that some things REALLY are, and it is actually badly confused.

What happens then if we read Mādhyamikas like Candrakīrti using Fine's distinction, that is, as contrasting a thin quantificational sense of "there are..." and an ontologically loaded sense of "exists"? If we understand the Madhyamaka critique of ontology as turning on panfictionalism or a global error theory, that distinction seems inapplicable. Instead of any innocently true statements using the thin sense of "there are...," we would just be left with a bunch of falsehoods, for there would be no *x*'s that are *F*; at most there would just wrongly *seem* to be such *x*'s. But if we go with a Tsongkhapa-style interpretation and say that many "there are…" statements are innocently true (i.e., "established by means of knowledge"), things could work out much better. We could have an intelligent interpretation of why Candrakīrti says that a Mādhyamika should content herself with *lokaprasiddha*, "what the world acknowledges," and not seek anything deeper in metaphysics – a Mādhyamika would restrict her acceptance of true statements to those with the quantificational "there are…" and eschew ontological talk about existence or constituents of reality as impossible and, in any case, not needed for the world to say and think truly what it does. Similarly Candrakīrti could maintain (as he does in *Prasannapadā* I) that he has no difficulty following, in an innocent fashion, the world's acceptance of universals (*sāmānyalakṣaṇa*) and particulars (*svalakṣaṇa*) alike;[28] or he could argue (as he in fact does in *Madhyamakāvatāra* VI) that the external world is unproblematically acceptable for him, that causality exists as accepted by the common man; he could even accept absences (*abhāva*) and negative facts as no less existent than anything else. The recurrent attempts of the metaphysician and epistemologist to try to do *better* or go *deeper* than the world might indeed be (as he says in *Catuḥśatakaṭīkā* 13) a type of intoxication (*smyos pa*) that makes them no longer even know what the world does and hence become "completely unversed in ordinary matters" (*'jig rten pa'i don dag la gtan ma byang ba*).[29]

This is, arguably, the Buddhist stance on metaphysics that would have the most radical impact cross-culturally. It would part ways with contemporary analytic metaphysics and would resemble, in some important respects, the later philosophy of Wittgenstein: diagnoses of intoxication coupled with description, rather than revision, of our thought and language.[30] Like Wittgenstein's quietism, an uncompromising Candrakīrtian stance will probably not readily enjoy favor in philosophical establishments nowadays. But that is hardly a reason for not giving it the genuine hearing it deserves.

Remaining Matters

Finally, there are two big themes that need to be at least mentioned here to flesh out the prospective picture of a Madhyamaka-inspired metametaphysics.

First, the question will still remain whether at least *some* metaphysics, East or West, couldn't still be pursued when stripped of the quest for underlying REAL entities. Some philosophers – especially those of a Quinean persuasion, who see philosophy as continuous with science – maintain that one can take up ontological questions by simply applying criteria of explanatory and predictive power, and especially parsimony. For them usual scientific methodology is thus extendable to metaphysics, while elucubrations about the absolute or the REAL are both impossible and superfluous. There are Mādhyamikas, notably

Svātantrikas (*not* Candrakīrtians), who seem to have gone in broadly this direction too, conserving some metaphysical debates; they argue for "deeper" customary truths about universals, the external world, mind, time, and so on, all the while remaining quietist about the REAL. The debate is sophisticated. Elliott Sober (2009) and Michael Huemer (2009) have examined the prospects for using parsimony arguments to settle metaphysical issues quasi-scientifically. Those prospects are not as rosy as W.V. Quine had hoped. In Tillemans (2016) I have argued that the doubters (including notably Candrakīrtians in their debates with Svātantrika coreligionists) may well be right to think that doing metaphysics is not merely a matter of epistemic business as usual – notably, parsimony arguments applied to decide typical problems of ontology would rely, after all, on unavowed intuitions about the REAL.[31]

Second, what would remain of traditional Buddhism if a thoroughgoing, modernized Candrakīrtian metametaphysics carried the day? My own view is that a systematic advocacy of *lokaprasiddha* impacts not just Buddhist metaphysics, but Buddhist ethics and religious dogmas as well.[32] It is implausible to think that one could rationally ground ethics on facts that are supposedly inaccessible to any human epistemic procedure, and are only knowable via scripture, if one also believes that morality and other customary truths are those that the world accepts, or should accept, by its own standards and epistemic practices. Customary truth as *lokaprasiddha* should thus lead to a major rethink: a Madhyamaka Buddhism without reliance on humanly inaccessible facts (*atyantaparokṣa*, literally "completely imperceptible") known only via scripture, especially karmic causality spanning multiple lives and multiple forms of existence. Many traditionalists will no doubt bridle at the suggestion that karma theory should ever be challenged, but such is the type of discussion needed for Buddhism to figure rationally in future cross-cultural philosophy.

Notes

1 The present article is a much reworked version of a lecture delivered at the symposium on "Buddhism and Contemporary Philosophy" at the University of British Columbia, Vancouver, Canada. I thank Evan Thompson, Jessica Main, Ashok Aklujkar, Koji Tanaka, and Bronwyn Finnigan for helpful feedback.
2 The term is that of David Chalmers *et al.* (2009). As they point out, the prefix "meta" is being used here as it is used in "meta-ethics" and "meta-semantics."
3 See Tillemans (2000, 22 n.84).
4 See n.15.
5 See later for an example from Dharmakīrti showing his use of the terms *asadartha* and *ābhāsa/pratibhāsa*. There are other well-known terms used similarly by adepts of the first style of argumentation: *prajñapti* (designations), *nāmamātra* (mere names). These terms too are typically used by Buddhist Ābhidharmikas

and Yogācāras to convey fictional status – such fictions are contrasted with what is a genuine entity (*vastu*), i.e., substantially existent (*dravyasat*).
6 See Tillemans (1984, 380). The Tibetan is: *gzhi lam rnam gsum chos can, bden par ma grub ste, bden grub kyi gcig dang bden grub kyi du ma gang rung du ma grub pa'i phyir.*
7 The Sanskrit text of this verse as quoted in Prajñākaramati's *Bodhicaryāvatārapañjikā* (ed. P.L. Vaidya 1960) 173, 17–18 is: *niḥsvabhāvā amī bhāvās tattvataḥ svaparoditāḥ/ekānekasvabhāvena viyogāt pratibimbavat//*.
8 See, e.g., Bhāviveka's reasoning against the Sāṃkhya as discussed by Candrakīrti in *Prasannapadā* 25, 9–26, 2: *na paramārthata ādhyātmikāny āyatanāni svata utpannāni/vidyamānatvāt/caitanyavad iti/*, "It is not ultimately so (*paramārthatas*) that the inner sense bases are produced from themselves, for they exist, just like consciousness." Note that while the use of *tattvatas, paramārthatas, svabhāvena* or some such equivalent term is probably more frequent in one branch of Indian Madhyamaka philosophy, the so-called Svātantrika school, Tibetan commentators, like Tsongkhapa and many others, add it to Prāsaṅgika–Madhyamaka argumentation abundantly too. We too do not restrict the use of REALLY to just one branch of the Madhyamaka. It might be thought that Candrakīrti's rejection of *paramārthatas* in this argument means he does not countenance qualifiers *at all* and could not use qualified argumentation. This is not right. While Candrakīrti does argue against using *paramārthatas* in the above argument from Bhāviveka, this can best be seen as a very specific case where (according to *Prasannapadā* 26, 2) it makes no sense – *kim arthaṃ punar atra paramārthata iti viśeṣaṇam upādīyate*, "But, in this context, why would one use the qualifier *paramārthatas*?" He goes on to say that even from a customary point of view (*saṃvṛtyāpi*) production from self makes no sense, so why bother with the qualifier "ultimately"? But there is no attempt to generalize here.

Note that the term *viśeṣa* (particularity) also figures in *Prasannapadā* I concerning the propriety of taking certain subject terms in a neutral general fashion (*sāmānyena*), or according to the particularities (*viśeṣa*) of the debaters' positions – Bhāviveka, as a Svātantrika-Mādhyamika, advocates the neutral manner and Candrakīrti, the Prāsaṅgika, says that neutrality is, in certain crucial cases, impossible. See *Prasannapadā* 26 et seq. See Tillemans (1990, 1:47 n.107) for a translation of the relevant passages. This is a specific debate between Indian Madhyamaka subschools as to whether certain terms can be accepted in common (*ubhayaprasiddha*) by both Mādhyamikas and metaphysical realists so that they can hence make "autonomous inferences" (*svatantrānumāna*). It does not imply that Prāsaṅgikas must reject all uses of qualifiers.

The distinction between argumentation styles that we are speaking of is not formulated as such in *Prasannapadā*. It comes from Madhyamaka philosophy as interpreted by Tibetans, especially those following Tsongkhapa; they speak of argumentation that is *dgag bya'i khyad par sbyar ba*, "with the added qualifier concerning what is being refuted" versus *dgag bya'i khyad par mi sbyar ba*, "without such an added qualifier." The Sa skya pa thinker Go rams pa bSod nams seng ge (1429–1489), in his *lTa ba'i shan 'byed*, maintained that Mādhyamikas should use the unqualified style of argumentation – the tetralemma (*catuṣkoṭi*) should be taken as a series of unqualified refutations of existence, nonexistence, both, or neither. See Cabezón and Dargyay (2007, n.180). Tsongkhapa and his dGe lugs pa followers, however, claimed that such an overly literal interpretation is uncharitable; he argued that the lemmas need to be qualified with REALLY if logical absurdities are not to result.

9   Jackson (1998, 4–5).
10 In Tillemans (2016, ch. 12), I emphasized that Buddhist metaphysics fulfills major requirements of Jackson's serious metaphysics. I now think that it is more important to be clear on where it is significantly different.
11 Dharmakīrti's *Pramāṇavārttika* 1.152: *na yāti na ca tatrāsīd asti paścān na cāṃśavat/jahāti pūrvaṃ nādhāram aho vyasanasaṃtatiḥ//*. On Dharmakīrti's life, oeuvre, and thought, see Tillemans (2011a).
12 Paṇḍita Aśoka's *Sāmānyadūṣaṇa* 101–102 (ed. H. Śāstrī), translated in Chakrabarti and Siderits' introduction to Siderits, Tillemans, and Chakrabarti (2011).
13 See Herzberger (1975).
14 On the *apoha* theory and Buddhist nominalism, its promises and problems, see Siderits, Tillemans, and Chakrabarti (2011) and Tillemans (2011a).
15 Dharmakīrti's *Pramāṇavārttikasvavṛtti* on verse 64 (ed. Gnoli 34–35): *kathaṃ idānīm ekasya vyāvṛttasyānyānanugamād anyavyāvṛttiḥ sāmānyam/tadbuddhau tathāpratibhāsanāt/na vai kiṃcit sāmānyaṃ nāmāsti/śabdāśrayā buddhir anādivāsanāsāmarthyād asaṃsṛṣṭān api dharmān saṃsṛjantī jāyate/tasyāḥ pratibhāsavaśena sāmānyaṃ sāmānādhikaraṇyaṃ ca vyavasthāpyate | asadartho 'pi/arthānāṃ saṃsargabhedābhāvāt/.*
16 *F*'s are supervenient on *G*'s just in case no two things can differ with respect to *F*-properties and not differ with respect to *G*-properties. In short, no *F*-differences without *G*-differences. Mind–matter, universals–particulars, ethical properties–physical properties, and many other such perennial dichotomies are the *F*'s and *G*'s for supervenience theorists.
17 See Tillemans (1999, ch. 10, 209–213).
18 Rejection of metaphysics was, of course, frequent in the twentieth century, whether with the logical positivists, the philosophy of the later Wittgenstein, or the ordinary language school. Arguably, the rebirth of modern metaphysics was with W.V. Quine's 1948 article "On What There Is," in which he argued that philosophy should adopt a univocal term "existence" and seek to determine just what one has to say exists when one speaks literally and in a univocal fashion. Cf. Putnam (2004, 78–79): "It [i.e., ontology] became respectable in 1948, when Quine published a famous paper titled 'On What There Is.' It was Quine who singlehandedly made Ontology a respectable subject." Quietists typically argue (see, e.g., Putnam 2004, 84–85) that this

univocality of "exists" demanded by ontology isn't forthcoming – it is, following Huw Price, even a kind of category mistake to say that something like January exists in the same sense of "exists" as atoms do. Or it is argued that the clear literal-versus-figurative contrast needed to say what there is will not be forthcoming (Yablo 1998). Another modern approach (e.g., Hirsch 2009, 2011; Price 2009) is to say that many metaphysical disputes are purely verbal disputes about the choice of language to use. These specific Western metaontological approaches are not, to my knowledge at least, ever explicitly developed by Buddhists, although they probably could be collaboratively. Other quietist approaches elaborated in the West may have affinities with Buddhist arguments. I have argued elsewhere that the critique of a "sideways on" perspective (see McDowell 1981) bears a significant resemblance to Buddhist critiques of "grasping at true existence" (*bden 'dzin*). See Tillemans (2016, ch. 12).

19 Nāgārjuna's *Vigrahavyāvartanī* 29–30 cited in Candrakīrti's *Prasannapadā* (ed. La Vallée Poussin) p. 16, lines 7–10: *yadi kācana pratijñā syān me tata eva* me baved doṣaḥ/nāsti ca mama pratijñā tasmān naivāsti me doṣaḥ//.* *Johnston and Kunst's edition (see Bhattacharya 1986) reads *eṣa* ("this"), and I've followed them here.

20 *Che ba'i bdag nyid can de dag//rnams la phyogs med rtsod pa med//gang rnams la ni phyogs med pa//de la gzhan phyogs ga la yod//.* Tibetan text in Lindtner (1990, 114).

21 For an attempt to interpret Madhyamaka as panfictionalism, see Garfield (2006).

22 Suppose that, to take a very simplified analogy, ordinary people believed firmly in the reality of square circles, or to borrow from Bertrand Russell, in a barber who shaved all and only those people in his village who didn't shave themselves. It would be pointless to construct a nominalism about square-circles or pursue the question whether the impossible barber is enduring or momentary, external, identical with, or different from his mind and body, and so on.

23 Cf. Stanley (2001, 46): "The problem facing a brute error theory of a discourse that is epistemically central…lies in explaining how a discourse laced through with falsity can nevertheless be useful."

24 Amber Carpenter (2015, 14–15) makes the same point about people being clearly presupposed in explanations that turn on human ends.

25 See Priest, Siderits, and Tillemans (2011).

26 See Fine (2009, 175).

27 Fine (2009, 176). The italics are his.

28 See Candrakīrti's *Prasannapadā* 1.75.2–4 (ed. La Vallée Poussin): *tasmāl loke yadi lakṣyaṃ yadi vā svalakṣaṇaṃ sāmānyalakṣaṇaṃ vā sarvam eva sākṣād upalabhyamānatvād aparokṣam/ataḥ pratyakṣaṃ vyavasthāpyate tadviṣayeṇa jñānena saha/*, "Therefore, in the world, when any and all subjects of characterization (*lakṣya*) whatsoever, be they particulars (*svalakṣaṇa*) or universals (*sāmānyalakṣaṇa*), are visible (*aparokṣa*) because they are directly perceived, they are therefore established as *pratyakṣa* ('perceptible'/'perceptions'), as are

the cognitions that have them as objects." See also Arnold (2005, 460–461). Essentially, Candrakīrti interprets the word *pratyakṣa* to mean both "perceptible" and "perception" (which is perfectly legitimate in Sanskrit) and says that universals and particulars alike are perceptible and that any cognitions that grasp them are perceptions. This, in effect, means that universals and particulars are on the same footing (contrary to Dignāga): both are customarily real and both are ultimately unreal. The passage has its parallel in Candrakīrti's *Catuḥśatakaṭīkā* 13, translated in Tillemans (1990, 1:175–179) and discussed on 41ff. See Dreyfus (1992, 42 n.58) for a summary of the point about Candrakīrti's recognizing universals and its dGe lugs interpretations.
29 Translated in Tillemans (1990, 1:177, 179) (sects. 8 and 17).
30 See, e.g., Wittgenstein (2009, sect. 124): "Philosophy must not interfere in any way with the actual use of language, so it can in the end only describe it. For it cannot justify it either. It leaves everything as it is."
31 See Tillemans (2016, ch. 12), "Serious, Lightweight or Neither: Should Madhyamaka go to Canberra?"
32 Note that much of Candrakīrti's (and Tsongkhapa's) Madhyamaka philosophy on typical Buddhist metaphysical issues – impermanence, the reality of universals, external objects, the special reflexive nature of mind, foundational status of perception, and sense data – does embrace the world and describe its thinking. Their hard revisionist edge comes on matters dogmatic and ethical. Crucially, these Mādhyamikas justify belief in accounts of karmic causality and retribution spanning multiple lives – whose truth is supposedly only known through scripture – by saying that such beliefs *can* still be in accord with the world's own conceptions of rational justification. For Candrakīrti's own failed attempts in *Catuḥśatakaṭīkā* 12 to show that belief in supra-sensible things like karma accords with *lokaprasiddha*, see Tillemans (2011b; 2016, ch. 8).

References

Abbreviations used in references: D = sDe dge Tibetan Tripiṭaka; P = Peking Tibetan Tripiṭaka.

Arnold, Dan A. 2005. "Materials for a Mādhyamika Critique of Foundationalism: An Annotated Translation of *Prasannapadā* 55.11 to 75.13." *Journal of the International Association of Buddhist Studies* 28(2): 411–467.

Bhattacharya, K. 1986. *The Dialectical Method of Nāgārjuna*. Translated from the original Sanskrit with introduction and notes by Kamaleswar Bhattacharya; text critically edited by E.H. Johnston and Arnold Kunst. Delhi: Motilal Banarsidass.

Cabezón, José I. and Geshé Lobsang Dargyay. 2007. *Freedom from Extremes: Gorampa's 'Distinguishing the Views' and the Polemics of Emptiness*. Studies in Indian and Tibetan Buddhism. Boston: Wisdom Publications.

Candrakīrti. *Catuḥśatakaṭīkā*. P. 5266, D. 3865. Sanskrit fragments edited by Haraprasād Śāstrī, in "Catuḥśatika of Ārya Deva." *Memoirs of the Asiatic Society of Bengal*, vol. III, 8, Calcutta, 1914. Chapters 12–13 translated in Tillemans (1990).

Candrakīrti. *Prasannapadā Madhyamakavṛtti*. P. 5260, D. 3860. Sanskrit edited by L. de La Vallée Poussin in *Mūlamadhyamakakārikās (Mādhyamikasūtras) de Nāgārjuna, avec le commentaire de Candrakīrti*. St. Petersburg: Bibliotheca Buddhica IV, 1903–13. Reprinted Osnabrück: Biblio Verlag, 1970.

Carnap, Rudolf. 1950. "Empiricism, Semantics, and Ontology." *Revue Internationale de Philosophie* 4: 20–40. Reprinted in *Meaning and Necessity*, 2nd edition (Chicago: University of Chicago Press, 1956).

Carpenter, Amber D. 2015. "Persons Keeping Their Karma Together." In *The Moon Points Back*, edited by Koji Tanaka, Yasuo Deguchi, Jay L. Garfield, and Graham Priest, 1–44. New York: Oxford University Press.

Chalmers, D., Manley, D., and Wasserman, R., eds. 2009. *Metametaphysics: New Essays on the Foundations of Ontology*. Oxford: Oxford University Press.

Dharmakīrti. *Pramāṇavārttika*. P. 5709, D. 4210. Sanskrit and Tibetan editions by Y. Miyasaka in *Acta Indologica* 2, Naritasan Shinshoji, Narita, 1972: 1–206.

Dharmakīrti. *Pramāṇavārttikasvavṛtti*. P. 5717.1, D. 4216. Sanskrit edited by Raniero Gnoli in *The Pramāṇavārttikam of Dharmakīrti: The First Chapter with the Autocommentary*. Serie Orientale Roma 23. Rome: Istituto Italiano per il Medio ed Estremo Oriente, 1960.

Dreyfus, Georges. 1992. "Universals in Indo-Tibetan Buddhism." In *Tibetan Studies: Proceedings of the 5th Seminar of the International Association for Tibetan Studies, Narita 1989*, vol. 1, 29–46. Narita: Naritasan Shinshoji.

Fine, Kit. 2009. "The Question of Ontology." In *Metametaphysics: New Essays on the Foundations of Ontology*, edited by David Chalmers, David Manley, and Ryan Wasserman, 155–177. Oxford: Oxford University Press.

Garfield, Jay L. 2006. "Reductionism and Fictionalism: Comments on Siderits's *Personal Identity and Buddhist Philosophy*." *American Philosophical Association Newsletter* (Newsletter on Asian and Asian-American Philosophers and Philosophy) 6.1 (Fall): 1–7.

Go rams pa bSod nams seng ge. *lTa ba'i shan 'byed = lTa ba'i shan 'byed theg mchog gnad kyi zla zer*. Sakya Students' Union edition, Sarnath, India, 1988. Tibetan text edited and translated in Cabezón and Dargyay (2007).

Herzberger, Hans. 1975. "Double Negation in Buddhist Logic." *Journal of Indian Philosophy* 3: 3–16.

Hirsch, Eli. 2009. "Ontology and Alternative Languages." In *Metametaphysics: New Essays on the Foundations of Ontology*, edited by David Chalmers, David Manley, and Ryan Wasserman, 231–259. Oxford: Oxford University Press.

Hirsch, Eli. 2011. *Quantifier Variance and Realism: Essays in Metaontology*. New York: Oxford University Press.

Horwich, Paul. 2006. "A World without Isms: Life after Realism, Fictionalism, Non-Cognitivism, Relativism, Reductionism, Revisionism, and So On." In *Truth and Realism*, edited by P. Greenough and M. Lynch, 188–202. Oxford: Clarendon Press.

Huemer, Michael. 2009. "When is Parsimony a Virtue?" *The Philosophical Quarterly* 59(235): 216–236.

Jackson, Frank. 1998. *From Metaphysics to Ethics*. Oxford: Oxford University Press.

Lindtner, Christian. 1990. *Nagarjuniana: Studies in the Writings and Philosophy of Nāgārjuna*. Delhi: Motilal Banarsidass. First published 1982 by Akademisk Forlag, Copenhagen, as volume 4 of Indiske Studier series.

McDowell, John. 1981. "Non-Cognitivism and Rule-Following." In *Wittgenstein: To Follow a Rule*, edited by Steven Holtzman and Christopher Leich, 141–162. London: Routledge and Kegan Paul.

Nāgārjuna. *Vigrahavyāvartanī*. P. 5228, D. 3828. Sanskrit text critically edited by E.H. Johnston and Arnold Kunst and translated by K. Bhattacharya. See Bhattacharya (1986).

Nāgārjuna. *Yuktiṣaṣṭikā*. P. 5225, D. 3825. Edited and translated in Lindtner (1990).

Paṇḍita Aśoka. *Sāmānyadūṣaṇa*. In *Six Buddhist Nyāya Tracts in Sanskrit*, edited by Haraprasād Śāstrī. Bibliotheca Indica 185. Calcutta: The Asiatic Society, 1910, reprinted 1989.

Price, Huw. 2009. "Metaphysics after Carnap: The Ghost Who Walks?" In *Metametaphysics: New Essays on the Foundations of Ontology*, edited by David Chalmers, David Manley, and Ryan Wasserman, 320–346. Oxford: Oxford University Press.

Priest, G., Siderits, M., and Tillemans, T. 2011. "The (Two) Truths about Truth." In *Moonshadows: Conventional Truth in Buddhist Philosophy*, by The Cowherds (= G. Dreyfus, B. Finnigan, J. Garfield, G. Newland, G. Priest, M. Siderits, K. Tanaka, S. Thakchoe, T. Tillemans, and J. Westerhoff), ch. 8. New York: Oxford University Press.

Putnam, Hilary. 2004. *Ethics without Ontology*. Cambridge, MA: Harvard University Press.

Siderits, M. 2003. *Personal Identity and Buddhist Philosophy: Empty Persons*. Ashgate World Philosophies Series. Aldershot, Hampshire: Ashgate.

Siderits, M., Tillemans, T., and Chakrabarti, A., eds. 2011. *Apoha: Buddhist Nominalism and Human Cognition*. New York: Columbia University Press.

Sober, Elliott. 2009. "Parsimony Arguments in Science and Philosophy: A Test Case for Naturalism." *Proceedings and Addresses of the American Philosophical Association* 83(2): 117–155.

Stanley, Jason. 2001. "Hermeneutic Fictionalism." In *Midwestern Studies in Philosophy, Volume XXV: Figurative Language*, edited by Peter A. French and Howard K. Wettstein, 36–71. Oxford: Blackwell.

Tillemans, Tom J.F. 1984. "Two Tibetan Texts on the 'Neither One nor Many' Argument for *Śūnyatā*." *Journal of Indian Philosophy* 12: 357–388.
Tillemans, Tom J.F. 1990. *Materials for the Study of Āryadeva, Dharmapāla and Candrakīrti: The Catuḥśataka of Āryadeva, Chapters XII and XIII, with the Commentaries of Dharmapāla and Candrakīrti: Introduction, Translation, Sanskrit, Tibetan and Chinese Texts, Notes*, two volumes. Wiener Studien zur Tibetologie und Buddhismuskunde 24(1–2). Vienna: Arbeitskreis für Tibetische und Buddhistische Studien. Reprinted in one volume by Motilal Banarsidass, Delhi, 2008.
Tillemans, Tom J.F. 1999. *Scripture, Logic, Language: Essays on Dharmakīrti and His Tibetan Successors*. Studies in Indian and Tibetan Buddhism. Boston: Wisdom Publications.
Tillemans, Tom J.F. 2000. *Dharmakīrti's Pramāṇavārttika: An Annotated Translation of the Fourth Chapter (parārthānumāna)*, vol. 1 (k. 1–148). Vienna: Verlag der Österreichischen Akademie der Wissenschaften.
Tillemans, Tom J.F. 2011a. "Dharmakīrti." In *Stanford Encyclopedia of Philosophy*. http://plato.stanford.edu/entries/dharmakiirti/
Tillemans, Tom J.F. 2011b. "Madhyamaka Buddhist Ethics." *Journal of the International Association of Buddhist Studies* 33(1–2): 353–372.
Tillemans, Tom J.F. 2016. *How do Mādhyamikas Think? And Other Essays on the Buddhist Philosophy of the Middle*. Studies in Indian and Tibetan Buddhism. Boston: Wisdom Publications.
Vaidya, P.L. 1960. *Śāntideva: Bodhicaryāvatāra, with the commentary Pañjikā of Prajñākaramati*. Buddhist Sanskrit Texts 12. Darbhanga: Mithila Institute of Post-Graduate Studies and Research in Sanskrit Learning.
Yablo, Stephen. 1998. "Does Ontology Rest on a Mistake?" *Proceedings of the Aristotelian Society, Supplementary Volume* 72: 229–261.
Wittgenstein, Ludwig. 2009. *Philosophische Untersuchungen (Philosophical Investigations)*. Translated by G.E.M. Anscombe, P.M.S. Hacker, and Joachim Schulte. Revised fourth edition by P.M.S. Hacker and Joachim Schulte. Oxford: Wiley-Blackwell.

6

Are Reasons Causally Relevant for Action? Dharmakīrti and the Embodied Cognition Paradigm

Christian Coseru

For Dharmakīrti – the influential seventh-century Indian Buddhist philosopher who, along with his predecessor Dignāga (480–540 CE), serves as a founding figure of the Buddhist logico-epistemological school – there is a special relationship between reasons and causes: specifically, Dharmakīrti and some of his followers, like many contemporary philosophers of a more naturalist persuasion, put forward the view that intuitions about causal chains of events *can* serve as reasons for effective action. The leading question of this essay is whether Dharmakīrti's account of reasoning could contribute to current debates in epistemology and philosophy of action. I will not address, therefore, exegetical questions about whether what we are dealing with here is some kind of sui generis naturalism, serious metaphysics, or something completely different.[1] Instead, what I propose to do is ask a series of questions about the relation between reasons and causes at work in Dharmakīrti's *kāryānumāna* argument (that is, the argument that an inference is sound only when one infers from the effect to the cause and not vice versa), and derive some conclusions about whether or not Dharmakīrti shares a common concern with current practitioners of naturalized epistemology.

Causality, Intentionality, and Mental Content

Dharmakīrti's work can be seen as extending the metaphysical and phenomenological concerns of Abhidharma, with its focus on mapping out the structure of our cognitive architecture and the function of its various constitutive elements (perception, attention, intentionality, etc.). By advancing a conception of causation that includes consciousness and cognition as causal efficient categories, Abhidharma presents us with a metaphysics of experience: the irreducible elements of existence (*dharmas*) are not essences or substances, but activities, properties, and patterns of connectedness.[2] The project of

Buddhist Philosophy: A Comparative Approach, First Edition. Edited by Steven M. Emmanuel.
© 2018 John Wiley & Sons, Inc. Published 2018 by John Wiley & Sons, Inc.

identifying and mapping out these irreducible elements (e.g., sensation, volition, attention, memory) shares many of the concerns of embodied and enactive cognitive science, even as it lacks the latter's empirical foundation.

One way to frame Dharmakīrti's project is as an attempt to situate these early Abhidharma explorations of the function of consciousness and cognition on a firm epistemological basis. Given a general concern with examining the sources of reliable cognition, Dharmakīrti's epistemological orientation (much like that of his predecessor, Dignāga) is naturalistic. Indeed, he articulates his account of language and inferential reason (as circumscribed by his *apoha* theory) largely on a model of embodied cognition, not unlike that pioneered in the work of Varela, Thompson, and Rosch (1991).[3] As a systematic inquiry into the foundations of knowledge, Buddhist epistemology thus aligns closely with contemporary naturalized epistemology. For the purpose of this analysis, I take naturalism to be a commitment to considering the empirical evidence from the sciences of cognition in settling questions about the acquisition of beliefs.[4] More broadly, naturalism refers to the notion that reality is exhausted by nature, although the question whether "nature" should include the mental is itself a part of a long-standing philosophical debate. Philosophers with weak commitments to naturalism typically operate with rather unrestricted notions of nature, whereas stronger adherents to naturalism define it more stringently. My position on naturalism, which I defend at length elsewhere,[5] closely aligns with the so-called 4E (embodied, enactive, embedded, and extended) approach to cognition: cognitive awareness is to be thought of not as an internal state of mind or brain locked into linear causal chains of sensory input and behavioral output. Rather, it is to be understood as a structure of comportment, an intentional and self-disclosing orientation and attunement to a world of actions, objects, and meaning.

Closely related to the question of how the intentionality or directness of mental states is at all possible is a more difficult question: How do mental states acquire their intentional content? That is, how do mental states come to be about something other than their own operations, and thus to serve as ground for effective action? No satisfactory answer to this question can circumvent debates about externalism versus internalism in epistemology. The question that I will pursue here, however, is more specific (and more apt to cut across this debate): Can such intentional content, in turn, play a causal role in explaining how acting toward some end is successfully accomplished? Specifically, if the justification for pursuing a certain course of action and the ensuing disposition to act are not simply outcomes of post hoc rationalization but integral elements of the causal web of events, then different chains of justification do not simply explain but enact different outcomes.

On the surface, it may seem as though this way of framing the problem of the relation between reasons and causes is trivial. Of course, thinking about raising my hand can cause my hand to go up. But insofar as actions are grounded in the physical-biological processes that realize them, it is not at all clear how and where reasons fit in the causal web. What makes Dharmakīrti's proposed solution to this conundrum interesting is not just his argument that reasons are causes (or, at least, are causally relevant for action), but his attempt to defend it on a strictly Abhidharmic (that is, reductionist) understanding of causation (on the model provided by the causal principle of dependent arising). If events arise due to a multitude of causes and conditions, then, the phenomenal primitives that mental states reduce to must play a constitutive role in the arising of these events. Buddhist moral psychology attests to the possibility of overcoming habitual modes of behavior. As such, it also provides reasons for valuing a certain course of action (viz., the Noble Eightfold Path), and expected outcomes (e.g., the goods that all Buddhist adepts seek). If, as Dretske (1989, 2) claims, reasons help us "to explain why we *should* do some of the things we do," then they are the causes for doing some of the things we do (even as they do not make explicit how our doings are behaviorally achieved).

One possible objection to this line of inquiry would be to say that the reductionist models of cognitive science differ in significant ways from those which are at work in the Abhidharma. The former are rooted in a variety of accounts of cognition in terms of functionalist, computational, and neurobiological models, to cite but a few, which may or may not be intertheoretically reducible. The latter offer at best a mereological account of whole–part relations, in which more complex entities (e.g., chairs) and cognitive events (e.g., pains) are explained in terms of either external conditioning factors (material elements) or internal dispositional constituents (phenomenal primitives). Since the only types of entities that are admitted to exist are those that cannot be further physically decomposed or dissolved through conceptual analysis, ultimately we are left with kind and quality terms. As Vasubandhu writes in the *Abhidharmakośa*: "When the apprehension of an entity persists after that entity has been reduced through conceptual analysis, that entity exists ultimately, e.g., *form*: while form may be reduced to atoms, and while we may exclude from it through cognitive analysis other qualia (such as taste, etc.), the apprehension of the proper nature of *form* persists" (Pradhan 1975, 334).

The Abhidharma tradition thus understands causality not in terms of relations between elements and compounds but in terms of a tripartite action–object–agent or cognition–cognized–cognizer model (*pramiti–prameya–pramātṛ*). It is this model of cognition that informs the view of Buddhist epistemologists such as Dharmakīrti.

A more serious objection comes in the form of arguments that invoke the causal closure of the physical domain to provide justification for treating mental events as causally inert. Although responses to this line of argumentation can vary widely, the notion that, as Dretske puts it, "what we believe, intend, and desire has no bearing on what we do" (Dretske 1989, 3) is deeply problematic. One solution is found in token-identity theories of the mental, which argue for the causal efficacy of mental events insofar as they are token-identical to physical events, a view known as *anomalous monism* (cf. Davidson 1970). The approach I favor follows closely Lowe's (2008) view that causation in the mental domain functions on principles of intelligibility (that is, on principles which make it perfectly intelligible for intentions to have a causal role in initiating behavior) rather than principles of mechanism (that is, on principles which explain how causation works in the physical domain). Mental events, thus, should be understood as causing actions not physical effects, since actions are not the sort of things studied by the natural sciences. Those actions will have their behavioral signatures when enacted, but *as actions* they cannot be understood in purely behavioral terms.

We can easily answer the first objection either by showing that the reductionist model of cognition at work in the Abhidharma is open to revision, or by pointing to 4E models of cognition to show that not all cognitive science is eliminativist. The second objection, as already noted, is considerably more difficult, in part because it invokes the casual closure of the physical domain as evidence for the epiphenomenal character of mental states. My proposed solution comes in the form of a new kind of naturalism: call it *phenomenological naturalism*. As I have argued elsewhere (Coseru 2015), phenomenological naturalism provides a way to articulate the relation between phenomenology and the project of naturalization that neither eliminates the first-person givenness of experience, nor collapses all of nature into what is experientially available. On this view, intentional mental states and their contents are structural features of our cognitive architecture. Insofar as our cognitions attain their objects, their features both map out the range of possibilities that are available to us, and structure the causal process that guarantees the effectiveness of our actions. Cognitive events, which arise as a result of the tight causal coupling between perception, reflection, and action, then, are not causally inert. Rather, they are constituted as causally relevant factors in the determination of action.

Cognition and Pragmatic Efficacy

Let me start with a general characterization of the Buddhist epistemological enterprise (*pramāṇavāda*) as a manifest form of epistemological optimism. Epistemological optimism is, generally speaking, the view that at least a subset of our cognitive modalities are reliable, and that it is actually possible to provide an explanatory account of how such modalities provide effective guidance for our actions. If Dharmakīrti is an epistemological optimist, which I think he is, then he must be held to task: he must show, first, how perception (one of the only two sources of knowledge he deems reliable) gives access to real particulars, and, second, how linguistic and conceptual practices can be pragmatically efficacious: that is, how they can lead to successful action given his generally nominalist stance.

For the purpose of this analysis, I will mainly focus on the second question, which requires that we briefly unpack some of the key aspects of Dharmakīrti's theory of inference. As is well known, Dharmakīrti's arguments in support of providing a metaphysical basis for inductive reasoning, especially as presented in the *Svārthānumana* chapter of the *Pramāṇavārttika* (Dharmakīrti 1957),[6] address a series of important and as yet unresolved issues regarding the foundational role of perception for knowledge. Resolving any of these issues would arguably have broader implications for our understanding and assessment of the nature and scope of the Buddhist epistemological enterprise.

I have two proposals here. My first proposal is that we seek to understand Dharmakīrti's innovative contributions to reasoning in epistemological rather than metaphysical terms: that is, in terms of how reasoning from evidence does and should proceed, rather than in terms of the justification of what kinds of things can be demonstrably said to exist. My second proposal is that we view Dharmakīrti's causal account of knowledge in terms of a certain conception of cognition as dynamically constituted and, thus, as a mode of engagement with situations and things.

Let me start with a brief summary of Dharmakīrti's innovative contribution to inductive reasoning. In response to Dignāga's (allegedly failed) attempt to resolve the problem of induction by means of the triple inferential method (*trairūpyahetu*), Dharmakīrti formulates his well-known principle that reasoning from the empirical data must be grounded on more than the simple observation and non-observation of occurring associations and dissociations, following the established method of *anvaya* (association of the evidence with the property to be established through it) and *vyatireka* (dissociation of the evidence with the property to be established). Dharmakīrti expands this method also to include a discussion of the *pakṣadharmatā*, the so-called evidence–subject relation, by means of which the trustworthiness of the former is established.

Consider the following key passage from *Hetubindu* 2.13 ("Drop of Reason" in Steinkellner 1967), in which the evidence–subject relation is spelled out in terms of the feature-placing power of reliable modes of apprehension:

> As previously stated, certainty [about the evidence–subject relation] is how perception and inference establish a quality of the subject, which serves as a property to be proven, such as, for instance, the determination that smoke is present in a locus or that the quality of being a product applies to sound. Thus, by means of perception there is the experience of a smoke possessing place whose distinctive character differs from everything else in its uniqueness. Given perceptual acquaintance with that place, there is, in a subsequent moment,

the cognition of evidence; this subsequent cognition is a type of recollection whose object is the difference [that enables the dissociation of smoke from non-smoke] on the basis of perceptual testimony.

Thus, when Dharmakīrti postulates that for a sound argument to obtain, two natural relations (between the evidence and what is to be established thereby) must be present, he is making a case for an enactive account of cognition. The two relations, of identity (*tādātmya*) and causal generation (*tadutpatti*), are effectively ways to state the token-identity of reasons and causes. Dharmakīrti's answer to the question of how these two natural relations are to be ascertained is framed by his defense of core Buddhist metaphysical principles, in this case, chiefly that of momentariness. It is here that Dharmakīrti's text raises three important issues concerning the nature of evidence and the role of perception in disclosing something essential about the order of the chain of events in the empirical domain. First, what is the nature of evidence or, more specifically, of the evidential property (*hetu*) for the thesis, or that which is to be established (*sādhya*)? Second, what would be the implication of asserting that the truth of the major premise can be known by perception? And finally, can a careful inspection of the effect, in the case of Dharmakīrti's *kāryānumāna* argument, be conducive to ascertaining the unique causal totality that is its source?

The answer to the first question is clear: only the two natural relations of identity and causal generation can serve as evidential property for the thesis. I will turn to these in a moment. The second question does not invite a straightforward answer. As Richard Hayes and Brendan Gillon (2008, 362) have recently explained, to claim that one can know the truth of the major premise by perception amounts to saying that whatever conclusion one may arrive at through inferential reasoning can also be known by perception. On this account, then, inferential reasoning would become a redundant source of knowledge.

As I have argued at length elsewhere (Coseru 2012, 115), it needn't be so, and this is where I think a naturalized account of reasons comes in handy: indeed, inferential reasons turn both toward ideal objects and toward the subjective modes of apprehension that ground our thought. When a proposition of the sort "sound is impermanent, because it results from effort" is judged true, it becomes true, logically speaking, *once and for all* such that its opposite is false. However, the problem is that "once and for all," or "perpetually" (*nityam*), is a subjective locution that belongs to the subjective experience of temporality. Furthermore, for any given system of reasoning, when we try to establish the truth of a proposition we invariably find ourselves having to turn away from the actual structure of the argument and appeal to experience or to a coherent system of beliefs (at least on a coherentist theory of truth). Models of embodied and embedded cognition developed in the last three decades[7] (and their adaptations in the Buddhist context[8]) suggest that perception is not simply a passive mode of apprehending objects and properties in the empirical domain – or what the Buddhist calls "unique particulars" – but an active process of involvement with situations and things.[9]

This need for grounding reason in experiential access to some presumably irreducible given (or to the givenness of experience itself) does not necessarily imply that Dharmakīrti is an epistemological foundationalist.[10] Here I want to make a different sort of claim, one that may suggest a bold answer to the third question: namely, that careful scrutiny of the effect can provide a basis for ascertaining the unique causal totality that is its source, but only for reasoning that is context-specific. I am prompted, thus, to ponder whether the inferential model at work in the Buddhist epistemological literature is best described as a system of pragmatic or context-dependent reasoning. Unlike deductive systems of semantic reasoning, which are context-free, pragmatic reasoning is largely inductive and encompasses the types of logic (nonmonotonic and paraconsistent) that represent reasoning from premises that are context-specific. On this model of pragmatic reasoning, while a given sentence φ may be a pragmatic consequence of a set of premises φ it need not be a pragmatic consequence of a larger set of premises $\varphi \cup \Psi$.[11]

Indeed, following Dignāga's inductive model of reasoning, we reason by first observing the occurrence of certain properties in an object or class of objects and the non-occurrence of those same properties when the object is absent. We establish that in order for a linguistic utterance to acquire the status of logical proof, the reason (*hetu*) must be present in the thesis (that is, in the position that is stated), be also present in similar positions, and be absent from all dissimilar positions. This is Dignāga's well-known model of the triple inferential mark (*trairūpya*), which operates by deriving hypothetical statements from past observations of the inductive domain. Consider again the example of produced phenomena such as sound: sound is impermanent because it is a product, and whatever is produced exists by virtue of its supporting causal and conditioning factors and ceases to exist with the cessation of its support. Conversely, a permanent object cannot be produced. That is, arguably, how we arrive at a logical reason. Thus, a proposition of the type "Sound is impermanent, because it results from effort" is true so long as we do not encounter an example of permanent, hence unproduced, sounds. Were we to come across such a counter-example, the proposition will be falsified.[12]

Now, Katsura has defined this type of logic as "hypothetical reasoning based on induction" (Katsura 2007, 76), claiming that while reasoning for oneself is essentially inductive, the presentation of arguments to others follows the deductive path. Indeed, to the extent that this system of reasoning, which is based on the observation and non-observation of evidence, is open to revision so as to accommodate cases where there is a violation of the linguistic convention, we may describe it as a system of pragmatic reasoning.

Dharmakīrti's attempt to ground reasoning on a stronger principle than mere observation and non-observation of the evidence led him to postulate that there must be some "essential connection" (*svabhāvapratibandha*) between the thesis and what is to be demonstrated. Although this essential connection is meant to address the problem of the uncertainty of hypothetical reasoning, it is not pragmatically neutral, since Dharmakīrti's ultimate criterion for truth is the causal efficacy of cognitions (*arthakriyā*).

A Theoretical Model for Causal Inference

Let's take a closer, if brief, look at Dharmakīrti's descriptive analysis of the role of causation for inference, as found in his principal work, the *Pramāṇavārttika* II.11–38, and its autocommentary, the *Svopajñavṛtti* (hereinafter abbreviated as PVSV; Pandeya 1989). First, in order to establish the sort of evidence that can serve as a warrant for sound inference and, at the same time, to rule out those instances of erratic attribution of a connection between evidence and the property to be proven, Dharmakīrti avails himself of various examples of things that are ordinarily thought of in conjunction: the act of speaking and passion, rice and cooking, a living body and breathing, perceptual awareness and the senses, and, of course, the stock example of fire and smoke.

The question that Dharmakīrti considers concerns the sort of properties, whether observed or unobserved, in similar or dissimilar cases, that can be counted as evidence for asserting a given thesis. How are such properties ascertained? That is, how does one come to know the truth of the major premise? Dharmakīrti makes use of the first two examples to argue against the principle that mere observation and non-observation of occurring associations and dissociations is a sufficient ground for sound inferential reasoning. In the case of the act of speaking and passion, observation of their occurring association is just a case of erratic evidence, for at most the act of speaking can serve as ground for inferring the presence of a speech organ and a capacity to communicate (PVSV 12.3), not of passion. Of course, here he is indirectly rejecting the notion that speech requires passion – seen as an affliction – for its cause: thus, buddhas, who are certainly observed to speak, cannot do so on account of something which they have overcome. In the case of rice and cooking, non-observation in dissimilar cases does not provide sufficient grounds for sound inference either: even though one may observe grains of rice cooking in a cauldron, one cannot thereby infer that all the grains of rice are cooked simply because they happen to be in the cauldron. Indeed, hypothetically speaking, some may be uncooked (PVSV 13.1).

How, then, can one escape the risk that there may be unobserved instances to the contrary, given that observation of a relation between things at a given place and time does not necessarily guarantee that the same relation will occur in other places and at other times? For Dharmakīrti the solution to this conundrum is appeal to rules of reasoning that best reflect the nature of causally efficient entities: that is, to the so-called natural relation (*svabhāvapratibandha*) between the properties of an inference. As he explains, one cannot infer from a cause to its effect, or from a causal totality (*kāraṇasāmagrī*) to an effect, because there is always the chance of impending factors preventing the arising of the given effect. Consider, for instance, cases when the rice in the cauldron is clumped. But Dharmakīrti does admit that one can infer from the effect to the cause, though only in a restricted case. As he writes in PVSV 12.4, "only an immediate effect enables the inference of a cause, because it is dependent on it."[13] The Sanskrit here for "immediate" is *nāntarīyakam*, which can also be translated as "inseparable" or "without interval," conveying the sense of tight proximity that is associated with causal–cognitive chains.

For Dharmakīrti, thus, an awareness of the causal totality can serve as a legitimate basis only for asserting that effects arise due to a variety of causes and conditions. Such awareness, however, may not be able to establish which specific effect arises due to which specific set of causes. Much like Dignāga before him, Dharmakīrti too is concerned with maximizing our predictive capacity to make sound inferences, the ultimate, and obvious, goal of which is achieving desired ends.[14]

Dharmakīrti's view of the role of causality for reasoning, then, may be summarized as follows: one can only legitimately infer from the effect to the cause, and only in the case of an immediately arising effect, since even knowing the causal totality for a given effect does not guarantee that impending factors would not preempt its arising. Now, a naturalized account of the *kāryānumāna* argument would have to take into account at least two things:

1) Empirical evidence that the reason, or that which is to be proven, acquires its evidential status as a result of factors that are inherent to our cognitive architecture, specifically to information processing systems that translate perceptual content into action.
2) A theoretically robust account of how intentional content, as the subjective basis for reasoning, can in turn play a causal role in explaining how acting toward some desired end is successfully accomplished.

As noted above, given different strategies of naturalization some may prove more effective than others. The strategy I favor takes the view that reasons can be naturalized both by bridging the gap between phenomenology and natural science, and by extending the concept of what counts as natural to include also the mental.[15] The general idea is that perceptual and mental processes have evolved to provide *effective* and *meaningful* interaction with the environment. Of course, these are, at best, working hypotheses and play at most a heuristic role. Nevertheless, they do provide an account of reasons that is both scientifically informed and phenomenologically constraining.

Recall our second leading issue: to say that the truth of the major premise can be known by perception is to put forth a particular view of perception – one which views perceptual awareness as a form of embodied action. On this view, perceptual awareness does requires input stimuli for its activation but the resulting perceptual content depends on a set of preconscious or preattentive processes of selection and grouping operating on the input data. These processes are generally thought to be representational: they *re-present* schematic components of perceptual experience following sensory-motor modalities. Perceptual awareness is thus inherently projective with the object of perception being the result of interactions between the input stimuli and dynamic information processes that are part of the architecture of sensory systems.[16]

To take just one example: evidence from neuroscience relating to cases of blindsight indicates that achieving a desired end, say navigating around objects in an environment without seeing them, can be achieved in the absence of any perceptual awareness of the objects, so long as the largely unconscious causal mechanisms that regulate sensorimotor intentionality remain functional. The philosophical upshot of this sort of phenomenon is that pragmatic reasoning of the sort that causes an individual to successfully reach an object even without being directly aware of it is possible by virtue of the fact that cognition is embodied and embedded within the environment of which it is a part.

On this account of embodied cognition, direct perceptual awareness, as conceived by the Buddhist, is an effective source of knowledge precisely because it is a form of embodied action. For to perceive is to understand how we cope with the environment we inhabit. We cannot cope very well if we take the world to be a vast agglomeration of entities that lack any reference to subjects of experience. This brings us to our third and final issue: can a careful inspection of the effect be conducive to ascertaining the unique causal totality that is its source?

Dharmakīrti argues that an inference from the cause to the effect is unsound. Now, what about inference from the effect to the cause? Consider the typical example of a park ranger: in spotting a column of fire rising above a mountain, she can legitimately infer that there is a fire, but not whether the fire is fueled by redwoods or by eucalypts. On closer inspection, she may detect from the peculiar color and odor of the smoke that it is eucalypts that fuel the fire, but still not know whether the fire was started by lightning or by embers drifting from a campsite. Closer inspection still may reveal that an arsonist in fact started the fire.

But this example, which I adopt and adapt here from Hayes and Gillon (2008), overlooks an important fact: the park ranger's experience. Unless this is her first day on the job, ideally she already has the sort of requisite knowledge and embodied skill demanded by the task at hand: ascertaining the unique causal totality of a given column of smoke. Her perception of smoke happens within a certain horizon of background intuitions about the height and distance of the smoke column, the time of day, current weather conditions, the location of campsites, the flammability of various tree species, and a recent history of arsonist attacks. It is this horizon of background intuitions that, on a 4E model of cognition, accounts for the efficacy of the inferential process.

Conclusion

A central principle of the embodied, enactive, embedded, and extended cognition paradigm is that at least a subset of our cognitive processes are not entirely internal but rather are co-constituted by external processes that extend into the environment. It is for this reason, I think, that Dharmakīrti's *kāryānumāna* argument could be interpreted as a species of what Keijzer and Schouten (2007) describe as *process externalism*: the view that reasons, as active forms of deliberation and cognitive engagement, depend on – and are continuous with – bodily processes that are embedded in the environment of which we are a part. Such an account steers clear of the typical conundrum of metaphysical interpretations: trying to square how someone like Dharmakīrti can argue for both external realism and some version of epistemic idealism.

Notes

1 For a review of the various positions that Dharmakīrti can be said to endorse, see Siderits (1999), Eltschinger (2010), and Tillemans (2014).
2 For a good overview of core aspects of the Abhidharma project, see Williams (1981), Cox (1995), and Ronkin (2005).
3 Conceived largely as a project of integrating phenomenological and epistemological theories into the framework of the natural sciences, this was also the first study to bring Buddhist philosophy of mind in conversation with the sciences of cognition.
4 This is largely a Quinean conception of naturalism. In his influential analysis of the failure of traditional epistemology to answer the problem of the foundation of our beliefs, Quine (1969) ended with a proposal that we abandon *a priori* reasoning and devote ourselves instead simply to studying the psychological processes by which we form beliefs. Strong defenders of naturalism, such as Kornblith (1999) and Stich (1990), have argued against rationality as a foundational principle for traditional epistemology. More moderate versions of naturalism, as one finds in Kim (1988) and Goldman (1992), allow for evaluative questions about rationality, justification, and knowledge to be pursued in a traditional manner.
5 See Coseru (2012, ch. 2).

6 On this aspect of Dharmakīrti's thought, see Hayes (1980), Gillon (1991), and Tillemans (2014).
7 See, for instance, Hurley (1998), Noë (2004), Gallagher (2006), and Thompson (2007).
8 See, for instance, MacKenzie (2009) and Chadha (2011).
9 Ganeri, for instance, suggests additional affinities between Dharmakīrti's account of perception and theories developed in recent years by Andy Clark and Christopher Peacocke (Ganeri 2011, 238).
10 I address this issue at length in Coseru (2009).
11 I derive this example of pragmatic reasoning from Bell (2001, 46ff.).
12 It may be worth noting here that arguments for the impermanence of sound are framed as Buddhist refutations of the characteristically Mīmāṃsaka proof about the infallibility of trustworthy verbal testimony (śabda-pramāṇa).
13 Translation, slightly altered, *per* Hayes and Gillon (2008, 340).
14 For now, I leave aside the question whether in framing the *kāryānumāna* argument as he does, Dharmakīrti's motive is ultimately soteriological. For more on this issue, see Steinkellner (1999).
15 For detailed accounts of how the conception of nature can be opened up to include consciousness and intentionality, see Smith (1999), who mainly uses Gibson's (1979) ecological approach to perception as a model.
16 See Palmer (1999).

References

Bell, J. 2001. "Pragmatic Reasoning: Pragmatic Semantics and Semantic Pragmatics." In *Modeling and Using Context*, edited by V. Akman, P. Bouquet, R. Thomason, and R.A. Young, 44–58. London: Springer-Verlag.
Chadha, M. 2011. "Self-awareness: Eliminating the Myth of the 'Invisible Subject.'" *Philosophy East and West* 61(3): 453–467.
Coseru, C. 2009. "Buddhist 'Foundationalism' and the Phenomenology of Perception." *Philosophy East and West* 59(4): 409–439.
Coseru, C. 2012. *Perceiving Reality: Consciousness, Intentionality, and Cognition in Buddhist Philosophy*. New York: Oxford University Press.
Coseru, C. 2015. "Perception, Causally Efficacious Particulars, and the Range of Phenomenal Consciousness." *Journal of Consciousness Studies* 22(9–10): 55–82.
Cox, C. 1995. *Disputed Dharmas: Early Buddhist Theories on Existence – an annotated translation of the section on factors dissociated from thought from Saṅghabhadra's Nyāyānusāra*. Tokyo: The International Institute for Buddhist Studies.
Davidson, D. 1970. "Mental Events." In *Experience and Theory*, edited by Lawrence Foster and J.W. Swanson, 79–101. London: Duckworth.

Dharmakīrti. 1957. *Pramāṇavārttika (tshad ma rnam 'grel)*. In *The Tibetan Tripitika, Peking Edition*, edited by D.T. Suzuki (P. 5709). Tokyo: Tibetan Tripitika Research Institute.
Dretske, F. 1989. "Reasons and Causes." *Philosophical Perspectives* 3: 1–15.
Eltschinger, Vincent. 2010. "Dharmakīrti." *Revue Internationale de Philosophie* 64(3): 397–440.
Gallagher, S. 2006. *How the Body Shapes the Mind*. New York: Oxford University Press.
Ganeri, J. 2011. "Apoha, Feature-Placing, and Sensory Content." In *Apoha: Buddhist Nominalism and Human Cognition*, edited by Mark Siderits, Tom Tillemans, and Arindam Chakrabarti, 228–246. New York: Columbia University Press.
Gibson, J.J. 1979. *The Ecological Approach to Visual Perception*. Dallas: Houghton Mifflin.
Gillon, Brendan S. 1991. "Dharmakīrti and the Problem of Induction." In *Studies in the Buddhist Epistemological Tradition: Proceedings of the Second International Dharmakīrti Conference, Vienna, June 11–16, 1989*, edited by E. Steinkellner, 53–58. Vienna: Verlag der Österreichischen Akademie der Wissenschaften.
Goldman, A. 1992. *Liaisons: Philosophy Meets the Social and Cognitive Sciences*. Cambridge, MA: MIT Press.
Hayes, R. 1980. "Diṅnāga's Views on Reasoning (*svārthānum āna*)." *Journal of Indian Philosophy* 8(3): 219–277.
Hayes, R. and Gillon, B. 2008. "Dharmakīrti on the Role of Causation in Inference as Presented in *Pramāṇavārttika Svopajñavṛtti* 11–38." *Journal of Indian Philosophy* 36: 335–404.
Hurley, S. 1998. *Consciousness in Action*. Cambridge, MA: Harvard University Press.
Katsura, S. 2007. "How Did the Buddhists Prove Something? The Nature of Buddhist Logic." *Pacific World* 3(9): 63–84.
Keijzer, F. and Schouten, M. 2007. "Embedded Cognition and Mental Causation: Setting Empirical Bounds on Metaphysics." *Synthese* 158: 109–125.
Kim, J. 1988. "What is 'Naturalized Epistemology'?" In *Philosophical Perspectives II: Epistemology*, edited by J.E. Tomberlin, 381–406. Atascadero: Ridgeview Publishing Company.
Kornblith, H. 1999. "In Defense of Naturalized Epistemology." In *The Blackwell Guide to Epistemology*, edited by J. Greco and E. Sosa, 158–169. Oxford: Blackwell.
Lowe, E.J. 2008. *Personal Agency: The Metaphysics of Mind and Action*. Oxford: Oxford University Press.
MacKenzie, Matthew. 2010. "Enacting the Self: Buddhist and Enactivist Approaches to the Emergence of the Self." *Phenomenology and the Cognitive Sciences* 9(1): 75–99.

Noë, A. 2004. *Action in Perception*. Cambridge, MA: MIT Press.
Palmer, S. 1999. *Vision: From Photons to Phenomenology*. Cambridge, MA: MIT Press.
Pandeya, R.C., ed. 1989. *Pramāṇavārttikam of Ārya Dharmakīrti: With the commentaries Svopajñavṛtti of the author and Pramāṇavārttikavṛtti of Manorathanandin*. Delhi: Motilal Banarsidass.
Pradhan, P. 1975. *Commentary on the Compendium of Superior Knowledge (Abhidharmakośabhāṣyam)*, revised 2nd edition, edited by A. Haldar. Patna: Kashi Prasad Jayaswal Research Institute.
Quine, W.V.O. 1969. "Epistemology Naturalized." In *Ontological Relativity and Other Essays*. New York: Columbia University Press.
Ronkin, N. 2005. *Early Buddhist Metaphysics: The Making of a Philosophical Tradition*. London and New York: Routledge-Curzon.
Siderits, M. 1999. "Apohavāda, Nominalism and Resemblance Theories." In *Dharmakīrti's Thought and Its Impact on Indian and Tibetan Philosophy: Proceedings of the Third International Dharmakīrti Conference, Hiroshima, November 4–6, 1997*, edited by S. Katsura, 349–362. Vienna: Verlag der Österreichische Akademie der Wissenschaften.
Smith, D.W. 1999. "Intentionality Naturalized?" In *Naturalizing Phenomenology*, edited by J. Petitot, F.J. Varela, B. Pachoud, and J.M. Roy, 83–110. Stanford: Stanford University Press.
Steinkellner, E., ed. 1967. *Dharmakīrti's Hetubinduḥ, Teil 1, tibetischer Text und rekonstruierter Sanskrit-Text*. Vienna: Österreichische Akademie der Wissenschaften.
Steinkellner, E. 1999. "Yogic Cognition, Tantric Goal, and Other Methodological Applications of Dharmakīrti's *kāryānumana* theorem." In *Dharmakīrti's Thought and Its Impact on Indian and Tibetan Philosophy: Proceedings of the Third International Dharmakīrti Conference, Hiroshima, November 4–6, 1997*, edited by S. Katsura, 349–362. Vienna: Verlag der Österreichischen Akademie der Wissenschaften.
Stich, S. 1990. *The Fragmentation of Reason*. Cambridge, MA: MIT Press.
Thompson, E. 2007. *Mind in Life: Biology, Phenomenology, and the Sciences of Mind*. Cambridge, MA: Harvard University Press.
Tillemans, Tom. 2014. "Dharmakīrti." In *The Stanford Encyclopedia of Philosophy*, edited by Edward N. Zalta. http://plato.stanford.edu/archives/spr2014/entries/dharmakiirti/
Varela, F.J., Thompson, E., and Rosch, E. 1991. *The Embodied Mind: Cognitive Science and Human Experience*. Cambridge, MA: MIT Press.
Williams, P. 1981. "On the Abhidharma Ontology." *Journal of Indian Philosophy* 9: 227–257.

7

Zen's Nonegocentric Perspectivism
Bret W. Davis

True life is beyond all meaning, and yet all meaning is constituted in relation to it.
—Nishitani[1]

Insofar as the word "knowledge" has any meaning, the world is knowable; but it is interpretable *otherwise, it has no meaning behind it, but countless meanings.—"Perspectivism."*
—Nietzsche[2]

Precisely because letting-be always lets beings be in a particular comportment that relates to them and thus discloses them, it conceals beings as a whole. Letting-be is intrinsically at the same time a concealing.
—Heidegger[3]

When one side is illuminated, the other side is darkened.
—Dōgen[4]

Ways of seeing mountains and water differ according to the type of being [that sees them]. … Do not stupidly assume that every kind of being uses as water what we view as water.
—Dōgen[5]

To study the Buddha Way is to study the self. To study the self is to forget the self. To forget the self is to be verified by the myriad things [of the world].
—Dōgen[6]

From the pine tree, learn of the pine tree.
—Bashō[7]

Buddhist Philosophy: A Comparative Approach, First Edition. Edited by Steven M. Emmanuel.
© 2018 John Wiley & Sons, Inc. Published 2018 by John Wiley & Sons, Inc.

This chapter approaches Zen, in part, from the perspective of Western discourses on perspectivism. It begins by examining the ambivalently egocentric character of Nietzsche's perspectivism, and later contrasts the egocentric perspectivism employed by Renaissance Western artists with the "floating perspective" developed by Song Chinese landscape painters. It also investigates the relevant Buddhist background of Zen, especially the perspectivism of the *Avataṃsaka Sūtra* and the Huayan school, which it compares and contrasts with that of Leibniz's monadology. Passing through some reflections on Cusanus, it ultimately looks to classical Zen masters such as Linji and Dōgen and to the Kyoto School Zen philosopher Nishitani Keiji in order to make its case.

At issue throughout is the question of what Zen can contribute to a cross-cultural dialogue on the nature of knowledge. The thesis is that the epistemology implied in Zen is a kind of perspectivism, and yet it differs significantly from the egocentric varieties of perspectivism that are prevalent in the Western tradition. The epistemology of Zen, it is argued, is a nonegocentric perspectivism. More precisely, the point is this: Rather than seeing things only from one's own habitually egocentric point of view, Zen cultivates one's ability to play the role of either "host" or "guest," as appropriate to the situation, and in general to empathetically and compassionately participate in the myriad perspectival openings onto the world that take place in singular events of interconnection.

The Ambivalence of Nietzsche's Perspectivism

The idea of perspectivism is often, and with good reason, associated with Nietzsche. So let us begin with him. Nietzsche reveals how perspectival delimitations are what make life livable and knowledge possible. Alexander Nehamas' elucidation is helpful here:

> To engage in any activity, and in particular in any inquiry, we must ultimately be selective. We must bring some things into the foreground and distance others into the background. We must assign a greater relative importance to some things than we do to others, and still others we must completely ignore. We do not, and cannot, begin (or end) with "all the data." This is an incoherent desire and an impossible goal. "To grasp everything" would be to do away with all perspectival relations, it would mean to grasp nothing, to misapprehend the nature of knowledge.[8]

After all, what would it be like to see a thing, or a person, all at once from everywhere? In this blinding cubist plenum, there would be no back and hence no real front, no inside and hence no real outside, no shadow and hence no real light. Nehamas illustrates this point with the example of painting:

"There is no sense in which painters…can ever paint 'everything' that they see. … [The] understanding of everything would be like a painting that incorporates all styles or that is painted in no style at all – a true chimera, both impossible and monstrous."[9] Taking a perspective on something not only limits what we can see, it also enables us to see in any meaningful sense in the first place. In thought as in perception, perspectival limitations are what allow us to have meaningful knowledge of anything. A perspective enables by delimiting knowledge.

Nietzsche does not just write about perspectivism; the polyvocal character of Nietzsche's texts themselves *enact* his "perspectivism." His texts are often a provocative amalgamation of aphoristic forces, forces which play off against one another to produce a dynamically ambiguous and often even ambivalent combination of perspectives.

Yet there is nevertheless a particularly dominant and dominating voice in Nietzsche's polylogue which speaks of the "will to power" as a drive to impose order on the chaos of perspectival multiplicity by submitting it to the command of a ruling perspective. Life itself, writes Nietzsche in *Beyond Good and Evil*, is "*essentially* appropriation, injury, overpowering what is alien and weaker; suppression, hardness, imposition of one's own forms, incorporation and at least, at its mildness, exploitation…life simply *is* will to power."[10]

To be sure, we also find in Nietzsche's texts a very different voice, one which calls for a nonwillful openness to perspectival plurality. Passages such as the following have allowed Nietzsche to be called a champion in the tradition of Keats' "negative capability"[11] and even "an unsung precursor of Heidegger's *Gelassenheit*."[12]

> Learning to see – habituating the eye to repose, patience, to letting things come to it; postponing judgment, learning to go around and grasp each individual case from all sides…the essence of which is precisely *not* to "will." … One will let strange, new things of every kind come up to oneself, inspecting them with hostile calm and withdrawing one's hand. To have all doors standing open, to lie servilely on one's stomach before every little fact, always to be prepared for the leap of putting oneself into the place of, or of *plunging* into, others and other things.[13]

This passage resonates well with the nonwillful and nonegocentric perspectivism found in Zen. And yet, in the same book Nietzsche contradicts this restraint of willing and this openness to perspectival multiplicity when he writes: "I want, once and for all, *not* to know many things. Wisdom sets limits to knowledge too."[14] He even affirms a kind of "*will* to ignorance."[15]

Why does Nietzsche want not only to recognize the limitations of knowledge, but also to limit knowledge? The following notebook entry is revealing here: "Not 'to know' but to schematize – to impose upon chaos as much regularity and form as our practical needs require."[16] Faced with the world's overwhelming and bewildering complexity, the practical desire to assert control by imposing a schematic order on its chaotic flow constricts Nietzsche's pluralistic openness. The will to ignorance for the sake of keeping things manageable counteracts Nietzsche's willingness to open "more eyes, different eyes," to "employ a variety of perspectives and affective interpretations in the service of knowledge."[17]

In the end there is a profound ambivalence to Nietzsche's perspectivism. On the one hand, it expresses an awareness of the always finite limitations of one's standpoint, and thus implies an openness to other points of view. Nietzsche, in fact, explicitly derides "the ridiculous immodesty that would be involved in decreeing from our corner that perspectives are permitted only from this corner." Rather, he claims, "the world has become 'infinite' for us all over again, inasmuch as we cannot reject the possibility that *it may include infinite interpretations*."[18] On the other hand, we are told that "*interpretation is itself a means of becoming master of something*."[19] It is our needs and drives that interpret the world, and since "every drive is a kind of lust to rule…each one has its perspective that it would like to compel all the other drives to accept as a norm."[20]

The "ego" for Nietzsche is not a given substance; it is a composite of competing and cooperating wills to power. It is thus composed, when it *is* successfully composed, by what Nietzsche calls "the great egoism of our dominating will."[21] Nietzsche's critique of the idea of the ego as an independent subject and substance, and his account of the construction of the composite ego, shares much with Buddhist doctrines of no-self (Skt *anātman*) and the five aggregates (Skt *skandhas*). Yet Nietzsche's frequent affirmations of egoism are at odds with the main thrust of Buddhism. In *Beyond Good and Evil*, Nietzsche writes: "I propose: egoism belongs to the nature of the noble soul – I mean that unshakable faith that to a being such as 'we are' other beings must be subordinate by nature and have to sacrifice themselves."[22]

Elsewhere I have examined in detail the deep ambivalences in Nietzsche's thought as they reveal themselves with remarkable clarity from the perspective of Zen.[23] Suffice it to say here that my sympathies with Nietzsche's radical openness to perspectival plurality are tempered by a dissatisfaction with his tendency to construe perspectival delimitation as necessarily an imposition of order on chaos by an egocentric force of will to power. In Zen I find a way of both appreciating perspectival plurality and engaging in perspectival delimitation in a manner that is neither willful nor egocentric.

Does a Buddha have (Perspectival) Omniscience?

In order to develop an understanding of Zen's perspectivism, we need to first consider the contradictory fact that there is a long tradition of attributing "omniscience" (Skt *sarvajñana* or *sarvākārajñatā*) to buddhas and bodhisattvas, which seems to suggest that enlightenment transcends the perspectival limits of human knowledge. At several places in the Pāli Canon, the Buddha is asked whether he has omniscience (Pāli *sabbaññutā*). He generally responds by saying that he does have "the threefold true knowledge," namely, "knowledge of the recollection of past lives," "knowledge of the passing away and reappearing of beings…according to their actions," and the liberating "knowledge of the destruction of the taints" that had bound him to samsara.[24] Yet he denies that he has omniscience in the strong sense of actual simultaneous knowledge of every fact in the past, present, and future. Bhikkhu Bodhi writes: "According to the exegetical Theravāda tradition the Buddha is omniscient in the sense that all knowable things are *potentially* accessible to him. He *cannot*, however, know everything *simultaneously* and must advert to what he wishes to know."[25] Perhaps this implies that a Buddha has what we might call *perspectival omniscience*, in the sense that he or she could potentially, albeit consecutively, see anything from any perspective.

In any case, the already strong Theravāda claim that a Buddha potentially and consecutively knows anything later gets inflated by some Mahāyāna Buddhist traditions into the claim that a Buddha actually and simultaneously knows everything. According to the *Avataṃsaka Sūtra* (which I single out here because it became the basis for the Chinese Huayan school, which in turn exerted a significant influence on Zen), in the last of the ten stages of development, a Bodhisattva attains "omniscient superknowledge…illuminating all worlds in the ten directions."[26] The "penetrating knowledge of enlightening beings [i.e., bodhisattvas] in this stage is infinite";[27] they "attain boundless knowledge comprehending all,"[28] and their "superknowledge of the celestial eye" enables them to witness the unfolding karmic processes of "sentient beings in worlds as many as atoms in untold buddha lands" in the entire past, present, and future.[29]

Perhaps such teachings of omniscience can be understood as pedagogical hyperbole meant to inspire and to intimate the unfathomable depths of both our present ignorance and potential enlightenment. More critically, they can be seen as part of what Paul Griffiths calls "the buddhalogical enterprise as an example of thinking motivated by the desire to limn maximal greatness."[30] The thought process would be: If knowledge is a virtue, then Buddha, the greatest of all beings, must possess the maximal degree of knowledge imaginable, which is omniscience. Griffiths points out that some of the digests of Mahāyāna doctrines of buddhahood (his focus is on Sanskrit and Tibetan texts stemming from the fourth through eighth centuries in India) argued for more modest interpretations of the Buddha's omniscience, either saying (as we have seen in the Pāli Canon) that the universality of the Buddha's knowledge is potential, rather than actual, or saying that he knew "everything important" rather than literally everything. Yet the dominant view in these digests is reported to be that "the scope of Buddha's awareness is universal in a very strong sense," including such claims as that the Buddha's universal awareness has always existed and that it involves "the simultaneous apprehension of everything in a single moment."[31]

Griffiths argues that such claims derive from a questionable attempt to attribute maximal greatness to the Buddha, as the Christian theological tradition has tended to do with God. He argues that the result is doctrinal incoherence or at least incongruity with core tenets of the Buddhist tradition. When pushed to the extreme, the doctrine of omniscience ends up "denying that Buddhas have conscious mental states, since having such states is just what it means for there to be something that it is like to be a particular being" with cognitive and perceptual limitations.[32] As we have seen, meaningful consciousness as we know it involves perspectival delimitation; it is indeed such delimitation that gives form and shape to anything that can be perceived or thought.

Perhaps a Buddha is liberated from only seeing the interconnections of the cosmos from his or her perspective, but would still see things, at any given time, from *a* perspective. In the Pāli Canon the Buddha explicitly acknowledges: "There is no recluse or brahmin who knows all, who sees all, simultaneously; that is not possible."[33] I will argue that the Zen tradition stays true to this early teaching. In fact, in the Zen tradition I find no interest whatsoever in omniscience, perspectival or otherwise. Although it developed under the influence of the Huayan school and thus the *Avataṃsaka Sūtra*, the lesson Zen takes from the latter is not that of omniscience, but rather mutual perspectival interrelation.[34]

Huayan's Jewel Net of Indra and Leibniz's Monadology

One of the most famous teachings from the *Avataṃsaka Sūtra*[35] that is developed into a central teaching of the Huayan school, is the Jewel Net of Indra. The universe is envisioned as a huge net, each knot of which contains a jewel that reflects, and is reflected in, all the others. The first patriarch of Huayan, Dushun (557–640), writes: "This imperial net is made all of jewels: because the jewels are clear, they reflect each other's images, appearing in each other's reflections upon reflections, ad infinitum."[36]

This may remind one of Leibniz's *Monadology*, in which he writes that "each simple substance has relations which express all the others, and that, consequently, is a perpetual living mirror of the universe."[37] Yet, there is a basic ontological difference between Huayan's and Leibniz's conceptions in that the latter thinks of monads as *independent substances that cannot affect one another.* In paragraph 7 of the *Monadology*, Leibniz claims: "There is…no way of explaining how a monad can be altered or changed in its inner being by any other creature, for nothing can be transposed within it… The monads have no windows through which anything can enter or depart." He goes on to say in paragraph 51 that it is only through the "intervention of God" that one monad could affect another; one monad only seems to cause changes in another due to the divine providence of the "*pre-established harmony* between all substances" (paragraph 78).

The need for divine intervention to orchestrate merely apparent interactions between independent substances (monads) is unnecessary in the case of the Huayan Buddhist teaching. Indeed the image of the Jewel Net of Indra, like other images such as the Tower of Maitreya, is meant to symbolize that "all beings, being interdependent, therefore imply in their individual being the simultaneous being of all other things."[38] In other words, such images are meant to portray the universe, or multiverse, as it is constituted by processes of "interdependent origination" (Skt *pratītya-samutpāda*; Ch. *yuanqi*; Jp. *engi* 縁起), the basic ontological tenet of Buddhism, which rejects precisely an ontology of independent substances such as that of Leibniz. In fact, in the end Dushun admits that the simile of the Jewel Net of Indra is merely an imperfect analogy; it is imperfect precisely insofar as it may be mistaken to suggest that beings are independent substances: "These jewels only have their reflected images containing and entering each other – their substances are [misleadingly portrayed as] separate. Things are not like this, because their whole substance merges completely."[39] What would be a merit of the image for Leibniz – the independent substantiality of the jewels – is a crucial demerit for Dushun.

Despite this fundamental ontological disagreement, Dushun nevertheless might have appreciated Leibniz's epistemological perspectivism. Leibniz writes:

> As the same city looked at from different sides appears entirely different, and is as if multiplied *perspectively*; so it also happens that, as a result of the infinite multitude of simple substances, there are as it were so many different universes, which are nevertheless only the perspectives of a single one, according to the different *points of view* of each monad.[40]

This helps us draw out an important implication of the Jewel Net of Indra, namely that each jewel reflects the whole *from its own unique perspective*. This is why the Huayan thinkers stress that the One harmoniously co-exists with the Many; the "oneness" of all things does not cancel out their "manyness," for the universe is at the same time a multiverse. The *Avataṃsaka Sūtra* says of Sudhana's experience of the Tower of Maitreya that "inside the great tower he saw hundreds of other towers similarly arrayed; he saw those towers as infinitely vast as space, evenly arrayed in all directions, yet these towers were not mixed up with one another, being each mutually distinct, while appearing reflected in each and every object of all the other towers."[41] Each tower houses all the others, each jewel reflects all the others, from its own unique perspective.

Fazang's Principal and Satellites, Linji's Host and Guests

Still, there is another limitation to images such as the Jewel Net of Indra, insofar as it might be taken to suggest that each jewel is locked in its own perspective. Such a perspectivism would, after all, remain egocentric. In fact, the perspectivism developed by the Huayan and Zen patriarchs affirms an ability to shift the focal point of experience, such that different points in the web of interconnections that make up the world can, in turn, take center stage. This is evident in the manner in which the third Huayan patriarch, Fazang, introduces the Jewel Net of Indra. He presents it as a teaching of how "principal and satellites reflect one another."

> This means that with self as principal, one looks to others as satellites or companions; or else one thing or principle is taken as principal and all things or principles become satellites or companions; or one body is taken as principal and all bodies become satellites. Whatever single thing is brought up, immediately principal and satellite are equally contained, multiplying infinitely.[42]

And so, while the self can and should at times become the focal point of a situation, such as when one raises one's hand to speak in a classroom, the focus will shift when another person or thing takes center stage. In such cases it is possible to experience oneself as no longer occupying the center of attention. The capacity for genuine empathy, after all, is also that of *ek-stasis* (literally "standing outside oneself"). Yet this capacity for ecstatic empathy, or kenotic (i.e., self-emptying) compassion, or in general the ability to play the role of guest, to listen, to be a catalyst and conduit for another's moment in the sun, requires a profound level of self-confidence.

The Huayan language of "host" (Ch. *zhu* 主) and "guest" (Ch. *bin* 賓 or *ke* 客) is taken up by the ninth-century Zen master Linji and, as we shall see later, by the twentieth-century Zen philosopher Nishitani Keiji. Linji, to be sure, in a certain sense privileges the role of "host" or "master" (*zhu* 主) over that of "guest." He associates the roles of host and guest with those of teacher and student, although he sees these roles as flexible and even reversible in the dynamic encounter of what came to be known as "Dharma combat," in which masters and students challenge one another to express their holistic understanding of the Dharma.[43] At one point Linji even associates the role of "guest" with that of a "servant" (Ch. *nu* 奴) who slavishly follows others,[44] and he repeatedly says that "lack of faith in oneself" or "lack of self-confidence" (Ch. *zixin-buji* 自信不及) is the main problem that ails us.[45] One of Linji's most famous teachings is: "Just make yourself master of every situation, and wherever you stand is the true [place]."[46] It is important to point out, however, that Linji is by no means counseling a self-assertion of one's own relative ego over others. It is by no means a matter of what Nietzsche calls a "sick selfishness" that says, "Everything for me."[47] A recent Zen master, Ōmori Sōgen, writes that Linji's notion of "becoming master wherever you are" is

> not a matter of selfishly asserting "me, me" all the time, but rather quite the opposite. It is a matter of negating the self in the ground of the self, of transcending the self and returning to the absolute, that is, of discovering the true self in something absolute, and of acting on the basis of its affirmation. If each of our actions is rooted in this kind of standpoint, it arises naturally from an absolute freedom.[48]

A true master is born only by way of undergoing what Zen calls "the great death" (Jp. *daishi* 大死) of the egocentric ego and returning to the empty ground of freedom and responsibility. Such a true master is self-confident enough to play the role of guest or even servant when and where appropriate. Indeed, the eighteenth-century Zen master Hakuin tells us in effect that, in the deepest sense, the true master is a servant to all beings: "You must resolve to withdraw yourself this very day, to reduce yourself to the level of a footman or a lackey, and yet bring your mind-master to firm and sure resolution."[49]

The true "master" of a situation thus need not always play the role of "host." He or she can also play the role of consummate guest. He or she can lead as well as follow, listen as well as speak. The Zen ideal of a relationship among equals is in fact a mutual exchange, a harmonious circulation, of the roles of guest and host (Jp. *hinju gokan* 賓主互換). The contemporary Zen philosopher Ueda Shizuteru writes, for example, that "the free exchange of the role of host is the very core of dialogue."[50]

Alberti's Egocentric and Guo Xi's Floating Perspectivism

In order to appreciate the fluidly pluralistic and nonegocentric nature of Zen's perspectivism, some further comparisons with elements of the Western tradition will be helpful. It is instructive to contrast the kind of perspectivism found in Daoist landscape paintings from the Song period in China with the kind of perspectivism established in the Renaissance by artists and authors such as Leon Battista Alberti. Alberti understands perspectival delimitation in an exclusively egocentric manner. Perspective in Western art in general is understood as the manner in which I see the world from my vantage point. This is readily apparent in the manner in which a landscape is enframed by a painter following Alberti's technique of linear perspective: The painter stands still, shuts one eye, and observes a landscape through a window fitted with a mathematical grid, which Alberti himself refers to as a "veil" constructed of intersecting lines of thread.[51]

It is not difficult to relate Alberti's vision of painting to what Heidegger calls "the age of the world-picture." "The fundamental event of the modern age," writes Heidegger, "is the conquest of the world as picture."[52] "Man becomes the relational center of that which is as such."[53] To be sure, the modern age may not be as metaphysically monolithic as Heidegger suggests. "That [Alberti's] representation of space does violence to the way we actually experience things was noted already by Leonardo da Vinci," who complained that Alberti's technique "reduces the viewing subject to a kind of cyclops, and obliges the eye to remain at one fixed, indivisible point."[54] As Merleau-Ponty more recently asks, "What would vision be without eye *movement*?"[55] Indeed we "normally see with two, constantly shifting eyes"[56] and with a "body" which is not only "an intertwining of vision and movement," but an intertwining of seeing and seen, self and world.[57]

Given his critique of the egocentric and avowedly Protagorian[58] world-picture of Alberti's "visual pyramid," viewed by an immobile cyclops through a mathematical grid, Merleau-Ponty would likely have been deeply sympathetic with what the Chinese artist and theorist Guo Xi called the "floating perspective" (Ch. *bao you yu kan* 飽游飫看) of Song landscape or "mountains and waters" (Ch. *shanshui* 山水) paintings (see Guo Xi's own masterpiece, "Early Spring"). Quoting Guo Xi, Francois Jullien writes:

> To paint the mountain will be to paint it as a "total" (*hun* [渾]) image, in its plentitude and compossibility... To paint is not to apprehend the mountain "in one locale" and from a "single corner." ... "The form of the mountain is to be seen on each of its faces." To paint the great image of the mountain is to deploy all of these many [perspectival aspects or] "so's," without any excluding any other.[59]

Shanshui painting is a spiritual exercise that requires a "fasting of the heart-mind" (Zhuangzi) in order to get back in touch with the flow of *qi* (氣), the psycho-physical breath-energy that circulates between and indeed mutually produces self and world. As Jullien puts it, the *shanshui* painter demonstrates the process through which, "by moving back inside us to the more primordial, more unappropriated, nonrigid state of breath-energy, we relate to external realities in an 'empty,' available way and enter into a relationship, not of knowledge, but of complicity with them."[60] How different is this fluid communion or respirational exchange with nature expressed in *shanshui* paintings[61] from the detached, rigid, and avowedly egocentric aims of painting by means of a mathematical window-grid of linear perspective!

Cusanus' Infinite Sphere Whose Center is Everywhere

To be sure, there is another side to the story of perspectivism in the West. In his illuminating study of the genesis of modernity, *Infinity and Perspective*, Karsten Harries points out how, since the Renaissance, and even especially in the Renaissance, "reflection on perspective leads quite naturally to the vision of an infinite universe that knows neither center nor circumference."[62] The seminal figure in Harries' account is Cusanus (Nicholas of Cusa), who developed the idea that "God is an infinite sphere, whose center is everywhere [and] whose circumference [is] nowhere."[63] Cusanus is said to have also advanced the concomitant claim that

> our experience of the world is limited by what happens to be our point of view and that we should not think that such a point of view gives us access to the way things really are: there are infinitely many other possible points of view, and to each corresponds a possible experience that would take itself to be the center.[64]

It is not surprising that Cusanus' idea of God as an infinite sphere whose center is everywhere has been taken up by Nishida Kitarō and Nishitani of the Kyoto School,[65] since it resonates well with Huayan and Zen conceptions of the universe as a multiverse of (potentially harmoniously) interactive and interexpressive monads. Yet this East Asian Buddhist perspectivism would question whether it is necessarily the case that egocentrism is "founded in the nature of experience itself, which *inevitably* places the experiencing subject at what it does indeed experience as the center" of the universe.[66] For Zen, this egocentrism well describes unenlightened experience, but not enlightened experience.

Harries notes that "the fundamental thought of *De Docta Ignorantia* came to Cusanus…while he was 'at sea in route back from Greece'…where he had worked toward the reunification of the Roman and Greek churches, toward a reconciliation of their different perspectives."[67] In *De Docta Ignorantia* Cusanus wrote that "it would always seem to each person…that he was at the 'immovable' center…and that all the other things were moved."[68] Having made a voyage to China and back across the Sea of Japan, Dōgen also refers to the experience of being on a boat. In *Genjōkōan* (The Presencing of Truth) he writes: "A person riding in a boat looks around at the shore, and mistakenly thinks that the shore is drifting along. When one fixes one's eyes closely on the boat, one realizes that it is the boat that is moving forward."[69] In other words, by "studying the self" one realizes that one is not the fixed center of the universe, and thus one becomes open to other provisional centers of the multiverse.

Harries himself says that what he calls "the principle of perspective" implies that "to think a perspective as a perspective is to be in some sense already beyond it, is to have become learned about its limitations."[70] Hence, Cusanus' *Docta Ignorantia* teaches us that "To become learned about one's ignorance is to become learned about the extent to which what we took to be knowledge is subject to the distorting power of perspective."[71] As Cusanus puts it, to have become aware of the manner in which each person places themselves at the center of the universe is to become aware that "the world-machine will have its center everywhere and its circumference nowhere, so to speak; for God, who is everywhere and nowhere, is its circumference and center."[72]

Harries understands the positive implications of "the principle of perspective" as indicating the manner in which we humans do have some ability to transcend our place and time through rational abstraction and through mystical experience.[73] I would add that we not only have some capacity for self-transcendence in these *vertical* senses, we also have the capacity for self-transcendence in a *horizontal* sense; that is to say, we are also able to escape from perspectival egocentricity through ecstatic empathy with other perspectives and the perspectives of others.

Ecstatic Empathy, Kenotic Compassion

Nietzsche asserts: "Egoism is the law of perspective applied to feelings."[74] Elsewhere he writes that "the kernel of the perspective view" implies that "a living creature is 'egoistic' through and through."[75] Yet what about such feelings as the cardinal Buddhist virtues of loving-kindness and compassion (Skt *maitrī-karunā*; Jp. *jihi* 慈悲)? Is perspectival knowledge always delimited by an egocentric will to power? Zen offers us an alternative Way of perspectival delimitation, one motivated more by ecstatic empathy, or kenotic compassion, rather than by egocentric willfulness. The capacity for ecstatic empathy would not involve an analogizing projection of the content of one's own mind onto others (as Theodore Lipps' theory of *Einfühlung* would have it), but rather an emptying of the heart-mind that allows it to be filled with an experiential content that is no longer determined merely by the way things appear to, and are emotionally reacted to from, one's own egocentric perspective.

Something similar is the other side of the openness of Keats' "negative capability." By not grasping after a single unifying perspective of "fact or reason," one is free to project oneself into various perspectives. With regard to Keats' idea of the "chameleon poet," Richard Woodhouse writes: "he will be able to throw his own soul into any object he sees or imagines."[76] Keats was reportedly influenced by William Hazlitt's theory of "sympathetic identification," which is claimed to be an essential function of the human mind. This ability to sympathetically identify (i.e., empathize) with other perspectives is said to be particularly pronounced in poets such as Shakespeare, of whom Hazlitt remarked: "He had only to think of anything in order to become that thing."[77]

In a similar vein, the haiku poet Bashō wrote:

> From the pine tree
>   learn of the pine tree,
> And from the bamboo
>   of the bamboo

Commenting on these lines, Nishitani writes:

> Our "knowing" rational order, or logos, always begins from and ends in the place where things speak of themselves... Its point of departure is where things are on their own home-ground, just as they are, manifest in their suchness.[78]

Heidegger said something similar when he defined "phenomenology" as "*apophainesthai ta phainomena* – to let what shows itself be seen from itself, just as it shows itself from itself."[79]

Yet what would it mean to know things just as they are? How could the subject completely jump out of its skin to become one with the object? In accord with Heidegger, Nishitani would reply: "we do not presuppose a separation of subject and object and then work toward their unification."[80] If we begin by hypostatizing a subject/object split, there is no way back out of this dichotomy. The problem with realism as well as with idealism, according to Nishitani, is the self-enclosure of willful subjectivity. He claims that even a dualistic realism ultimately lapses into a closet subjective idealism, insofar as it falls prey to what he calls the "paradox of representation" – for "even the very idea of something independent of representation can only come about as a representation."[81]

If we begin as a self-enclosed subject attempting to know objects as independently subsisting things-in-themselves, we begin too late, that is to say, we don't begin at the beginning, at the originary interrelational experience of being-in-the-world. The unique "suchness" of a thing is not the fixed essence of an independent substance that is isolated from us and from other things, but rather what I would call *a singular event of interconnection*. Such nondual events can be reduced to "objectivity" no more than they can be reduced to "subjectivity." They are rather originary events of interconnection from which both subjects and objects are but *a posteriori* abstractions. To know a thing just as it is, to let things show themselves from themselves, is to *ecstatically participate in the perspectival opening of a singular event of interconnection*.

Nishida advanced the epistemic ideal of "seeing a thing by becoming it" (Jp. *mono to natte miru* 物となって見る).[82] Yet, according to Nishida, this is not simply a matter of passive receptivity; it is not a matter of a "passive intellect" (Gk *nous pathetikos*)[83] that knows forms by receiving their impressions on its *tabula rasa*. Rather, it entails a dynamic process of what Nishida calls "acting-intuition" (Jp. *kōi-teki chokkan* 行為的直観).[84] The paradigm for Nishida here is neither detached observation nor mechanical production, but rather artistic creation or *poiesis*. Intuition takes place only in the process of this creative activity. Nevertheless, the return to a nonwillful participation in this poietic event of delimitation does require on the part of the self a radical self-emptying, an ability to stand outside the ego and let things, as events of interconnection, speak for themselves.

The human self is, on the one hand, persistently tempted to close in on itself as an ego-subject of will; and yet, on the other hand, it is also capable of opening itself up to other perspectives by way of a self-emptying. We are capable not only of willful appropriation but also of nonwillful letting-be. The latter stance of kenotic openness, which Nishitani calls the Zen "standpoint of emptiness (Skt *śūnyatā*; Jp. *kū* 空)," is said to be a "standpoint of radical deliverance from self-centeredness" that "implies an orientation directly opposed to that of will."[85] Only when the fundamental craving of the ego-self is radically negated can one become a "self that is not a self," that is to say, a self that discovers itself only in its openness to and ecstatic interrelation with others. Only when "the self is a self absolutely made into a nothingness" does one attain to "a standpoint where one sees one's own self in all things, in living things, in hills and rivers, towns and hamlets, tiles and stones, and loves all these things 'as oneself.'"[86]

The Multiverse of Perspectival Events of Interconnection

Insofar as we can empty ourselves and empathize with other perspectives, we cease to "know" them as "objects." Rather, as we enter into and participate as guests in their middle-voiced occurrence, perhaps all we can say, borrowing Heidegger's language, is that a thing "things" in its own way, gathering the world and serving as its temporary focal point. As Dōgen says, "a bird flies, just like a bird."[87] Of an intimate kind of "knowing of non-knowing" that would abandon egocentric objectification to empathize with the middle-voiced occurrence of things on their own "home-ground" (Jp. *moto* もと), Nishitani writes:

> The thing in itself becomes manifest at bottom in its own "middle," which can in no way ever be objectified. Non-objective knowledge of it, the knowing of non-knowing, means that we revert to the "middle" of the thing itself. It means that we straighten ourselves out by turning to

what does not respond to our turning, orienting ourselves to what negates our every orientation. Even a single stone or blade of grass demands as much from us.[88]

Yet what is meant by a "single stone or blade of grass"? Nishitani draws on the same radicalization of the Buddhist ontology of "interdependent origination" that was expressed in the simile of the Jewel Net of Indra when he writes: "even the very tiniest thing…displays in its act of being the whole web of mutual interpenetration that links all things together."[89] Each and every "thing" is, as what I am calling a singular event of interconnection, a focal point that gathers the whole world. To know such a singular thing as it is, to let it show itself from itself, does not mean to see it as a substance subsisting on its own, unrelated to us and to other things. Rather, it means to see it as the host that invites us and all other things to be its guests; it means to see it as the focal point around which is gathered the entire interrelational universe.

While, on the one hand, the Huayan and Zen vision of "one in all and all in one" does deny *independent* or *isolated* individuality, on the other hand it stresses, as a crucial correlate of the interdependent unity of the world, the uniqueness of each and every thing as a singular event of interconnection that opens onto the world from its own unique perspective. In Nishitani's words, "It is not possible for there to be two things that are exactly the same. For there to be two such identical things, there would have to be two worlds that were entirely the same."[90] Everything is unique insofar as it is an opening onto everything else from its own perspective. Each thing, we might say, as a singular event of interconnection, swallows up the whole universe in its perspectivally constituted world. The universe is thus made up of infinitely many mutually interpenetrating worlds. In other words, the universe is a unity of multiverses and the multiverse is a multitude of universes.

Dōgen writes:

> besides appearing as round or square, there are unlimited other virtues of the ocean and of the mountains, and there are worlds in all four directions. And you should know that it is not only like this over there, but also right here beneath your feet and even in a single drop [of water].[91]

William Blake unknowingly echoes this last thought when he beckons us "To see a World in a Grain of Sand."[92] The *Avataṃsaka Sūtra* multiplies the point to reach its logical conclusion: "The lands on a point the size of a hairtip/ Are measureless, unspeakable;/So are the lands on every single point/ Throughout the whole of space."[93] Each thing, as a singular event of interconnection, is a perspectival opening onto every other such thing in the universe qua multiverse.

Nishitani on the Mutual Circulation of Host and Guest

Nishitani elaborates on the Huayan and Zen ideas of "mutually circulating interpenetration" (Jp. *ego-teki sōnyū* 回互的相入) and the dynamic interchange between roles of "host" and "guest," or "master" and "attendant," as follows.[94] On the one hand, since each nodal point in the web of interconnectedness can be seen as the center from whose perspective the whole is reflected, each point has the potential to be seen as the "host" or "master" of all others. On the other hand, any given thing can be seen in a position of "guest" or "attendant" to another thing, insofar as it is seen from that thing's perspective as a constitutive element supporting its existence. In the perspectival interchange of this dynamic "circuminsession" or "mutually circulating interpenetration," "all things are in a process of becoming master and attendant to one another."[95]

The existential question is how to participate in this cosmic process wherein all supports one and one supports all. The answer we get is that one must learn to be both master and attendant, host and guest, of all other things. Nishitani writes: "The gathering together of the being of all things at the home-ground of the being of the self can only come about in unison with the subordination of the being of the self to the being of all things at their home-ground."[96] The true master, who can serve as host for all other beings, is also capable of placing himself in the role of guest with regard to all other beings.

In contrast to a crude "master morality" of will to power, where an egoistic drive would seek to unilaterally impose its perspective on others, a Zen "master"[97] would be able to freely assume, as the situation demands, either perspectival role of master or attendant, host or guest. At times, one is called on to clear a path and to lead others; at other times, one should give way to others, following and supporting their lead. At times, one should speak; at other times, listen. Or, in a dialogue, one should practice the art of alternating between speaking and listening, letting the matter itself take center stage. The nonwillful "standpointless standpoint" of Zen is thus fixated neither on activity nor on passivity; it is rather a pivot of flexibility, that is, a responsive ability to shift perspectival roles as the situation itself shifts.[98]

Motivated by a primal vow to liberate all sentient beings from suffering, the Zen adept would be a master of compassion. Having emptied herself of attachment to any particular perspective, starting with that of her own egocentric will to power, she would release an innate ability to kenotically empathize with the widest variety of perspectives, balancing their claims and emphasizing each in its proper time and place. In tune with a fluid and ungraspable Way rather than a doctrinal system of knowledge, her acts would embody the practical wisdom Buddhists call "skillful means" (Skt *upaya kaushalya*; Jp. *hōben* 方便), a kind of *phronēsis* of compassion. She would possess neither knowledge of everything nor even dogmatic certainty of anything. Rather, she would intuitively know how to follow and further a dynamic Way, a Way that gives way to different perspectives in different situations. Her wisdom would reside not only in an awareness of the limits of this or that claim to knowledge; it would also reside in an intuitive ability to effectively and compassionately participate in the perspectival delimitation of events of interconnection, that is, to nonwillfully and nonegocentrically take part in the myriad ways in which the myriad things give themselves to be known.

Notes

1   *Nishitani Keiji chosakushū* [*Collected Works of Nishitani Keiji*] (Tokyo: Sōbunsha, 1987), vol. 10, p. 204; Nishitani Keiji, *Religion and Nothingness*, translated by Jan van Bragt (Berkeley: University of California Press, 1982), p. 182. Note that Japanese names are written in the order of family name followed by given name.
2   *Kritische Studienausgabe Friedrich Nietzsche: Sämtliche Werke*, edited by Giorgio Colli and Mazzino Montinari (New York: De Gruyter, 1980), 12:7[60]. Translations of passages from Nietzsche's notebooks are taken from *The Will to Power*, translated by Walter Kaufmann and R.J. Hollingdale (New York: Random House, 1967), in this case p. 267 (§481).
3   Martin Heidegger, *Pathmarks*, edited by William McNeill (Cambridge, UK: Cambridge University Press, 1998), p. 148.
4   "The Presencing of Truth: Dōgen's *Genjōkōan*," translated by Bret W. Davis, in *Buddhist Philosophy*, edited by Jay Garfield and William Edelglass (Oxford: Oxford University Press, 2009), p. 256.
5   Dōgen, "*Sansuigyō*: The Sutra of Mountains and Water," translated by Gudo Wafu Nishijima and Chodo Cross, in *Shōbōgenzō: The True-Dharma Eye Treasury* (Berkeley: Numata Center for Buddhist Translation and Research, 2007), vol. 1, pp. 221, 224.
6   "The Presencing of Truth: Dōgen's *Genjōkōan*," 156.
7   As quoted in Nishitani, *Religion and Nothingness*, 195.
8   Alexander Nehamas, *Nietzsche: Life as Literature* (Cambridge, MA: Harvard University Press, 1985), p. 49.
9   Ibid., 50–51.
10 *Basic Writings of Nietzsche*, edited and translated by Walter Kaufmann (New York: Random House, 1968), p. 392 (§259).
11 David C. Wood, *The Step Back: Ethics and Politics after Deconstruction* (Albany: SUNY Press, 2005), p. 196 n.6. Keats spoke of a "negative capability" for "being in uncertainties, mysteries, doubts, without any irritable reaching after fact and reason" ("Letter from John Keats to George and Tom Keats, 21 December 1817," in *Romanticism: An Anthology*, 2nd edition, edited by Duncan Wu [Malden: Blackwell, 1998], p. 1019). For Keats, this poetic "humility and capability for submission" to the uncertainties and mysteries of life was more noble and

valuable than the "philosophic mind" which uses "consequitive [i.e., consecutive, logical] reasoning" to chase after certainty and knowledge.

12 David Farrell Krell, *Intimations of Mortality: Time, Truth, and Finitude in Heidegger's Thinking of Being* (University Park: The Pennsylvania State University Press, 1986), p. 136. On Heidegger's turn from will to *Gelassenheit* (releasement or "letting-be"), see my "Will and *Gelassenheit*," in *Martin Heidegger: Key Concepts* (New York: Routledge, 2014).

13 Friedrich Nietzsche, *Twilight of the Idols*, in *The Portable Nietzsche*, translated by Walter Kaufmann (New York: Viking Penguin, 1982), p. 511.

14 Ibid., 467.

15 *Kritische Studienausgabe Friedrich Nietzsche*, 11:26[294]; *Will to Power*, 328 (§609).

16 *Kritische Studienausgabe Friedrich Nietzsche*, 13:14[152]; *Will to Power*, 278 (§515).

17 Friedrich Nietzsche, *Genealogy of Morals*, in *Basic Writings of Nietzsche*, 555 (§3.12).

18 Friedrich Nietzsche, *The Gay Science*, translated by Walter Kaufmann (New York: Random House, 1974), p. 336 (§374).

19 *Kritische Studienausgabe Friedrich Nietzsche*, 12:2[148]; *Will to Power*, 342 (§643).

20 *Kritische Studienausgabe Friedrich Nietzsche*, 12:7[60]; *Will to Power*, 267 (§481).

21 *Kritische Studienausgabe Friedrich Nietzsche*, 13:14[27]; *Will to Power*, 230 (§426).

22 Nietzsche, *Beyond Good and Evil*, in *Basic Writings of Nietzsche*, 405 (§265).

23 See my "Zen after Zarathustra: The Problem of the Will in the Confrontation between Nietzsche and Buddhism," *Journal of Nietzsche Studies* 28 (2004): 89–138. Also, in response Graham Parkes' critique of this article, see my "Nietzsche as Zebra: With both Egoistic Antibuddha and Nonegoistic Bodhisattva Stripes," *Journal of Nietzsche Studies* 46/1 (2015): 62–81.

24 *The Middle Length Discourses of the Buddha*, 2nd edition, translated by Bhikkhu Ñāṇamoli and Bhikkhu Bodhi (Boston: Wisdom, 2001), p. 626; see also ibid., 588, 655.

25 Ibid., 1276, emphasis added.

26 *The Flower Ornament Scripture: A Translation of the Avatamsaka Sutra*, translated by Thomas Cleary (Boston: Shambhala, 1993), p. 791.

27 Ibid., 794.

28 Ibid., 817.

29 Ibid., 862–865.

30 Paul Griffiths, *On Being Buddha: The Classical Doctrine of Buddhahood* (Albany: The State University of New York, 1994), p. 59.

31 Ibid., 169–172.

32 Ibid., 193.

33 *The Middle Length Discourses of the Buddha*, 735.

34 Zen is deeply influenced by early Daoist thought, especially that of the *Zhuangzi*, in addition to Huayan and other schools of Buddhism. Although Zhuangzi is frequently interpreted as a skeptic, I would argue that it is better

to characterize him as a perspectival pluralist. See *The Complete Works of Chuang Tzu*, translated by Burton Watson (New York: Columbia University Press, 1968), especially ch. 2. The influence of the *Zhuangzi* presumably helps account for the fact that Zen takes up the idea of mutual perspectival interrelation rather than any doctrine of omniscience from the *Avataṃsaka Sūtra*.

35 See *The Flower Ornament Scripture*, 215, 226, 232.
36 Tu Shun, "Cessation and Contemplation in the Five Teachings of the Hua-yen," in Thomas Cleary, *Entry into the Inconceivable: An Introduction to Hua-Yen Buddhism* (Honolulu: University of Hawaii Press, 1983), p. 66.
37 Gottfried Leibniz, *Monadology*, paragraph 56, in *Classics of Western Philosophy*, edited by Steven M. Cahn (Indianapolis: Hackett, 1977), p. 471.
38 Cleary, *Entry into the Inconceivable*, 7.
39 Tu Shun, "Cessation and Contemplation in the Five Teachings of the Hua-yen," in Cleary, *Entry into the Inconceivable*, 68.
40 Leibniz, *Monadology*, paragraph 57, in *Classics of Western Philosophy*, 471.
41 *The Flower Ornament Scripture*, 1490.
42 Fa-tsang, "Cultivation of Contemplation of the Inner Meaning of the Hua-yen: The Ending of Delusion and Return to the Source," in Cleary, *Entry into the Inconceivable*, 168.
43 See *The Record of Linji*, translated by Ruth Fuller Sasaki, edited by Thomas Yūhō Kirchner (Honolulu: University of Hawaii Press, 2009), pp. 133–134, 232, 245–246.
44 Ibid., 188.
45 Ibid., 155.
46 Ibid., 186.
47 Nietzsche, *Thus Spoke Zarathustra*, in *The Portable Nietzsche*, 187.
48 Ōmori Sōgen, *Rinzairoku kōwa [Lectures on The Record of Linji]* (Tokyo: Shunjūsha, 2005), p. 95.
49 Hakuin, *Hebi-ichigo* [Snakes and Wild Strawberries], as quoted in Nishitani, *Religion and Nothingness*, 276.
50 *Ueda Shizuteru shū* [Collected Writings of Ueda Shizuteru] (Tokyo: Iwanami, 2002), vol. 10, p. 281. See my "Conversing in Emptiness: Rethinking Cross-Cultural Dialogue with the Kyoto School," in *Philosophical Traditions* (Royal Institute of Philosophy Supplement 74), edited by Anthony O'Hear (Cambridge, UK: Cambridge University Press, 2014).
51 Leon Battista Alberti, *On Painting*, translated by Cecil Grayson (New York: Penguin, 1991), pp. 65–67. See also Albrecht Dürer's woodcut depictions of artists using Albertian perspective devices: "Man Drawing a Lute" and "Artist Drawing a Nude with Perspective Device."
52 Martin Heidegger, *The Question Concerning Technology*, translated by William Lovitt (New York: Harper & Row, 1977), p. 134.
53 Ibid., 128.

54 Hubert Damisch commenting on Da Vinci's *Treatise on Painting*, as quoted in Karsten Harries, *Infinity and Perspective* (Cambridge, MA: The MIT Press, 2001), p. 76.
55 Merleau-Ponty, "Eye and Mind," in *The Primacy of Perception*, edited by James Edie (Evanston: Northwestern University Press, 1964), p. 162.
56 Harries, *Infinity and Perspective*, 77.
57 Merleau-Ponty, "Eye and Mind," 162–163.
58 See Harries, *Infinity and Perspective*, 67; and Alberti, *On Painting*, 8.
59 François Jullien, *The Great Image Has No Form, or On the Nonobject through Painting*, translated by Jane Marie Todd (Chicago: University of Chicago Press, 2009), p. 55.
60 Ibid., 171–172.
61 Compare this with Merleau-Ponty's statement: "There really is inspiration and expiration of Being, action and passion so slightly discernible that it become impossible to distinguish between what sees and what is seen, what paints and what is painted" ("Eye and Mind," 167).
62 Harries, *Infinity and Perspective*, 64.
63 Ibid., 59.
64 Ibid., 38.
65 See *Nishida Kitarō zenshū* [*Complete Works of Nishida Kitarō*] (Tokyo: Iwanami, 1987), vol. 7, p. 208; ibid., vol. 11, pp. 130, 423; and *Nishitani Keiji chosakushū*, vol. 10, pp. 164, 178, 290; Nishitani, *Religion and Nothingness*, 146, 158, 263.
66 Harries, *Infinity and Perspective*, 38, emphasis added.
67 Ibid., 32.
68 As quoted in ibid.
69 "The Presencing of Truth: Dōgen's *Genjōkōan*," 257.
70 Harries, *Infinity and Perspective*, 42.
71 Ibid., 43.
72 Ibid., 32.
73 Ibid., 160–165.
74 Nietzsche, *The Gay Science*, 199 (§162).
75 *Kritische Studienausgabe Friedrich Nietzsche*, 11:36[20]; *Will to Power*, 340 (§637).
76 Quoted by Walter Jackson Bate in *John Keats* (Cambridge, MA: Harvard University Press, 1963), p. 261.
77 Quoted by Bate in *John Keats*, 260.
78 Nishitani, *Religion and Nothingness*, 195.
79 Martin Heidegger, *Being and Time*, translated by Joan Stambaugh, revised by Dennis J. Schmidt (Albany: SUNY Press, 2010), p. 32; the Greek phrase has been Romanized.
80 Nishitani, *Religion and Nothingness*, 107.
81 Ibid., 108.
82 *Nishida Kitarō zenshū*, 10: 473.

83 See Aristotle, *De Anima*, Bk. III, ch. 5 (430a10–25).
84 *Nishida Kitarō zenshū*, 10: 107–218, 541–571; also ibid., 11: 438.
85 Nishitani, *Religion and Nothingness*, 250–251.
86 Ibid., 281.
87 Dōgen, "Zazenshin" [The point of zazen], *Dōgen Zenji goroku* [Recorded Words of Dōgen], edited by Kagamishima Genryū (Tokyo: Kōdansha, 1990), p. 184.
88 Nishitani, *Religion and Nothingness*, 140.
89 Nishitani, *Religion and Nothingness*, 150.
90 *Nishitani Keiji chosakushū*, 14: 126.
91 "The Presencing of Truth: Dōgen's *Genjōkōan*," 257. For more on Dōgen's perspectivism, see my "The Philosophy of Zen Master Dōgen: Egoless Perspectivism," in *The Oxford Handbook of World Philosophy*, edited by Jay Garfield and William Edelglass (New York: Oxford University Press, 2011).
92 William Blake, *The Poetry and Prose of William Blake*, edited by D.E. Erdman (New York: Doubleday, 1970), p. 118.
93 *The Flower Ornament Scripture*, 892.
94 See also my "Kū ni okeru deai: Nishitani Keiji no Zen tetsugaku ni okeru 'ware to nanji' no ego-teki kankei" [Encounter in Emptiness: The Mutually Circulating I-Thou Relation in the Zen Philosophy of Nishitani Keiji], *Risō* 689 (2012): 114–131.
95 Nishitani, *Religion and Nothingness*, 149.
96 Ibid., 249.
97 Note that the English phrase "Zen master" usually translates *rōshi* (老師), which literally means "elder teacher." However, as we have seen, Linji and others adopt the Huayan word for "master" (Ch. *zhu* 主). Here I am bringing these two senses together.
98 According to Zhuangzi, the Daoist sage dwells at the empty "hinge of the Way" (Ch. *daoshu* 道樞), and so can harmoniously coordinate the tensions between perspectival contrarieties. "When the hinge is fitted into the socket, it can respond endlessly" (*Complete Works of Chuang Tzu*, 40).

8

Rhetoric of Uncertainty in Zen Buddhism and Western Literary Modernism

Steven Heine

Uncertainty as a Model of Self-Realization

This chapter examines the role of the rhetoric of "uncertainty" that was initially generated in the voluminous kōan collections of Zen Buddhism composed and catalogued during the cultural heights of Song dynasty (960–1277) China, as seen in relation to some key aspects of the movement of literary modernism as representations of comparable trends in Western thought. The principle of uncertainty in Zen indicates a resourceful approach to gaining philosophical awareness conducive to spiritual liberation that is characterized by fundamental ambiguity and purposeful inconclusiveness. This outlook places full responsibility for attaining self-realization on an individual trainee, who through engaging multiple discursive perspectives without fixation or limitation gains spontaneous freedom from intellectual fetters and emotional attachments.

In particular, I analyze the role of the evaluative (Ch. *pingchang*; Jp. *hyōshō* 評唱) form of kōan commentary presented in the *Blue Cliff Record* (1128) and related texts from the era. Kōan commentators during the Song dynasty did not try to offer definitive explications or solutions for enigmatic kōan cases but, rather, a way of exploring and making an assessment of various viewpoints that serves as a model for self-reliance in attaining spiritual awareness. Their highly stylized prose and poetic remarks on encounter dialogues seek to upend dramatically or reverse radically staid and stereotypical opinions via a Zen adept's symbolic ability to "overturn a trainee's meditation seat and chase away the great assembly,"[1] or more expansively to "reverse the flow of the great seas, topple Mount Sumeru [the mythical cosmic Buddhist summit], and scatter the white clouds."[2]

That approach stressing the ongoing need to subvert and invert conventional interpretations of kōans in order to stimulate self-reflection has a resonance with the notion of epiphany established by James Joyce in *Dubliners* and other works, including *Ulysses*. Joyce highlights the way an instantaneous awakening emerges based on insight into the unconscious implications of everyday actions and words. His inventive narrative style unfolds the experience of an epiphany, a term he singlehandedly transformed from its prior usage in medieval religious ritual to refer to personal spiritual cognizance. This enables the reader to gain in sudden yet momentous fashion a profound understanding of a character's deeper motives or reactions that are deliberately suppressed or otherwise remain hidden from view in the story's action.

Both the traditional East Asian and contemporary Western views emphasize the crucial role of observing and contemplating the inner meaning of fine details of human behavior and expressive interaction in order to trigger a sudden moment of self-discovery. Such a breakthrough is most compellingly disclosed in a highly refined literary fashion featuring innovative rhetorical devices, including wordplay, allusions, paradoxes, contradictions, and other examples of deliberately elusive and ambiguous writing that is indirect, incomplete, and inconclusive yet conveys pointedly the heart of the matter. This approach surpasses ordinary conceptual structures, which are incapable of capturing the true meaning of mystical insight.

I developed this topic while trying to come to terms with two separate but intertwining hermeneutic issues in regard to analyzing the meaning and significance of Zen kōans. One issue involves providing an interpretation of the creativity of evaluative commentaries. As there is no simple translation or explanation for this complicated discursive method, I came to favor the notion of uncertainty by borrowing from various usages of the term in the modern West. The second hermeneutic matter has to do with responding to the perennial question about why it is that so many aspects of Zen literature and art produced by what seems to have been a reclusive, utopian, medieval mystical sect originating a millennium ago enjoy so much correspondence to contemporary culture. Elements from Zen are continually being appropriated and adapted in diverse ways through scholarly translations and artistic innovations. In responding to the query, I argue that understanding the social environment of Song China, during which highly educated literati at once gained mobility in the court and sought solace from pervasive anxiety through sophisticated Buddhist-based literary pursuits, makes it clear that Zen's rhetoric of uncertainty originally flourished in a historical setting known for imaginative forms of self-expression that is much more similar to our times than generally recognized.

Both of these interpretative issues point to the importance of appreciating the function of self-realization in Zen that is comparable to literary modernism. The *Ten Oxherding Pictures* is another twelfth-century Zen text frequently adopted by interpreters today that provides a sequence of images and poems exploring the transformation of a seeker who finds and tames an ox symbolizing the attainment of enlightenment. During the middle of the path, the bull is tagged with a nose ring, an image frequently evoked in kōan commentaries, but then no longer requires this device when it is able to act in full harmony with the pursuer. An ad for a recent Japanese edition of this text tried to capture the essence of this work by using a bilingual phrase: "Search for Your Own Bull" (*Sagashite goran kimi no ushi*).[3] This demonstrates that Zen uncertainty represents the disclosure of an individual's chronicle about struggling with the feeling of doubt before undergoing a breakthrough to awakening, which has an affinity with contemporary literary modes of gaining spiritual realization through indirect forms of creativity.

How does one attain a sufficient degree of confidence in his or her capacity to embrace uncertainty as the key to an experience of liberating? Zen master Xuedou, who in eleventh-century China was one of the two authors of the multilayered *Blue Cliff Record* along with Yuanwu a hundred years later, writes that the effort to reach enlightenment is symbolized by the image of seizing a precious gem from the jaws of a proverbial undersea dragon. This effort has left Xuedou in a perpetual state of angst that is a crucial yet constructive part of uncertainty. According to Xuedou's four-line verse:

> For twenty long, hard years I have suffered,
> By dredging up time and again from the blue dragon's cave for your sake.
> Such is the grief that can hardly be recounted;
> If you want to be a clear-minded Zen monk, you'd better not take this lightly!

Yuanwu then comments, first by playfully calling into question Xuedou's claim that he reached enlightenment, and next by proclaiming an ultimatum that each reader must find the proper pathway and be able to disclose what the jewel really means through his own efforts.

The notion of uncertainty as an innovative interpretative tool for deconstructing each and every standpoint put forth indicates that the *Blue Cliff Record* endorses indeterminacy on experiential and literary levels as the key to undergoing enlightenment. There is no attempt on the part of either Xuedou or Yuanwu – in fact, such an effort is deliberately avoided and disputed – to reach a firm or clear-cut conclusion that may become the source of a preoccupation or attachment. However, an emphasis on uncertainty is not intended to indicate a form of nihilism, pessimism, or radical relativism that abandons the quest for awakening. The *Blue Cliff Record* is especially buoyant and optimistic that each and every person has the potential to develop the skill or knack for attaining and conveying insight, and is thereby able to become an adept in his or her own way. As Yunmen declares in case 6, "Every day is a good day," regardless of extenuating circumstances or divisions and distinctions made in ordinary life.

Therefore uncertainty can be referred to more positively as the expressive activity (*hyōgen sayō*), borrowing a Nishida Kitarō philosophical notion, of "sharpening a (critical discursive) sword" (*jifeng*, Jp. *kippō* 機鋒, literally a "crossbow arrow" hitting its mark or any "razor-like device" that cuts through obstacles). This term implies a quick-witted talent for answering effectively no matter the situation and breaking any impasse that emerges in Zen's combative spiritual encounters. That notion is supported by the verse and capping phrases on case 75, which declares: "Observe carefully the interaction of action points [between interlocutors]! (One entry, one exit. Two adepts are both parrying with the same staff, but which one is really holding it?)."[4] By indicating a vivid, alert, and timely elucidation of words and gestures, Zen expressions are deployed either sparingly but with great precision and effect or with parsimony yet a generosity of spirit by nimbly communicating clever retorts that at first disarm the adversary in a dialogue, yet in the end disclose deeper wisdom available to all parties.

Evaluative Method of Kōan Commentary

The evaluative method of kōan commentary, or *pingchang*/*hyōshō*, literally indicates a "critical responsive (*ping*/*hyō*) calling out or singing (*chang*/*shō*)," and implies the variability and adaptability a Zen adept exhibits in his teaching style. Rather than functioning as a form of literary criticism in the conventional sense of offering an objective analysis, evaluative commentary represents the standpoint of assessing through judgments made yet continually modified or overturned how and to what extent the discourse of a kōan case features a creative use of language, which is unimpeded by the constraints of logic and rationality so that the record can succinctly and immediately cut through obstacles and untie the bonds of ignorance.

Evaluative commentary is the rhetorical vehicle used to express uncertainty in that whatever standpoint is provisionally upheld at any given juncture in interpreting a kōan, which is designed to foster disturbance by challenging commonly accepted notions of reality or expectations about the capacity of thought, is invariably disputed or confirmed in ironic or deliberately disingenuous fashion. However, uncertainty must not be posited as an end in itself as this perspective also needs to be overthrown from its pedestal. Yuanwu comments several times on the perpetual deconstructive process by citing an old Chinese saying, "The correct question is situated within the answer, and the answer is situated within the question."[5]

As Yuanwu remarks of the provisional quality of discourse in a passage in case 8 of the *Blue Cliff Record* that greatly influenced Dōgen's "Being-Time" ("Uji") fascicle of the *Treasury of the True Dharma-Eye* (*Shōbōgenzō*), "Sometimes a phrase is like a lion crouching on the ground; sometimes a phrase is like the Diamond King's jewel sword; sometimes a phrase cuts off the tongues of everyone on earth; and sometimes a phrase follows the waves and pursues the currents."[6] These images refer to the variability of teaching styles that must be constantly redesigned and refashioned so as to correspond to the learning requirements of disciples.

Moreover, Donghan Liangjie suggests in the *Jewel Mirror Samadhi* (Ch. *Baojing Sanmei*; Jp. *Hōkyō Zanmai*), "Meaning does not abide in words, but a pivotal moment of change brings forth truth" 意不在言.来機亦赴 (alternatively: "Because intention is not evident in speaking, truth appears when one reaches the point of change").[7] According to this standpoint, a particular instance of verbal exchange must be comprehended in terms of a broader sense of expressiveness that encompasses nonverbal demonstrations, such as examples of masters striking and slapping disciples during an encounter, as well as more passive gestures like shaking one's sleeve or raising the ceremonial fly-whisk to indicate a comeback or rebuttal or to cast a dismissive tone. In Dongshan's saying, the character 機 (Ch. *ji*; Jp. *ki*) – also the first syllable in the compound *jifeng* used extensively by Yuanwu – indicates a transformative opportunity realized by summoning one's utmost proficiency in smashing through all barriers.

The notion of uncertainty conveys a spiritual condition of upholding and perpetuating the interior illumination of Zen ancestors gained through undergoing experiential upheavals and reversals. This indicates that the primary aim of the *Blue Cliff Record* is to acknowledge a foundational ambivalence and irreconcilability while engaging and trying in utter frustration yet with graceful acceptance to reconcile perennial philosophical issues that are crucial elements of the quest for spiritual awakening. The ability to turn the tables by circling around an adversary or dialogical partner while finding areas of cooperation for mutual benefit enables a crossing of the proverbial Zen checkpoint known symbolically as the Dragon's Gate.

The *Blue Cliff Record*'s method begins by identifying problematic stances derived from conceptually or volitionally based explanations of kōans that are generally either too literal or overly abstract. For example, Yuanwu complains in case 3 that in his day people were often saying of a famous phrase attributed to master Mazu, though without any firm basis, that the "Sun-faced Buddha represents the left eye, whereas the Moon-faced Buddha is the right eye."[8] Yuanwu similarly grouses in his comments on case 56 that when a teacher once hit a disciple seven times, learners spent their time wondering unproductively why it was not eight times or six times, as if determining the exact number might make a difference.

Xuedou's verses consistently demonstrate that the poet-monk functions as an active and inspired interpreter, rather than a passive observer or distant reflective voice, by suggesting in dramatic fashion the merit of his own approach, the aim of which is to challenge any and all opinions, including those of masters portrayed in kōan narratives. In case 30, in which Zhaozhou answers a monk's query with the non sequitur, "Zhen province produces big radishes," Xuedou follows up his four-line ode with the exclamatory, "Thief! Thief!"[9] Examples of Xuedou's facility with paradox appear in cases 28 and 50 when he refers to seeing the Big Dipper in the north by looking to the south, yet indicates that while its handle hangs down below and is available to be grasped it remains ever elusive and out of reach.

To show that Xuedou's expressions must not be either taken at face value or reified but are, like all other sayings and doings cited in the text, subject to criticism, Yuanwu adds to case 30, "Well! It's none other than Xuedou himself who is the one being held in stocks, thus giving evidence of his crime."[10] In many instances, such as cases 4, 19, and 24, Yuanwu offers great praise for Xuedou's literary composition, which he says is "consummately accomplished" and "the best of its kind," since only Xuedou truly understands kōans in an appropriately effective manner. Yet, Yuanwu's approval is almost always peppered with disclaimers. In case 78 when Xuedou tells his followers, "Although you've washed in fragrant water I'll spit right in your face," Yuanwu notes, "Too bad! He adds a layer of mud on dirt and should know better than to defecate on pure soil."[11] Yuanwu's testing and contesting with alternative attitudes and outlooks does not stop there. In case 56 he takes Xuedou to task for attributing a Zen saying cited in the verse to the wrong teacher, while in case 79 in which master Touzi strikes an unwary monk Yuanwu demands with irony, "[The inquirer] deserved to be hit, but why did Touzi stop before his staff was broken?"[12]

The *Blue Cliff Record*'s creative interpretative approach based on the appraisals of the evaluative method is also revealed in the verse and prose comments to case 1. This involves first patriarch Bodhidharma's conversation in which he tells the Emperor there is "nothing holy" and he does "not know his own name," and then departs the territory to return to his homeland, a loss the ruler deeply regrets. Xuedou begins the poem in an evaluative fashion through upending expectations by reversing stereotypes and demanding members of the audience make their own assessment by saying, "The holy truths are empty/How do you understand this?"[13] He then addresses the Emperor with, "Stop your vain yearning!"[14] At the end of his poetic remarks Xuedou turns to the assembly after the line, "Looking around to the right and to the left," and asks boldly, "Is there any patriarch here?" while answering himself with, "There is. Call him over so he can wash my feet!"[15] Yuanwu reacts by suggesting that Xuedou is the one who "deserves a beating of thirty blows of the staff." Yet, Yuanwu further comments that "by his acting in this [deliberately eccentric] way, still [Xuedou] has made an accomplishment."[16]

My view that the *Blue Cliff Record* is founded on expressing the rhetoric of uncertainty is intended to encompass but not be limited to the Zen emphasis on undergoing a profound experience of existential doubt, which destabilizes and undermines all assumptions and presuppositions that otherwise obstruct the journey toward religious awakening that consists of freedom from such fetters. According to the commentary on case 51, an unenlightened person is one whose "eyes go blurry and sightless, so they only know how to answer a question by raising a question or react to an answer by giving an answer, but without realizing how much they are being swayed by the views of others."[17] The passage reflects the negative meaning of uncertainty in the sense of one who is unsure and unstable while wavering aimlessly among attitudes that are influenced by external factors. However, this condition functions as a stage on the path in that it causes the need for everyday awareness to be tossed upside-down and cast topsy-turvy by a worthy teacher's elusive instructions that set the stage for a total reorientation of standpoints. According to one of the frequently used capping phrases, such an insecure and apprehensive person "falls back three thousand miles" prior to attaining recovery and redemption by being able to overcome all impediments.

Such a reversal represents a bottoming out that ultimately results in the positive meaning of uncertainty, which pertains to the open-ended outlook of the Zen adept who confidently embraces all possible perspectives without clinging to one side or the other while exercising supreme agility along with the ability to adjust to circumstances at the spur of the moment. Yuanwu further writes in case 51, "Whoever upholds Zen teaching is able to discern how to take charge of a situation [or seize an opportunity] by knowing when to advance or retreat, how to distinguish true from false, and understanding whether to kill or give life or to capture or let go [of the disciple]."[18] According to the verse comment on case 52 in which the master's response to a disciple's question uses concrete everyday imagery, the best approach is "not to make a show of transcendence and, in that way, you reveal true loftiness"; that is, by resisting the urge to appear overly clever, crafty, or mannered, an authentic teacher displays his or her wisdom through rhetorical prowess.

Therefore, in contrast to the unenlightened "one who needs to be punished by having their meditation seat overturned," since their stereotypes must be shifted upside-down, Yuanwu maintains that the enlightened master represents "one who is able to reverse the flow of the great seas to topple Mount Sumeru."[19] In his evaluative reactions Yuanwu uses the same verb 倒 (overturn, topple), which indicates falsity in traditional Buddhist scriptures, to suggest both the negative and positive meanings of the impact of uncertainty. Whichever consequence the act of capsizing represents depends on whether the state of being uncertain befalls a learner who stands prior to and awaits the experience of awakening or is enacted by an adept existing in the aftermath of said experience. In either instance the term suggests a diversion, inversion, or subversion that epitomizes upending fetters and, thereby, gaining liberation from conventional views by virtue of the Zen master's facility with utilizing diverse sorts of discursive devices. These techniques are apropos to the conditions and circumstances of trainees, who may need to be either symbolically captured and slain if they are incorrigibly stubborn in their fixations or released and given a new lease on life if they are already making good progress in the path toward self-discovery.

According to the commentary on case 2, Zhaozhou is considered an exemplary adept whose agility in responding in compelling and unflappable ways to challenging questions posed by disciples reveals the rhetoric of uncertainty by means of a dynamic approach to teaching that is singularly unbound by the need to resort to any particular technique, such as the extreme methods that were typical of Linji and Deshan, who frequently struck and screamed:

> Zhaozhou never used beating or shouting to deal with people and only evoked everyday speech, but there was no one in the world who could manage to get the best of him. This was all because he never made typical kinds of calculating judgments. Instead, on the basis of having attained a great self-liberation, he could take up the matter at hand from a sideways standpoint or use an inverted (upside-down) perspective by either going against or going along [with the needs of a student] to help them attain great freedom.[20]

While discussing in case 45 the way Zhaozhou responds to a challenge by dodging with dexterity a monk's bullet-like probing inquiry Yuanwu comments: "See how at the ultimate point where it seems impossible to make a turn 轉 he does find a place to turn, and this act spontaneously covers the whole universe. If you are not able to make such a turn then you will not get stuck wherever you set foot on the path."[21]

The components of the turnabout experience expressed in the *Blue Cliff Record* include in a more or less sequential pattern:

1) Transmission of truth takes place by engaging with examples of untruth, or communication that uses various sorts of indirection ranging from metaphor and parable to obscure allusion or obtuse references, and to non sequitur or absurdity, silence, nonverbal gestures or symbols, or natural or innocuous sounds; illumination occurs through disclosing a level of insight that has always been available in everyday experience but was long hidden by ignorance and attachment.
2) Tendentious tendencies on the part of dialogue participants are exposed at each and every turn as seemingly impenetrable obstacles and obstructions, so that a dramatic reversal is needed to force change to occur by ending the gridlock derived from stubborn insistence in regard to any and all one-sided or partial views.
3) Topsy-turvy sayings and doings create a profound sense of doubt, or generate what is often referred to as the Zen malady (comparable to Kierkegaard's "sickness unto death" as the cause of anxiety and dread); it is necessary for

one to have their fixations drastically confronted and overturned so that barriers or checkpoints are transformed from an impediment, whether conceptual or practical, into a vehicle for realization.[22]

4) Tension between dialogue partners is dialectical, as reflected in the teacher's ability to mix censure, reprimand, dismissal, and rejection with acceptance, tolerance, admiration, and praise by virtue of a compassionate lowering oneself to the "in-the-mud (or weeds)" level of the trainee's ignorant standpoint in order to help ripen and polish their understanding.

5) Turnabouts occurring in a dialogue reveal the adept's knack for maneuvering, so that in case 10 involving master Muzhou, a disciple of Huangbo (and Dharma brother of Linji), an inquiring "monk is speechless and at a loss: he is no longer able to turn the circumstance freely. On the other side, Muzhou is neither scared nor stuck. He waits in confidence for the opportune moment. When the moment comes, he recognizes it immediately and turns it around."[23]

6) Transformational experiences are continually deepened in the aftermath of awakening as the master seeks ways to describe the mystery through evoking serene natural imagery or to apply the metaphorical acupuncture needle exactly where it hurts most but without wounding healthy tissue; this effort culminates in his ability to criticize all those who have gone before by uttering the equivalent of the German saying, "Others think this, but I (*Aber Ich*) think..." and then taking the challenge to the audience/reader by demanding, "What do you think?"

This teaching results in a trainee transitioning from the desperation of "fishing for a whale but coming up with a frog" to the triumph of "buying iron but getting gold." As Xuedou says in the verse comment on case 10, "Adepts know how to seize the opportunity for change,"[24] while also implying that Muzhou, the apparent victor in the dialogue, is just as blind as the anonymous disciple. This stands in contrast to case 9 in which he suggests that both Zhaozhou and his monk-adversary are winners for "showing their ability in direct encounter."[25] However, blindness, which can symbolize delusion, also has virtue in representing transcendent wisdom as in the non-preferential sense that "justice is blind."[26]

As Yuanwu's comments on case 45 indicate, the opposite of Zhaozhou's turnabout approach, which is eminently capable of moving in different directions depending on pedagogical demands, and thus the bane of Zen practitioners everywhere who are seeking to overcome their own limitations, is the fixed and obstructive standpoint of calculation that derives from what the text calls the inauthentic mentality of "being unconcerned" (*wuji*). This refers to a passive and inactive state of expecting enlightenment to occur automatically rather than being vigilant and vigorous in actualizing attainment. The *Blue Cliff Record* commentary mockingly says, "These days everyone makes unconcern the basis of understanding. Some suggest, 'Since there is neither delusion nor enlightenment it is not necessary to go on seeking Buddha.'"[27]

One example of uncertainty, as found in a couple of dozen kōans, usually takes the form of final remark by Yuanwu on the case or verse, of the declaration, "I strike," which represents the commentator's entering or intruding directly into the topic raised by the dialogical encounter in his own inimitable way but without indicating a firm conclusion. His aim is not to persuade the audience to adapt a particular viewpoint that may become the source of an attachment but, rather, to encourage and demand that they think through the answer for themselves.

The need for readers to understand kōans in their own fashion is addressed in case 20 when Yuanwu lists six different masters before his day who had responded to the quixotic exchange cited as the main case, and then makes it clear he does not agree with any of these but instead offers his own alternative interpretation of the topic. While Xuedou's verse is highly commended as superior to other versions Yuanwu also prods the reader to question its meaning. At the end of the section of his prose commentary on the poem he follows up several rhetorical queries with the exhortation, "When you reach the pathway, who else is there to point to the matter at hand?"[28]

Song Dynasty Resonances with Modernism

An understanding of the significance of uncertainty expressed through the evaluative commentary of the *Blue Cliff Record* as developed in the context of Song Chinese intellectual history is enhanced by seeking out reverberations with contemporary Western worldviews beginning in the nineteenth century that are often at least indirectly influenced by the influx of East Asian writings and ideas. The Song dynasty, an era when the creative impulse evident in religion was expressed through literary, fine, and performing arts, featured meritocracy reached through the educational exam system as well as some indicators of the arising of democracy. These conditions fostered a focus on erudition enhanced through leisure activities spent, not as a mindless passing or killing of time for the sake of entertainment, but in order to heighten self-awareness through intense personal reflections on selfhood in communion with nature.

This state of aesthetic spirituality was accompanied by an admiration and appreciation for those talented individuals who could bridge sacred pursuits with secular accomplishments, while fearing the possible consequences of social upheaval or political turmoil. Possible exile or imprisonment could be a consequence of imminent dangers of invasion from the north or through coming in conflict with current Chinese leadership, which often reacted strongly to domestic turmoil if linked to the kind of foreign threats that might lead to the fall of the empire. This caused a sense of melancholy and world-weariness based on sensitivity to the fleetingness of opportunities for gaining spontaneous flashes of insight through an instantiation of mystical insight. Analyzing the Song worldview that informed the composition of kōan commentaries suggests the following elements:

a) The main goal was to gain self-knowledge realized by means of creative self-expression, sometimes free from and sometimes adhering to literary rules and regulations in a way that can be likened to harmonizing with a song, chant, ode, or recitation, or listening to a tune played with a wind, percussion, or string instrument.

b) This involved undergoing a profound experience of doubt and anxiety leading to physical in addition to psychological symptoms associated with the "Zen illness" that could be intense and prolonged, and could make one feel that he or she put his life at stake in the pursuit of knowledge that sometimes had "real world" implications since Yuanwu and other masters underwent extensive periods of persecution and exile.

c) The goal was reached by seizing opportune moments (Ch. *jiyuan*; Jp. *kien* 機緣) during the course of verbal and nonverbal exchanges or testing situations in order to develop an intensely intimate yet forbearing mentor–mentee relationship that fostered spiritual growth through spontaneous awakening, rather than the gradual accumulation of evidence or data lacking intuitive awareness.

d) There was no specific religio-literary destination, as realization required that one continued to probe further by looking into a matter from all sides and every angle (upside down, inside out, sideways, and backwards), whereby a single word or phrase, or sound or gesture, becomes an entryway for demonstrating what can be compared to the knack of a card player finding his way out of being dealt a losing hand in knowing "when to hold 'em and when to fold 'em."

e) The result was an ambiguous and inconclusive state of mind based on making one's own personal judgment through an assessment in accord with circumstances by accepting, sometimes reluctantly, alternative views while also severely criticizing those who fall into the trap of conceptualization and cliché or use idle contrivances.

f) Adepts were expected to be able to persuade others by example while admitting that, ultimately, literary and artistic expression is a matter of the scattering of sand into the eyes of the reader, although this could not be helped as teachers hoped to inspire without predetermining their learners' power of observation and insight.

One caveat in my approach, as indicated, is that there is no term used in the *Blue Cliff Record* or other Zen records that can be translated as "uncertainty." The modern construction *buqueding* 不確定 (Jp. *fukakutei*) comes close in implying what is not to be relied on or what cannot be known in a definitive way, while the traditional Japanese term *hakanai* 儚い (はかない) suggests a sorrowful acceptance of what is invariably absent, lost, missing, or inconclusive. Part of the impetus for using the term is that uncertainty corresponds to or evokes some contemporary Western attitudes about accepting chaos and finding purpose through abandoning the pursuit of certitude, ranging from scientific investigation in theoretical physics to literary modernism and philosophical existentialism. These outlooks stress awareness of the limits of human knowledge as well as the incapacity of speech acts in conveying information or achieving articulation. Such a view reflects a different state of mind than mere inaccuracy or indecision in the ordinary sense because it represents a sense of confidence and prescience while recognizing indeterminacy.

The term uncertainty is perhaps best known today from Werner Heisenberg's principle as part of quantum mechanics, which argues that only probabilities can be calculated. Unlike Isaac Newton's clockwork universe, where everything follows clear-cut laws on how to move and prediction is fairly easy if you know the starting conditions, the uncertainty principle enshrines a level of ambiguity and indecision into the theory of physics. Calculation of either position or momentum will be inaccurate in that the act of observation itself affects the situation by skewing the particle being detected, thus delimiting the possibility of exactitude.[29]

Perhaps more pertinent to the meaning of Zen rhetoric are various cultural notions that emphasize the role of uncertainty in terms of personal growth in seeking spiritual realization. For example, a professor of leadership studies, Richard Shell, in an unorthodox recent approach to self-attainment, celebrates the "power of uncertainty," and says of the viewpoint of his book *Springboard: Launching Your Personal Search for Success*, "You don't need to avoid uncertainty... The truth of the matter is that nobody is certain."[30] A sophisticated philosophical outlook was developed by nineteenth-century poet John Keats in the theory of "negative capability" that links the indeterminacy of finding a single fixed truth, which Keats felt was being pursued in futility by some of his colleagues, to the inexhaustible richness and aptitude of an individual to perceive, think, and function beyond any presupposition. Keats' notion further captures the rejection of the constraints of any particular context and the ability to experience phenomena free from the bonds of conventional epistemology, or the assertion of one's own will and individuality upon their activity.[31]

In that vein, though not necessarily through direct influence, American author Stephen Crane once told an editor of his struggles with creative writing, "I cannot help vanishing and disappearing and dissolving. It is my foremost trait."[32] Similarly in *On Late Style* Edward Said examines the production of great modern Western writers, artists, and musicians at the end of their lives and shows that, rather than the resolution of a lifetime's artistic endeavor, most of the late works are rife with unresolved contradiction and almost impenetrable complexity.³³ Their artistic genius was evident through foreshadowing in their word of future developments in respective disciplines, even if this stood in contrast to general tastes and expectations.

Perhaps the single main example of a Western like-mindedness with Zen rhetoric of uncertainty involves novelist James Joyce, who epitomized the movement known as literary modernism with his early collection of short stories, *Dubliners*, published in 1914, and his massive tome *Ulysses*, published in 1922. This was around the same time as comparable literary developments with fusing form and function to capture and convey interiority in the literature of T.S. Eliot, William Faulkner, Eugene O'Neill, Virginia Woolf, and others who innovated expressionism or stream of consciousness. Like his peers Joyce experimented with style and typography including the use of discontinuity, the juxtaposition of contradictory or ironic narrative elements such as the uninterrupted depiction of feelings and an unreliable or perspective-bound narrator, and intertextuality through the use of classical allusions as well as borrowings with wordplays from other languages, cultures, and texts. Critic L.J. Morrissey notes that the narration in the first story in *Dubliners* first reveals but then withdraws judgments and confidences just when the reader needs the most help in building to the denouement, so that "the method of telling itself forces us to judge, to interpret, to participate in the text."³⁴

Joyce's primary contribution to modernist discourse that touches base with classical Zen experience is his formation of the notion of epiphany, which is comparable to *satori* and represents an idea he almost single-handedly transformed from an obscure medieval theological term to a vital aspect of contemporary spirituality attained through literary refinement and aesthetic sensibility. Each of the fifteen stories of *Dubliners* is composed so as to crescendo in the revelatory experience of an epiphany. In these writings, to at least one of the characters based on the fine details of conversation or observation and in an altogether unexpected and unintended way through a sudden awareness of quiddity or what Joyce calls the "whatness" of a single common object that has become radiant, in a moment suddenly and open-endedly the meaning of all things emerges in a way that is crystal clear in its uncertain and ephemeral nature. The theme is perhaps best summed up by a passage in *Ulysses*, which was originally conceived as the sixteenth story of *Dubliners*. This occurs in Episode 3, *Proteus*: "remember your epiphanies on green oval leaves, deeply deep, copies to be sent if you died to all the great libraries of the world."³⁵ A Joycean scholar further notes:

> By the time he scrawled those words, James Joyce had long been working to claim the term "epiphany" on behalf of secular literature. Hitherto, the word had an ancient, and predominantly religious, history. It has its genesis in ancient Greece (ἐπιφάνεια), where it was used beautifully to refer to the first glimmer of dawn, the first sight of the enemy in battle,

or the first vision of a god. It became Judaised in 2 Maccabees, when it was used to describe the God of Israel, and was Christianised in 2 Timothy, where it mainly referred to the Second Coming; thereafter it came to describe the personal realisation that Christ was the Son of God.[36]

An interesting Zen connection with the early Greek meaning of the term as the first glimmer of a truth that is about to unfold, whether in the human or natural realm, is expressed in case 41 of the *Blue Cliff Record*, in which Zhaozhou asks about "one who has died the great death and returns to life" and Touzi says, "He must not go by night; he must get there in daylight."[37] A modern Chinese scholar suggests this rendering (emphasis added): "He is not permitted to walk in the night, but must get there *as soon as the day starts to become bright*."[38]

The main link with kōan literature is that Joyce rejected his Catholic upbringing to apply the term epiphany to the humanist context of self-awareness as "a sudden spiritual manifestation, whether in the vulgarity of speech or of gesture or in a memorable phase of the mind itself. [Joyce] believed that it was for the man of letters to record these epiphanies with extreme care, seeing that they themselves are the most delicate and evanescent of moments."[39] For Joyce, as for Xuedou and Yuanwu, revelation occurs in the context of a brief, cryptic exchange in which the delivery of truth is indirect and unintended, and by no means apparent in the words themselves. This requires a reading between the lines to realize a fleeting visionary instant, as when one suddenly becomes aware that a romance is exposed as hollow at the core or, indeed, never really existed, although this is not seen until a flash of understanding occurs based on a stray comment or unconscious body language. That approach resembles the works of Marcel Proust, for whom the scent of a blossom, or just an appropriately inspired recollection of this sensation, could instantly trigger new levels of memory and self-awareness.

An intriguing affinity with the breakthrough type of turnaround experience depicted in the poetic or narrative remarks of the *Blue Clue Record* occurs in the final passage of "The Dead," the fifteenth story of *Dubliners*, that evokes mystical hearing associated with the lyricism of natural events. Joyce writes with deceptively simple eloquence of the main character's experience of epiphany as a kind of cosmic resonance in dealing profoundly with newfound understanding based on a revelatory view of his wife's past: "His soul swooned slowly as he heard the snow falling faintly through the universe and faintly falling, like the descent of their last end, upon all the living and the dead."[40]

However, a basic difference with some of the melancholy implications in Joyce's worldview, which focuses on everyday narratives rather than the adventures of mystical pilgrims, is the conviction as expressed in several Yunmen dialogues of the fundamental level of self-attainment that constitutes the universal potentiality of Buddha-nature. This is conveyed in case 27 on the "Golden breeze" that constitutes the body even when trees wither and leaves fall, case 83 on "Buddhas and pillars communing" symbolizing the unity of ultimate and mundane reality, and case 86 in which Yunmen proclaims, "Everyone has a light," although he acknowledges the conundrum that it appears dark and dim as soon as you try to look right at it. This difficulty occurs, he suggests in Joycean fashion, because the function of gazing without genuine insight represents a futile attempt to reduce the pure subjectivity of awareness that encompasses objectivity into a mere entity that stands over and is opposed to the perceiver, thereby distorting what should be characterized as a fundamentally holistic act of perception.[41]

Uncertain of Uncertainty

One way to look at the perpetual pedagogical conundrum regarding knowledge related to language is to consider the observation made by Ernst Cassirer in *Language and Myth* about how a sense of intellectual frustration and futility becomes a necessary psychological stage that gives way to an undying effort to gain understanding. Cassirer writes: "All the energy devoted to [trying to resolve a basic quandary] seems only to lead us about in a circle and finally leave us at the point from which we started. And yet the very nature of such fundamental problems entails that the mind, though it despairs of ever finally solving them, can never quite let them alone."[42] Cassirer's view is complemented from an opposing angle through a comment offered in a preface to the *Blue Cliff Record* by Zhou Chi (Yucen Xiuxiu) from a 1305 edition that presumes full awareness as a base condition of human experience, but highlights impediments that all too easily obstruct it from being manifested:

> Human mind and the way are one; the way and myriad things are one. This oneness fills cosmic space – is there anywhere that the way is not found? When ordinary people look for it they can only see what they see and not what they do not see. They seek [the way] from others and leave it to others to tell them about it. This is like [Su Shi's] metaphor of the sun. In turning an object of inquiry over and over in their minds to try to figure it out, investigators move further away and lose sight of it all the more.[43]

Su Shi's parable of the sun is similar to the classic fable of blind men trying to understand an elephant by mistaking each part for the whole (e.g., a leg as a tree). The thoughts of Cassirer and Zhou coincide in suggesting that the more we seek to express, the greater the distance from the object, but this is exactly the impulse that drives our continual striving.

In order to show the complexity of uncertainty so that the notion is not reduced to a simplistic interpretation, it is helpful to distinguish between three levels of Zen ambiguity based on using the model of "toward awakening (satori) and from awakening" (*satori e, satori kara*); that is, by distinguishing whether one is still on the path of striving to achieve self-realization (*satori e*) or one has already attained this goal (*satori kara*) and is endeavoring to teach it persuasively to sometimes stubborn or seemingly incorrigible disciples.[44] As Musō Soseki writes based on his understanding of a passage from Yuanwu's comments, "For one who has yet to attain realization, it is better to study the intent [or meaning] than to study the words; for one who has attained realization, it is better to study the words than to study the intent."[45]

The first level of uncertainty, or its negative meaning, refers to the pre-satori experience that is characterized by feeling a vague sense of underlying doubt or disturbance about unchallenged assumptions so that one must cling to meaning while forgetting words as empty containers of intentionality. Feelings of instability and unsettledness persist but are productive in pointing beyond ordinary barriers to the possibility of attaining transcendence. The second level, or the positive meaning of uncertainty, involving the post-satori experience, reflects the flexibility of the master in trying to determine the most appropriate instructional method that best addresses the pedagogical stage of his trainees. This involves dazzling the reader with elegant language that indulges their current deficient level of understanding by allowing for a gradual process of growth, or puzzling the learner through compelling him to abruptly cast aside misconceptions while spontaneously accepting and adapting to a higher truth.

In addition to pre-satori uncertainty about how to gain awakening and post-satori uncertainty about how to lead followers, the third level of uncertainty is hermeneutic reflexivity. Objective observers researching the history and ideology of the text continually face indecisiveness about how to read and appreciate the complex quality of the *Blue Cliff Record*. This is due to the text's facility in evoking eloquent prose and poetic rhetoric that is obscurely rooted in Song dynasty locutions so as to craft a vision of the "knack" (another rendering of *ji*) for expressing Zen awakening and how to get it. I express this ongoing quandary through postulating a faux dialogue: "What about uncertainty? What about it? You tell me. I am uncertain. About? I am uncertain about uncertainty. Are you certain of that? Certainly (not)."

I conclude by citing the poems of two Zen masters from Kamakura era (1185–1333) Japan, who inherited the legacy of the Song Chinese views. Dōgen wrote a verse explaining that, long after he was enlightened and had begun teaching a large group of disciples in the mountains of Japan, he was continually filled with self-doubt that enhanced his illumination:

> For so long living in this world without attachments;
> Since giving up the use of paper and pen,
> I see flowers and hear birds without feeling much.
> While dwelling on this mountain, I am embarrassed by my own lack of talent.[46]

A similar verse by Musō Soseki conveys what it means to be creatively uncertain in communing with the ephemeral beauty of nature:

> Autumn-colored word-branches dropping many leaves,
> Frosty clouds carrying rain pass through this nook in the mountains.
> Everyone is born with the same sort of eyes –
> So why don't we all see the kōan that is right in front of us (*genjōkōan*)?[47]

Notes

1. T48:148c20 (T refers to the traditional Sino-Japanese Buddhist canon, *Taishō Shinshū Daizōkyō*); all *Blue Cliff Record* passages cited have been checked against Thomas Cleary and John C. Cleary, trans., *The Blue Cliff Record*, 3 vols (Boulder, CO: Shambhala, 1977). Some materials in this chapter draw from Steven Heine, *Chan Rhetoric of Uncertainty in the Blue Cliff Record: Sharpening a Sword at the Dragon Gate* (New York: Oxford University Press, 2016).
2. T48:160a116–17. I agree with Thomas Cleary's comments in the introductory essay to his translation of the *Book of Serenity* (Hudson, NY: Lindisfarne, 1990), 39: "In the Chan understanding, no expression or view can ever be complete, and Chan literature explicitly warns that dialogue and difference among Chan adepts are not to be understood in terms of either/or, win/lose choices… sayings are not necessarily direct comments on or illustrations of the statements they are added to; sometimes they are designed to shift the reader into a different viewpoint or shed light on the same point from a different angle."
3. John Cage's eccentric drawings of the series are one of countless contemporary examples; see Stephen Addiss and Ray Kass, *John Cage: Zen Ox-Herding Pictures* (New York: George Braziller, 2009). In a similar vein, William Scott Wilson, translator of *Bushidō* works, said that avid readers in Japan are likely also to listen to Sinatra's "I Did It My Way."
4. T48:203a8–9.
5. T48:150a03.
6. T48:148a22–24.
7. T47:525c27.
8. T48:142c21.
9. T48:170a1.
10. Ibid.
11. T48:205b14.
12. T48:205c7.
13. T48:141a2.
14. T48:141a7.
15. T48:141a08–10.
16. T48:141a09–10.

17 T48:186a17–18.
18 T48:186a16–17.
19 T48:160a16.
20 T48:142c28–a3.
21 T48:182a04–5.
22 See Jeffrey Broughton, trans. with Elise Yoko Watanabe, *The Chan Whip Anthology: A Companion to Zen Practice* (New York: Oxford University Press, 2014).
23 Caifang Zhu, "The Hermeneutics of Chan Buddhism: Reading Koans from *The Blue Cliff Record*," *Asian Philosophy* 21/4 (2011): 387.
24 T48:150b23.
25 T48:149c18.
26 See Katsuki Sekida, *Two Zen Classics: Mumonkan and Hekiganroku*, ed. A.V. Grimstone (New York: Weatherhill, 1977), 176.
27 T48:182b4–5.
28 T48:161c12.
29 Alok Jha, "What is Heisenberg's Uncertainty Principle?," *The Guardian* (November 10, 2013); www.theguardian.com/science/2013/nov/10/what-is-heisenbergs-uncertainty-principle (accessed December 6, 2014).
30 "I really feel like part of my mission is to be the person who says, 'It's OK. Be uncertain. Everybody's uncertain. Don't feel inadequate. Embrace it. Go with it. Let that lead you to the interesting stuff'"; cited by Dave Zeitlin, *The Pennsylvania Gazette* (September/October 2013): 46–51.
31 Roberto Unger, *False Necessity: Anti-Necessitarian Social Theory in the Service of Radical Democracy*, revised edition (London: Verso, 2004), 279–280.
32 Caleb Crain, "The Red and the Scarlet: The Hectic Career of Stephen Crane," *New Yorker* (June 30, 2014).
33 Edward Said, *On Late Style: Music and Literature Against the Grain* (New York: Vintage, reprinted 2007).
34 "Joyce's Revisions of 'The Sisters': From Epicleti to Modern Fiction," *James Joyce Quarterly* 24/1 (1986), as cited by Brenda Maddox, "Introduction," *Dubliners* (New York: Bantam, reprinted 1990, from 1914), xvii.
35 Jake Wallis Simons, "James Joyce's *Ulysses*: The Beginning of an Epiphany," *The Independent* (January 25, 2012).
36 Note that in 361 CE the Roman historian Ammianus Marcellinus used the word for the first time to refer to a Christian feast (*epiphanion*). In the centuries that followed it was mainly used in connection to a variety of Christian festivals, which were celebrated differently, and at various times, by the different churches.
37 T48:178c17–18.
38 *Zhongguo Chanzong Dianji Congkan: Biyanlu* (Henan Zhengzhou: Zhongzhou guji chubanshe, 2013), 222.
39 See Ilaria Natali, "A Portrait of James Joyce's Epiphanies as a Source Text," *Humanicus* 6 (2011): 1–25.

40 Joyce, *Dubliners*, 192.
41 To comment briefly on another parallel, Joyce's allusive literature is compared to Yuanwu's approach, whereas his main follower, Samuel Beckett, who assisted with research for the writing of *Finnegan's Wake*, is similar in his postwar turn to minimalism based on his epiphany while mourning for his mother's death to the burning of Yuanwu's text by his main disciple, Dahui.
42 Ernst Cassirer, *Language and Myth* (New York: Dover, 1953), 31.
43 T48:139b3–6.
44 Ishii Shūdō's final (farewell) lecture at Komazawa University, Tokyo (January 24, 2014), "Saishū Kōgi: Chūgoku Zen to Dōgen Zen – Sono Renzoku to Hirenzoku to ("Chinese Chan and Dōgen Zen: Regarding Their Continuities and Discontinuities"); cited by permission of author.
45 Thomas Yuhō, trans., *Dialogues in a Dream* (Kyoto: Tenryū-ji Institution for Philosophy and Religion, 2010), 102.
46 *Dōgen Zenji Zenshū*, ed. Kawamura Kōdō *et al.*, 7 vols (Tokyo: Shunjūsha, 1988–1993), 4:290.
47 Cited in David Pollack, *Zen Poems of the Five Mountains* (New York: Crossroad, 1985), 37 (with alteration).

9

From the Five Aggregates to Phenomenal Consciousness: Toward a Cross-Cultural Cognitive Science[1]

Jake H. Davis and Evan Thompson

Buddhism originated and developed in an Indian cultural context that featured many first-person practices for producing and exploring states of consciousness through the systematic training of attention. In contrast, the dominant methods of investigating the mind in cognitive science have emphasized third-person observation of the brain and behavior. In this chapter, we explore how these two different projects might prove mutually beneficial, in particular for investigating the relationship between attention and consciousness. We ask not only what Buddhism can do for scientists but also what science can do for Buddhists. How might Buddhist theory and practice be useful to cognitive scientists working to understand the mind? And how might cognitive science help Buddhists to deepen their understanding of their own tradition?

In a ground-breaking article on meditation and the neuroscience of consciousness, neuroscientists Antoine Lutz and Richard Davidson, together with Buddhist scholar John Dunne, stress that in order to investigate properly a given type of meditation practice, scientists must take account of the traditional theoretical frameworks used to conceptualize and teach that practice (Lutz, Dunne, and Davidson 2007). We follow their lead and focus here on both traditional formulations and recent scientific investigations of "mindfulness" meditation. In this form of practice, meditators aim to cultivate a lucid awareness of their moment-to-moment bodily, emotional, perceptual, and cognitive processes. For this reason, mindfulness meditation may be especially relevant to contemporary scientific and philosophical debates about the nature of attention and its relationship to consciousness. Moreover, because of the widespread application of mindfulness meditation in secular settings such as healthcare, this form of practice is already the subject of a burgeoning field of investigation within psychology and neuroscience.

Mindfulness meditation is formulated in the early dialogues containing the Buddha's teachings, as preserved in the Chinese, Sanskrit, and Pāli texts of

Buddhist Philosophy: A Comparative Approach, First Edition. Edited by Steven M. Emmanuel.
© 2018 John Wiley & Sons, Inc. Published 2018 by John Wiley & Sons, Inc.

the various East and South Asian Buddhist traditions. Yet it is teachers from Theravāda Buddhist countries such as Sri Lanka, Thailand, and Burma who, drawing from the Pāli texts, have most explicitly emphasized mindfulness practice. For this reason and for the sake of simplicity, we make reference especially to Pāli textual sources and terminology in this chapter. Nevertheless, it should be borne in mind that similar practices are found in other Buddhist traditions, especially Tibetan and Chan/Zen traditions.

Situating Buddhist views within recent scientific debates about consciousness allows us to see how these views might be tested experimentally and thereby opens up new understandings of what these ancient teachings mean for us today. At the same time, understanding the conceptual frameworks of the Buddhist teachings can help scientists to refine the theoretical frameworks they bring to scientific research on meditation and consciousness. This opportunity is lost if we simply apply existing scientific frameworks to interpret data from experiments on meditation practices.

A case in point is the issue of how to conceptualize "mindfulness" in a way that can bridge between Buddhist theory and cognitive science, and we address this issue first. We continue this cross-cultural project by exploring how to bring the theoretical frameworks of cognitive science into conversation with one traditional and foundational Buddhist model of the mind. We then discuss several ways in which recent studies of meditation may shed new light on the relationship between attention and consciousness. Reciprocally, understanding these experimental results in the light of Buddhist theory may suggest new avenues for scientific research. Finally, we point to one such area for future investigation, the central question of how the particular forms of attention training involved in mindfulness meditation might alter and attenuate habitual emotional reactions.

The Meaning of Mindfulness

Buddhist teachings include many methods for training practitioners' habits of mind. The strong emphasis on moral conduct, for example, can be seen as a means for protecting oneself from unwholesome mental states (greed, hatred, and delusion). Cognitive science has yet to study ethical training and its mental effects, so investigations of dedicated practitioners of Buddhist monastic vows – from a social neuroscience perspective, for example – might prove fruitful. Many Buddhist techniques of reflection, such as reflection on the inevitability of death (*maraṇasati*), act as a complement to ethical training. This general type of reflective intervention, however, has been popular in modern forms of cognitive therapy, so scientific investigations may have less to learn from the investigation of specifically Buddhist methods of reflection than from other types of Buddhist mental practices.

The term "meditation" is generally used to refer to a third category of practices involving attention training techniques aimed at directly cultivating particular positive mental states. These practices range from cultivating states such as loving-kindness, or literally friendliness (*mettā*), to practices aimed simply at cultivating a settled and unified state of mind (*samādhi*) through concentration on a visualized image of a colored disk or a light. In these forms of meditation, practitioners counteract mind-wandering by repeatedly bringing the mind back to the subject of meditation. The use of such methods of attention training for developing altered states of consciousness through strong concentration was widespread at the time of the Buddha. Buddhist texts relate how before his enlightenment the Buddha studied techniques for concentrating the mind under teachers such as Āḷāra Kālāma and Uddaka Rāmaputta (MN.36). Yet these early Buddhist texts also emphasize that the method of mind training that the Buddha went on to discover for himself was novel, with results that differ importantly from those that were being taught by his contemporaries. Of the many types of mental cultivation employed in various cultural contexts, we focus here on the Theravāda Buddhist practice of mindfulness meditation.

The Theravāda practice of mindfulness meditation can be broadly characterized by the aim to cultivate attention to one's own present experience. Because this practice includes returning the mind again and again to present-moment experience, mindfulness meditation includes an element of concentration, though different teachers emphasize this concentrative aspect to differing degrees. In other concentrative practices, one might return the attention again and again to a particular feeling of friendliness, or a particular mental image of color or light, thereby cultivating the continuity and stability of a particular object in the mind. In contrast, mindfulness practice aims to develop a settled type of attention on objects that are constantly changing. Present experiences of heat or cool in the body, of anger or of joy, of concentration or of distractedness, constantly arise and pass away again. Indeed, Buddhist teachings claim that experiencing for oneself in this direct and focused way the impermanent and unstable nature of all aspects of experience brings about a profound change in how one relates to oneself and others.

The majority of psychological and neuroscientific studies of mindfulness meditation to date have been based on data from participants in the Mindfulness-Based Stress Reduction (MBSR) program. This eight-week program was pioneered by Jon Kabat-Zinn at the University of Massachusetts Medical School in Worcester, Massachusetts in 1986. The program has been replicated and adapted widely and is now offered in the secular context of hospitals and clinics around the world. Studies comparing participants in the MBSR program with control groups have shown mindfulness practice to correlate with significant reductions in suffering associated with various illnesses (e.g. Grossman *et al.* 2007). Mindfulness-Based Stress Reduction has also been associated with structural changes in the brain (changes to gray matter concentration or the density of cell nuclei) (Hölzel et al. 2011a; for a review see e.g. Hölzel et al. 2011b).

To study the effects of such therapeutic interventions on the brain and the rest of the body, scientists need to employ conceptual constructs of the phenomenon under investigation that guide where and how they look. Thus, in studying the health benefits and neural mechanisms of mindfulness meditation, scientists have had to ask what precisely mindfulness is (Davidson 2010). As Kabat-Zinn notes in a recent article, he used the term "mindfulness" in his presentations "as a place-holder for the entire dharma," that is, as an umbrella term meant to point in a secular, accessible way toward the many varied techniques employed in a diverse array of Buddhist traditions (Kabat-Zinn 2011, 290). Kabat-Zinn had been influenced by Korean Zen Buddhist teachings as well as by formulations of mindfulness meditation by Theravāda Buddhist teachers, who draw more explicitly on texts from the Pāli discourses such as the *Mahāsatipaṭṭhāna Sutta* or "Longer Discourse on Mindfulness" (DN.22). But many of those trained to teach MBSR to patients, as well as the scientists studying such interventions, have had little or no direct contact with the Buddhist traditions from which the mindfulness technique is derived. As a result, attempts in the scientific literature to formulate what mindfulness is have often proceeded in almost total independence from theoretical formulations of mindfulness practice contained in Buddhist textual traditions. In the absence of references to such traditional canonical sources, there has been an inordinate focus on one particular phrase Kabat-Zinn used in his seminal introductory guide for practitioners to describe mindfulness, namely, "paying attention in a particular way: on purpose, in the present moment, and nonjudgmentally" (Kabat-Zinn 2004, 4). Thus Bishop and colleagues, in proposing an operational definition of mindfulness for clinical psychology, summarize the literature by noting that "mindfulness has been described as a kind of nonelaborative, nonjudgmental, present-centered awareness in which each thought, feeling, or sensation that arises in the attentional field is acknowledged and accepted as it is" (Bishop et al. 2004, 232).

When specific references do occur in the scientific literature to the Buddhist textual sources, these references often consist in noting that the term "mindfulness" is a translation of the Pāli term *sati*. In Buddhist theory, however, the term *sati* carries connotations of memory and remembrance, making attempts to understand mindfulness as a present-centered, nonelaborative, and nonjudgmental attention appear inaccurate and confused (Bodhi 2011; Dreyfus 2011). Indeed, the term "mindfulness" seems to have been chosen by early translators of the Pāli texts because they saw parallels not with a notion of nonjudgmental present-centered attention, but rather between the Christian ethical notion of conscience and the textual usage of *sati* in the context of holding in mind and being inspired by certain truths, for the sake of improvement of one's ethical character (Gethin 2011). The broad usage of the term *sati* is perhaps best captured by the colloquial English notion of "minding." The Pāli texts employ *sati* in reference to everything from "minding" one's livestock (MN.19) to "minding" one's meditation object in practices such as loving-kindness (Sn.115), in addition to using *sati* specifically in the context of mindfulness meditation or, more literally, in the *establishment of sati (sati-upaṭṭhāna)*.[2] As one prominent translator of the Pāli texts notes, in the traditional formulation of mindfulness meditation in *Mahāsatipaṭṭhāna Sutta*, *sati* is only one of a number of factors present (Bodhi 2011). The role of *sati* in minding or being attentive to the object of meditation is thus claimed to be separate from and complementary to a number of other factors. A meditator engaged in mindfulness meditation is described as dwelling watching the object of meditation (*anupassī viharati*), with ardent effort (*ātāpī*), clear awareness (*sampajāno*), as well as attentiveness (*satimā*), and in this way removing desire and discontent in regard to the world (*vineyya loke abhijjhā-domanassaṃ*).

Careful understanding of the textual sources in the context of recent scientific research can suggest a way forward for psychological conceptualizations of mindfulness meditation, and thereby for scientific investigations employing these theoretical constructs. In its general sense of "minding" something, *sati* clearly can involve elaborative and evaluative cognitive processes. In the role *sati* plays in the context of mindfulness meditation, however, the involvement of memory may be of a more limited and specific kind. Thus Dreyfus (2011), in a discussion based on Pāli texts as well as Indian Mahāyāna Abhidharma sources, argues that *sati* consists in "retentive focus," the ability of the mind to hold its object and not float away from it, a conception close to the cognitive psychology construct of working memory (see later). Like Dreyfus, we believe that the technical vocabularies used in cognitive science can provide a greater degree of precision for characterizing mindfulness than can the operational definition of mindfulness in clinical psychology (notwithstanding the usefulness that definition may have for therapeutic purposes). Moreover, the cognitive science vocabulary can help to capture the care and precision with which the Buddhist terms are used in their native philosophical context.

Consider how selective attention is currently conceptualized in cognitive science. Two types of attention, which rely on distinct neural systems but also share a common neural network, have been distinguished by cognitive neuroscientists (Corbetta and Shulman 2002). If we ask you to switch your attention from the words on this page to the sensations in your right hand, and you comply, you are employing so-called top-down, endogenous orienting. Scientists distinguish this voluntary form of attention from so-called bottom-up, stimulus-driven attention, which is activated when a strong or salient stimulus, such as a loud siren or a flash of light, grabs your attention. Top-down attention depends on generating and maintaining a "control set" that specifies in advance what you are to select; thus, when you switched your attention to the sensations in your right hand, you did so by forming an attentional control set on the basis of our instructions. The maintenance of an attentional control set depends crucially on working memory, the ability to retain task-relevant information on a short-term basis. Working memory has been shown to play an important role in visual selective attention (De Fockert *et al.* 2001) and seems to play a similar role in directing bodily awareness. In a paradigm developed by Ruth Schubert and colleagues, subjects are instructed to attend either to the left or right hand, while tactile stimulation is applied to left and right index fingers with the mechanical pins of a Braille stimulator (Schubert *et al.* 2006, 2008, 2009). In a series of studies integrating behavioral tasks with multiple neuroimaging methods, Schubert and colleagues found evidence that selective, top-down spatial attention, for instance to the left hand, functions to increase subjects' ability to detect and report on weak stimuli by directly amplifying early sensory responses to stimuli in this area of the body and inhibiting responses to other areas. Desimone and Duncan's (1995) well-known "biased-competition" model of attention makes sense of such results by suggesting that representations in early sensory areas compete with one another for access to downstream resources, such as those involved in the ability to have conscious access to the sensory response and to report on it, while top-down modulation by attentional control sets serves to bias these competitions in favor of certain sensory responses. In a more recent proposal, Rolls (2007, 442) draws on the biased-competition model to suggest that attention is an emergent process, in which feedback and feedforward effects between working memory areas and sensory processing areas settle into an optimal configuration for energy minimization. In this light we may hypothesize that when meditators apply instructions to attend to the sensations of the breath in mindfulness practice, working memory plays a role in specifying how attention is to be directed. This suggestion is consistent with results showing that, following a course in the MBSR program, participants show increased performance on tasks measuring such top-down orienting (Jha, Krompinger, and Baime 2007), as well as enhanced activity in brain areas specific to interoceptive attention (Farb, Segal, and Anderson 2013a, 2013b).

In the canonical formulation of *satipaṭṭhāna* or "establishing *sati*" (DN.22; MN.10), meditators are instructed to pay attention to every aspect of daily life; in going, for instance, the ardent meditator knows "I am going." Likewise, one influential form of mindfulness practice descended from the Mahasi Sayadaw of Burma and popularized by American teachers such as Joseph Goldstein and Sharon Salzberg employs mental noting: at introductory stages of practice, meditators are instructed to use mental labels to note everything from the movement of the breath to perceptual processes such as seeing and hearing, and even mental states such as boredom, interest, restlessness, or joy. Such minimal conceptual labels might seem insufficient for developing the penetrative understanding, *paññā*, that mindfulness is said to bring. In light of the cognitive science of attention reviewed above, however, we can understand meditators' use of labels such as "I am going" not as a phenomenological analysis of experience, nor as a metaphysical analysis of the nature of reality, but rather as holding in working memory a mental representation that functions to direct top-down attention in ways that can have transformative effects.

A Buddhist Model of the Mind

The five aggregate model of the mind, found across many Buddhist philosophical traditions, parallels a number of distinctions drawn in cognitive science (Varela, Thompson, and Rosch 1991). In the Pāli texts these five aggregates (*khandas*) are listed as *rūpa, vedanā, saññā, saṁkhāra,* and *viññāṇa.* It would be nice if we could simply list what each of these words refers to in easily accessible English terms. How best to interpret the meaning of each of these Buddhist terms, however, raises substantive philosophical issues and is not easily decided.

In the list of the five *khandas,* the first, *rūpa,* is often understood as referring simply to the physical matter of the body. Understood in this way, the physicality of the body would seem to fall outside of the psychological realm. In the Pāli dialogues, however, this term is used to connote not only the body's solidity and extension, but also its mobility, temperature regulation, fluid and digestive systems, as well as its processes of decay. For this reason, textual scholars such as Sue Hamilton have suggested that *rūpa* is better understood as referring to the "lived body rather than simply its flesh" (Hamilton 2000, 29). On this reading, the conceptual framework of the five *khandas* anticipates a number of recent proposals on which the tight coupling between body and brain constitutes an organism as a functional unity and underwrites emotion, cognition, and consciousness (Parvizi and Damasio 2001; Craig 2002). On such empirical grounds a strong argument has also been mounted that psychological processes are fundamentally grounded on life-regulation processes of the body interacting dynamically with its environment (Thompson 2007; see also Colombetti and Thompson 2008; Cosmelli and Thompson 2009).

Bodily changes such as the contraction of the gut in fear or the flush of blood in anger are an important aspect of emotional responses. Indeed, William James (1884) proposed that emotions essentially are such bodily reactions, an idea that still plays an important role in emotion theory today; for example, neuroscientist Antonio Damasio (2000) and philosopher Jesse Prinz (2004) have both argued that emotions are constituted in part by bodily reactions. But emotion theorists also recognize a second aspect of emotion, one that takes us from *rūpa* construed as the living body to *vedanā,* the second of the five *khandas* in the Buddhist model of the mind. This second aspect is the feeling tone proper to an emotion. Some emotions feel pleasant and others feel unpleasant.

When we consciously feel joyful, the experience is pleasant, and when we feel fearful, the experience is unpleasant. Psychologists call this aspect of emotion its affective valence or hedonic tone (see Colombetti 2005 for the complicated history behind this concept of "valence").

The notion of affect valence provides a close analogue to the Buddhist notion of *vedanā*. In the *Khajjaniya Sutta* (SN.III.86–7), *vedanā* is defined as feeling pleasure, feeling pain, or feeling neither-pleasure-nor-pain. In the case of both concepts, valence and *vedanā*, the feeling tone of pleasant versus unpleasant versus neutral is closely related to action tendencies of approach versus avoidance. From the modern neuroscience perspective, the bodily responses constitutive of an emotion, including an emotion's valence and action tendency, can be activated even when we do not report consciously feeling the emotion (LeDoux 2000). For example, we may exhibit bodily responses associated with fear, even though we do not report seeing anything fearsome or feeling fearful. Such implicit emotional responses can serve to reinforce or inhibit behaviors leading to pleasant or unpleasant states, and thus influence decision-making. Thus, like *vedanā*, valence motivates us at implicit as well as explicit levels, and influences our decisions about mundane matters, such as how much soda-pop to drink or what brand of mobile phone to buy, as well as our decisions about more profound moral choices (Loewenstein and Lerner 2003; Rozin 2003).

In understanding the function of meditative training in bringing about personal transformation, the habits of mind that dispose an individual to perceive and react to the world in certain distinctive ways are of obvious importance. These habits of mind fall under the third of the five aggregates, *saṁkhāra*. Most broadly, this category can be understood as comprising all volitional activities. These include volitions that lead to outward action – the type of volition we normally think of as the will. But they also include more internal processes, such as attention, *manasikāra*, literally "making-in-the-mind." Thus we can understand *saṁkhāra* as referring to implicit and habitual processing routines that shape how we perceive and behave, and that typically escape explicit, cognitive awareness.

Importantly, these habits of mind not only shape our inner and outer actions, but are themselves formed through the repetition of certain kinds of inner and outer volitional activities. Thus, in addition to conditioning the other four aggregates, the *saṁkhāras* involve dynamic self-reference and self-conditioning: habits are formed and conditioned by habits (SN.III.22).[3] This conception parallels recent models of cognitive events as self-forming processes arising from nonlinear interactions between components at neural and motor levels (for a review, see Cosmelli, Lachaux, and Thompson 2007). Complex (nonlinear) dynamical systems have a feature known as sensitive dependence on initial conditions: a minute change in conditions at one point in time can greatly shift the trajectory of the system down the line. Similarly, the dynamic self-formation of the *saṁkhāras* allows for the possibility of radical transformation of one's personality traits. In the particular case of mindfulness meditation, the suggestion is that by intentionally attending to present experience instead of dwelling in reactivity to the remembered past or the imagined future, we can radically transform the habits of attention that surface at moments of feeling threatened or tempted, and thereby transform the way we react outwardly to such situations.

Within this category of habits of mind, the role of attention is of particular interest for our purposes in this chapter. In the *Mahāhatthipadopama Sutta* of the Majjhima Nikāya, for example, we find the following claim:

> If the internal eye-organ is intact, but an external form does not come into its range... If the internal eye-organ is intact, and an external form does comes into its range, but there is not the bringing together born from that (*tajja samannāhāra*), there is not the appearance of a degree of consciousness born from that (*tajja viññāṇabhāga*). But when the internal eye-organ is intact, and an external form does come into its range, and there is the bringing together born from that, there is the appearance of a degree of consciousness born from that.
>
> (MN.28)

Despite other Pāli texts that omit the factor of "bringing together," *samannāhāra*, in the account of perceptual processes, this factor is clearly crucial in the above formulation: an external form coming into the range of an intact eye is said to result in a share or degree of consciousness only with the addition of this factor of bringing together. The traditional Pāli commentary glosses *samannāhāra* as here meaning *manasikāra* (attention).[4] As the above formulation suggests, *manasikāra* is understood in this theoretical framework as a universal kind of attention necessary for any moment of consciousness (see also Bodhi 2000, 81). It may therefore correspond in a rough way with the basic kind of alertness required for consciousness that Parvizi and Damasio (2001) hypothesize to be dependent on subcortical structures such as the thalamus and brainstem, and that occurs independently of the direction of this consciousness to particular objects through selective attention.

This core level of consciousness, which we discuss briefly below, stands in contrast to the more cognitive functions that allow one to identify, recall, and report what one experiences. These cognitive processes are the function of the fourth aggregate, *saññā*. In the *Khajjaniya Sutta*, *saññā* is defined as cognizing (*sañjānāti*) that there is blue, that there is red, yellow, or white. The term *saññā* is often glossed as "perception," but this interpretation is inadequate. As the Pāli scholar Peter Harvey explains, *saññā*

> is only one part of the perceptual process and...one can have a *saññā* of a mental object but cannot, in English, be said to "perceive" such an object...

> [T]he word *"saññā"* and its verbal form *"sañ-jānāti"* clearly refer to some kind of knowledge or knowing which is done in an associative, connective, linking (*sa-*) way.
>
> *(Harvey 1995, 141)*

The Pāli texts contain some intriguing statements that suggest *saññā* may be akin to what philosopher Ned Block (2007, 2008) calls "cognitive access," defined as the ability to recall, report, and deliberate on a perceptual event. In the *Nibbedhika Sutta* (AN.VI.63), for instance, the Buddha defines *saññā* as that which results in spoken communication (*vohāra*): "As one identifies (*sañjānāti*) it, so one says 'I saw thus.'"

Saññā is differentiated in the Buddhist model of the mind from *viññāṇa*, the fifth aggregate, often glossed as "consciousness." It is tempting to relate this notion to what Block calls "phenomenal consciousness" (Block 1995, 2007, 2008). Whereas phenomenal consciousness consists in "what it is like" for a subject to have or undergo an experience, cognitive access consists in having the content of an experience enter working memory so that one can identify and report on this content. Given this distinction, *viññāṇa*, defined as a moment of either visual, auditory, tactile, olfactory, gustatory, or mental awareness, would be analogous to phenomenal consciousness, whereas *saññā*, defined as a recognitional ability, would be analogous to cognitive access.

Yet this tentative analogy between Pāli Buddhist and cognitive science conceptions of consciousness needs refinement. Block conceives of phenomenal consciousness as a state of experiencing in a rich and vivid way certain objects or properties, for instance a state of seeing red. Without such a notion of phenomenally conscious states as essentially including modality-specific content, it would make little sense to suggest, as Block does, that phenomenal consciousness might be realized by certain patterns of recurrent neural activity in visual areas of the brain (Block 2005). In contrast, recall Parvizi and Damasio's suggestion that there is a basic, core level of consciousness, dependent on the thalamus and brainstem, that occurs independently of selective attentional processes in higher cortical areas (Parvizi and Damasio 2001). This core or ground floor level of consciousness depends on a basic kind of alerting function distinct from the higher-level mechanisms of selective attention that come into play in determining what one is conscious of. On this view, the fact *that* there is a phenomenal feel – the fact that there is *something* it is like for a subject – depends on the basic alerting function. In contrast, the *content* of phenomenal consciousness – *what* it is like for a subject – depends also on how this consciousness is directed to particular objects and properties through selective attention. Put another way, the particular contents of phenomenal consciousness can be seen as modifications or modulations of a basal level of awareness dependent on the alerting function (see also Searle 2000).

We suggested above that the Pāli Buddhist concept of *manasikāra* may be analogous to this alerting function, rather than to selective attention. Correspondingly, *viññāṇa* may be best understood from this cognitive science perspective as analogous to a basal level of awareness common to all phenomenally conscious states.

We need to be cautious, however, in drawing any of the foregoing parallels between the fourth and fifth aggregates and cognitive science conceptions of cognitive access and consciousness. Currently there is no consensus in cognitive science about whether phenomenal consciousness and cognitive access are two different phenomena, or whether phenomenal consciousness depends constitutively on cognitive access.[5] On the one hand, it seems odd to say that you can have a conscious experience that you do not know you are having. And if knowing that you are having a certain experience, such as a visual experience of the color red or a tactile experience of hardness, requires the cognitive functions of identifying the object or properties being experienced, then it seems problematic to postulate a type of experience that occurs independent of cognitive access. Furthermore, given that the principal scientific criterion for the presence of consciousness is behavioral report, and behavioral report requires cognitive access, how could such a subjective experience ever be investigated?

On the other hand, it seems unsatisfactory to assume, in advance of the evidence, that having a conscious experience consists wholly in various cognitive operations such as identifying its content or identifying oneself as having experienced that content. Proponents of drawing a distinction between phenomenal consciousness and cognitive access need only posit that some instances of phenomenal consciousness happen not to be cognitively accessed; they need not posit that there are subjective experiences that the subject cannot access or know about. Indeed, one function of phenomenal consciousness may be to make its content accessible for encoding in working memory, for the purposes of identification, recall, deliberation, and report (Prinz 2005). Certain experiences may be too fleeting and rapid to stabilize in working memory, as various kinds of evidence have sometimes been taken to suggest (see Kouider *et al.* 2010; Block 2011). Nevertheless, such experiences may not be inaccessible in principle; for instance, it may be possible to gain greater cognitive access to them through the kind of mental training central to mindfulness meditation.

We believe this last point indicates a major shortcoming in the current debates about consciousness within cognitive science. These debates have proceeded without significant consideration given to the possibility that specific forms of mental training, such as mindfulness meditation practices, might be able to produce new data about the relationship between attention and consciousness. Here is an area where Buddhist theory has much to contribute to cognitive science. We take up this topic in the next section.

Attention and Consciousness

Attention and consciousness seem to be tightly interlinked in normal subjects in everyday conditions of perception. Therefore, empirical research has focused on subjects in conditions outside the normal range in order to test whether consciousness can occur in the absence of attention, and whether attention can occur without consciousness. Yet little agreement exists on what the research to-date shows. Does it confirm the commonsense idea that we must be conscious of something in order to attend to it, as philosopher Christopher Mole (2008, 2011) contends? Or is it rather the other way round, that attention is a prerequisite for consciousness, as neuroscientist Stanislave Dehaene and his colleagues have argued (Dehaene et al. 2006)? Or is attention both necessary and sufficient for consciousness, as philosopher Jesse Prinz (2011) maintains? Alternatively, are attention and consciousness doubly dissociable, such that there can be attention without consciousness and consciousness without attention, as neuroscientists Christof Koch and Naotsugu Tsuchiya (2007) propose? In these debates, cognitive scientists have appealed to studies on various kinds of alterations or disruptions to normal visual consciousness, such as occur in binocular rivalry, blindsight, and the so-called attentional blink. As we now discuss, in each of these cases, studies of meditation may offer important additional information relevant to the ongoing debates.

In normal vision, the brain receives visual images from each eye that present slightly differing perspectives on the same scene. In the paradigm known as binocular rivalry, however, each eye is presented with a different image at the same time. For example, one eye may receive the image of a house while the other eye receives the image of a face. Subjects generally report seeing one image at a time but also that their perception switches unpredictably between the two images. Two kinds of results from empirical studies of binocular rivalry are relevant for our purposes here. On the one hand, the visual image that is not consciously seen provokes significant neural responses selective to its particular features. For example, the image of a fearful face has been found to activate the amygdala, an area of the brain associated with perceiving emotionally salient stimuli (Williams et al. 2004). On the other hand, voluntary shifts in attention have been shown to affect which image becomes consciously seen (Ooi and He 1999). Moreover, in an intriguing study, Olivia Carter and her colleagues found that long-term Tibetan Buddhist practitioners of concentration meditation were able to change the perceptual switching rate when they viewed the images while practicing this type of meditation (with eyes open focused on the display as the meditative object) (Carter et al. 2005). A large number of the practitioners reported that the amount of time one image remained perceptually dominant increased considerably while practicing concentration meditation as well as immediately after meditation.

Three individuals reported that the image remained completely stable with no switching for an entire five-minute period of concentration meditation. In some cases, one of the two images was completely dominant; in other cases, the non-dominant image remained faintly or partially visible behind the dominant one, so that the conscious perception was of two superimposed images. As Carter and her colleagues observe, "These results contrast sharply with the reported observations of over 1000 meditation-naïve individuals tested previously." Thus, it may be that meditative training of voluntary attention enables long-term practitioners of concentration meditation to stabilize consciousness of one or the other image in a way that normal subjects are unable to do.

In an important review article, Lutz and colleagues suggest that, in addition to the top-down orienting network, which voluntarily allocates selective attention to a chosen object, concentration or "focused attention" styles of meditation involve a "monitoring" function necessary to detect when attention has wandered away from the chosen object (Lutz et al. 2008). Lutz and colleagues distinguish such "focused attention" practices from "open monitoring" practices, which may involve focused attention training at early stages of practice, but use the development of the monitoring skill to be able eventually to drop any intentional selection or deselection within the field of present experience. Instead, in open monitoring styles of practice, meditators aim to remain attentive to whatever arises in moment-to-moment experience, without becoming lost in mind-wandering. Open monitoring styles of meditation include certain Tibetan Buddhist and Chan/Zen practices, as well as mindfulness meditation derived from Theravāda Buddhist sources. According to traditional descriptions, at advanced stages of this style of practice the attentiveness to whatever arises continues without the effortful and relatively slow process of selection and deselection, so that the practice becomes agile and effortless.

In this connection, a recent neuroimaging study offers suggestive results (Manna et al. 2010). Antonietta Manna and her colleagues used functional magnetic resonance imaging (fMRI) to monitor Theravāda Buddhist monks expert in both concentration and mindfulness practices, as contrasted to a group of lay novice practitioners. In the expert meditators, the brain activity patterns in open monitoring meditation resembled those of the resting state, whereas the activity patterns in both of these states contrasted sharply with those in focused attention meditation on the breath. Manna and colleagues interpret this finding as suggesting that "open monitoring ('mindfulness') is also reflected and thus practiced in ordinary non-meditative conditions" (Manna et al. 2010, 52).

This result suggests another proposal for the meaning of mindfulness (as discussed above), seen especially in relation to cognitive science issues about the relationship between attention and consciousness. We noted above that in the Pāli Buddhist framework a basic and universal kind of attention, *manasikāra*, is held to be necessary for consciousness. The scholar-practitioner Anālayo suggests that *sati* "can be understood as a further development and temporal extension of this type of attention [*manasikāra*], thereby adding clarity and depth to the usually too short fraction of time occupied by bare attention in the perceptual process" (Anālayo 2004, 59). Whereas the focusing of attention in concentration practices involves activation of top-down orienting networks, mindfulness practice may consist in enhancing the processes involved in sustaining alert consciousness more generally. If this were the case, then we should expect that long-term, trait increases in one's consciousness of subtle stimuli (as opposed to transitory state increases) would be evident even in resting states.

Scientists who argue that distinct neural systems subserve selective attention and consciousness (e.g., Koch and Tsuchiya 2007) also appeal to pathological cases, in particular a condition known as blindsight. As a result of damage to the visual cortex, patients in this condition report having no visual experience in affected areas of the visual field, but they can nonetheless detect and discriminate features of the presented stimuli that they deny seeing. Kentridge, Heywood, and Weiskrantz (1999) found that in one blindsight patient, top-down attention could be cued so as to increase detection and discrimination of stimuli that were not consciously seen, even when the cue itself was not consciously experienced. Corbetta and Schulman (2002) suggest that damage to neural systems involved in stimulus-driven alerting is responsible for this condition, while orienting systems remain intact. This hypothesis is consistent with the suggestion that a basic kind of alerting is necessary for phenomenal consciousness, whereas top-down orienting is not. Yet because brain damage can have unknown, non-specific effects, it is difficult to generalize from findings in pathological populations to claims about attention and consciousness in normal populations. In order to triangulate more precisely which functions are inhibited in pathological conditions such as blindsight, it may be helpful to have evidence from the other end of the spectrum, that is, from a pool of individuals with attentional abilities significantly greater than normal. Experienced Buddhist meditators may provide such a pool.

Earlier, when discussing the five aggregate model of the mind, we noted that in order to be able to recall and report on events, one needs to have identified them at the time they occurred: "As one identifies (*sañjānāti*) it, so one says 'I saw thus' " (A.VI.63). Attentiveness plays a role here, too. For example, studies of the so-called "attentional blink" require that one identify two visual targets (such as letters, words, or images) presented within 200–500 milliseconds of each other in a rapid sequence of other distracting visual stimuli. Subjects often notice the first target but fail to notice the second one. The standard explanation is that detecting the first target uses up the available attentional resources, so the second target is missed and not reported. A recent study showed that the ability to detect the second target was greatly improved after a three-month intensive mindfulness meditation retreat, and that this improvement correlated with EEG measures showing more efficient neural responses to the first target (Slagter *et al.* 2007). Importantly, the participants were instructed not to meditate during the task, so the improved performance indicates that mindfulness meditation has lasting effects on attention outside of the context of meditation practice. The authors of this study suggest that mindfulness meditation may lead to less elaborative cognitive processing of the first visual target – less "mental stickiness" to it – and that this reduction facilitates the ability to identify and report the second rapidly occurring target.

Support for this suggestion comes from recent work on mind-wandering and its association with the brain's so-called default mode network. The default mode network comprises a set of brain regions active in the resting state but whose activity decreases during externally directed and attention-demanding perceptual tasks (Buckner, Andrews-Hanna, and Schacter 2008); these regions have also been shown to be active during mind-wandering (Mason *et al.* 2007; Christoff *et al.* 2009), including mind-wandering during focused attention meditation conditions (Hasenkamp *et al.* 2012). Training in mindfulness meditation is associated with decreases in default mode network activation (Brewer *et al.* 2011; Berkovich-Ohana, Glicksohn, and Goldstein 2012) and with corresponding increased activation in visceral and somatic areas associated with interoception (Farb *et al.* 2007, 2010; Farb, Segal, and Anderson 2013b).

Such decreases in elaborative thought and corresponding increases in interoceptive awareness are relevant to understanding the role of mindfulness practice in increased emotional awareness. In a recent study, mindfulness meditators showed significantly more coherence between physiological changes and their subjective awareness of emotional responses than did either professional dancers (ballet and modern dance), or control subjects with no meditation or dance experience (Sze *et al.* 2010). Mindfulness meditators were more aware of their visceral responses and thereby more aware of their emotions. In another study, Silverstein *et al.* (2011) report evidence of increased interoceptive awareness in female undergraduates engaged in mindfulness training. These authors suggest that women who were distracted by emotionally driven self-evaluative thoughts were much slower in registering their bodily reactions, as measured by reaction time in rating physiological response to sexual stimuli, whereas mindfulness meditation training increased awareness of bodily reactions by decreasing self-evaluative thoughts. Finally, in another study, although both experienced and beginning mindfulness meditators reported that the emotional intensity of positively and negatively valenced pictures was attenuated during mindfulness practice, the attenuation was associated with different brain activity patterns in the two groups (Taylor *et al.* 2011). Whereas the experienced meditators showed decreased default mode network activity without a corresponding decrease in brain areas associated with emotional reactivity, the beginning meditators showed no decrease in default mode network activity but rather a decrease in the left amygdala, a brain area associated with reactivity to emotionally salient stimuli. While increased emotion regulation in beginning meditators may depend partly on changes in how they think about the situations encountered, the attenuated subjective experience of emotional reactions in advanced practitioners seems to be related instead to a decrease in elaborative thought. One possible interpretation of these results is to suggest that it is precisely in virtue of being more aware of their own emotional reactions that advanced mindfulness practitioners are able to disrupt habitual emotional reactivity, and thus attenuate the subjective intensity of emotional response to pleasant or unpleasant situations.

Conclusion

As we have seen, the establishment of mindfulness begins by relying on working memory in order to maintain an attentional set for orienting voluntary, selective attention to a given object, such as the present sensations of breathing. One effect of this practice is to enable increased cognitive access by facilitating identification of what is observed, as well as later recall and report. Eventually, however, it is the reduction in elaborative cognitive processing – in thoughts about the imagined past or mentally projected future, especially self-related thoughts – that allows for increased phenomenal consciousness of current stimuli. According to this conception, mindfulness can be seen as a developed form of the basic alerting mechanisms necessary for any moment of consciousness, rather than as a function of top-down orienting or of cognitive access.

Understanding mindfulness as a strategy of decreasing elaborative thought and enhancing phenomenal awareness helps to distinguish it from more cognitive strategies, such as changing how one thinks about the challenging or distressing situations one encounters in daily life. Such cognitive strategies are widespread in clinical psychology, and they have influenced how the practice of mindfulness has been received. One example is a recent trend in clinical psychology toward emphasizing the ability of mindfulness to facilitate specifically positive reappraisal. For instance, Garland and colleagues give the example of mindfulness allowing individuals to reappraise a serious heart condition as "an opportunity to change their lifestyle and health behaviors rather than as a catastrophe portending imminent doom" (Garland, Gaylord, and Fredrickson 2011, 60). We believe, however, that the tendency to assimilate mindfulness meditation to this type of intervention carries the risk of missing its radical promise.

Buddhist teachings do include many types of cognitive reflections; we noted above the practice of remembering or reflecting on death (*maraṇasati*). As the Pāli term for this practice indicates, such reflections require *sati*, in the sense of attentiveness. In light of the analysis offered above, however, we can draw a sharp distinction between such practices of reflection and mindfulness meditation (*satipaṭṭhāna*). In reflection practices, working memory functions to maintain in mind thoughts with a particular content, for instance about the inevitability of one's death, and thereby engender a certain type of emotional response. Working memory also plays an important role in concentration, by maintaining an attentional set for orienting to a particular meditation object. In the context of mindfulness meditation, however, we have suggested that the function of such orienting is to reduce elaborative cognitive processing and thereby allow for increased phenomenal consciousness of current stimuli.

Moreover, traditional Buddhist presentations do not support a conception of mindfulness as biasing subjects specifically toward positive appraisal of life situations. We have seen that on both Buddhist and empirical models, organisms respond to the constant flow of pleasant and unpleasant valence, *vedanā*, with habitual reactive routines of craving and aversion. In the Buddhist context, latent craving and aversion are said to result in perceptual distortions (*saññā-vipallāsa*), which when elaborated lead to distortions of thought (*citta-vipallāsa*) and, when such thought patterns become habitual, to distortions of view (*diṭṭhi-vipallāsa*) (see e.g. the translator's introduction to Olendzki 2010). This Buddhist viewpoint finds a parallel in the empirical context, where affective bias is taken as underlying emotional distortions of attention and memory (Elliott *et al.* 2010). Thus the role of mindfulness meditation in dispelling emotional distortions may rest on its ability to attenuate both positive and negative affective biases.

These points suggest two ways in which mindfulness may achieve the traditional goal of "seeing things as they are" (*yathābhūtañāṇadassana*). One function of mindfulness is to counteract not knowing. Under normal circumstances we miss much of what is going on. By increasing phenomenal consciousness of subtle changes in our bodies and in our environments, we may make this information available to be encoded in working memory and thus to be identified, deliberated on, and expressed to others. A second function of mindfulness is to counteract knowing wrongly. Through attenuating affective bias, we can gradually replace emotionally distorted perceptions, thoughts, and views with undistorted cognitions. These two functions of mindfulness are mutually reinforcing. Accordingly, we can understand Buddhist teachings as claiming that our normal modes of mind-wandering involve the proliferation of distorting emotional reactivity, but that we can attenuate the affective biases on which this reactivity depends by sustaining a bare and lucid phenomenal consciousness of present stimuli. If so, one of the most interesting questions for future research will be to address in psychological and neural terms exactly how this transformative mechanism works.

Notes

1 The original version of this chapter was first published in *A Companion to Buddhist Philosophy* by Emmanuel (2013).
2 The term *satipaṭṭhāna* has commonly been rendered as a (plural) noun, the (four) "foundations of mindfulness." But the primary sense of the term is verbal and refers to the active practice of establishing mindfulness, as noted recently by prominent translators such as Bhikkhu Bodhi (2011) and Thanissaro Bhikkhu (see the translator's introduction to Thanissaro Bhikkhu 2011). For a critique of the more standard gloss of *satipaṭṭhāna* as "foundations of mindfulness" and the commentarial derivation of the term from *paṭṭhāna* on which this gloss is based, see Anālayo (2004, 29–30).
3 SN.III.22, "*saṅkhāre saṅkhārattāya saṅkhatamabhisaṅkharonti.*"
4 MN-a.II.229. This interpretation is confirmed by the use of these terms as synonyms in the suttas, as at MN.65 (Harvey 1995, 129–130).
5 For a sampling of the debate, see Lamme (2003), Block (2005, 2011), Kouider *et al.* (2010), and Cohen and Dennett (2011).

References

Anālayo. 2004. *Satipaṭṭhāna: The Direct Path to Realization*. Cambridge: Windhorse Publications.
Berkovich-Ohana, A., Glicksohn, J., and Goldstein, A. 2012. "Mindfulness-Induced Changes in Gamma Band Activity: Implications for the Default Mode Network, Self-Reference and Attention." *Clinical Neurophysiology* 123(4): 700–710. doi:10.1016/j.clinph.2011.07.048
Bishop, S.R., Lau, M., Shapiro, S., Carlson, L., Anderson, N.D., Carmody, J., et al. 2004. "Mindfulness: A Proposed Operational Definition." *Clinical Psychology: Science and Practice* 11(3): 230–241. doi:10.1093/clipsy.bph077
Block, N. 1995. "On a Confusion About a Function of Consciousness." *Behavioral and Brain Sciences* 18: 227–247.
Block, N. 2005. "Two Neural Correlates of Consciousness." *Trends in Cognitive Sciences* 9(2): 46–52. doi:10.1016/j.tics.2004.12.006
Block, N. 2007. "Consciousness, Accessibility, and the Mesh Between Psychology and Neuroscience." *Behavioral and Brain Sciences* 30(5–6): 481–548. doi:10.1017/S0140525X07002786
Block, N. 2008. "Consciousness and Cognitive Access." *Proceedings of the Aristotelian Society (Hardback)* 108(1pt3): 289–317. doi:10.1111/j.1467-9264.2008.00247.x
Block, N. 2011. "Perceptual Consciousness Overflows Cognitive Access." *Trends in Cognitive Sciences* 15(12): 567–575. doi:10.1016/j.tics.2011.11.001
Bodhi, Bhikkhu, ed. 2000. *A Comprehensive Manual of Abhidhamma*. 1st BPS Pariyatti edition. Seattle: Pariyatti Publishing.

Bodhi, Bhikkhu. 2011. "What Does Mindfulness Really Mean? A Canonical Perspective." *Contemporary Buddhism* 12(1): 19–39. doi:10.1080/14639947.2011.564813

Brewer, J.A., Worhunsky, P.D., Gray, J.R., Tang, Y.-Y., Weber, J., and Kober, H. 2011. "Meditation Experience is Associated with Differences in Default Mode Network Activity and Connectivity." *Proceedings of the National Academy of Sciences* 108(50): 20254–20259. doi:10.1073/pnas.1112029108

Buckner, R.L., Andrews-Hanna, J.R., and Schacter, D.L. 2008. "The Brain's Default Network." *Annals of the New York Academy of Sciences* 1124(1): 1–38. doi:10.1196/annals.1440.011

Carter, O.L., Presti, D.E., Callistemon, C., Ungerer, Y., Liu, G.B., and Pettigrew, J.D. 2005. "Meditation Alters Perceptual Rivalry in Tibetan Buddhist Monks." *Current Biology* 15(11): R412–R413.

Christoff, K., Gordon, A.M., Smallwood, J., Smith, R., and Schooler, J.W. 2009. "Experience Sampling During fMRI Reveals Default Network and Executive System Contributions to Mind Wandering." *Proceedings of the National Academy of Sciences* 106(21): 8719.

Cohen, M.A. and Dennett, D.C. 2011. "Consciousness Cannot Be Separated from Function." *Trends in Cognitive Sciences* 15(8): 358–364. doi:10.1016/j.tics.2011.06.008

Colombetti, G. 2005. "Appraising Valence." *Journal of Consciousness Studies* 12(8–10): 103–126.

Colombetti, G. and Thompson, E. 2008. "The Feeling Body: Toward an Enactive Approach to Emotion." In *Body in Mind, Mind in Body: Developmental Perspectives on Embodiment and Consciousness*, edited by W.F. Overton, U. Muelle, and J. Newman, 45–68. Mahwah: Erlbaum.

Corbetta, M. and Shulman, G.L. 2002. "Control of Goal-Directed and Stimulus-Driven Attention in the Brain." *Nature Reviews Neuroscience* 3(3): 201–215.

Cosmelli, D. and Thompson, E. 2009. "Embodiment or Envatment? Reflections on the Bodily Basis of Consciousness." In *Enaction: Towards a New Paradigm for Cognitive Science*, edited by J. Stewart, O. Gapenne, and E.A. Di Paolo. Cambridge, MA: The MIT Press.

Cosmelli, D., Lachaux, J.P., and Thompson, E. 2007. "Neurodynamical Approaches to Consciousness." In *The Cambridge Handbook of Consciousness*, edited by P.D. Zelazo, M. Moscovitch, and E. Thompson. Cambridge, UK: Cambridge University Press.

Craig, A.D. 2002. "How Do You Feel? Interoception: The Sense of the Physiological Condition of the Body." *Nature Reviews Neuroscience* 3(8): 655. doi:10.1038/nrn894

Damasio, A.R. 2000. *The Feeling of What Happens: Body and Emotion in the Making of Consciousness*. New York: Mariner Books.

Davidson, R.J. 2010. "Empirical Explorations of Mindfulness: Conceptual and Methodological Conundrums." *Emotion* 10(1): 8–11.

De Fockert, J.W., Rees, G., Frith, C.D., and Lavie, N. 2001. "The Role of Working Memory in Visual Selective Attention." *Science* 291(5509): 1803–1806. doi:10.1126/science.1056496

Dehaene, S., Changeux, J., Naccache, L., Sackur, J., and Sergent, C. 2006. "Conscious, Preconscious, and Subliminal Processing: A Testable Taxonomy." *Trends in Cognitive Sciences* 10(5): 204–211. doi:10.1016/j.tics.2006.03.007

Desimone, R. and Duncan, J. 1995. "Neural Mechanisms of Selective Visual Attention." *Annual Review of Neuroscience* 18(1): 193–222.

Dreyfus, G. 2011. "Is Mindfulness Present-Centred and Non-judgmental? A Discussion of the Cognitive Dimensions of Mindfulness." *Contemporary Buddhism* 12(1): 41–54. doi:10.1080/14639947.2011.564815

Elliott, R., Zahn, R., Deakin, J.F.W., and Anderson, I.M. 2010. "Affective Cognition and Its Disruption in Mood Disorders." *Neuropsychopharmacology* 36(1): 153. doi:10.1038/npp.2010.77

Farb, N.A.S., Segal, Z.V., Mayberg, H., Bean, J., McKeon, D., Fatima, Z., and Anderson, A.K. 2007. "Attending to the Present: Mindfulness Meditation Reveals Distinct Neural Modes of Self-Reference." *Social Cognitive and Affective Neuroscience* 2(4): 313.

Farb, N.A.S., Anderson, A.K., Mayberg, H., Bean, J., McKeon, D., and Segal, Z.V. 2010. "Minding One's Emotions: Mindfulness Training Alters the Neural Expression of Sadness." *Emotion* 10(1): 25–33.

Farb, N.A.S., Segal, Z.V., and Anderson, A.K. 2013a. "Attentional Modulation of Primary Interoceptive and Exteroceptive Cortices." *Cerebral Cortex* 23(1): 114–126.

Farb, N.A.S., Segal, Z.V., and Anderson, A.K. 2013b. "Mindfulness Meditation Training Alters Cortical Representations of Interoceptive Attention." *Social Cognitive and Affective Neuroscience* 8(1): 15–26.

Garland, E.L., Gaylord, S.A., and Fredrickson, B.L. 2011. "Positive Reappraisal Mediates the Stress-Reductive Effects of Mindfulness: An Upward Spiral Process." *Mindfulness* 2(1): 59–67. doi:10.1007/s12671-011-0043-8

Gethin, R. 2011. "On Some Definitions of Mindfulness." *Contemporary Buddhism* 12(1): 263–279. doi:10.1080/14639947.2011.564843

Grossman, P., Tiefenthaler-Gilmer, U., Raysz, A., and Kesper, U. 2007. "Mindfulness Training as an Intervention for Fibromyalgia: Evidence of Postintervention and 3-Year Follow-Up Benefits in Well-Being." *Psychotherapy and Psychosomatics* 76(4): 226–233. doi:10.1159/000101501

Hamilton, S. 2000. *Early Buddhism: A New Approach: The I of the Beholder*. Richmond, Surrey: Curzon Press.

Harvey, P. 1995. *The Selfless Mind: Personality, Consciousness and Nirvana in Early Buddhism*. Reissue. London: Routledge.

Hasenkamp, W., Wilson-Mendenhall, C.D., Duncan, E., and Barsalou, L.W. 2012. "Mind Wandering and Attention During Focused Meditation: A Fine-Grained Temporal Analysis of Fluctuating Cognitive States." *NeuroImage* 59(1): 750–760. doi:10.1016/j.neuroimage.2011.07.008

Hölzel, B.K., Carmody, J., Vangel, M., Congleton, C., Yerramsetti, S.M., Gard, T., and Lazar, S.W. 2011a. "Mindfulness Practice Leads to Increases in Regional Brain Gray Matter Density." *Psychiatry Research* 191(1): 36–43. doi:10.1016/j.pscychresns.2010.08.006

Hölzel, B.K., Lazar, S.W., Gard, T., Schuman-Olivier, Z., Vago, D.R., and Ott, U. 2011b. "How Does Mindfulness Meditation Work? Proposing Mechanisms of Action From a Conceptual and Neural Perspective." *Perspectives on Psychological Science* 6(6): 537–559. doi:10.1177/1745691611419671

James, W. 1884. "What is an Emotion?" *Mind* 9(34): 188–205.

Jha, A.P., Krompinger, J., and Baime, M.J. 2007. "Mindfulness Training Modifies Subsystems of Attention." *Cognitive, Affective, & Behavioral Neuroscience* 7(2): 109–119.

Kabat-Zinn, J. 2004. *Wherever You Go, There You Are*. New York: Hyperion.

Kabat-Zinn, J. 2011. "Some Reflections on the Origins of MBSR, Skillful Means, and the Trouble with Maps." *Contemporary Buddhism* 12(1): 281–306. doi:10.1080/14639947.2011.564844

Kentridge, R.W., Heywood, C.A., and Weiskrantz, L. 1999. "Attention Without Awareness in Blindsight." *Proceedings of the Royal Society of London. Series B: Biological Sciences* 266(1430): 1805–1811. doi:10.1098/rspb.1999.0850

Koch, C. and Tsuchiya, N. 2007. "Attention and Consciousness: Two Distinct Brain Processes." *Trends in Cognitive Sciences* 11(1): 16–22.

Kouider, S., Gardelle, V. de, Sackur, J., and Dupoux, E. 2010. "How Rich is Consciousness? The Partial Awareness Hypothesis." *Trends in Cognitive Sciences* 14(7): 301–307. doi:10.1016/j.tics.2010.04.006

Lamme, V.A.F. 2003. "Why Visual Attention and Awareness are Different." *Trends in Cognitive Sciences* 7(1): 12–18.

LeDoux, J.E. 2000. "Emotion Circuits in the Brain." *Annual Review of Neuroscience* 23: 155–184.

Loewenstein, G. and Lerner, J.S. 2003. "The Role of Affect in Decision Making." In *Handbook of Affective Sciences*, edited by R.J. Davidson, K.R. Scherer, and H.H. Goldsmith. New York: Oxford University Press.

Lutz, Antoine, Dunne, J.D., and Davidson, R.J. 2007. "Meditation and the Neuroscience of Consciousness." In *The Cambridge Handbook of Consciousness*, edited by P.D. Zelazo, M. Moscovitch, and E. Thompson. Cambridge, UK: Cambridge University Press.

Lutz, A., Slagter, H.A., Dunne, J.D., and Davidson, R.J. 2008. "Attention Regulation and Monitoring in Meditation." *Trends in Cognitive Sciences* 12(4): 163–169. doi:10.1016/j.tics.2008.01.005

Manna, A., Raffone, A., Perrucci, M.G., Nardo, D., Ferretti, A., Tartaro, A., et al. 2010. "Neural Correlates of Focused Attention and Cognitive Monitoring in Meditation." *Brain Research Bulletin* 82(1–2): 46–56. doi:10.1016/j.brainresbull.2010.03.001

Mason, M.F., Norton, M.I., Van Horn, J.D., Wegner, D.M., Grafton, S.T., and Macrae, C.N. 2007. "Wandering Minds: The Default Network and Stimulus-Independent Thought." *Science* 315(5810): 393–395. doi:10.1126/science.1131295

Mole, C. 2008. "Attention and Consciousness." *Journal of Consciousness Studies* 15(4): 86–104.

Mole, C. 2011. *Attention is Cognitive Unison: An Essay in Philosophical Psychology*. New York: Oxford University Press.

Olendzki, A., trans. 2010. "Vipallasa Sutta: Distortions of the Mind." *Access to Insight*. www.accesstoinsight.org/tipitaka/an/an04/an04.049.olen.html

Ooi, T.L. and He, Z.J. 1999. "Binocular Rivalry and Visual Awareness: The Role of Attention." *Perception* 28(5): 551–574.

Parvizi, J. and Damasio, A. 2001. "Consciousness and the Brainstem." *Cognition* 79(1–2): 135–160.

Prinz, J.J. 2004. *Gut Reactions: A Perceptual Theory of Emotion*. New York: Oxford University Press.

Prinz, J.J. 2005. "A Neurofunctional Theory of Consciousness." In *Cognition and the Brain: The Philosophy and Neuroscience Movement*, edited by A. Brook and K. Akins, 381–396. Cambridge, UK: Cambridge University Press.

Prinz, J.J. 2011. "Is Attention Necessary and Sufficient for Consciousness?" In *Attention: Philosophical and Psychological Essays*, edited by C. Mole, D. Smithies, and W. Wu, 174–204. New York: Oxford University Press.

Rolls, E. 2007. *Memory, Attention, and Decision-Making: A Unifying Computational Neuroscience Approach*, 1st edition. New York: Oxford University Press.

Rozin, G. 2003. "Introduction: Evolutionary and Cultural Perspectives on Affect." In *Handbook of Affective Sciences*, edited by R.J. Davidson, K.R. Scherer, and H.H. Goldsmith. New York: Oxford University Press.

Schubert, R., Blankenburg, F., Lemm, S., Villringer, A., and Curio, G. 2006. "Now You Feel It – Now You Don't: ERP Correlates of Somatosensory Awareness." *Psychophysiology* 43(1): 31–40.

Schubert, R., Ritter, P., Wüstenberg, T., Preuschhof, C., Curio, G., Sommer, W., and Villringer, A. 2008. "Spatial Attention Related SEP Amplitude Modulations Covary with BOLD Signal in S1: A Simultaneous EEG–fMRI Study." *Cerebral Cortex* 18(11): 2686.

Schubert, R., Haufe, S., Blankenburg, F., Villringer, and Curio, G. 2009. "Now You'll Feel It, Now You Won't: EEG Rhythms Predict the Effectiveness of Perceptual Masking." *Journal of Cognitive Neuroscience* 21(12): 2407–2419.

Searle, J.R. 2000. "Consciousness." *Annual Review of Neuroscience* 23(1): 557–578. doi:10.1146/annurev.neuro.23.1.557

Silverstein, R.G., Brown, A.-C.H., Roth, H.D., and Britton, W.B. 2011. "Effects of Mindfulness Training on Body Awareness to Sexual Stimuli: Implications for Female Sexual Dysfunction." *Psychosomatic Medicine* 73(9): 817–825. doi:10.1097/PSY.0b013e318234e628

Slagter, H.A., Lutz, A., Greischar, L.L., Francis, A.D., Nieuwenhuis, S., Davis, J.M., and Davidson, R.J. 2007. "Mental Training Affects Distribution of Limited Brain Resources." *PLoS Biology* 5(6): e138. doi:10.1371/journal.pbio.0050138

Sze, J.A., Gyurak, A., Yuan, J.W., and Levenson, R.W. 2010. "Coherence Between Emotional Experience and Physiology: Does Body Awareness Training Have an Impact?" *Emotion* 10: 803–814. doi:10.1037/a0020146

Taylor, V.A., Grant, J., Daneault, V., Scavone, G., Breton, E., Roffe-Vidal, S., et al. 2011. "Impact of Mindfulness on the Neural Responses to Emotional Pictures in Experienced and Beginner Meditators." *NeuroImage* 57(4): 1524–1533. doi:10.1016/j.neuroimage.2011.06.001

Thanissaro Bhikkhu, trans. 2011. "Maha-satipatthana Sutta: The Great Frames of Reference." *Access to Insight*. www.accesstoinsight.org/tipitaka/dn/dn.22.0.than.html

Thompson, E. 2007. *Mind in Life: Biology, Phenomenology, and the Sciences of Mind*. Cambridge, MA: Belknap Press.

Varela, F.J., Thompson, E., and Rosch, E. 1991. *The Embodied Mind: Cognitive Science and Human Experience*. Cambridge, MA: The MIT Press.

Williams, M.A., Morris, A.P., McGlone, F., Abbott, D.F., and Mattingley, J.B. 2004. "Amygdala Responses to Fearful and Happy Facial Expressions Under Conditions of Binocular Suppression." *The Journal of Neuroscience* 24(12): 2898–2904. doi:10.1523/JNEUROSCI.4977-03.2004

10

Embodying Change: Buddhism and Feminist Philosophy
Erin A. McCarthy[1]

This chapter focuses on women's bodies in Buddhism and works toward revalorizing that tradition.[2] My aim in bringing Buddhist philosophy into conversation with contemporary feminist philosophy is to advance both fields and advance their aim to relieve suffering in the world. Traditionally, with its tendency toward dualistic thinking, Western philosophy has marginalized the body and deemed it inferior to mind. Much feminist philosophy critiques this sort of dualism, so it makes sense to turn toward nondualistic traditions – such as those in Buddhism I shall discuss – for ways to rethink body so as to make it non-limiting for women.

Links between feminism and Buddhism date back almost to its birth. Although the Buddha initially refused to ordain women, expressed a general reluctance to do so, and imposes extra precepts and eight heavy rules on female monastics, the fact remains that in the end he *did* ordain women and stated unequivocally that they can attain enlightenment. He did this at a time when women could not be fully ordained as monastics in most other religions. While there are legitimate grievances to be raised about the way in which the Buddha treated women, his decision to ordain women was radical and speaks to a deep, abiding openness and sense of equality in the tradition.

This is not to suggest that Buddhism has been immune to patriarchy. Women have been viewed as inferior, simply by virtue of being women, in Buddhism as elsewhere. The prevailing misogyny of Indian culture at the time of the Buddha did not disappear when he declared that women too could become enlightened. And it is important not to romanticize Buddhism or view nondualism as a panacea. We cannot ignore the women whose names have been left off the lineage charts, the women whose work was and continues to be invisible. Nor can we ignore the way women's questions down the centuries have been marginalized in Buddhist traditions – as they have been in the West.

Buddhist Philosophy: A Comparative Approach, First Edition. Edited by Steven M. Emmanuel.
© 2018 John Wiley & Sons, Inc. Published 2018 by John Wiley & Sons, Inc.

Although feminism has a good deal to teach Buddhism, the opposite is also true – that they are congenial, rather than antithetical. Viewing Buddhism from the standpoint of feminism can help free it from its patriarchal past and allow it to face up to the harmful things that have been said or done in the Buddha's name, and recover the openness which the Buddha expressed. My goal, in other words, is to reappropriate the past – to perform what Rita Gross terms a feminist revalorization of Buddhist tradition. As Gross states: "To revalorize is to have determined that, however sexist a religious tradition may be, it is not irreparably so. Revalorizing is, in fact, doing that work of repairing the tradition, often bringing it much more into line with its own fundamental values and vision than was its patriarchal form" (Gross 1993, 3). This requires the sort of praxis that inspires both Buddhism and feminism – putting ideas into action, seeing what works and what doesn't, and returning to refashion theory over and over again to ensure it is truly liberating. It is in this spirit that this chapter attempts to revalorize the views of women's bodies in Buddhism in light of contemporary feminist philosophy.

Women's Bodies in Buddhism: A Brief Overview

Although, philosophically, Buddhism maintains that the enlightened body is beyond gender, the tradition has invariably presented the enlightened body as male. As Miriam Levering points out, "As in the case of the God of Western theology, sophisticated Buddhists knew that buddhas were in some sense beyond gender, yet they said repeatedly that a male body presented him best to the human imagination, and many would certainly have been startled by a reference to the Buddha as female" (Levering 1997, 137). So the Buddha's decision to fully ordain women notwithstanding,

> the door was still left open to speculation about the limitations of the "female nature," a theme prominent in the androcentric and misogynist views that were to become increasingly characteristic of the tradition as the monastic order became more institutionalized and male dominated in the first several centuries following Sakyamuni's death.
>
> *(Sponberg 1992, 12–13)*

There is no shortage of literature – particularly in early Buddhism – that states unequivocally that in order to become enlightened one must first possess a male body. *The Sutra on Changing the Female Sex* states, for example:

> If women can accomplish one thing (Dharma), they will be freed of the female body and become sons. What is that one thing? The profound state of mind which seeks enlightenment. Why? If women awaken to the

thought of enlightenment, then they will have the great and good person's state of mind, a man's state of mind, a sage's state of mind... If women awaken to the thought of enlightenment, then they will not be bound to the limitation of a woman's state of mind. Because they will not be limited, they will forever separate from the female sex and become sons.

(Paul 1981, 65)

Diana Paul argues that in one sense this was liberating for women, for a woman

could free herself from her sexual nature without postponing her becoming a Bodhisattva until rebirth as a man. She was no longer biologically determined by her body, not a victim of her bodily needs... She emerges from her sexual identity as a female by mentally becoming a man in this lifetime.

(Paul 1981, 66)

However, Paul argues that this is ambiguous: "innate psychological characteristics of maleness and femaleness are denied *philosophically* since females can change into males psychologically. *Yet* the male symbol is still ranked higher than the female, and women have to exert more effort to overcome their physical needs" (Paul 1981, 67). Even when women are said not to require transformation into the male form, they still aren't equal as *women*. Equality attaches only to men.

In the early sutras we also find women ranked lower than men because of their female form, that is, their embodiment as women. Consider the following from the *Aṅguttara Nikāya*:

Monks, I see no other single form so enticing, so desirable, so intoxicating, so binding, so distracting, such a hindrance to winning the unsurpassed peace from effort...as a woman's form. Monks, whosoever clings to a woman's form – infatuated, greedy, fettered, enslaved, enthralled – for many a long day shall grieve, snared by the charms of a woman's form... Monks, a woman, even when going along, will stop to ensnare the heart of a man; whether standing, sitting or lying down, laughing, talking or singing, weeping, stricken or dying, a woman will stop to ensnare the heart of a man. ... Verily, one may say of womanhood: it is wholly a snare of [the Tempter,] Mara.

(Sponberg 1992, 20)

On the one hand, the Buddha is cautioning against desire and attachment and thereby underlining his teachings on the five *skandhas* – that what we consider to be our "self," including the form (*rūpa*) in which we find ourselves embodied in this lifetime, is not permanent and so ought not to be an object of attachment. On the other hand, the passage goes beyond saying that monks should not be attached to the form of women to imply that woman's form itself is evil – that there is something inferior, perhaps inherently bad, about women's bodies. The image of woman as a temptress entrapping men is nefarious. The claims about the form of woman, her *rūpa*, quickly give way to generalizations about what it is to *be* a woman: posing a threat to man no matter what she is doing: sitting or lying down, laughing, talking or singing, weeping, and so on. As Alan Sponberg points out:

> Although the early Mahayana reaffirmed the basic principle of soteriological inclusiveness with its universalization of the bodhisattva path, a religious ideal it held open to all – men and women, monastic and lay – this rejection of institutional androcentrism did not entail a corresponding rejection of ascetic misogyny.
>
> *(Sponberg 1992, 21)*

Sponberg goes on to cite several examples from the Mahāyāna *Maharatnakata* which express the view that: "Women can ruin the precepts of purity"; women are more detestable than the dead dog or snake; "Because of them one falls into evil ways. There is no refuge"; and so on (Sponberg 1992, 21–22). This shifts somewhat, however, as the Mahāyāna concept of emptiness develops. According to Sponberg,

> in their attempt to reaffirm the early principle of soteriological inclusiveness some factions of the Mahayana were inspired to develop that original principle toward a much more actively egalitarian view, an affirmation of nondualistic androgyny, which had strong roots in the newly emerging Mahayana philosophy of emptiness.
>
> *(Sponberg 1992, 24)*

Take, for example, the *Vimalakīrti Sūtra*. After Sariputra asks an enlightened goddess living in the house to change out of her female state (form) and into a male state, assuming any woman would naturally want to do so if she could, we read:

> "For the past twelve years I have been trying to take on female form, but in the end with no success. What is there to change? If a sorcerer were to conjure up a phantom woman and then someone asked her why she didn't change out of her female body, would that be any kind of reasonable question?"
>
> "No," said Shariputra. "Phantoms have no fixed form, so what would there be to change?"
>
> The goddess said, "All things are just the same – they have no fixed form. So why ask why I don't change out of my female form?"

At that time the goddess employed her supernatural powers to change Shariputra into a goddess like herself, while she took on Shariputra's form. Then she asked, "Why don't you change out of this female body?"

Shariputra, now in the form of a goddess, replied, "I don't know why I have suddenly changed and taken on a female body!" The goddess said, "Shariputra, if you can change out of this female body, then all women can change likewise. Shariputra, who is not a woman, appears in a woman's body. And the same is true of all women – though they appear in women's bodies, they are not women. Therefore the Buddha teaches that all phenomena are neither male nor female."

Then the goddess withdrew her supernatural powers, and Shariputra returned to his original form. The goddess said to Shariputra, "Where now is the form and shape of your female body?"

Shariputra said, "The form and shape of my female body does not exist, yet does not not exist."

The goddess said, "All things are just like that – they do not exist, yet do not not exist. And that they do not exist, yet do not not exist, is exactly what the Buddha teaches."

(Watson 1997, 90–91)

We notice here that the goddess refuses to transform herself into a male body because all forms are ultimately empty, so there is no "female body." The goddess mocks Sariputra for clinging to form. Whether one is in a female or male body is immaterial, as she so deftly illustrates by switching bodies with him. The goddess has no need to embody a male form to demonstrate her enlightened state. Our outward embodiments are impermanent and empty – from the perspective of an enlightened being, one's form is immaterial so focusing on the supposed necessity of being embodied in male form to be enlightened is, as she so effectively demonstrates here, nonsense.

Jump ahead several centuries and we see the effect of this emphasis on emptiness regarding attitudes toward women in the work of medieval Japanese philosopher Dōgen.

Dōgen's Feminism

While at first glance it may seem odd to draw on a thirteenth-century Zen master to promote the aims of contemporary feminism, Dōgen's views about women, as I have urged elsewhere, are feminist.[3] He does not think that by virtue of being women, women are any less capable of attaining enlightenment than men. Nor does he think that women's bodies are the cause of the downfall of monks on the path to enlightenment, or are inherently impure or evil. In contrast to the "Eight *Garudhammas*" or eight heavy rules – the special rules the Buddha put in place when he established the female monastic order which say that when monks and nuns are together, monks are always above nuns – Dōgen writes:

> If you encounter someone who maintains the great dharma, having received the acknowledgment – "You have attained my marrow" – whether the person is a pillar or a lantern, a buddha, wild fox, demon, man or woman, you should keep your body and mind on the zazen seat and attend to the person even for immeasurable eons.
>
> *(Dōgen 2010, 73)*

Anyone who clings blindly to rules and regulations – even those attributed to the Buddha – does not, according to Dōgen, truly understand the Buddha way. He admonishes them, calling them "foolish people [who] have neither seen nor heard the buddha way" (Dōgen 2010, 74). Further challenging the notion that the most junior monk is senior to the most senior nun, he says:

> It is an excellent custom of study that when a nun has attained the way, attained dharma, and started to teach, monks who seek dharma and study join her assembly, bow to her, and ask about the way. It is just like finding water at the time of thirst.
>
> *(Dōgen 2010, 74)*

Rather than treat nuns as inferior Dōgen says monks seeking enlightenment should acknowledge and learn from teachers regardless of their gender. If a nun has attained enlightenment, she ought to be bowed down to – the physical form of a teacher in no way diminishes their knowledge of the dharma. Dōgen is unequivocal in his belief that what is important is the understanding of the dharma, not gender. Later, alluding to the *Lotus Sūtra* in which a half-dragon/half-girl who is seven years old attains enlightenment, he says:

> Even seven-year-old girls who practice buddha dharma and express buddha dharma are guiding teachers of the four types of disciples [monks, nuns, laymen and laywomen]; they are compassionate parents of sentient beings.
>
> *(Dōgen 2010, 77–78)*

Another powerful expression of Dōgen's feminism in *Shōbōgenzō* could easily be read as a commentary on the contemporary objectification of women. As if in response to the view of women expressed in early Buddhist scripture, and prevalent in the Japan of his time, he says bluntly and unequivocally: "Those who are extremely stupid think that women are merely the objects of sexual desire and treat women in this way. The Buddha's children should not be like this" (Dōgen 2010, 79).

Dōgen also challenges the belief that women need to be embodied as men before they can attain enlightenment. He says:

> [T]hose who are called laity in Song China are people who have not left their households. Some of them are married and have their abodes. Others are celibate but may still have much worldly concern. However, monks with cloud robes and mist sleeves visit laypeople who have clarified dharma, bow to them, and inquire about the way, just as they do to masters who have left their households. They should also do so to accomplished women and even to animals.
> *(Dōgen 2010, 77)*

Dōgen makes it clear that women are fully capable not only of attaining enlightenment as women, but also of being dharma teachers of monks, whether or not they have chosen the monastic path.

In "Twining Vines," discussing the transmission from Bodhidharma, the first Patriarch of Zen, to his students – one of whom was the nun Zongchi – Dōgen again disputes the notion that women's bodies are in themselves impure or in need of transformation in order to be enlightened. He first states:

> Investigate these words of Bodhidharma: *You have attained my skin... flesh...bones...marrow.* These are the ancestor's words. All four students had attainment and understanding. Each one's attainment and understanding is skin, flesh, bones, and marrow leaping out of body and mind; skin, flesh, bones and marrow dropping away body and mind. Do not see or hear the ancestor with a limited understanding of these statements.
> *(Dōgen 2010, 480)*

Dōgen puts all of Bodhidharma's students on the same level – including Zongchi to whom Bodhidharma said "You have my flesh" – admonishing those who think that "skin and flesh are not as close as bones and marrow" (Dōgen 2010, 480). He has no time for those critics who claimed that the transmission that Zongchi received was somehow lesser than that received by Bodhidharma's other students. For him, Zongchi is on the same level as the other three male disciples.

Given the ways in which women's bodies were viewed in Buddhism, Dōgen's remarks are especially significant. He insists Zongchi's body is not an impediment to her enlightenment, not a barrier to her understanding. Nor was it necessary for her to transform into a man physically or psychologically in order to be enlightened – even though, as we know, Dōgen views the body as an integral part of practice-enlightenment: "Reflect that the teaching of the oneness of body and mind is always being expounded in the buddha dharma" (Dōgen 2010, 15). When Bodhidharma says to Zongchi "You have my flesh" it is especially significant since it implies her flesh is Bodhidharma's flesh. In her embodied female form, in *her* very body, to paraphrase Hakuin, she had Bodhidharma's flesh, she was a buddha.[4] For Bodhidharma, and for Dōgen, the body of a woman on the path was in no way tainted. It was equally capable of enlightenment without having to erase its difference as a woman.

As Watsuji Tetsurō explains it in *Purifying Zen: Shamōn Dōgen*, "To reject women's salvation is to throw away half of humanity. This cannot be called compassion" (Tetsurō 2011, 87); and "All people deserve to be treated equally because all of them can take this body-mind, which is no different from rice or flax or bamboo or bulrushes, and make it a receptacle of the Dharma" (Tetsurō 2011, 88).

Nondualism

Dōgen's teachings about women are representative of his radical nondualism – Zen's "not one, not two." Ultimately in Zen, both body and mind drop off, and the enlightened being is said to be beyond gender. However, Zen's nonduality means that one's gender does not simply get discarded. As Taigen Dan Leighton explains:

> Dōgen's nonduality is not about transcending the duality of form and emptiness. This deeper nonduality is not the opposite of duality, but the synthesis of duality and nonduality, with both included, and both seen as ultimately not separate, but as integrated.
>
> *(Leighton 2004, 35)*

The "with both included" is particularly of interest for feminist philosophy. Too often, woman's subjectivity is subsumed by man's subjectivity in the guise of oneness or universality, and difference gets left out entirely. By contrast, the nonduality we find in Dōgen and Zen holds open a space for difference, without falling prey to the harmful dualisms that place one gender (or race, or class, or sexuality) in a position of power or privilege over another. Iris Marion Young describes the harm dualistic thinking can do as follows: "the 'feminine' signifies a relational position in a dichotomy, masculine/feminine, where the first is more highly valued than the second, and where the second is partly defined as a lack with respect to the first" (Young 2005, 5). Here Young echoes Simone de Beauvoir's contention that woman as subject is a lack, defined only as "not man."[5] Young explains that

> [this] dichotomy lines up with others that have a homologous, hierarchical logic, such as mind/body, reason/passion, public/private, hard science/soft science, and dozens of other value laden dichotomies whose

discursive application has practical effects in personal lives, workplaces, media imagery, and politics, to name only a few social fields.

(Young 2005, 5)

We have already seen how this hierarchical logic affected women in Buddhism – especially in its early phases – and how Dōgen's Zen rejects this hierarchical logic. To illustrate what revalorization through a comparative feminist philosophical lens looks like, we now turn to one of the most pervasive images in Buddhism – that of maternal imagery, with a focus on the maternal body.

Revalorizing the Maternal Body

It is a puzzling contradiction that the same female body identified in early scripture as impure, disgusting, vile, and a burden to be overcome, is also what makes one of the most pervasive symbols of enlightenment in Buddhism possible – the maternal body. As Reiko Ohnuma points out in her book *Ties That Bind: Maternal Imagery and Discourse in Indian Buddhism*:

> Symbolically, motherhood was a double-edged sword, sometimes extolled as the most appropriate symbol for buddhahood itself, and sometimes denigrated as the most paradigmatic manifestation possible of the attachment to the world that keeps all benighted beings trapped within the realm of rebirth. Motherhood was a lightning rod, a privileged symbol used in an iconic fashion to stand for both the best and the worst.
>
> *(Ohnuma 2012, 5)*

Early Mahāyāna introduces the *Tathāgatagarbha* or Buddha womb teaching. (*Tathagata* means the enlightened one, or the thus come one, and *garbha* is Sanskrit for womb). As Leighton explains it:

> According to the *Śrīmālā Sutra*, … this womb of buddhas is the basis, support, and foundation of the world of samsara, the conditioned realm of suffering… The whole world is depicted as a womb, nurturing the development and emergence of new buddhas, but this imagery is also reversed in Tathagatagarbha theory inasmuch as *garbha* can mean both womb and embryo. So the awakening buddha is also like a womb giving birth to the awakened land of a buddha field, the realm of environment constellated simultaneously with a buddha's awakening.
>
> *(Leighton 2007, 16)*

In the excerpt below, for example, woman's body is the metaphor for the ideal for bodhisattvas – as the place in which the "world's light of saving grace" is found:

> "I see with my Buddha eye
> That in the bodies of all beings
> There lies concealed the buddhagarbha…"
>
> "I see that all kinds of beings
> Have a buddhagarbha hidden by kleśas."
>
> "I see that all beings
> Are like infants in distress.
> Within their bodies is the tathāgatagarbha,
> But they do not realize it.
> So I tell bodhisattvas,
> 'Be careful not to consider yourselves inferior.
> Your bodies are tathāgatagarbhas;
> They always contain
> The light of the world's salvation.'"
>
> *(Grosnick 1995, 96–101)*

The *womb* of the Buddha is within every body, in fact *is* every body, the sutra tells us. Notice it is not the seed, not the sperm, as we might expect of a tradition with patriarchal tendencies, but the *womb*. The whole of this lengthy sutra, directed to male monastics, is focused on something that is unique to women's embodiment. For it is by virtue of containing the "womb of the buddhas" that bodies themselves contain "the world's light of saving grace." True, this view is hard to square with calling the vagina, the pathway to the womb, "the mouth of poisonous black snakes" or "charcoal pits of blazing fire," but if we read the passage above through contemporary lenses we begin to see how we might revalorize it and use it to support and advance feminism in the tradition.

Leighton writes:

> The buddha womb is the container of potential buddhas and is endowed with the capacity to give birth to buddhas. Similarly, the world of a spiritual text is a womb that can give birth, through the agency of interpretation, to a multiplicity of awakening and healing meanings. So one can see sutras themselves as wombs of buddha, available to give birth to awakening teachings and insights. And in the other direction, in accord with the reversible meaning of garb as both womb and embryo, awakened interpretation can thus create (or re-create) the sutra as an awakening buddha field.
>
> *(Leighton 2007, 17)*

Either way – garbha as womb or embryo – it is *only* woman's body that makes this metaphor possible.

Bringing feminist philosophy into the conversation as we have done here, revalorizing the texts, recovering women's bodies to see them also as sources of enlightenment is one among the multiplicity of "awakening and healing meanings" that can emerge from texts such as these. Yet, we must proceed with caution. As Laura Green observes, feminist philosophers who wish to revalorize the maternal body this way face a dilemma:

> The question seems to be one of conceptual comportment: what would it mean, philosophically, to take the female embodied self – particularly in its capacity for birthing as norm – whilst at the same time resisting any claim to "authenticity"? Furthermore, how might this be achieved without turning "woman" into a utopian, sentimentalized and abstract category, and one which is somehow also "unknowable"?
>
> *(Green 2011, 145)*

This, in fact, is what seems to have happened in the Buddhist tradition. Once the maternal body is deliberately disconnected from real women and their experience, it is turned into an abstract category for men – almost something mysterious, rather than being a source of valorization for women. For example, in the *Tathāgatagarbha Sutra* cited above, we also find this passage:

> "It is like an impoverished woman
> Whose appearance is common and vile,
> But who bears a son of noble degree
> Who will become a universal monarch.
> Replete with seven treasures and all virtues,
> He will possess as king the four quarters of the earth.
> But she is incapable of knowing this
> And conceives only thoughts of inferiority."
>
> *(Grosnick 1995, 101)*

The suggestion here is that despite the fact that the woman grew the king, carried and nourished him in her body for nine months, she remains inferior, indeed an ignorant vessel. Her value and capability is dismissed and she is common, vile, and ignorant, as though she had nothing to do with bringing him into the world.

Bringing a feminist philosophical perspective into conversation with Buddhist philosophy, particularly its nondualism, opens a way forward to not get stuck in any one conceptualization of feminine or masculine, as Dōgen urges, but to still acknowledge difference and the lived experience of being in differently sexed bodies. This can ensure that we neither end up essentializing women, or making women so abstract and universal that the concept becomes mysterious and unknowable. As noted, Dōgen's nondualism is a helpful starting point. Re-reading the way maternity is characterized in this sutra and in other Buddhist texts allows us to extend our thinking, allowing us to conceive of the maternal as extending beyond the bearing of children. We can explore how woman might make or find meaning in this expanded, enlightened notion of maternity whether or not she actually bears children, and how this reimagined maternity might liberate or enlighten all sentient beings. By revalorizing this notion – recognizing that comments such as those in the sutra above, for example, are at least not telling the whole story, if not simply false, reintegrating women's voices into the tradition, and calling out the misogyny and patriarchy – *Tathāgatagarbha* becomes a metaphor that includes women and the creative maternal dimension rather than excluding them.

And where does this creative maternal dimension come from – what is it about women that can give birth? The womb. It needs to be empty, and it empties itself every month, in order to create life; sometimes it is closed, sometimes it is open – mostly, we can say, it is not quite closed and the womb is the source for all (human) beings in the world. Furthermore, it is a place where mother and child, self and other are intimately interconnected but at the same time where each maintains its difference. French philosopher Luce Irigaray writes about this alternative to dualistic subject–object relations as the "placental economy." In this model, "the mother's self and the other that is the embryo" manage to negotiate the space of the same (the maternal body) and the other (the embryo), the "difference between the 'self' [maternal body] and other [embryo] is…continually negotiated" (Irigaray 1993, 41). Drawing on the Buddhist concept of emptiness (*śūnyatā*), Japanese philosopher Nishida Kitaro's explanation of absolute nothingness sounds strikingly similar to the placental economy – a place wherein there is deep interdependence and yet difference is maintained. As Bret Davis explains it:

> The alterity of the other person is thus recognized not by way of penetrating laterally through the walls of the ego, but rather by way of passing through an opening in one's own depths. I paradoxically encounter the irreducible exteriority of the other person in the depths of myself; I discover that others are always already in me. This inclusion of alterity is not a reduction of the other to the self; to the contrary, it is an originary expropriation of the self. In its innermost depths the self is exposed to alterity, and so to know oneself is to be open to others.
> *(Davis 2014, 318–319)*

This space of nothingness, this space of wisdom, of *prajñā*, where the other is in me, can be symbolized as womb – its emptiness a place in which two come together as one without either subsuming the other. It is in this nothing, this emptiness, where we find the ground of all distinctions and at the same time discover the nonduality of self and other. As I read them, Irigaray and Nishida both conceptualize the kind of emptiness that Buddhism maintains is the source of all creation, the source of enlightenment, the *Tathāgatagarbha*.

In closing, I'd like to turn from texts to an image. I suggest that we read the *ensō*, the iconic Japanese Zen symbol of emptiness, as womb. The *ensō* is sometimes closed, sometimes open, source of life and creativity, and each one is unique. As John Daido Loori explains: "On the one hand it is just a circle painted with one brushstroke, in a single breath. On the other hand, it is the representation of the totality of the great void" (Loori 2007, xii). And it is that emptiness – of the womb, of the *ensō* – that is the source of all life and out of which *everything* is born. It is the source, we might say, of the maternal creative dimension which, if we bring feminist philosophy together with Buddhism, belongs to everyone.

If we bring together the image of the *ensō* with feminist philosophical thought and with the revalorizing of women's bodies and the maternal in Buddhism as I have suggested here, we can begin to revalorize women's bodies in the tradition in a way that is liberatory. Imagined this way, the maternal creative dimension of being, the *Tathāgatagarbha*, is inherent in all beings, and we honor its roots, its source in the female body rather than forgetting, denying, repressing,

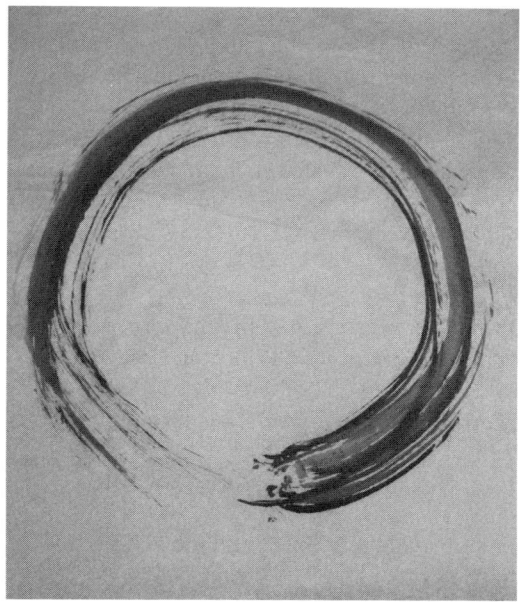

Erin McCarthy, *Ensō*, 2014.

or universalizing it out of existence. After this re-reading, this revalorizing, anyone can look at women's bodies and see a concrete exemplar worthy of emulation regardless of gender. At the same time, the female body becomes worthy of our esteem rather than disgust. And finally women can see in the *ensō* the source of the saving grace of all beings in themselves.

Notes

1 I am grateful to Paul Forster for comments on drafts of this chapter.
2 This chapter moves beyond my previous work on Dōgen and feminist philosophy by going further back in the Mahāyāna tradition (see McCarthy 2014).
3 See McCarthy (2014).
4 Interestingly, there is emerging evidence that Prajñatara, Bodhidharma's teacher, was actually a woman. In the Korean Zen tradition, it is claimed, this is well established, but it seems to have become lost during the transmission of Zen to China. See www.zenwomen.com/2010/04/prajnatara.html (accessed November 11, 2016).
5 For more on this see McCarthy (2012).

References

Davis, Bret. 2014. "Ethical and Religious Alterity: Nishida after Levinas." In *Kitarō Nishida in der Philosophie des 20. Jahrhunderts*, edited by Rolf Elberfeld and Yōko Arisaka, 313–341. Freiburg/Munich: Alber Verlag.
Dōgen. 2010. *The Treasury of the True Dharma Eye: Zen Master Dōgen's Shōbōgenzō*, edited and translated by Kazuaki Tanahashi. Boston and London: Shambhala.
Green, Laura. 2011. "A 'Fleshy Metaphysics': Irigaray and Battersby on Female Subjectivity." *Women: A Cultural Review* 22(2–3): 143–154. doi:10.1080/095740 42.2011.561115
Grosnick, William H. 1995. "The *Tathāgatagarbha Sutra*." In *Buddhism in Practice*, edited by Donald Lopez, 92–106. Princeton: Princeton University Press.
Gross, Rita. 1993. *Buddhism After Patriarchy: A Feminist History, Analysis, and Reconstruction of Buddhism*. Albany: SUNY Press.
Irigaray, Luce. 1993. *je, tu, nous: Toward a Culture of Difference*. New York: Routledge.
Leighton, Taigen Dan. 2004. "Dōgen's Cosmology of Space and the Practice of Self-Fulfillment." *Pacific World* 6: 27–43.
Leighton, Taigen Dan. 2007. *Visions of Awakening Space and Time: Dōgen and the Lotus Sutra*. Oxford: Oxford University Press.

Levering, Miriam. 1997. "Stories of Enlightened Women in Ch'an and the Chinese Buddhist Female Bodhisattva/Goddess Tradition." In *Women and Goddess Traditions: In Antiquity and Today*, edited by Karen L. King, 137–176. Minneapolis: Fortress Press.

Loori, John Daido. 2007. Foreword to Audrey Yoshiko Seo, *Ensō: Zen Circles of Enlightenment*. Boulder: Shambhala.

McCarthy, Erin. 2012. "From Beauvoir to Irigaray: Making Meaning out of Maternity." In *Beauvoir and Western Thought from Plato to Butler*, edited by Shannon Mussett and William Wilkerson. Albany: SUNY Press.

McCarthy, Erin. 2014. "A Zen Master Meets Contemporary Feminism: Reading Dōgen as a Resource for Feminist Philosophy." In *Buddhist Responses to Globalization*, edited by Leah Kalmanson and James Mark Shields. Lanham: Lexington Books.

Ohnuma, Reiko. 2012. *Ties That Bind: Maternal Imagery and Discourse in Indian Buddhism*. New York: Oxford University Press.

Paul, Diana. 1981. "Buddhist Attitudes Toward Women's Bodies." *Buddhist and Christian Studies* 1: 63–71.

Sponberg, Alan. 1992. "Attitudes Toward Women and the Feminine in Early Buddhism." In *Buddhism, Sexuality and Gender*, edited by Josâe Ignacio Cabezâon, 3–36. Albany: SUNY Press.

Tetsurō, Watsuji. 2011. *Purifying Zen: Watsuji Tetsurō's Shamōn Dōgen*, translated by Steve Bein. Honolulu: University of Hawaii Press.

Watson, Burton, trans. 1997. *The Vimalakirti Sutra*. New York: Columbia University Press.

Young, Iris Marion. 2005. *On Female Body Experience: Throwing Like a Girl and Other Essays*. Oxford: Oxford University Press.

11

Buddhist Modernism and Kant on Enlightenment
David Cummiskey

Some claim that the European Enlightenment, with its emphasis on the triumph of reason over religious authority, and the Buddhist concept of enlightenment, as a transformative awakening, have nothing in common – indeed I have been told that "it is a mere coincidence that they share a similar sounding word"; that asking how they are related is nothing but a "conceptual confusion," an equivocation that is on a par with confusing the bank of a river with a bank for cash deposits.[1]

Of course, the two historical traditions are indeed different in countless ways. The European Enlightenment was rooted in the acceptance of the new scientific method, the industrial revolution, the emergence of politically powerful merchant classes, the resulting disruption of established social hierarchies, factional religious disputes, and bloody religious wars. For complex socio-cultural reasons, and philosophical reasons too, a skepticism and rejection of religious authority and traditional hierarchies became increasingly widespread. The enlightenment instead emphasized relying on one's own judgment and this fueled the nascent and emerging republican sentiments for representative government.

In contrast, Buddhism began over 2,000 years ago as a monastic tradition focused on the ultimate goal of achieving nirvana, which is understood to be a release from samsara, that is, the otherwise endless cycle of suffering and rebirth. From its humble beginnings, Buddhism spread and diversified into one of the major world religions with perhaps 500 million people across the globe identifying as Buddhist. Indeed, there are a vast diversity of Buddhist religious sects, and each has its own favorite doctrines and texts, traditions and rituals.

Unlike the European Enlightenment, the objection might continue, Buddhism is a sectarian religion, not a scientific and secular rejection of religious authority. The practice of Buddhism involves superstitions, folk rituals, prayer, and worship of buddhas and bodhisattvas all of which contrasts with the rationalism of the European Enlightenment. In addition, the monastic pursuit of personal

Buddhist Philosophy: A Comparative Approach, First Edition. Edited by Steven M. Emmanuel.
© 2018 John Wiley & Sons, Inc. Published 2018 by John Wiley & Sons, Inc.

enlightenment is clearly distinct from the emphasis on the socio-cultural and historic shift from religious authority to the dominance of science and reason that is central to the Enlightenment.

This is all true. Nonetheless, one of the many contemporary offshoots of the early Buddhist teachings is the contemporary tradition of Engaged Buddhism and Buddhist Modernism (which is explained below); and it is this offshoot and version of Buddhism that is most familiar and popular in the West. In Europe or America, when a colleague or student asks about the *relationship between European and Buddhist enlightenment*, they are (most likely) asking about Buddhist Modernism, and not monastic Buddhism and the early Buddhist teachings. Clearly, they are not asking about the Buddhist doctrine of rebirth or nirvana as the escape from the twelvefold chain of dependent origination, or the monastic code of conduct, and they are also not asking about the practice of Buddhism as a living religion that shapes local cultural practices.

In contrast to the many Buddhist religious and cultural traditions, when it comes to the contemporary Modernist, Engaged-Buddhist conception of enlightenment and the European enlightenment, especially Kant's conception of *enlightenment*, we will see that these two traditions do have much in common. The clear mistake is instead thinking that the two traditions simply share a similar sounding word (by an accident of translation) and shared metaphors of "light" and "awakening."

What is Buddhist Modernism?

Buddhist Modernism is the most common and familiar form that Buddhism takes in the West. It is a mistake, however, to call the Buddhist Modernist tradition "Western Buddhism" (McMahan 2008). First, Buddhists throughout Asia also embrace this Modern form of Buddhism, and second, the leading figures of Buddhist Modernism are not Europeans – consider, for example, that three of the most influential figures in "Western Buddhism" are the Dalai Lama (1999, 2005), Thich Nhat Hanh (1998, 2016), and Chogyam Trungpa (1973, 1984, 1991). In addition, when people learn about Buddhism and ask how it is related to the Enlightenment, they are not confused by the use of the same word; they are especially struck by the similarity between Buddhist philosophy and Western non-religious traditions like *secular humanism*. This cross-cultural similarity is both *historical and doctrinal*. Buddhist Modernism is itself, *in part*, a product of the engagement between Buddhism and the European Enlightenment; for a systematic account of the history, see David McMahan's *The Making of Buddhist Modernism* (2008). Nonetheless, it is also doctrinal; the elements of Buddhist Modernism (which are outlined below) have deep textual and historical roots in the early teachings, Theravada, and Mahayana traditions. Buddhist Modernism highlights and emphasizes some Buddhist doctrines and themes, reinterprets others, and minimizes or ignores others. This is unavoidable. As the Zen philosopher Dōgen teaches (Dōgen 2012), "Whenever one side is illuminated, the other side is darkened" (Edelglass and Garfield 2009, 256). Buddhist Modernism illuminates (and darkens) distinctive aspects of the Buddhist canon. All forms of Buddhism have taken particular shapes that respond to the local cultures. All of the current sects of Buddhism have also developed their distinctive doctrines in response to other cultures and traditions. Chinese, Japanese, Thai, Tibetan, and all other Buddhisms include an intercultural fusion of Buddhism with other traditions. Although Buddhist Modernism is *in part* a product of engagement with the West, it is also clearly Buddhist nonetheless.

One more point of clarification. Buddhist Modernism is not itself supposed to be a Buddhist sect or tradition. It is instead a broad and overarching analytical category that is useful in distinguishing different contemporary strands of Buddhism. As a particular example, Engaged Buddhism is a paradigmatic Buddhist Modernist approach (Queen 2000). Another specific example of Buddhist Modernism is the explicit modernizing of Thai Buddhism that started under King Chulalongkorn. The cosmopolitan and democratic turn in Tibetan Buddhism under the Dalai Lama, which has surely been influenced by his exile, is another clear example. The historical interaction between the European West and Buddhist cultures is a complex and interesting story of mutual influence and integration (McMahan 2008). Our focus, however, is instead on the core philosophical elements of Buddhist Modernism.

Buddhist Modernism has the following six features:

1) *Meditation and mindfulness are the central focus of Engaged Buddhism and Buddhist Modernism.* Unlike Modernism, Buddhism as a living religion is more focused on rituals and worship, and on actions that contribute to good rebirth. Buddhist cultural traditions also emphasize and rely on the life and the past lives of the Buddha (as recounted in the Jataka tales) as a source of moral guidance and wisdom. Although in Buddhist cultures, some lay-Buddhists do practice meditation, meditation is not a common lay-practice and is instead associated with a more committed monastic practice.

   In contrast, for Engaged Buddhists, meditation and mindfulness are the major focus of daily Buddhist practice, and mindfulness is meant to permeate all aspects of one's daily life and work. For Buddhist Modernists, meditation, mindfulness, and non-violence are the heart and soul of Buddhism. This is a significant difference from the traditional more monastic focus of Buddhism. For early Buddhism, the community of monks, the Sangha, constitutes the core of the Buddhist community, and a layperson gains merit and good karma by supporting the community of monks (and through wholesome action). For many Engaged Buddhists, the concept of the Sangha is expanded from the community of monks to include all self-identified and practicing Buddhists.

As a distinct but related part of this reorientation, both Thich Nhat Hanh and Chogyam Trungpa explicitly emphasize the Third Noble Truth, instead of the First Noble Truth. The First Noble Truth is the truth of the unavoidability of suffering, unease, and dissatisfaction. The Third Noble Truth is the possibility of the release from suffering, the end of delusion and craving that results from an awakened mind. According to early Buddhist teaching, dependent origination is essentially related to the impermanence of all things and it is thus the source of suffering (and holds us in the cycle of rebirth). For Engaged and Modernist Buddhists, the more important point is that suffering results from the primal confusion of self/other (subject/object dichotomy), and its related egocentrism, and the solution to suffering is a cognitive and emotional recognition and internalization of dependent origination and our interdependence. Greater mindfulness, achieved through increased wisdom and insight meditation, is the essence and nature of awakening. The Dalai Lama (1999) also advocates for a "spiritual revolution" and shift in our consciousness (our heart-mind) that follows from the recognition of our webs of interconnection and common humanity, which he argues leads to boundless compassion. Recognizing the truth of dependent origination, he tells us, ends anger, greed, and delusion, and thereby calms our minds and generates a profound inner peace. In short, meditation and mindfulness are the means to a more enlightened, peaceful, and contented existence.

2) *Buddhist Modernists emphasize Buddhist moral psychology and the Inner Science of the Mind, which includes a highly developed (empirical) science of cognition and emotion.* Even the earliest Buddhist teachings include a complex moral psychology and cognitive science. Buddhaghosa in particular developed an elaborate account of intention and of the complex interrelationship between different mental states (Buddhaghosa 2003; Heim 2013). Buddhism also anticipates the recent scientific insights into the embodied nature of cognition, the fractured and multiple processing systems of the brain/mind, and the cognitive theory of the emotions (Dalai Lama 2005). These scientific principles provide the empirical and verifiable basis for the above claims about the benefits of meditation and the nature of the will and consciousness (Varela, Thompson, and Rosch 1991; Davis and Thompson 2014). The conception of embodied cognition is an offshoot of early Buddhist philosophy and a corollary of the Buddhist theory of the self as constituted by the five *skandhas* (aggregates or bundles), which are physical body, feeling/sensation, perception, volition/emotion, and conscious awareness. Early Buddhist teachings argue, via introspection and insight meditation, first, that there is no core self that survives or unifies the flow of mental states that constitute our mental and bodily existence, and second,

that there is no unified center of will or executive control that might constitute our true self (Siderits 2007, 32–69). Instead the self is a "convenient designator" for the changing and transient coalition of mental aggregates that shapes action and experience. One of the major points and transformative aspects of Buddhist meditation is developing and internalizing these insights into the nature of the self. These insights in turn alter one's fundamental moral orientation and experience of the world. This aspect of Buddhist doctrine is important in our discussion below of Buddhist and Kantian enlightenment.

3) *Buddhist Modernism emphasizes Buddhism as philosophy.* Philosophical reflection and insight is at the core of Buddhism from the start, but it is not always a focus of Buddhist religious and cultural traditions. The early Pāli Canon was divided into three baskets, the Tripitaka. The three baskets are the Sutras, which are closest to scriptures, the Vinaya, which is the Monastic Code of Discipline, and the Abhidharma, which is the philosophical texts and commentary on the dharma and the Buddha's teachings. Not surprisingly, the lay-practice of Buddhism as a religion focuses on the Sutras, and largely ignores the philosophical analysis of the dharma. And, of course, the Sutras and Vinaya Code are at the core of monastic Buddhism. The attention to the Abhidharma is more varied and less central to religious practice and ritual. The monastic community preserves Buddhist philosophy but it is more difficult and abstract and thus less definitive of Buddhism as lived religion.

The Pāli Tripitaka was first recorded and maintained at the Aluvihara Rock Temple in Sri Lanka. When I visited Aluvihara and asked the Abbot of the monastery about the Abhidharma, he waved his hands dismissively and said it is too confusing and not important and that I should focus on the Sutras. In contrast, however, Tibetan Buddhist monks are often philosophical scholars and the Dalai Lama has a commanding understanding of Tibetan Buddhist philosophy. In predominantly Buddhist countries, however, most lay-Buddhists and many monks do not study Buddhist philosophy or cognitive science. Western Buddhists are often surprised to discover that most lay-Buddhists do not practice meditation or care about Buddhist philosophy.

Nonetheless, at roughly the same time as Greek philosophy in the West, Buddhism launched one of the world's earliest and richest philosophical traditions. Buddhist philosophy includes epistemology, metaphysics, philosophy of language, logic, and especially theories of personal identity, cognition, and moral philosophy and a related moral psychology (see Siderits 2007; Garfield 2015). In short, Buddhist philosophy and cognitive science are central to Buddhism in general, but emphasized by Modernists in particular.

4) *Buddhist Modernists emphasize the "Four Immeasurables," which are the practice of loving-kindness, sympathetic joy, caring-compassion, and equanimity.* Although all Buddhist traditions also emphasize these virtues,

Buddhist Modernists place primary emphasis on the cultivation of virtue (and the correlative principle on not harming sentient creatures), and significantly less emphasis on moral rules and the precepts (including monastic practice and the Vinaya monastic moral code of conduct). Although they do not have a monastic focus, Buddhist Modernists may still participate in meditation workshops and longer Buddhist retreats (see PlumVillage.org, for example). The point and focus of these retreats is to be more awake, mindful, and enlightened when one returns to the routine daily life of work, community, and family. The goal is to be more compassionate as one continues as a full participant in one's community, family, and work.

5) *Buddhist Modernists also embrace democratic values and declarations of human rights.* So far, all of the distinctive elements that are emphasized by Buddhist Modernism are also found in Buddhism more generally. The nature and standing of rights is the exception to this claim. Classical Buddhism does not defend either democratic values or human rights. Indeed, it is widely agreed that Buddhist texts have no concept of individual human rights, understood as claim-rights or trumps that protect the individual from the demands of the common good (Keown, Prebish, and Husted 1998). Indeed, it is a common characteristic of all pre-modern cultures that they do not include justifications of human rights, especially universal rights to liberty and property. This is true of both Western and Buddhist cultures. Rights-based theories of justice are a modern and contemporary phenomenon. Traditional Buddhist cultures focus on role-based responsibilities and duties, and Buddhist ethics in particular is concerned with wholesome actions and opposed to unwholesome ones. Similarly, the contemporary focus on individual rights also emerged only recently in the West. For example, Aristotle did not develop a conception of universal human rights, but contemporary Aristotelian virtue ethicists all embrace human rights.

Nonetheless, the question of the place of rights in Buddhism is important *because* many believe that the recognition of universal human rights is a product of and the crowning jewel of the European Enlightenment.

Is there a foundation for human rights in Buddhist theory in particular? Or is it instead an *ad hoc* "Western" addition to Buddhism? I have argued elsewhere that the Buddhist conception of the self as constituted by a web of interdependent relationships is at odds with recent attempts to ground rights (and justice) on the distinctness and separateness of persons (Cummiskey 2010). Instead, a Buddhist conception of rights should recognize that human rights are instrumental means, but nonetheless usually an essential institutional means, which advance the Buddhist's ends of compassion and care for others (Garfield 2015). For Buddhism, compassion is conceptually prior to rights claims. In addition, the capacity to achieve enlightenment (wisdom and boundless compassion), and our common "Buddha-nature" (in some traditions), provides the basis of our equal moral standing and significance. In contrast, as we will discuss below, for Kant, autonomy is the basis for the dignity of humanity. This contrast, and important difference between Kant and Buddhism, will be explored more fully in the rest of the chapter.

It is nonetheless worth emphasizing that the Buddha rejected caste-based societies and embraced a more egalitarian moral ideal. This is especially true of the monastic community. When it comes to the background society and political philosophy, traditional Buddhism defends a conception of enlightened monarchy. In contrast, Buddhist Modernists almost universally embrace human rights, a vision of more mindful and compassionate politics, and democratic values. Although this is not our focus here, developing a contemporary, distinctly Buddhist political theory is an ongoing project of Buddhist Modernism (see Cummiskey 2014).

6) Finally, *and most importantly for our discussion of the nature of enlightenment, for Buddhist Modernism, the Buddhist teachings are a system of testable beliefs (and not based on appeal to authority and a leap of faith).* The Buddhist dharma, the teachings, forms a comprehensive philosophical doctrine rooted in arguments and empirical science. Modernists emphasize that the Buddha insisted that people should not accept his arguments and doctrines based on his authority alone, but rather that his followers should constantly test his teachings "as the wise would test gold by burning, cutting, and rubbing it (on a piece of touchstone), so you are to accept my teachings after examination and not merely out of regard for me" (from the Kalama Sutta).

This last teaching, which Kant echoes, is absolutely central to Buddhist Modernists. Unlike many Buddhist religious traditions, they insist that Buddhist doctrines must be based on independent verification and rigorous philosophical analysis. In categorically rejecting all dogma and all bald appeals to authority, Buddhist Modernists instead embrace Kant's deceptively simple "motto" of the European Enlightenment, "to have courage to use your own understanding." This is already a first and fundamental point of agreement, a shared European and Buddhist conception of enlightenment. Kant and Buddhists ask the question "What is enlightenment?" and both agree that it begins with the simple directive *to think for oneself.*

What is Enlightenment?

Let us explore this point of agreement more fully. Is this again a mere trivial similarity that hides a deeper and more fundamental disagreement? What more precisely are the points of similarity and difference between contemporary Buddhist conceptions of enlightenment and Kant's conception of enlightenment? Rather than focusing on the historical period known as the Enlightenment, the question is what is enlightenment.

For Kant, enlightenment involves first and foremost thinking for oneself, but that just shifts the question: what is involved in thinking for oneself? Kant argues, first, that passively letting others control what one is thinking is a form of *immaturity*. If others tell me what to think, and limit what I am allowed to think, then they stand above me like a parent to a child. When it comes to fundamental personal, moral, and religious questions, if I defer to another, it would seem that I take them to be more enlightened. If I am to think for myself about fundamental personal, moral, religious, and scientific questions, then I also must be permitted to decide what I think is plausible and believable and not have this determined by moral and religious authorities. *Religious freedom* is a necessary condition of enlightenment and it is thus also a political precondition for enlightenment. This is why the emergence of religious freedom and tolerance is central to the European Enlightenment period.

Is this sufficient? What is it to think for oneself? Is the goal nothing more than rejecting authority? Although freedom from the control of others, negative freedom, is necessary, if one's thinking is simply uncontrolled, then it is also random, lawless, and *ungoverned by reason*. As such it also lacks any legitimacy and authority. Kant thus concludes that in order to think for oneself, one must also follow the dictates of reason.

Maturity (and enlightenment) requires that one thinks for oneself, and (as Kant argues elsewhere) thinking imposes its own constraints and limits. For Kant, thinking for oneself does not involve thinking whatever one wants. Just as there is more to freedom of the will than simply following one's inclinations (for Kant), so too there is more to thinking for oneself than believing whatever one happens to want to believe. Indeed, Kant agrees with Rousseau's famous claim that "to be driven by appetite alone is slavery, and obedience to the law one has prescribed for oneself is liberty" (Rousseau 1762, bk. I, ch. VIII). For Kant, *thinking for oneself* essentially involves thinking and thus following the dictates of reason. Thinking is itself rule-governed, and thinking for oneself, as opposed to deferring to others, involves believing on the basis of rational norms and reasons. This is in one sense trivially true but it is nonetheless significant.

When it comes to morality, Kant insists that people have the capacity to set themselves ends and to act on principle, and that this is the source of our freedom and our value. When our desires and natural inclinations conflict with our aspirations and principles, they are actually a *hindrance to our freedom*. This is clearest when one is overcome by desire and acts against one's deeper goals or higher aspirations. If I eat compulsively or "lose" my temper, I am not in control, and I am not free. I cannot here adequately reconstruct Kant's argument from freedom to morality. Let us simply note that for Kant, thinking for oneself requires inner freedom and rejecting egoism (which he calls *the principle of self-love*). Reason has its own norms and these norms have their own inner authority. Neither our actions nor our beliefs should be subservient to our inclinations. For Kant, the mistake of all previous theories of morality was attempting to ground moral motivation on the person's contingent desires and inclinations. The idea that rational conduct is subservient to passions and desires undermines freedom and morality, Kant argues. The will is not limited to serve only as a tool of self-love. It instead is capable of a higher vocation that frees it from mere "heteronomy" and makes self-rule, autonomy, possible. Heteronomy of the will, that is, treating reason as the slave of self-love and the passions, is for Kant the primal confusion. Enlightenment includes and requires a transformation of one's orientation from self-love to recognition of and respect for our common humanity (for more, see Cummiskey 1996).

This conception of the inclinations, as hindrances to freedom and reason, is in many ways analogous to the Buddhist view that we need to free ourselves from our "afflictive emotions" (Dalai Lama 1999). The afflictive emotions include jealousy, anger, and hatred. These emotions systematically disrupt our judgment and disturb our inner calm; they make us less mindful and less perceptive; and they thus typically harm both oneself and others. For Buddhists, as for Kant, morality also involves overcoming the afflictive emotions and a transformation in one's motivational structure.

Transforming one's moral orientation is central to Buddhist practice. The point of insight meditation is to help one overcome *entrenched habits of mind* and develop greater awareness of oneself and others. More philosophically, the emotions of anger and selfishness are rooted in the *primal confusion* of the *subject–object duality*. More specifically, we take our particular standpoint to be ontologically significant – but it is not! And this primal confusion is thus also the root of egoism, attachment, and selfishness. This is also referred to by Buddhists as *twofold self-grasping*: First, one spontaneously takes the perspective of "I" as a *privileged subject*, and second, one thus sees *everything else as situated in relation to oneself* (Garfield 2015).

In order to overcome this deeply engrained perspective on the world, one must engage in both *philosophical reflection* and *meditation*, which is meant both to enable and to internalize philosophical insights. One must also change and *discipline one's actions*. In short, increased enlightenment requires increased wisdom, moral restraint, and meditation. (These are the three parts of the Noble Eightfold Path.) The goal, however, is not just better behavior. The goal is a fundamental *phenomenological* transformation that leads to a new way of seeing and responding in the world.

This Buddhist conception of moral development is characteristic of Buddhist Modernism (see, e.g., Thich Nhat Hanh 1988) but it is also thoroughly based in Nāgārjuna's philosophy (150–250 CE; Nāgārjuna 1995) and Śāntideva's classic work *Bodhicaryāvatāra: A Guide to the Bodhisattva Way of Life: How to Live an Awakened Life* (685 CE and see Garfield 2015, ch. 9). The Buddhist focus on transformation, transcendence, and awakening one's mind is precisely what seems to many to make it so different from the European Age of Enlightenment, which was a socio-cultural transformation of society. However, this distinction is misleading. What distinguishes the "Age of Enlightenment" is the focus on individual enlightenment. The study of European history focuses on the sociological, cultural, and political changes, but the defining feature of the age is the focus on the capacity of each citizen to take charge and responsibility for their own life and to decide fundamental religious and moral questions using their own reason. This brings us back to Kant's definitive and influential essay, "An Answer to the Question: What is Enlightenment?" (Kant 1784).

To further explore Kant's answer and its commonality with the Buddhist Modernist conception of the awakened mind, we turn to Kant's views on *Education* (Kant 1960). It is here that Kant sketches the precondition necessary for enlightenment (which Buddhists would characterize using their concept of dependent origination). Kant's *moral anthropology* is too often neglected, to the detriment of Kant studies. *Kant's Impure Ethics: From Rational Beings to Human Beings* by Robert Louden (2000) provides the most sustained and philosophically richest discussion of Kant's understanding of human nature, socialization, and moral development. Kant follows Rousseau in taking seriously the importance of the philosophy of education and arguing that right education is essential to moral development. Indeed for Kant, education is *uniquely essential* for humans, because human beings need to develop through four stages of development: humans must be *disciplined, cultivated, civilized, and moralized*.

Briefly, the first stage of education is *discipline* and this begins with training and reinforcing behaviors in infants and small children. This first stage is often ignored but it is clearly the first step in socialization and a precursor of moral development. The next stage is *cultivation*, which involves developing and perfecting skills. Through the cultivation of skills, we further develop a disciplined mind and character that is now also informed by instrumental reason; and in this way, Kant argues, we are reshaping our untutored nature to advance an end. The capacity to take the necessary means to our ends is constitutive of practical reason. Through discipline and cultivation, we develop our nascent will and thus the capacity to take the necessary and indispensable means to advance our ends. This is Kant's formulation of the "hypothetical imperative." A mature person also has the capacity to choose and endorse ends, but one must first learn the basic self-control to pursue an end over time and in light of adversity. The cultivation of skills must next be complemented by what Kant calls "*civilization*" – for Kant to be civilized is to *prudently develop the responses and behaviors that are agreeable to others*. For Kant, *prudence and good manners* are two sides of the same coin. Notice that *being civilized is essentially social*. It involves not simply the maturity of the individual but also the development of the "species" (or at least the narrower community with which one interacts). Civilization is thus a social accomplishment of many individuals acting in concert and harmony.

The hardest step for individuals and humankind, Kant argues, is the transition from being civilized to being "*moralized*" – which parallels the transition in Kant's practical philosophy from *prudence and self-love* to *ethics and morality*. For Kant, the full maturity of the human race, the shedding of our self-imposed immaturity, and the actualization of our capacity for autonomy are all one and the same, and they constitute enlightenment. The maturity of the human race, its enlightenment, requires a fundamental transformation in orientation. The enlightened person rejects the principle of self-love and embraces and internalizes the authority of morality.

In both his writings on the doctrine of virtue and his writings on educating the whole person, Kant is explicit that the transition from being civilized to being moralized involves *a transformative reorientation of the self*. At its core, the transformation involves an inner "disposition" to choose ends. This transformation requires (what the Dalai Lama calls) an inner "spiritual revolution" (which is not a religious conversion). Kant writes: "The most difficult condition of the human race is the crossing-over from civilization to moralization."

What does this involve? Kant writes that the human being "should acquire the disposition to choose nothing but good ends. Good ends are those which are necessarily approved by everyone and can simultaneously be ends of everyone" (quoted by Louden 2000, 42). We see here that Kant's famous categorical imperative is not a sterile rule for testing maxims. It must instead become a settled disposition that shapes one's consciousness.

The crucial concept here is that of a *disposition*, and as Louden explains, a disposition for Kant is not a mere habit. It is "a mechanism by way of sense" and as such it is more than just a way of thinking; it is a way of seeing and being in the world. It involves nothing less than a person's basic orientation to life (Louden 2000, 42). The phenomenological transformation of how the enlightened person experiences the world is analogous to the account of the awakened mind that we find in Śāntideva (685 CE), and the account of moral phenomenology echoed in Jay Garfield's compelling reconstruction of Śāntideva (Garfield 2015, ch. 9). Barbara Herman explains that Kant's categorical imperative does not provide a decision procedure for actions, but instead provides "rules of moral salience" that enable us to immediately recognize and respond to the morally salient features of a deliberative field (Herman 1993).

The Kantian vs. Scottish Enlightenment

But wait, one might object, Kantian ethics is based on *the priority of the individual and the significance of the autonomous agent*! This is fundamentally at odds with Buddhist conceptions of *interdependence, dependent origination, and rejection of the autonomous self*.

In response, first, this is an interesting substantive philosophical dispute about the nature of enlightenment; it is not a case of two views talking past each other, confused over a similar-sounding word or references to light as a metaphor. Indeed, there are lengthy discussions in the Buddhist canon of agency, executive function, and the nature of freedom and responsibility (e.g., Goodman 2002; Sridharan 2013; Repetti 2014). On this substantive question, though, many Buddhist philosophers are closer to the Scottish Enlightenment (Hume and now Parfit, instead of Kant and Korsgaard, for example). Kant aims to show that morality is and must involve a rational and categorical necessity. Hume, in contrast, famously argues that reason is and ought to be the slave of the passions.

Hume (2006) argues that reason is a mere tool of desire (or passion or inclination). Reason is important because it discerns facts and causal relations between facts, and reason also establishes abstract logical relations between ideas, but reason cannot motivate us to do anything (or even to refrain from acting) without a prior, antecedent desire (*Treatise* III iii 3). Reason judges either matters of fact or relations of ideas. The justification of an action, however, cannot be reduced to either a mere matter of fact or relations of ideas. The wrongfulness (or unwholesomeness) of an action eludes us until we turn to our own sentiments and attitudes (*Enquiry* Section I and Appendix I). Hume's method is very similar to the Buddhist method in analyzing the self. For Hume, we first break down the capacity of reason and the distinctions and relations of ideas. Hume identifies seven relations of ideas: Resemblance, Identity, Relations of time and place, Proportion in quantity and number, Degrees in any quantity, Contrariety, and most importantly, Causation. Although we will not explore this here, the similarity to the Buddhist method of exploring the mind is clear and fascinating. Returning to the question of whether reason alone can provide moral distinctions: Can reason, so understood, motivate without desire? It is clear that without any human sentiments or preferences, reason alone compares and sorts ideas and establishes relations. But all of this rational processing is inert and provides no basis for distinguishing right from wrong, virtue from vice until it considers the effects of actions and outcomes on our passions and desires. We are motivated by our desires and passions. Reason's role is to help us judge whether a recommended course of action causes suffering or happiness. Indeed, Hume argues that the virtues are simply character traits that are useful or immediately agreeable to self and others.

The final distinction between virtue and vice comes from a sentiment or feeling of sympathy for others but reason must first prepare the way for us to experience appropriate sympathetic responses. Through reason we learn the facts and the causal effects of our actions. Although reason alone does not distinguish right from wrong, it is a necessary precondition for right conduct and virtue. Hume's analysis of the role of reason and sympathy is more in line with Buddhism, which emphasizes the importance of wisdom and compassion as essential to enlightenment.

To sum up, on the foundations of moral judgment, and on the necessity of emotive engagement, Hume and the Scottish Enlightenment also rejects Kant's rationalism and are much more aligned with Buddhist Modernism. There are clearly important differences in the Kantian, Humean, and Buddhist conceptions of the person, reason, and agency. As a result there are substantive disagreements about the *answer* to the question, "What is enlightenment?" Both Kant and Buddhists, however, are concerned with the same question, and concerned for the same reasons, and agree that enlightenment involves a fundamental reorientation of self that avoids the primal confusion of solipsistic egocentrism and heteronomy.

As a final note on this point, in addition to its parallels to Hume, the Buddhist conception of the mind, as a bundle of interacting cognitive functions, is often compared with recent accounts of embodied cognition (Varela, Thompson, and Rosch 1991). Depending on how one interprets Kant's transcendental idealism and conception of autonomy, Buddhist Modernism may be *more naturalistic and scientific* than Kant. At any rate, Buddhist Modernism is clearly sufficiently committed to the empirical, scientific vein of the Age of Reason.

On the other hand, although the Buddhist embodied conception of the self fits well with scientific models, Buddhists also need fairly robust accounts of agency and responsibility, and this is thus a lively focus of contemporary Buddhist philosophy. In short, the nature of embodied autonomy is one of the more interesting philosophical questions for both Kantians and Buddhists of all types. For the purpose of this discussion, however, the primary point is that the debate between Kant and Buddhism/Hume is an internal debate over the nature of enlightenment itself.

Returning to Kant, we should not overstate the supposed difference in the traditions by overemphasizing the alleged individualism of Kant's conception of enlightenment. We have already seen that Kant emphasized the need for education, the social nature and preconditions for civilization, and moral development. In this respect Kant's views on moral development and the preconditions for autonomy are actually similar to communitarians (Taylor 1985). Kant's conception of morality is itself social at its essential core. As Bristow (2011) explains, in his *Stanford Encyclopedia of Philosophy* entry on the Enlightenment,

> [Kant's conception of enlightenment] proposes, instead, a vision of human beings who are able...to step back from their particular situations and inclinations, in order *to construct an intersubjective order of co-existence, communication and cooperation on terms that all can accept.*
> (Bristow 2011, emphasis added)

Kant's maxim of enlightenment is "To think for oneself" and for Kant this involves the public use of one's reason freed from all authority and addressing the world at large. Following Onora O'Neill (1989), we can see that this maxim of enlightenment is completed by Kant's second maxim (from the *Critique of Judgment*) – "To think from the standpoint of everyone else" (quoted by O'Neill 1989, 46 [Kant, *Critique of Judgment* V 294]). We are to reflect on our own judgment from the perspective of everyone else. Kant's third maxim, "To always think consistently," seems easiest but is actually "the hardest of attainment." (The three rules of thinking are straightforward applications of the formulations of Kant's categorical imperative: Autonomy of thought, Treat other thinkers as subjects too, and Consistency in thinking is as important as consistency in willing.) In short, Kant's conception of enlightenment is not overly individualistic or ahistorical.

Conclusion

There remains a fundamental difference and substantive dispute between Kant and Buddhist Modernism. For Buddhists, unlike Kant, the key to awakening is the realization of the fundamental interdependence and interconnectedness of human beings (and indeed of all existence); our fundamental equality is rooted in our common susceptibility to suffering, and not in our autonomy and capacity to reason; and rational insight alone is not enough to achieve a systematic reorientation of one's thinking and action. Overcoming self-love and partiality requires retraining the mind through meditative practice, which leads to a transformation of consciousness, which includes a more mindful awareness of interdependence. Buddhism defends the more plausible position: selfishness, anger, and hatred are rooted in our (natural?) egocentric orientation, and mere reason cannot overcome these passions. We have already seen that Kant thinks that "The most difficult condition of the human race is the crossing-over from civilization to moralization." Śāntideva's account (685 CE) of the difficult path to an awakened mind provides a more compelling and psychologically realistic account of how one transcends the "primal confusion" of egocentrism and heteronomy. Wisdom/reason alone is not enough; one also needs to retrain the habits of the mind through moral practice, and perhaps also years of meditative practice.

Again, this is an internal dispute about the best means to a more enlightened self. And here, we find a common spirit and hope that a more enlightened existence will also lead to a better, more satisfying life. William Bristow concludes his discussion of Kant as follows: "The faith of the Enlightenment – if one may call it that – is that the process of enlightenment, of becoming progressively self-directed in thought and action through the *awakening* of one's intellectual powers, leads ultimately to a better, more fulfilled human existence" (Bristow 2011, emphasis added). Kant and Modern Buddhists share a conception of enlightenment and a conviction that awakening one's mind will lead to a better, more fulfilling life.

Note

1 With thanks to Burt Louden, Paul Schofield, and Rachel Neckes for helpful comments on this chapter, and Mark Okrent for his dismissive skepticism, which helped inspire it. For examples of the dismissive attitude see, for example, http://ask.metafilter.com/216044/How-does-the-Buddhist-understanding-of-enlightenment-compare-with-the-Western-Age-of-Enlightenment (accessed 14 November 2016).

References

Bristow, William. 2011. "Enlightenment." In *The Stanford Encyclopedia of Philosophy*, edited by Edward N. Zalta. http://plato.stanford.edu/archives/sum2011/entries/enlightenment/

Buddhaghosa. 2003. *The Path of Purification*, translated by Bhikkhu Nanamoli. Colombo: Pariyatti Publishing.

Cummiskey, David. 1996. *Kantian Consequentialism*. New York: Oxford University Press.

Cummiskey, David. 2010. "Competing Conceptions of the Self in Kantian and Buddhist Moral Theories." In *Cultivating Personhood: Kant and Asian Philosophy*, edited by Stephen R. Palmquist. Berlin: Walter de Gruyter.

Cummiskey, David. 2014. "Comparative Reflections on Buddhist Political Thought: Asoka, Shambhala, and the General Will." In *A Companion to Buddhist Philosophy*, edited by Steven M. Emmanuel, 536–551. Malden: Wiley-Blackwell.

Dalai Lama XIV (Tenzin Gyatso). 1999. *Ethics for the New Millennium*. New York: Riverhead.

Dalai Lama XIV (Tenzin Gyatso). 2005. *The Universe in a Single Atom: The Convergence of Science and Spirituality*. New York: Random House.

Davis, J. and Thompson, E. 2014. "From the Five Aggregates to Phenomenal Consciousness: Towards a Cross-Cultural Cognitive Science." In *A Companion to Buddhist Philosophy*, edited by Steven M. Emmanuel, 585–597. Malden: Wiley-Blackwell.

Dōgen. 2012. *Textual and Historical Studies*, edited by Steven Heine. New York: Oxford University Press.

Edelglass, William and Garfield, Jay. 2009. *Buddhist Philosophy: Essential Readings*. New York: Oxford University Press.

Garfield, Jay. 2015. *Engaging Buddhism and Why it Matters to Philosophy*. New York: Oxford University Press.

Goodman, Charles. 2002. "Resentment and Reality: Buddhism on Moral Responsibility." *American Philosophical Quarterly* 39(4): 359–372.

Heim, Maria. 2013. *The Forerunner of All Things: Buddhaghosa on Mind, Intention, and Agency*. New York: Oxford University Press.

Herman, Barbara. 1993. *The Practice of Moral Judgment*. Cambridge, MA: Harvard University Press.
Hume, David. 2006. *Treatise* and *Enquiry*, reprinted in *Moral Philosophy*, edited by Geoffrey Sayre-McCord. Indianapolis: Hackett Publishing.
Kant, Immanuel. 1784. "An Answer to the Question: What is Enlightenment?" In *Perpetual Peace and Other Essays*, translated by Ted Humphrey (Indianapolis: Hackett Publishing, 1983).
Kant, Immanuel. 1960. *Education*. Ann Arbor: The University of Michigan Press.
Keown, D.V., Prebish, C.S., and Husted, W.R., eds. 1998. *Buddhism and Human Rights*. Richmond: Curzon Press (New York: Routledge, 2015).
Louden, Robert B. 2000. *Kant's Impure Ethics: From Rational Beings to Human Beings*. New York: Oxford University Press.
McMahan, David. 2008. *The Making of Buddhist Modernism*. New York: Oxford University Press.
Nāgārjuna. 1995. *Mūlamadhyamakakārikā: The Fundamental Wisdom of the Middle Way*, translated by Jay Garfield. New York: Oxford University Press.
Nhat Hanh, Thich. 1988. *Interbeing: Fourteen Guidelines for Engaged Buddhism*. Berkeley: Parallax Press.
Nhat Hanh, Thich. 2016. *Plum Village: Mindfulness Practice Center*. http://plumvillage.org/
O'Neill, Onora. 1989. *Constructions of Reason: Explorations of Kant's Practical Philosophy*. Cambridge, UK: Cambridge University Press.
Queen, Christopher, ed. 2000. *Engaged Buddhism in the West*. Somerville: Wisdom Publications.
Repetti, Riccardo. 2014. "Recent Buddhist Theories of Free Will: Compatibilism, Incompatibilism, and Beyond." *Journal of Buddhist Ethics* 21: 280–352.
Rousseau, J.J. 1762. *On the Social Contract*, edited by Donald Cress (Indianapolis: Hackett Publishers, 1987).
Siderits, Mark. 2007. *Buddhism as Philosophy*. Indianapolis: Hackett Publishing.
Sridharan, Vishnu. 2013. "The Metaphysics of No-Self: A Determinist Deflation of the Free Will Problem." *Journal of Buddhist Ethics* 20: 287–305.
Taylor, Charles. 1985. "Atomism." *Philosophy and the Human Sciences, Philosophical Papers* 2, 187–210. Cambridge, UK: Cambridge University Press.
Trungpa, Chogyam. 1973. *Cutting Through Spiritual Materialism*. Boston: Shambhala Press.
Trungpa, Chogyam. 1984. *Shambhala: The Sacred Path of the Warrior*. Boston: Shambhala Press.
Trungpa, Chogyam. 1991. *Meditation in Action*. Boston: Shambhala Press.
Varela, F., Thompson, E., and Rosch E. 1991. *The Embodied Mind: Cognitive Science and Human Experience*. Cambridge, MA: MIT Press.

12

Compassion and Rebirth: Some Ethical Implications

John Powers

Buddhism as a Salad Bar

Buddhism has its origins in ancient India with the awakening (*bodhi*) of the Buddha, Siddhārtha Gautama (ca. 563–483 BCE). Following this experience, he traveled around northern India, sharing his insights with anyone who cared to listen. His Dharma later spread throughout Asia, and in recent times Buddhism has been embraced by millions of people in Western countries. Many of these converts are attracted by a vision of Buddhism according to which it is fundamentally different from Judeo-Christian traditions that require adherence to dogmas that run contrary to empirical evidence. Buddhism, on this view, is "rational" and "scientific."

Adherents of this version of Buddhism often adopt an eclectic approach: Buddhism's myriad traditions offer a range of therapeutic techniques that can help contemporary humans deal with the problems of the modern world, reduce their stress, lower their heart rates, and improve their relationships with others. These techniques were developed in India and other regions of Asia as aspects of individual integrated systems of theory and practice, but people who adopt this ecumenical approach pick and choose what most appeals to them, and often mix Buddhist ideas with elements of other religions, psychotherapy, and New Age concepts.

This is a uniquely modern and Western approach. Prior to the "discovery" by nineteenth-century European scholars of a tradition they labeled "Buddhism," few of the people to whom it was applied thought that their religious beliefs and practices were related to those in other areas of what is now conceived as the Buddhist world. As Coleman (2001) notes, the idea that there is a common thread running through the Buddhism of Southeast Asia, India, East Asia, and the Tibetan cultural area is a recent innovation, and this eclectic vision also incorporates insights from non-Buddhist sources: "it is not at all uncommon

Buddhist Philosophy: A Comparative Approach, First Edition. Edited by Steven M. Emmanuel.
© 2018 John Wiley & Sons, Inc. Published 2018 by John Wiley & Sons, Inc.

for teachers from two different traditions to lead a retreat together or for a teacher to give a dharma talk that not only quotes other Buddhist traditions but Christians, Muslims, and contemporary psychologists as well...they are beginning to form a distinct Western tradition all its own" (Coleman 2001, 16–17).

The Western converts who are shaping this new interpretation of an ancient tradition are often well educated and feel no need to blindly accept archaic notions like Mt. Meru, the mythical *axis mundi* described in Indian scriptures that sits at the center of the flat disk of the world, at the base of which four continents are arrayed along the cardinal points of the compass. Anyone who flies in a plane can empirically disprove this cosmology, and modernist Buddhists reject it in favor of scientific evidence. Citing such clearly deficient teachings in canonical texts, many Buddhists adopt a pragmatic, nontraditional attitude: contemporary practitioners should feel free to decide what works for them and jettison whatever they regard as cultural baggage, prescientific notions, or ineffective techniques.

Some take things even further: Stephen Batchelor (1997), for example, conceives the Buddha as someone who rejected beliefs that were common during his time, used reason and direct perception to figure out how the world works, and shared his ideas with others. He only asked that his followers consider what he had to say and compare this with what they could observe with their senses and verify through reasoning. Batchelor advocates "Buddhism without beliefs." He admits that the Buddha often spoke of unverifiable doctrines such as rebirth (Pāli *punabbhava*; Skt *punarbhava*; lit. "re-becoming"), but he only did so as a skillful device. He really "regarded speculation about future and past lives to be just another distraction" (Batchelor 1997, 35).

The Buddha's sermons included statements that he had directly realized the operations of karma and rebirth, but Batchelor thinks that "in accepting the idea of rebirth, the Buddha reflected the worldview of his time" (Batchelor 1997, 36). In other words, he spoke of rebirth as a practical heuristic device that accorded with his audiences' entrenched beliefs, but if we apply his more central admonition to reflect critically and employ empirical evidence, we will realize that many of the doctrines of developed Buddhist schools are "based on speculation" (Batchelor 1997, 36). Modern, rational people can confidently reject the dross of ancient dogma and apply the Buddha's essential insights to their lives. Like diners choosing from various ingredients on offer in a salad bar, Buddhists should take whatever appeals to them and create individualized programs of practice that meet their specific needs and that satisfy their spiritual appetites.

Rebirth in the Pāli Canon

Batchelor's Buddha was as a thoroughgoing rationalist, and he asserts that the Buddha "did not claim to have had an experience that granted him privileged, esoteric knowledge of how the universe ticks" (Batchelor 1997, 5). This is not, however, the way in which the Buddha is reported in Buddhist texts. In the *Numerical Discourses*, the Buddha claims that "the Tathāgata has fully awakened to the origin of the world. The Tathāgata has fully awakened to the cessation of the world...in this world...whatever is seen, heard, sensed, cognized, reached, sought after, examined by the mind – all that the Tathāgata has fully awakened to" (Bhikkhu Bodhi 2012, 410). In the *Middle Length Discourses*, the Buddha describes the process of his awakening experience: in the first watch of the night, he purified his mind with the attainment of profound meditative absorptions (*jhāna*). He then gained "true knowledge" of the specific details of many thousands of his own past lifetimes that had occurred during innumerable eons of cosmic contraction and expansion (Bhikkhu Bodhi 1995, 341).

In the second watch of the night, he acquired the "divine eye" (*dibba-cakkhu*), a supernormal ability that surpasses the senses of all other beings, through which he perceived the workings of the universe. He directly observed the multiple rebirths of countless other sentient beings, and he understood the consequences of their wholesome and unwholesome actions from one life to the next. In the third watch, he acquired certain knowledge of the four noble truths (*ariya-sacca*) and fully comprehended the causes for attainment of liberation from the cycle of rebirth (*saṃsāra*). Despite Batchelor's confident assertions that the Buddha was not a mystic and did not claim any extraordinary abilities, the Buddhist canon is replete with counterexamples. His attainment of awakening was the result of meditative practice over many lifetimes, during which his insight deepened and he acquired supernatural powers. In his final life, much of his time was spent in meditative retreat, and accounts from the canon report that he regularly entered into states of absorption. Through his meditative attainments, he fully comprehended karma and rebirth, and he conveyed his insights to his followers as accurate descriptions of real processes that would help them in turn to follow the path to liberation.

The core problem the Buddha identified was suffering or unsatisfactoriness (*dukkha*). He declared that all life involves suffering, and he divided it into three types: (i) suffering of change: the unhappiness that results from being forced to endure negative experiences or when one loses something that one values; (ii) suffering of pain, as when one is hit with a club or suffers from disease; and (iii) pervasive suffering: the fact that the universe is constituted in such a way that discontent is inevitable. Suffering was the first "noble truth" that he taught during his first sermon ("Discourse Turning the Wheel of Dharma"), and the Buddha followed this with an analysis of its underlying cause. Suffering, he declared, results from desire: because we wish for possessions and cling to them, because we yearn for things like wealth, sex, fame, or power in the hope that these will provide happiness, we are inevitably disappointed. No amount of material things or sensual pleasures can fully satisfy the craving that motivates these attitudes, and anything that we do acquire will inevitably be lost at some point. All of our hopes and desires, our property and relationships, our joys and sorrows, end at death, but the residual karmas and mental attitudes that underlie them propel us forward toward a new birth, one that inevitably involves more unsatisfactoriness.

In the third noble truth, the Buddha indicated that a solution is possible: through mental training, one can reduce desire and the afflicted mental states that give rise to it and attain a state of equanimity. This is achieved by the fourth noble truth, the "truth of the path," which involves cognitive reorientation. By changing one's views, goals, speech, and livelihood, and engaging in certain types of meditative practice, it is possible to overcome suffering. During the training period, one engages in meditation. This involves, among other things, applying antidotes that lessen the strength of the three primary afflictions (*kilesa*): anger, desire, and obscuration. Meditators familiarize themselves with objects of observation (*ālambana*) that lead to greater peace and equanimity and also progressively enhance such positive qualities as generosity and morality. The end result of this training, according to the Pāli Canon, is *nibbāna* (nirvana), a state of perfect peace that transcends suffering.

Rebirth is central to the Buddha's vision of suffering as the core existential problem. Human life is brief, but rebirth is beginningless, and each being has suffered in every possible way innumerable times. Birth is painful, life is punctuated by experiences of emotional trauma, loss, physical discomfort, separation from people and things that are valued, sickness, and a range of other physical and psychological maladies. Death is also generally painful, both emotionally and physically, and because the process is repeated endlessly the Buddha urged people to consider the facts as he presented them and make an informed decision to pursue a path that can lead to a final liberation from all suffering.

Very Hidden Phenomena

For many modernist Buddhists, however, this contradicts the Buddha's pragmatist and empiricist stance. The operations of karma cannot be verified by sensory data, nor can rebirth. When beings die, their bodies decay, and no intersubjectively available evidence has ever been presented to substantiate the notion that there is any continuity of consciousness, as Buddhist texts claim. According to the Pāli Canon's descriptions, after physical functioning ceases, the "stream of consciousness" (*viññāṇa sota*, *Dīgha Nikāya* 3.105) or "evolving consciousness" (*saṃvattanika viññāṇa*, *Majjhima Nikāya* ii.256; see Bhikkhu Bodhi 1995, 1311 n.1011) continues to change from moment to moment and is propelled forward by one's karma toward a future life situation that is concordant with one's morally relevant volitional actions in past lives. Negative karmic seeds will give rise to painful circumstances, while positive ones will result in pleasurable outcomes.

The Buddha claimed that he had attained an advanced level of awareness through which he was able to perceive these operations with direct perception, but for most beings karma and rebirth are "very hidden phenomena" (Skt *atyanta-parokṣa*). Non-virtuoso Buddhists must accept the Buddha's descriptions on faith because they cannot replicate his observations. There is, of course, a promise that they might do so in the future if they are sufficiently diligent in their practice: the faculty of yogic direct perception (*yogi-pratyakṣa*), through which patterns of causation that operate below the range of the senses can be known, is latent in all sentient beings and can be developed through meditative practice. Like a scientist who verifies the existence of microorganisms in a glass of water with a microscope that enhances her senses, a Buddhist practitioner can cultivate the ability to directly comprehend the subtle workings of karma that are opaque to most people. Claims to this effect are common among advanced meditators. Tibetan lamas, for example, often inform their students about how past actions led to present situations or provide purportedly authoritative statements regarding the rebirth situations of their relatives or friends.

For many contemporary Buddhists, however, these ideas sound like mystical hogwash and blind faith. The Buddha – a paragon of rational empiricism – could not have enjoined his followers to act in this way. Buddhadāsa Bhikkhu (1906–1993), a Thai monk who propounded a rationalist interpretation of Buddhism, claimed that the Buddha taught "no-self" (Skt *anātman*; Pāli *anattā*), which denies any substantial, ongoing entity or soul: "because there is no one born, there is no one who dies and is reborn. Therefore, the whole question of rebirth is quite foolish and has nothing to do with Buddhism...in the sphere of the Buddhist teachings there is no question of rebirth or reincarnation" (Buddhadāsa 1994, 4–5). The goal of the path, as Buddhadāsa understands it, is *nibbāna*, which he describes as a state beyond all suffering that also transcends ordinary conceptions of happiness.

In accordance with Theravāda tradition, Buddhadāsa's vision of the path is mainly concerned with individual effort and its outcomes. People who follow the Buddha's teachings are motivated by their experience of suffering and the promise that it can be reduced or eliminated through the techniques he taught. Along the way, they might, as Buddhadāsa himself did, instruct others and share their insights, but this is not an integral element of their path. The goal is release from one's experience of suffering, and each being must accomplish this through individual effort.

Buddhadāsa's interpretations of Buddhism have generated considerable interest among modernist followers of the tradition but, not surprisingly, are rejected by others who uphold more orthodox views. Bhikkhu Bodhi (2005), for example, thinks that jettisoning the doctrine of rebirth "would virtually reduce the Dhamma to tatters...the conception of rebirth is an essential plank of its ethical theory, providing an incentive for avoiding evil and doing good."

Humans, he asserts, have a "deep intuitive sense" that the universe is morally coherent: good actions should lead to positive results, while wickedness should be punished. But there are numerous examples of people like Stalin or Mao Zedong who were responsible for many deaths and great suffering but died in their sleep at an advanced age with no apparent retribution for the evil they perpetrated. Virtuous people may suffer pain or disappointment, and many die without enjoying the sort of rewards that their good deeds deserve.

Bhikkhu Bodhi believes that "it is only too obvious that such moral equilibrium cannot be found within the limits of a single life." Rebirth is required for our sense of a morally coherent cosmos to be fulfilled. The underlying order he postulates may be invisible to our senses and contravened by scientific evidence, but this does not mean that it is not real: "beyond the range of normal perception, a moral law holds sway over our deeds and via our deeds over our destiny. It is just the principle of kamma, operating across the sequence of rebirths, that locks our volitional actions into the dynamics of the cosmos, making ethics an expression of the cosmos's own intrinsic orderliness."

But can merely wishing that the universe should correspond to human desires for justice and appropriate recompense for actions make it so? Is a deep intuition that this is really the way things are sufficient to overturn the evidence of our senses, which reveals that every being who has ever lived has either died or is currently undergoing a process of aging that will result in the same fate? No one, no matter how virtuous, has ever escaped death and the physical decomposition that follows it. Bhikkhu Bodhi points out that contemporary rationalists who adopt a materialist stance generally accept scientific pronouncements about quarks, quantum physics, chemical laws, and operations of cells that they cannot verify with their senses, and in some cases not even with available scientific instruments. Why not believe what the Buddha said about rebirth, which accords with our intuitive inclinations and makes moral behavior coherent?

Ethical Behavior and Its Consequences

This sort of appeal is unlikely to sway a committed rationalist materialist, but it might be sufficient for traditional Buddhists. But is it even necessary for Buddhist ethics? If there is no substantial self, why should it matter whether or not a later moment of a psycho-physical continuum suffers for negative actions committed by former moments? Or that deeds have concordant consequences? Could the very practice of virtue be its own reward? Even if the universe only imperfectly metes out justice that accords with the karmas that occasion it, can't an individual still decide to engage in ethical behavior and strive to benefit others?

Alasdair MacIntyre's distinction between external and internal goods may be relevant here. In *After Virtue*, MacIntyre distinguishes two kinds of outcomes of engaging in a regimen of practice. External goods are connected with the practice "by the accidents of social circumstance"; these may be such things as wealth, fame, or power (MacIntyre 1984, 188). They may accrue to an individual in a number of ways, including achieving excellence in a particular endeavor, or through immoral actions such as embezzlement, robbery, and so on. There is no necessary relation between their acquisition and moral behavior, no matter how exalted.

The second sort of goods can only be gained by participating in the practice and becoming accomplished in it. MacIntyre gives the example of playing chess: a person who wishes to achieve goods relevant to chess must participate in the practice, learn its rules, submit to instruction by experts, and work at it for an extended period of time. Through this, her technique will improve, and her excellence will be recognized by the chess community. External and internal goods differ in that the latter accrue to oneself alone, while the former will eventually become someone else's property: one will spend one's money in various ways, and after death one's estate will pass on to others. Moreover, when one person acquires them, there is less available for others. But with internal goods "their achievement is a good for the whole community who participate in the practice" (MacIntyre 1984, 190–191).

Systems of practice have associated virtues that are acquired by those who participate in them. Someone who plays a team sport well, for example, will develop such qualities as courage in the face of adversity, magnanimity in defeat, teamwork, and persistence in training. A person who is dedicated to moral cultivation will become compassionate, generous, and ethical and will develop other virtues that are the outcomes of the practice and that are valued by the community. These attributes will benefit society and also enhance the individual's character.

This requires a certain humility because at the beginning one must submit to the authority of the community of practitioners, receive instruction from experts, and accede to evaluation: "a practice involves standards of excellence and obedience to rules as well as the achievement of goods" (MacIntyre 1984, 190). While external goods may be achieved in a variety of ways, internal goods can only result from the practice itself: "a virtue is an acquired human quality the possession and the exercise of which tends to enable us to achieve those goods which are internal to practices and the lack of which effectively prevents us from achieving any such goods...we have to accept as necessary components of any practice with internal goods and standards of excellence the virtues of justice, courage, and honesty" (MacIntyre 1984, 191). These virtues also define how we relate to others and become part of the mosaic of a society. The healthy functioning of communities necessitates wholesome practices as a prerequisite.

The Practice of Compassion

None of this requires rebirth. An individual who commits to cultivation of moral virtues may as a result progressively develop good qualities and contribute to the collective good, and the resultant internal "goods of excellence," as MacIntyre later termed them (Knight 1998, 55), can be evaluated independently of whether or not she is rewarded with external "goods of effectiveness." In the context of Buddhist ethics, this might be sufficient for the system described in the Pāli Canon, which aims at nirvana. With its attainment, the individual psycho-physical continuum that has engaged in practice comes to an end, and there will be no rebirth. As an *arhat* (an adept destined for nirvana), one generates no new karma. While volitional residue from the past remains, there will be physical embodiment, but when karma is exhausted, there will no longer be any basis for continued existence.

In Mahāyāna practice, however, this is insufficient for a truly moral life. The Mahāyāna ideal, the bodhisattva, undergoes the profound existential transformation of the "mind of awakening" (*bodhicitta*), which is prompted by a realization that all beings are subject to the same sufferings that provided motivation for one's own quest to transcend the problems of cyclic existence. The bodhisattva has an expansive view of the universe: all beings have been involved in processes of birth, death, and rebirth since beginningless time, and so all have been in every possible relationship with me. Every sentient being has been my mother, father, best friend, favorite pet, spouse, and child. My mothers in particular have been particularly kind and have selflessly sacrificed for me. As Tsongkhapa (1357–1419) the founder of the Gelukpa (dGe lugs pa) order, expresses this attitude:

> From one's own viewpoint, because one has cycled beginninglessly, there are no sentient beings who have not been one's friends hundreds of times. Therefore, one should think, "Whom should I value?" "Whom should I hate?"... Imagine your mother very clearly in front of you. Consider several times how she has been your mother numberless times, not only now, but from beginningless cyclic existence. When she was your mother, she protected you from all danger and brought about your benefit and happiness. In particular, in this life she held you for a long time in her womb. Once you were born, while you still had new hair, she held you to the warmth of her flesh and rocked you on the tips of her ten fingers. She nursed you at her breast...and wiped away your excrement with her hand. In various ways she nourished you tirelessly. When you were hungry and thirsty, she gave you drink, and when you were cold, clothes, and when poor, money. She gave you those things that were precious to her. ... When you suffered with a fever she would rather have

died herself than have her child die; and if her child became sick, from the depths of her heart she would rather have suffered herself than have her child suffer.

(Ba so et al. 1972, 572.5)

The bodhisattva comprehends the moral implications of this scenario: all beings have been equally kind during past lives, and they have sacrificed greatly to help her. Thus she owes a debt of gratitude to them, and she resolves to repay it by working tirelessly to help them overcome suffering. After considering how best to achieve this, she embarks on the path to buddhahood, because buddhas are the sort of beings who are best equipped to help others. After giving rise to the mind of awakening, the bodhisattva trains for at least three incalculable eons (*asaṃkhyeya-kalpa*, the period between the arising of the universe and its destruction) in the six perfections (*pāramitā*): generosity, ethics, patience, effort, concentration, and wisdom. When these qualities have been developed to the highest possible degree, one attains buddhahood and uses the vast store of merit one has accumulated during countless lifetimes of practice, coupled with supreme wisdom (*prajñā-pāramitā*) guided by great compassion (*mahākaruṇā*), to skillfully benefit them.

This scenario obviously requires rebirth. The obligations that follow from the past kindness of others make no sense in the context of a single life. I owe my mother a debt of gratitude for giving me life and for raising me, but the same cannot be said for the billions of people I will never meet who live in distant parts of the world. I may have a general sense of a common humanity and a wish that they be happy, but Tsongkhapa's practice for developing *bodhicitta* cannot produce the sort of visceral sense of deep connection between myself and them without something more than the fact that we inhabit the same planet and share some common DNA. The problems become even more acute when we consider other mammals, or reptiles, fish, insects, and other life forms: the bodhisattva ideal embraces all of them, but in the context of a single brief existence that terminates with death the possibility of forming the sort of commitment to their happiness required of a bodhisattva seems remote.

A further problem arises when one considers the task of a bodhisattva: to work for as long as necessary so that all sentient beings might be free from suffering. Given the short duration of a human life and the limited capacities of even the most advanced Buddhist practitioners, any rational bodhisattva who considers the countless numbers of suffering beings and the sheer impossibility of positively affecting more than a few thousand during the course of one's existence in the world should probably conclude that the goal is hopeless. Unless one's work can be carried out over the course of many lifetimes and in various parts of the world (or universe) in a variety of life situations, it would make far more sense for someone who is committed to making a positive difference in the world to lower expectations and commit to achievable goals. Ending the sufferings of sentient beings even in a single world in one human lifetime is so far beyond any conceivable being's capacity (even that of a buddha, who only has about forty years to affect others following awakening) that trying to do so would be an impracticable, dispiriting task.

Jay Garfield: Team Buddha

In Indian Mahāyāna literature, the bodhisattva is depicted as a hero, someone who commits to countless lifetimes of training in order to benefit as many sentient beings as possible. Bodhisattvas "put on the great armor" and acquire incalculable stores of merit through their acts of self-abnegation and their willingness to give away whatever is necessary to alleviate others' suffering – even their own lives. The *8,000 Line Perfection of Wisdom Discourse* describes the ideal attitude:

> Bodhisattvas, great beings, should train in this way: "In order to benefit all the world…I will lead the immeasurable realms of sentient beings to final nirvana." Bodhisattvas, great beings, should begin applying themselves in that way to establishing all virtuous roots, but should not be conceited because of this. … These supreme beings thoroughly lead the world and are a great benefit to the world. Therefore, they should always and uninterruptedly train well in the six perfections.
>
> *(Vaidya 1960, 116ff.)*

In the *Compendium of Training*, Śāntideva characterizes this as a solitary path, one in which trainees receive teachings and encouragement from other bodhisattvas and from buddhas, but ultimately each bodhisattva has to cultivate her own virtues; no one else can bring one's generosity, ethics, or wisdom to perfection:

> The bodhisattva is alone, with no…companion, and puts on the armor of supreme wisdom. He acts alone and leaves nothing to others, working with a will that is firm with courage and strength. He is strong in his own strength…and thinks: "I will help all sentient beings to obtain whatever they need to obtain." … Bodhisattvas think: "All creatures are in pain; all suffer from bad and hindering karma. … All that mass of pain and evil karma I take in my own body. … I resolve to do so; I endure it all. I do not turn back or run away, I do not tremble…I am not afraid…nor do I despair. I must definitely bear the burdens of all sentient beings…for I have resolved to save them all, I must set them all free, I must save the whole world from the forest of birth, aging, sickness, and rebirth, from

misfortune and wrongdoing, from the round of birth and death, from the dangers of error. I work to establish the kingdom of perfect wisdom for all sentient beings. I care not at all for my own liberation. I must save all sentient beings from the river of rebirth with the raft of my omniscient mind. I must pull them back from the great precipice. I must free them from all misfortune, ferry them over the stream of rebirth. For I have taken upon myself, by my own will, the whole of the pain of all living things.

(Bendall 1897–1902, 278–283)

According to Jay Garfield (2002), this attitude, which is extolled throughout Mahāyāna canons and commentarial literature, is misguided and ignores the philosophical implications of the doctrines of no-self and emptiness (*śūnyatā*). He regards the notion of the heroic bodhisattva cultivating the perfections over the course of eons in order to benefit others as "a subtle form of self-grasping" (Garfield 2002, 70). The problem, as he sees it, is that it implicitly assumes at least a functional individual, one that is superimposed on the momentary events of a particular psycho-physical continuum. Garfield proposes to free "the morally central notion of bodhicitta from unnecessary and perhaps implausible metaphysical and cosmological baggage" (Garfield 2002, 76). The idea of rebirth cannot be reconciled with Buddhism's empiricist and rational stance. It requires acceptance of metaphysical beliefs that are not in evidence, and it also muddies the moral waters. All that we can be certain of is the present existence; moral cultivation, as well as our efforts on behalf of sentient beings, must occur within this context.

Garfield believes that the grandiose aspirations found in Mahāyāna literature obscure the essentials of bodhisattva practice: "The aim and motivation of bodhicitta is the alleviation of the suffering of all sentient beings. That is beyond question. It also includes the view that only a buddha could accomplish that task, given its stupendous difficulty" (Garfield 2002, 81). But, he adds, there is no reason to assume that this must be pursued in a solitary manner. Moreover, the notion that *I* must be the savior of all sentient beings implies a concept of selfhood and individual striving that is incompatible with no-self. Who exactly is this bodhisattva, and what connection is there between the buddha at the end of the process and the bodhisattva who first gives rise to bodhicitta? Why should the bodhisattva's path and cultivation of virtues be conceived as singular?

Garfield proposes a radically new model, according to which a community of practitioners pools its efforts over generations, gradually improving in generosity, ethics, patience, wisdom, compassion, and other virtues. The end result is the emergence of a buddha, one who stands on the shoulders of previous bodhisattvas, who selflessly cultivated virtue in order that, long after their demise and physical decomposition, someone might attain the supreme state and complete the task of alleviating the suffering of sentient beings. This, Garfield contends, is superior to the view advanced by Tsongkhapa:

> Knowledge and compassion deepen over the generations, and after a time, some individual attains Buddhahood as a consequence of the accumulation of causes by others. Call this a transpersonal model of attainment, as opposed to the intrapersonal model embraced by the dGe lugs pa tradition.
>
> *(Garfield 2002, 81)*

Garfield is unconcerned that adherents of Buddhist traditions reject his proposed modifications to their systems. They have failed to grasp the implications of Nāgārjuna's (ca. 150–250 BCE) analysis of no-self and emptiness and have effectively smuggled in a virtual self to the detriment of both philosophical consistency and effective practice.

Garfield is no doubt correct that the traditional notion of a single bodhisattva conceived as a coherent psycho-physical continuum of momentary events is at least implicitly at odds with Buddhism's rejection of a self. But is Garfield's vision of the path plausible? I contend that it is not. First, his belief that virtue may be cumulative cannot be supported by any available evidence. As MacIntyre points out, acquisition of virtue is internal; no matter how wise or compassionate I become, this cannot be transferred to anyone else. Each person has to do the work. If, for example, a million athletes were to spend three hours every day lifting weights in order that someone in the next generation might surpass them, their efforts would be in vain. Their insights regarding technique, diet, training regimens, and so on might help to enhance future performance, but the strength gained by the time they spend in the gym and their repetitions of bench presses cannot be passed on to others.

The same is true for virtue and its cultivation. Human consciousness is not like a computer's hard drive, and I cannot download my good qualities into someone else's psycho-physical continuum any more than I can help them to run faster by doing sprints. Garfield points out that scientists and philosophers make discoveries that would not be possible without the previous work of others in their fields. Einstein's special theory of relativity was his insight, but he could not have generated this idea without the research of earlier generations of scientists. But this is irrelevant to moral cultivation: a virtuous person may – and often does – inspire others, but her moral development takes place in her own brain. Others may hear her inspiring words and witness her noble actions, but each person must cultivate moral attitudes individually. No one can transfer a fully developed moral sensibility. This can only be accomplished by the day-to-day (and according to traditional Buddhism lifetime-to-lifetime) training of confronting difficult situations, making decisions, evaluating them in light of outcomes, and gradually advancing in this practice.

Unlike external goods, the internal "goods of excellence" that result may benefit a community due to the salubrious outcomes of one's actions and the ways in which they might motivate others, but there is no reason to imagine that such qualities can be transmitted, any more than the enhanced physical strength that results from weight training.

Even it were possible, history provides no reason to believe that virtue improves over time. The Buddha lived and taught more than 2,500 years ago, and following his death the Dharma spread throughout Asia and later to most countries around the world. At any given time there are probably millions of committed Buddhists practicing meditation and cultivating virtue with the aim of benefitting others and ending their suffering. Despite this effort, there is no evidence that Buddhists (or majority Buddhist countries) are becoming more ethical, more compassionate, or more wise – or that in each generation a particular person reaps the benefits of this collective effort and surpasses previous practitioners in virtue. The suffering of sentient beings remains pretty much constant. There are still wars, famines, genocides, racism, and other causes of discontent, and Buddhist adepts are not reducing their scale or the misery they cause.

A comparison of today's news with events of a century ago provides no compelling evidence that the moral cultivation of Buddhist meditators is having any discernible effect on the world or that the aggregate of suffering is diminishing. Even if one accepts Steven Pinker's (2011) conclusion that the period since World War II has been one of the most peaceful in history measured in global terms, Pinker does not believe that there has been a progressive improvement since the Buddha's time, nor is there any evidence that might link the relative improvement he sees in this short period to the efforts of Buddhist meditators. He attributes it to better systems of governance, improved legal systems, and abandonment of institutionalized violence by civil authorities. These are aspects of Western societies and are notably absent in many countries with Buddhist majorities or governments that espouse Buddhism, and Pinker believes that the negative tendencies that gave rise to the greater sufferings of the past persist in the consciousnesses of modern humans. They are only ameliorated by institutional improvements, not by any alteration in how our minds work.

Even more significant problems loom for Garfield's bodhisattva. As Garfield correctly notes, the first goal of the training is to end the sufferings of all sentient beings. Beyond that, the bodhisattva wants to help them to have happiness and the causes of happiness. But in light of the ubiquitousness of discontent, the short span of one human lifetime is insufficient to achieve anything more than a limited (and often temporary) improvement for a few beings. Stories of the Buddha's life report that several dozen followers became *arhat*s and thus passed beyond suffering. In the intervening centuries, there have presumably been other practitioners who have emulated their example and attained at least a significant reduction of discontent.

But such meager results are a poor return for the prodigious effort involved in Buddhist practice and the deprivations that a bodhisattva must endure. The vast majority of the myriads of sentient beings who inhabit the world at any given time will be utterly unaffected and will continue to suffer. Most will be unaware of the existence of the bodhisattva.

Mood-altering drugs might help: bodhisattvas could make bulk purchases of tranquilizers or antidepressants and distribute them to beings in distress. Or they might accumulate money and sponsor relaxing vacations for stressed humans or purchase domestic animals to save them from slaughter. Traditional Buddhist methods are more problematic; meditation practice is time-consuming, difficult, and often ineffective. Many people work at it for years with no significant reduction of stress or other sources of discontent. Moreover, Buddhist cultivation is not a once-and-for-all solution to pain; unlike an operation to set a broken bone, for example, unless one continues to meditate throughout one's entire life, it is likely that the beneficial effects of practice will diminish or cease.

This still falls well short of the bodhisattva vow to do whatever one can to end the suffering of all sentient beings. If one were to be reborn, one could devote future lifetimes to helping many other transmigrators, but Garfield's bodhisattva knows that rebirth is a fiction that cannot be entertained by anyone who truly understands the implications of Nāgārjuna's analysis of emptiness. The existential clock is ticking, and the prospects for any significant reduction of aggregate suffering are miniscule.

If one draws out the ramifications of a commitment to end the sufferings of others coupled with rejection of rebirth, a hypothetical unwanted conclusion presents itself for a bodhisattva who knows that rebirth will not occur: mass murder. The bodhisattva, confident that the present life is the only one, does not have to worry that beings who suffer now will experience further torment after death. The results of their karmas terminate when their hearts stop beating, and nothing is carried over to future lives, except perhaps in the memories of those who knew them. Mood-altering drugs have side effects and lead to reduced cognitive functioning. Meditation is difficult and its results are uncertain. But if the bodhisattva kills beings, their suffering comes to an end. A dead being has no possibility of ever again experiencing pain, loss, bereavement, disappointment, frustration, or any of the myriad ills that befall the living. Nirvana, as we saw above, is the final end of all suffering, and in the absence of rebirth, death is its functional equivalent.

An unambitious bodhisattva might be content with becoming a serial killer or helping beings by acquiring automatic weapons and opening fire in a crowded place. But one who is motivated to end the suffering of the maximum possible number of beings could engineer a military coup in a nuclear-armed nation like Pakistan that has refused to rule out the first strike option. The dictator bodhisattva could launch warheads at India, calculating their delivery in such a way that it can respond by firing its own missiles. If a few could be sent toward China in order to engineer a regional war, roughly one third of the world's population might be affected, and hundreds of millions of humans would never again have to endure the sufferings of embodied existence. Countless other life forms would also be destroyed in the exchange and thus also released from pain. If other bodhisattvas could be convinced to join in, they could take control of nuclear arsenals in other countries and expand the conflagration to the other continents.

Of course, there would still be millions of sentient beings left in the world, but the nuclear fallout would kill many of them as a result of global weather patterns. Many would suffer horribly in the short term, but the resulting world would be largely depopulated, and the sum total of misery would be significantly reduced. The happiness of the nonhumans that remain would probably be greatly enhanced in the absence of people killing, eating, and otherwise harming them.

Such a conclusion is, of course, abhorrent for any Buddhist practitioner or tradition, and this is one reason why insistence on the reality of rebirth is a common stance among Buddhist teachers. This sort of hypothetical, drawn out from the philosophical implications of the opponent's stance, is the kind of dialectic beloved by the Tibetan Gelukpa order; it uses Nāgārjuna's reductio approach to show the opponent that the premises he thought were acceptable lead inevitably to conclusions at odds with Buddhist ideals and tenets.

Rebirth is required in order for the universe to have the sort of moral equilibrium advocated by Bhikkhu Bodhi above. If the deceased beings were to be reborn, the bodhisattva would have immeasurably increased the world's suffering, and any residual karmas would manifest in future lives. No real reduction in suffering would be accomplished, and the bodhisattva's actions would be utterly counterproductive. The mass-murdering bodhisattva would also reap the consequences of unskillful actions that were motivated by compassion but profoundly misguided.

A bodhisattva might, of course, recoil from the horrific consequences of mass murder and decide instead to focus on improving the happiness of as many beings as possible. But given the ubiquitous nature of suffering and the fact that situations are uncertain and prone to give rise to unsatisfactoriness at any moment, the potential for positive outcomes is limited. If rebirth is a fiction, it is possible to bring about a significant reduction in aggregate suffering through mass murder, but even a buddha cannot do very much to foster genuine and lasting happiness.

Conclusions

Garfield presents his vision of the bodhisattva path as a rejection of the subtle self-grasping that he believes lies at the heart of the traditional Mahāyāna conception of the bodhisattva, but for most Buddhists a decision to commit oneself totally to helping others in innumerable ways for as long as it takes to end the sufferings of all beings is the most selfless possible attitude. If one takes seriously the discourses attributed to the Buddha in Pāli and Sanskrit sources, there is no doubt that rebirth and its consequences are integral to his vision of the path, nor does this literature provide any indication that he did not believe his teachings to be veridical. Successive generations of Buddhist adepts have also claimed to have corroborated his descriptions of the operations of karma and rebirth through direct perception resulting from years of meditative practice. A Buddhist who rejects rebirth on empiricist grounds cannot see the microorganisms in a glass of water with his senses alone, but he probably accepts that they exist. For most Buddhists, the fact that the Buddha declared that rebirth is a fact is probably enough for them to believe in this doctrine and his pronouncements regarding karma and its operations. If a person sees value in engaging in Buddhist meditation for her own purposes, such as reducing stress, there is probably no need to bother with such things, but Mahāyāna practice would be incoherent without rebirth. It might be possible to adopt an agnostic approach and train as if rebirth will take place, but it is difficult to see how this could provide the sort of motivation required for bodhisattva training and the sacrifices it entails.

A further problem arises in the context of therapy. People with psychological problems go to therapists because they are unable to resolve them on their own, relying solely on their own resources. For Buddhists, the first act of commitment to the practice is generally "taking refuge" in the three jewels (Buddha, Dharma, and Monastic Community). This is an admission that one has not done very well on one's own in dealing with one's mental afflictions and that one requires help. Submitting to their authority and receiving instruction is a necessary first step, and it requires a certain humility to rely on others more advanced than oneself in relevant techniques.

Eclectic Buddhism, which picks and chooses whatever doctrines and practices one finds appealing, is like a self-help approach to suffering. It implicitly assumes that the person who is suffering is better qualified to make decisions regarding therapy than professional therapists. From its inception, however, Buddhism has rejected this notion. A common analogy is a person who has fallen into a hole: others in the same hole are unlikely to be of much help. The best source of release is someone who stands outside it and has the resources to rescue those who are unable to save themselves.

In traditional Buddhism, one's present situation is the result of habit-formation over the course of innumerable lifetimes, during which one has engaged in unskillful actions and created counterproductive proclivities. It is impossible for most beings enmeshed in their own sufferings and negative emotions to gain the sort of objectivity and insight necessary to reverse this process. And once they accept their limitations and submit to the authority of teachers with greater insight and experience than them, the training period is long and arduous.

It is easy to retrogress at any time, and a skillful guru is required to ensure that one stays on the path and avoids its pitfalls. Beings caught up in ignorance, craving, hatred, delusion, and other unwholesome mental states are poor judges of their problems and psychological needs. For people in this situation, imagining that they are better able to choose what to believe or practice than adepts who have attained advanced levels of the path is probably the greatest possible form of self-cherishing from the perspective of traditional Buddhism.

References

Ba so Chos kyi rgyal mtshan, sDe drug mkhan chen Ngag dbang rab brtan, 'Jam dbyangs bzhad pa'i rdo rje, and Bra sti dge bshes Rin chen don grub. 1972. *Four Intertwined Annotations on the Great Exposition of the Stages of the Path [Lam rim mchan bzhi sbrags ma]*. Delhi: Chos 'phel legs ldan.

Batchelor, Stephen. 1997. *Buddhism without Beliefs: A Contemporary Guide to Awakening*. New York: Riverhead Books.

Bendall, Cecil, ed. 1897–1902. *Çikṣāsamuccaya: A Compendium of Buddhistic Teaching Compiled by Çāntideva, Chiefly from Earlier Mahāyāna-sūtras*. St. Petersburg: Imperial Academy (Bibliotheca Buddhica vol. 1).

Bhikkhu Bodhi. 1995. *The Middle Length Discourses of the Buddha: A New Translation of the Majjhima Nikāya*. Boston: Wisdom Publications.

Bhikkhu Bodhi. 2005. "Does Rebirth Make Sense?" *Access to Insight*. www.accesstoinsight.org/lib/authors/bodhi/bps-essay_46.html (accessed July 29, 2015).

Bhikkhu Bodhi. 2012. *The Numerical Discourses of the Buddha: A Translation of the Aṅguttara Nikāya*. Boston: Wisdom Publications.

Buddhadāsa Bhikkhu. 1994. *Heartwood of the Bodhi Tree: The Buddha's Teachings on Voidness*, edited by Santikaro Bhikkhu. Boston: Wisdom Publications.

Coleman, James W. 2001. *The New Buddhism: The Western Transformation of an Ancient Tradition*. New York: Oxford University Press.

Garfield, Jay L. 2002. "Nāgārjuna's Theory of Causality: Implications Sacred and Profane." In *Empty Words: Buddhist Philosophy and Cross-Cultural Interpretation*, 69–85. New York: Oxford University Press.

Knight, Kelvin. 1998. *The MacIntyre Reader*. Notre Dame: University of Notre Dame Press.

MacIntyre, Alasdair. 1984. *After Virtue*, 2nd edition. Notre Dame: University of Notre Dame Press.

Pinker, Steven. 2011. *The Better Angels of Our Nature: Why Violence Has Declined*. New York: Viking.

Vaidya, P.L. ed. 1960. *Aṣṭasāhasrikā Prajñāpāramitā with Haribhadra's Commentary Called Āloka*. Darbhanga: Mithila Institute.

Further Reading

Analayo, Bhikkhu. 2015. *Compassion and Emptiness in Early Buddhist Meditation.* Cambridge: Windhorse Publications.

Brassard, Francis. 2000. *The Concept of Bodhicitta in Śāntideva's "Bodhicaryāvatāra."* Albany: SUNY Press.

Broughton, Jeffrey Lyle. 2009. *Zongmi on Chan.* New York: Columbia University Press.

Chakrabarti, Kisor Kumar. 1999. *Classical Indian Philosophy of Mind: The Nyāya Dualist Tradition.* Albany: SUNY Press.

Chappell, David, ed. 1983. *T'ien-t'ai Buddhism: An Outline of the Fourfold Teachings.* Tokyo: Daiichi Shobō.

Clayton, Barbra. 2006. *Moral Theory in Śāntideva's Śikṣāssamuccaya: Cultivating the Fruits of Virtue.* New York: Routledge.

Cleary, Thomas F. 1995. *Entry into the Inconceivable: An Introduction to Hua-Yen Buddhism.* Honolulu: University of Hawaii Press.

Cook, Francis H. 1989. *Sounds of Valley Streams: Enlightenment in Dōgen's Zen.* Albany: SUNY Press.

Cowherds, The, eds. 2015. *Moonpaths: Ethics and Emptiness.* New York: Oxford University Press.

De Jong, J.W. 1977. *Nāgārjuna's Mūlamadhyamakakārikā Prajñā Nāma.* Revised by Christian Lindtner, 2004. Chennai: Adyar Library.

Dreyfus, Georges B.J. 1997. *Recognizing Reality: Dharmakīrti's Philosophy and Its Tibetan Interpretations.* New Delhi: Sri Satguru Publications.

Duckworth, Douglas, *et al.* 2016. *Dignāga's Investigation of the Percept: A Philosophical Legacy in India and Tibet.* New York: Oxford University Press.

Dunne, John D. 2004. *Foundations of Dharmakīrti's Philosophy.* Boston: Wisdom Publications.

Faure, Bernard. 2009. *Unmasking Buddhism.* Malden: Wiley-Blackwell.

Ganeri, Jonardon. 2007. *The Concealed Art of the Soul: Theories of Self and Practices of Truth in Indian Ethics and Epistemology.* New York: Oxford University Press.

Buddhist Philosophy: A Comparative Approach, First Edition. Edited by Steven M. Emmanuel.
© 2018 John Wiley & Sons, Inc. Published 2018 by John Wiley & Sons, Inc.

Garfield, J.L., Tillemans, T.J.F., and D'Amato, M. 2009. *Pointing at the Moon: Buddhism, Logic, Analytic Philosophy*. New York: Oxford University Press.

Gimello, R.M. and Gregory, P., eds. 1983. *Studies in Ch'an and Hua-Yen*. Honolulu: University of Hawaii Press.

Hadot, Pierre. 2002. *What is Ancient Philosophy?* Cambridge, MA: Harvard University Press.

Hayes, Richard P. 2013. *Dignāga on the Interpretation of Signs*, 2nd edition. New York: Springer.

Heine, Steven. 1994. *Dōgen and the Kōan Tradition: A Tale of Two Shōbōgenzō Texts*. Albany: SUNY Press.

Hoffman, F.J. 1987. *Rationality and Mind in Early Buddhism*. Delhi: Motilal Banarsidass.

Jackson, Roger Reid. 1983. *Is Enlightenment Possible?: An Analysis of Some Arguments in the Buddhist Philosophical Tradition with Special Attention to the Pramāṇasiddhi Chapter of Dharmakīrti's Pramāṇavārttika*. Madison: University of Wisconsin-Madison.

Jayatilleke, K.N. 1963. *Early Buddhist Theory of Knowledge*. London: George Allen & Unwin.

Johansson, R.E.A. 1969. *The Psychology of Nirvana*. London: George Allen & Unwin.

Johansson, R.E.A. 1979. *The Dynamic Psychology of Early Buddhism*. Oxford: Curzon Press.

Kalupahana, D.J. 1992. *A History of Buddhist Philosophy: Continuities and Discontinuities*. Honolulu: University of Hawaii Press.

Kapstein, Matthew. 2001. *Reason's Traces: Identity and Interpretation in Indian and Tibetan Buddhist Thought*. Studies in Indian and Tibetan Buddhism. Boston: Wisdom Publications.

Karma Phuntsho. 2005. *Mipham's Dialectics and the Debates on Emptiness*. London: Routledge.

Keown, D. 2003. *Dictionary of Buddhism*. Oxford: Oxford University Press.

King, Winston L. 2001 [1964]. *In the Hope of Nirvana: The Ethics of Theravada Buddhism*. Seattle: Pariyatti Press.

Kraft, Kenneth, ed. 1992. *Inner Peace, World Peace: Essays on Buddhism and Nonviolence*. Albany: SUNY Press.

Kuijp, Leonard W.J. van der. 1983. *Contributions to the Development of Tibetan Buddhist Epistemology from the Eleventh to the Thirteenth Century*. Wiesbaden: Franz Steiner.

LaFleur, W.R. 1988. *Buddhism: A Cultural Perspective*. Englewood Cliffs: Prentice-Hall.

Lang, Karen. 2003. *Four Illusions: Candrakīrti's Advice to Travelers on the Bodhisattva Path*. New York: Oxford University Press.

Loizzo, J. 2007. *Nāgārjuna's Reason Sixty (Yuktiṣaṣṭikā) with Candrakīrti's Reason Sixty Commentary*. New York: The American Institute of Buddhist Studies at Columbia University.

Matilal, Bimal K. 1971. *Epistemology, Logic, and Grammar in Indian Philosophical Analysis*. The Hague: Mouton.
Ñāṇananda, Bhikkhu. 1986. *Concept and Reality in Early Buddhist Thought*. Kandy, Sri Lanka: Buddhist Publication Society.
Odin, Steven. 1995. *Process Metaphysics and Hua-Yen Buddhism: A Critical Study of Cumulative Penetration vs. Interpenetration*. New Delhi: Sri Satguru Publications.
Pettit, John. 1999. *Mipham's Beacon of Certainty: Illuminating the View of Dzogchen, the Great Perfection*. Boston: Wisdom Publications.
Ruegg, David Seyfort. 1981. *The Literature of the Madhyamaka School of Philosophy in India*. A History of Indian Literature, vol. 7, fasc. 1. Wiesbaden: Harrassowitz.
Ruegg, David Seyfort. 2002. *Prolegomena to Madhyamaka Philosophy, Studies in Indian and Tibetan Madhyamaka Thought, Part II*. Vienna: Arbeitskreis für Tibetische und Buddhistische Studien Universität Wien.
Saratchandra, E.R. 1958. *Buddhist Psychology of Perception*. Colombo, Sri Lanka: Associated Newspapers of Ceylon.
Siderits, M. 2016. *Studies in Buddhist Philosophy*, edited by Jan Westerhoff. New York: Oxford University Press.
Siderits, M., Thompson, E., and Zahavi, D. 2011. *Self, No Self? Perspectives from Analytical, Phenomenological, and Indian Traditions*. New York: Oxford University Press.
Sparham, Gareth. 2005. *Tantric Ethics*. Boston: Wisdom Publications.
Tola, F. and Dragonetti, C. 1995. *Nāgārjuna's Refutation of Logic*. Delhi: Matilal Banarsidass.
Tsomo, Karma Lekshe, ed. 2000. *Innovative Buddhist Women: Swimming Against the Stream*. Richmond, Surrey: Curzon Press.
Vidyabhusana, Satis Chandra. 2002. *A History of Indian Logic: Ancient, Mediaeval and Modern Schools*. Delhi: Motilal Banarsidass.
Walser, Joseph. 2005. *Nāgārjuna in Context: Mahāyāna Buddhism and Early Indian Culture*. New York: Columbia University Press.
Williams, Paul. 2000. *Buddhist Thought: A Complete Introduction to the Indian Tradition*. London: Routledge.
Wright, Dale S. 2009. *The Six Perfections: Buddhism and the Cultivation of Character*. New York: Oxford University Press.
Yotsuya, K. 1999. *The Critique of Svatantra Reasoning by Candrakīrti and Tsong-kha-pa: A Study of Philosophical Proof According to Two Prāsaṅgika Madhyamaka Traditions of India and Tibet*. Stuttgart: Franz Steiner Verlag.
Ziporyn, Brook. 2016. *Emptiness and Omnipresence: An Essential Introduction to Tiantai Buddhism*. Bloomington: Indiana University Press.

Index

Note: page numbers in **bold** refer to illustrations, page numbers in *italics* refer to information contained in tables.

4E approach to cognition   110

a
a posteriori   135
Abhidharma (higher teachings)
    68–71, 88–9, 94, 98, 109–12, 209
absolute idealism   29–30, 31, 35–9
  as panpsychism   30
  singular (nondual)   29, 30
acting-intuition   136
action   12, 17, 109–20, 213
  embodied   118
  justification   216
  moral consequences   57
  pursuing a course of   110
aesthetic meaning   48–9, 53
affective bias   181
afflictions, three primary   224
agency   54, 217
Āḷāra Kālāma   167
Alberti, L.B.   131–2
alerting function   174–5, 178
Aluvihara Rock Temple, Sri Lanka   209
ambiguity   7, 159–60
ambivalence   124–6, 149
American Philosophical Association (APA)   1–2, 4
amygdala   176, 179–80
Anālayo   177–8
analogy, medical   13, 18
analytic philosophy   97–9
androcentrism   190, 192
androgyny, nondualistic   192
anger   22, 24, 213, 218, 224
anomalous monism   112
antireflexivity (AR)   64–7, *65*, 70, 77–9, 81
antisymmetry (AS)   64–6, *65*, 67, 70, 75, 78–81
anxiety   146, 152, 155
APA *see* American Philosophical Association
aphoristic forces   125
apoha-style nominalism   92, 93, 110
Aquinas, T.   4, 73
AR *see* antireflexivity
arhats   228, 233
Aristotelians   13
Aristotle   4, 45, 73, 74–6, 210
  Categories   74
Armstrong   73
art   58, 124–5, 131–2, 135
"art of living"   12
artistic creation   136

Buddhist Philosophy: A Comparative Approach, First Edition. Edited by Steven M. Emmanuel.
© 2018 John Wiley & Sons, Inc. Published 2018 by John Wiley & Sons, Inc.

AS *see* antisymmetry
Asaṅga   69
Asia   68
Asian philosophy   2, 4
Atisha, *Lamp for the Path to Enlightenment...*   18, 24
atomism (A)   66, 67, 98
attachment   191–2, 197, 213
attention   169–73, 175–81
  "biased-competition" model   170
  bottom-up, stimulus-driven   169
  and consciousness   165, 175, 176–80
  focused attention practices   177
  habits of   173
  selective   174–5, 177, 178, 180
  to the present   15–16, 25
  top-down, endogenous orienting   169–70, 171, 177, 178, 180
  universal   173, 175, 177–8
  visual selective   170
attention training techniques   167
  see also meditation
"attentional blink"   176, 178–9
Aurelius, Marcus   14
autonomy   211, 215, 217, 218
  embodied   217
Avataṃsaka Sūtra   124, 127–9, 137
awakening   147, 149, 151, 153, 159–60, 214, 218, 223, 228–9
  see also transcendence
awareness
  bodily   170
  cognitive   172
  emotional   179–80
  universal   127–8
  see also self-awareness
axis mundi   222

b

Baggini, J.   5
Barnes, E.   80
Bashō   123, 135
Batchelor, S.   222, 223
"being in"   74
"being said of"   74
"being-in-the-world"   135
beliefs   12, 17
Bendall, C.   231
Bhagavad Gita   4
Bhāviveka   89, 94
Bhikkhu Bodhi   127, 225–6, 235
binocular rivalry   176
biological emergence   51–3
biological patterns   53
biology, evolutionary   52–3, 55
Bishop, S.R.   168
Blake, W.   137
blindsight   118, 178
Bliss, R.L.   80
Block, N.   174
Blue Cliff Record –50, 7, 145, 147, 152–6, 158–60
bodhicitta ("mind of awakening")   228, 229, 231
Bodhidharma   150, 195–6
Bodhisattvas   205, 228, 229–36
  female   191
  and gender   191, 192, 198
  ideal   24
  omniscience   126–7
  and women's bodies   191, 192, 198
bodily awareness   170
body   54, 55
  disposition   58
  enlightened   190–1
  as inferior to the mind   189
  lived   171
  male   190–1
  marginalization   189
  see also women's bodies
body-mind   54
Bohn, E.D.   80
Bowdoin College   1
Bradley, F.H.   6, 30, 32

Brahamanical tradition   92
  and karma   57
  and metaphysics   47
  and supernaturalism   59
brain   173–4, 179–80
  default mode network   179
  and mental phenomena   45, 46, 54
  and Mindfulness-Based Stress
    Reduction   168
brain damage   178
brainstem   173, 174
breath-energy (*qi*)   132
breathing techniques   170
Bristow, W.   217, 218
Buddha (Siddhārtha Gautama)   18, 19,
    49–60, 68, 207, 209, 221, 222, 233
  and attention training
    techniques   167
  attitude towards women   189, 190,
    191, 193
  and awakening   223
  and the caste system   211
  consciousness   128
  dharma   70
  empiricism   224, 225
  first sermon of   223
  and the four noble truths   223–4
  insight   222
  and karma   57–8
  middle way of   47
  and mindfulness meditation   165–6
  perception of karma and rebirth   225
  and perspectival omniscience   126–8
  pragmatism   224
  psycho-ethical therapy   59–60
  as rationalist   222, 225
  and rebirth   225, 226, 236
  and *sañña*   174
  and supernaturalism   59
  testing of the teachings of   211
  universal awareness   127–8
  see also Dharma
Buddha Way   123, 194

Buddha womb teaching
    (*Tathāgatagarbha*)   197–8
Buddha-nature   158–8, 211
Buddhadāsa Bhikkhu   225
Buddhaghosa   208
buddhahood/Buddhahood   229, 232
  striving for   18–19, 21–2, 24
buddhas   205, 229, 230, 235
  and gender   190, 195–6
  and *Tathāgatagarbha*   197
Buddhism   5–6
  Classical   210
  and a cross-cultural approach to
    cognitive science   7, 165–82
  eclectic approach to   221–2, 236–7
  empiricist stance   231
  Engaged   206, 207–8
  ethics   221–37
  and feminist philosophy   189–202
  heterogeneity   6
  and metametaphysics   6, 87–104
  and metaphysics   87–104
  and panpsychism   29–41
  and philosophy as way of life
    11–27, 209
  political theory   210–11
  rationalist interpretation   221, 222,
    225, 231
  Thai   207
  Yogācāra   29–30, 34, 35–9
  see also early Buddhism; Huayan
    school; Mahāyāna Buddhism;
    Theravāda school (Way of the
    Elders); Tibetan Buddhism; Zen
    Buddhism
Buddhist coherentism   71–2
Buddhist Modernism   7, 205–19, 225
  definition   206–11
  engagement with the West   206–7
  features   207–11
  influences on   206–7
  and rebirth   8
Burma   170

C

Cameron, R.   78
Canberra school   90
Candrakīrti   94, 98, 99
Candrakīrtians   100
caring-compassion   209–10
Carnap, R.   97
Carter, O.   176–7
Cassirer, E.   159
caste system   211
categorical imperative   215, 218
causal agents   49
causal efficacy   116–17
causal generation   114
causal inference   116–19
causal processes   30, 36, 37, 38, 56
causal relations   70
causal totality   117, 118
causality   49–51, 109–20
   Leibniz on   76–7
   physical   56
   psychological   56–7
   tripartite model   111
cause and effect   30, 115, 117, 118
causes   6
   and reasons   109–20
Chan Buddhism   68, 166, 177
   see also Zen Buddhism
change   49–50, 53, 60
chaos   125–6
Chatterjee, A.J.   39
Chengguan   72
China   68
Chinese Buddhism *see* Huayan school
Chogyam Trungpa   206, 208
Christianity
   and conscience   168
   and the omniscience of God   128
Christians   222
Chulalongkorn   207
civilization, Kant on   214–15, 217, 218
Classical Buddhism   210
Clayton, Philip   48

clinical psychology   168, 169, 180
cogito   31
cognition   39, 109
   4E approach to   110
   causal efficacy   116
   and the dependent nature   38
   embedded   110, 112, 114, 118
   embodied   109–20, 217
   enactive account of   114
   and matter   36
   and objects   35
   and perception   37
   and pragmatic efficacy   112–16
   as subject   37
"cognitive access"   174, 175, 180
cognitive awareness   172
cognitive reorientation   224
cognitive science   112
   and Buddhist Modernism   208–9
   cross-cultural approach to   7, 165–82
   reductionist models   111
coherentism (C)   66, 67, 80
   Buddhist   71–2
Coleman, J.   221
Common Era   68
communication   53
compassion   7, 138–9, 208, 216, 227–30, 232, 235
   caring-compassion   209–10
   and gender   196
   and human rights   210–11
   impartial   21, 24
   kenotic   130, 134–6, 138
   and rebirth   8
   universal   21, 22, 24, 25
complexity   126
concentration meditation   167, 176–7
conceptual practices   112–13
conditionality   56
Confucianism   3, 68
Confucius   4
connectedness   64, 67
conscience   168

consciousness   109–10, 165–6,
    173–80, 232
  altered states of   167
  and attention   165, 175, 176–80
  Buddha consciousness   128
  continuity after death   224
  core level   173–5
  Dignāga on   37
  emergence   53–6
  exploration   165
  foundational consciousness   38–9
  "hard problem" of   36
  "internal"   38
  neuroscience of   165
  phenomenal consciousness   174–5,
    178, 180–1
  as physical phenomenon   32
consummate nature   38
contingencies   76–7
continuity, principle of   51–3
Corbetta, M.   178
Coseru   7
cosmology   24, 76
cosmos, focusing attention on the
    15, 25
Crane, S.   156
creativity   146, 147, 155, 156–7, 161
  artistic   136
cross-cultural cognitive science
    7, 165–82
cross-cultural dialogue   5
cross-cultural metaphysics   87,
    99, 100
crypto-dualism   33
cultivation (philosophy of
    education)   214
cultural artifacts   38
Cusanus   124, 133–4
  De Docta Ignorantia   133–4

d

Dalai Lama   16, 17, 206–9, 213, 215
Damasio, A.   171, 173, 174
dao   71

Daoism   68, 71
Daoist landscape paintings   131–2
Darwin, C.   52
Darwinian theory   52–3
Dasgupta, S.   80
Davidson, R.   165
Davis, B.   200
de Beauvoir, S.   196–7
death   224, 226
  contemplation of the certainty
    of   19
  and the end of suffering   234–5
  reflection on   166, 180–1
deductive reasoning   115
default mode network   179
Dehaene, S.   176
delusion   166, 208, 237
democracy   154
democratic values   210–11
Democritus   98
demons   50
dependent arising
  doctrine of   47, 50–1, 59, 60
  twelvefold formula of   50
dependent nature   38
dependent origination
  (*pratītyasamutpāda*)   68–9,
    208, 215
depth   4
Descartes, R.   4, 31, 45
Deshan   152
Desimone, R.   170
desire   12, 14–15, 17, 23, 191, 213
  as hindrance to freedom   212–13
  and reason   216
  removal through meditation   169
  and suffering   223–4
detachment   16
determinism   57–8
Dewey, J.   47, 49, 51–5
  and continuity   51–2
  and humans and nature   53–4
  middle way of   47
  and religious meaning   58–9

Deweyan pragmatism 6
  comparison with early Buddhism 47–8
  emergent naturalism in 45–61
DeWitt Hyde, W. 1
Dharma (teachings of the Buddha) 69–70, 130, 209, 221, 225, 233
  and gender 194, 195, 196
  as system of testable beliefs 211
"Dharma combat" 130
Dharmakīrti 7, 35, 37, 88–9, 91–2, 94, 109–20
dialogue 13–14
Dignāga 6, 35–7, 89, 109, 110, 113, 115, 117
disciples 149, 153
discipline 214
discursive analysis 16
disposition 215
Dōgen 7, 123–4, 133, 136–7, 148, 160, 193–7, 199–200, 207
dogma 211, 221, 222
Dongshan Liangjie 149
doubt 152, 155, 160
Dragon's Gate 149
dream argument 35
Dretske, F. 111
Dreyfus, G. 169
drives 125, 138
drugs, mood-altering 234
dualism 31, 33, 35, 36, 37, 58, 189
  Buddha's rejection of 55–6
  and the Middle Way 45–7
  non-naturalist 55
  as unscientific 45–6
  see also nondualism
duality 37
dukkha see suffering
Duncan, J. 170
Dunne, J. 165
Dushun 72, 128, 129
dynamism 138–9

e
early Buddhism
  comparison with Deweyan pragmatism 47–8
  emergent naturalism in 45–61
East Asia 68
education, Kant on 214–15, 217
EEG *see* electroencephalogram
ego 131
  death of the egocentric ego 131
  Nietzsche and the 126
ego-self 136
egocentrism 131, 133–4, 138, 208, 217–18
egoism 126, 134, 213
eight causes 58
Eight *Garudhammas* (eight heavy rules) 193–4
Einstein, A. 232
ek-stasis (standing outside oneself) 130
electroencephalogram (EEG) 179
eliminativism 93
Eliot, T.S. 157
embodied action 118
embodied autonomy 217
embodied cognition 109–20, 217
embodiment
  female 191, 196, 198, 199
  male 193, 195
emergence 37
emergent naturalism 6
  biological emergence 51–3
  and causality 49–51
  definition 48–9
  in early Buddhism and Deweyan pragmatism 45–61
  emergence of consciousness 53–6
  emergence of mind 53–6
  emergent levels of reality 49–51, 55
  and karma 56–8
  and moral agency 56–8
  ontological claims 48–9

principle of continuity 51–3
and religious meaning 58–60
emotion 208–9
  affective valence/hedonic tone 171–2
  afflictive 213, 218, 224
  emotional awareness 179–80
  emotional distortions 181
  emotional responses 171, 179–81
  emotional stimuli 176
empathy 7, 130
  ecstatic 130, 134–6, 138
empirical evidence 117
empiricism
  and panpsychism 32
  radical 32
empiricists 73
emptiness 7, 24–5, 192–3, 231–2, 234
  as dependent designation 71
  and "placental economy" 200–1
  standpoint of 136
encoding 175
energy 45, 46, 52
Engaged Buddhism 206, 207–8
enlightenment 7, 19–21, 23–4, 47, 127, 133, 146–7, 160, 209
  achieving well-being through 17
  and Buddhist Modernism 211, 215–18
  and change 60
  "Chinese" simultaneous enlightenment approach 16
  definition 211–15
  and emptiness 201
  and the European Enlightenment 205–6
  and human rights 211
  "Indian" gradual enlightenment approach 16–17
  Kantian 206, 209, 211–18
  Scottish Enlightenment 215–18
  spirit of 24
  symbols of 197
  and thinking for oneself 211, 212–13, 217–18
  women and 189, 190–1, 193–201
ensō 201, **202**
Epictetus, *Handbook* 14, 24
Epicureans 6, 12–16
  "fourfold remedy" 14
Epicurus 13, 14, 18
epiphany 7, 145–6, 157–8
epistemological foundationalism 115
epistemological optimism 112
epistemological perspectivism 124, 129
Epistemological school 88–9
epistemology 4, 7, 112–13
  naturalized 109–10
  and philosophy as way of life 13, 25
equality 218
  gender 191, 194
equanimity 209–10
essences, dependence 77
ethical discipline 21
ethical training 21, 22, 166, 168–9
ethics 4, 221–37
  Confucian 3
  and karma 58
  and panpsychism 33–4
  and philosophy as way of life 13, 24
  and physicalism 46
European Enlightenment
  and Buddhist enlightenment 205–6
  and Buddhist Modernism 206
  definition 211–15
  and human rights 210
evidence–subject relations 113–14
evil 225, 226
  women's bodies as 192, 193, 195–6, 197
evolutionary biology 52–3, 55
existence 47, 49

experience   47–8, 56
  and determinism   58
  and matter   36
  reduction   46
experiential metaphysics   32
experiential world   30–4, 68–9
extendability (E)   64–7, 65, 71, 75, 78
extended objects   35–6
extended things   35–6
external goods   227, 233
  of effectiveness   228
external objects   89
external realism   35, 36
external relations   29
external world   35, 38, 99, 100

f
F's   87–9, 91–3, 94, 96–7, 99
facts   216
fatalism   57
Faulkner, W.   157
Fazang   68, 71, 72, 130–1
feedback   170
feedforward   170
female monastic order   189, 194
  see also nuns
"female nature"   190
femaleness   191
feminine, the   7, 196, 199–200
feminist philosophy   7, 189–202
  Dōgen's   193–6, 197, 199–200
  and revalorization of the maternal body   197–202
  and *Tathāgatagarbha*   197–8
  and Zen nondualism   192, 196–7, 199–200
FEs see foundational elements
Fine, K.   78, 80, 96, 97–8
five *skandhas/khandas*   54, 126, 171-80, 191–2, 208, 208–9, 210, 216, 217
"floating perspective"   124, 131–2
flux   71

fMRI see functional magnetic resonance imaging
form   111
  emptiness of   193
foundational consciousness   38–9
foundational elements (FEs)   66, 67
foundational object   66
foundationalism (F)   66, 67, 71, 73, 76, 77–9, 80
"Four Immeasurables"   209–10
  see also loving-kindness
Four Noble Truths   208, 223–4
free will   57, 212
freedom   212–13, 217
functional magnetic resonance imaging (fMRI)   177

g
Garfield, J.   4, 215, 230–5
Garland, E.L.   180
"gathering virtue"   21
Geluk order   17
Gelukpa order (Tibetan)   228, 235
gender equality   191, 194
gender issues   7, 189–202
generalizability   88, 97
generosity   21
"ghost in the machine"   31
Gillon, B.   114, 118
global error theory   98
global literacy   1
globalization   3
globalized philosophical curriculum   3–4
gnosis   37
God   37, 59, 66, 67, 73, 190
  dependence of everything on   76–7
  existence of   76, 77
  as infinite sphere   133, 134
  intellect   76, 77
  and monads   129
  omniscience   128
goddesses   192–3

gods   50, 59, 72
Goldstein, J.   179
Gombrich, Richard   57, 58
good   225, 226
good ends   215
grand theory   92–4
great chain of being   73
"great death, the"   131
Great Treatise on the Stages of the Path to Enlightenment, The (Tsongkhapa)   11–13, 17, 18–23
Great Treatise (Tsongkhapa)   6
greed   166
Greek culture   1
Greek philosophers   2, 11, 12, 23, 24, 25
Green, L.   199
Griffin, D.R.   33
Griffiths, Paul   127, 128
Grosnick, W.H.   198, 199
Gross, R.   190
grounding   73–4, 76, 79–80
"guest," position of   7, 130–1, 136, 138–9
Guo Xi   131–2
gurus   237

h

Ha-shang   16, 21, 23, 25
Hadot, P.   11–17, 20, 23–5
Hakuin   131, 196
Hamilton, S.   171
happiness   15, 223, 225, 235
Harries, K.   133–4
Hartshorne, C.   33
Harvey, P.   173–4
hatred   166, 213, 218, 237
Hayes, R.   114, 118
Hazlitt, W.   134–5
heart-mind   134
Heidegger, M.   123, 125, 132, 135, 136
Heisenberg, W.   156
Hellenistic philosophers   6, 16, 24

Hempel, C.   34
"Hempel's dilemma"   34
Herman, B.   215
Herschock, P.D.   5
Herzberger, H.   91
heteronomy   213, 217, 218
Heywood, C.A.   178
Horwich, P.   96
"host," position of   6, 130–1, 138–9
Huangbo   153
Huayan school   68, 71–2, 124, 127, 128–9, 130, 133, 137–8
Huemer, M.   100
human affairs, insignificance of   15, 16
human person, the   53–6
human rights   210–11
humanism, secular   206
Hume, D.   4, 73, 216–17
hypostates   73
"hypothetical imperative"   214

i

"I"   15
  as privileged subject   213
lamas   225
idealism   88–9, 135
  absolute   29–30, 31, 35–9
  and dualism   33
  and external realism   36
  and materialism   33–4
  and metaphysics   47
  and the mind   29, 31, 33
  subjective   29, 30, 31, 35–9
  transcendental   217
ideas   216
identity   114
ignorance   133
illumination   149, 160, 207
imagined nature   38
immaturity   212, 215
impartite objects   89, 93, 98
impermanence   49, 68–9, 167, 191, 208

inclinations   212–13, 216
inclusiveness   4
incompleteness   7, 49
independent existence, myth of   31
independent verification   211
India   68, 221
Indian tradition   3, 16–17
individualism   217, 218
individuality, transcendence   15
inductive reasoning   113, 115
inference, theory of   6, 109, 110, 113, 114, 116–19
infinite   126, 133, 137
infinite regress, vicious   78
infinitism (I)   67, 71, 78
  metaphysical   80
Inner Science of the Mind   208–9
insight   22–3, 25, 60, 155, 223
insight meditation   213
intelligibility, principles of   112
intention   57, 208
intentionality   109–12
interconnection   136–7, 139, 218
  singular event of   135, 137
interdependence   129, 208, 215, 218
interdependent origination   129, 137
internal goods   227, 232–3
  of excellence   228, 233
internal relations   29, 36, 39
interoception   179
interpenetration, mutually circulating   138–9
interpretation   126
intuition   136, 139
Irigaray, L.   200, 201
Islamic scholarship   2, 3

j
Jackson, Frank   90–1, 92–3
James, W.   30, 32, 171
Jenkins, C.S.   79
Jo nang pa   94
Joyce, J.   7, 145–6, 157
  Dubliners   145, 157, 158
  Ulysses   146, 157–8
joyous perseverance   22
Jullien, F.   132
justice   210, 226

k
Kabat-Zinn, J.   167, 168
Kamakura era   160–1
Kamalaśīla   16–17
Kant, I.   4, 73
  and autonomy   211
  and education   214–15, 217
  and enlightenment   206, 211–18
  and morality   212–17
Kantian enlightenment   206, 209, 211–18
karma   19–20, 24, 207, 230
  awareness of   225, 236
  cessation   228
  and emergent naturalism   56–8
  and rebirth   223, 224–5, 226, 228, 234–6
kāryānumāna argument   109, 114, 117, 119
Katsura, S.   115
Keats, J.   125, 134, 156
Keijzer, F.   119
Kentridge, R.W.   178
Khajjaniya Sutta   172, 173
Kierkegaard, S.   152
"knowing of non-knowing"   136–7
knowing wrongly   181
knowledge   135
  empirical   32
  and enlightenment   127
  limitations of   125
  limits to   125–6
  and omniscience   126–8
  and perception   113–14, 118
  and perspective   125, 134

threefold true 127
  as virtue 127
known objects 35
kōans 7, 145–54
  evaluative commentaries 145–54
Koch, C. 176
Korean Zen Buddhism 168
Kyoto School 124, 133

l
laity 195
Leibniz, G. 73, 76–7, 124, 128–9
Leighton, T.D. 196, 197, 198
Leonardo da Vinci 132
letting-be 123, 136
Levering, Miriam 190
Lewis, David 90
liberation 18–20, 22–4, 50, 59, 138
  from suffering 223, 224
  and metaphysics 90
  of women 191
life, organic 52
life-world 37
linear perspective 131–2
linguistic meaning 53
linguistic practices 112–13, 115
Linji 124, 130–1, 152, 153
Lipps, Theodore 134
lishi wuai 72
"living well" 11
logic 4, 51, 115
logico-epistemological school 109
logos 135
lokaprasiddha 100
loops 65, 66, 67, 79
Loori, J.D. 201
Louden, R. 214, 215
loving-kindness 134, 167, 169, 209–10
Lowe, E.J. 80, 112
Lutz, A. 165, 177

m
MacIntyre, A. 227, 228, 232
Madhyamaka (Middle Way) 17–18, 45–7, 52, 54, 59, 68, 70–1, 94, 96–7
Mādhyamikas (followers of the Middle Way) 17–18, 94–6, 98–100
Mahāsatipaṭṭhāna Sutta 169, 173
Mahasi Sayadaw 170
Mahāyāna Buddhism 18, 19, 21, 24, 68, 228
  Abhidharma 169
  and bodhisattvas 230–1, 235, 236
  and Buddha omniscience 127
  and Buddhist Modernism 206
  Chinese forms 68, 71
  and gender issues 192
  and rebirth 236
  Yogācāra 29
  see also Madhyamaka; Mādhyamikas
Majjhima Nikāya 173
Makkhali Gosāla 57
male body 190–1
male domination 190
maleness 191
manasikāra (attention) 173, 175, 177–8
Manna, A. 177
Manorathanandin 88
Many, and the One 129
Mao Zedong 226
maraṇasati (reflection on death) 166, 180–1
masculine, the 7, 196, 199–200
mass murder 234–5
masters 130–1, 138, 149–51, 153, 160–1
materialism 31–3
  and dualism 33
  and idealism 33–4
  metaphysics 47
  strangeness of 32

materiality   35
maternal body, revalorization
      197–202
matter   31, 32, 33, 34, 35, 52
   and cognition   36
   and experience   36
   and mind   33, 34, 36, 37
   mind–matter unity   33, 34
   and physicalism   45, 46
Matthews, F.   33–4
maturity   212, 214–15
Mazu   149
MBSR (Mindfulness-Based Stress
      Reduction)   167–8
McMahan, David   206
meaning   123, 125
   aesthetic   48–9, 53
   and emergent naturalism   48–50,
      53, 58–60
   religious   58–60
   social   53
mechanism, principles of   112
medical analogies   13, 18
meditation   14, 60, 165–7, 234
   and Buddha   223
   and Buddhist Modernism
      208–9, 210
   concentration meditation   167,
      176–7
   and desire   169
   on the emptiness of the self   7
   and "I" as privileged subject   213
   insight meditation   213
   and lay-Buddhists   209
   mindfulness meditation   7, 165–70,
      173, 175, 177–81
   open monitoring types   177
   on the self/"I"   15
   serenity meditation   6, 22–3, 25
   and yogic direct perception
      225, 236
meditative stabilization   22
mental, the   34, 111–12, 117

mental content   109–12
mental cultivation/training   167,
      175, 224
   see also meditation
mental phenomena   45, 46, 48, 54–5
mental states   89, 166, 208, 237
meritocracy   154
Merleau-Ponty, M.   132
Meru, Mount   222
metametaphysics   87–104
metaontology   6, 87
metaphysical dependence   6, 63–83
   in Buddhist traditions   67–72,
      80–1
   fruits of dialogue   80–1
   grounding   73–4, 76, 79–80
   ontological dependence   73–4, 77,
      79, 80
   structural features   64
   taxonomy   63–7, 65, 70, 71, 72,
      75–8, 80
   in Western traditions   73–81
metaphysical infinitism   80
metaphysical realism   88–9, 97
metaphysics   6, 24, 45–61, 87–104,
      109, 114
   contemporary   45–6
   dualist   35, 45–6, 52
   early Buddhist   6
   experiential   32
   and inductive reasoning   113
   legitimacy   90–3
   naturalistic   46, 47
   as necessary   90–3
   and panpsychism   32
   and philosophy as way of life   13
   physicalist   45–6
   pluralistic   51
   polarization   45
   and pragmatism   47
   qualified argumentation   87–90, 94,
      96–9
quietism   94–9

serious 90–1, 92–3
unqualified argumentation
  87–90, 94
and Yogācāra 36–7
Middle Way school (*Madhyamaka*)
  17–18, 45–7, 52, 54, 59, 68, 70–1,
  94, 96–7
see also Mādhyamikas (followers of
  the Middle Way)
Mīmāṃsaka Kumārila Bhaṭṭa 92
mind 7, 29–33, 36–9, 51, 159
  and absolute idealism 31
  Buddhist model of the 54, 126,
    171–80, 217
  emergence 53–6
  five aggregates (*khandas*) model of
    the 54, 126, 171–80
  habits of 172, 173
  and idealism 29, 31, 33
  investigation in cognitive
    science 165
  and materialism 33
  and matter 33, 34, 36, 37
  and panpsychism 29–31
  reduction to matter 33
  settled and unified state of 167
  and subjective idealism 29, 31
  and suffering 59
  supermind 37
  training 167, 175, 224
  and Yogācāra 29
  see also body-mind
"mind of awakening" (*bodhicitta*)
  228, 229, 231
mind–body dualism 45, 54, 55
mind–body problem 36
mind–matter unity 33, 34
mind-wandering 167, 177,
  179, 181
mindfulness
  and Buddhist Modernism/Engaged
    Buddhism 208
  definition 168

and knowing wrongly 181
meaning of 166–71
mindfulness meditation 7, 165–70,
  173, 175, 177–81
Mindfulness-Based Stress Reduction
  (MBSR) program 167–8
"minding" 169
misogyny 189, 190, 192, 200
Mole, C. 176
Moliya Sīvaka 58
momentariness 114
monadology 124, 128–9
monads 76, 128–9, 133
monarchy, enlightened 211
monastic orders
  gender issues 189, 190–5
  see also monks; nuns; Sangha;
    Tsongkhapa
monism 36
  dual-aspect 37
  neutral 36, 38
monks 16, 60, 177, 225
  and Buddhism as philosophy 209
  dis-attachment from women's form
    191–2
  and enlightenment 205–6
  gender issues 189, 190–5
  see also Sangha; Tsongkhapa
mood-altering drugs 234
moral agency 56–8
moral conduct 59–60, 166
moral cultivation 227, 228, 232, 233
moral development 23–4, 213–14,
  217, 232
moral judgement 216–17
moral psychology 59, 111, 208–9,
  213–14
moral responsibility 57
moral virtues 21, 23
morality 19–20, 226–9, 231–3, 235
  Kantian 212–17
moralization, Kant on 214, 215,
  217, 218

Morganti, M. 78, 80
Morrissey, L.J. 157
mothers 228–9
multiculturalism 4
multiverse 129, 133, 136–7
murder, mass 234–5
Muslims 222
Musō Soseki 160, 161
"mutually circulating interpenetration" 138–9
Muzhou 153
mystical insight 155

n
Nāgārjuna 31, 68, 94, 213, 232, 233, 235
  Mūlamadhyamakakārikā 70–1
nāma-rūpa 54
natural science 45–7, 52, 117
natural world 47, 50, 53, 55, 57, 60, 77
naturalism 47, 110
  eliminative 48
  phenomenological 112
  and physicalism 48
  reductive 48
  and supernaturalism 59
  see also emergent naturalism
naturalistic metaphysics 46, 47
naturalization 117
nature 49, 52–5, 160–1
  and karma 57
  and meaning 58
necessary conditions 31
negative argumentation 87–8
"negative capability" 134, 156
Nehamas, A. 124–5
"neither one nor many" argument 88, 89
Neo-Platonists 73
Net of Indra 72, 128–30, 137
neural sciences 45
neuroimaging 170, 177
neuroscience 118, 165, 172
New York Times (newspaper) 2

Newton, I. 156
Nhat Hanh, Thich 206, 208
nibbāna 60
  see also nirvana
Nietzsche, F. 7, 123, 124–6, 131, 134
nihilism 89
nirvana 19–20, 22, 205–6, 224–5, 228, 230, 234
  see also nibbāna
Nishida Kitarō 133, 135–6, 148, 200, 201
Nishitani Keiji 123–4, 130, 133, 135–9
no-self 126, 225, 231, 232
nominalism 89, 91–3, 113
  apoha-style 92, 93, 110
non-experience 33, 34
non-knowing, knowing of 136–7
non-observation 115–16
non-substances 74–5
nondualism 33
  Zen 192, 196–7, 199–200
nonegocentric perspectivism 7, 123–43
nonexistence 88–9, 91
nonwillfully 125, 136, 138, 139
not knowing 181
novelty, formation 52, 53
nuns 195–6
  see also female monastic order

o
objectivity 16, 135
  methodological 34
  ontological 34
objects 35–9, 136
  and cognition 35
  extended 35–6
  foundational 66
  known 35
  as observer-dependent 35
  of phenomenal reality 72
  and subjects 135
  of ultimate reality 72
obscurations 224

observation   30, 31, 115–17
observer-dependence   35
Ohnuma, R.   197
omniscience, perspectival   126–8
Ōmori Sogen   131
One, the (God)   73
One, and the Many   129
O'Neill, E.   157
O'Neill, O.   217–18
ontological dependence   73–4, 77, 79, 80
ontological emergence, strong   49, 56, 57
ontological seriousness   90
ontology   87, 91, 94–9, 129, 137
   see also metaontology
"open monitoring"   177
order   125–6, 135, 226
organic/psycho-physical level   51
other   208

p
Pāli Canon   7, 18, 50, 59–60, 127–8, 165–6, 168–9, 171, 173–5, 177–8, 180–1, 209, 222–4, 228, 236
Pāli scholars   173–4
pain   223, 224
painting   124–5
Paṇḍita Aśoka   91
panfictionalism   94–5, 98
panphysicalism   33
panpsychism   6, 29–41
   as absolute idealism   30
   definition   29, 33, 34
   and empiricism   32
   and ethics   33–4
   and metaphysics   32
   monism   36
   nonduality   33
   singular (nondual)   30
   strong form (animistic panpsychism) 29–30, 31
   weak form (relational panpsychism) 30, 31

parables   159
"paradox of representation"   135
parsimony, quantitative   78
particulars   89, 91–3, 95, 98–9, 112
   unique   115
partite objects   89, 93, 98
parts (*skandhas*)   69, 191–2, 208, 208–9, 210, 216, 217
Parvizi, J.   173, 174
passions   12, 14, 15, 17, 23, 116
passivity   136
path, the   224, 225, 236, 237
patience   21–2
Patriarchs of Zen   195
patriarchy   130, 189, 198, 200
Paul, D.   191
peace, inner   208
perception   30, 35–8, 173, 176–7
   and cognition   37
   and knowledge   113–14, 118
   and real particulars   112
perceptual distortions   176–9, 181
personal growth   156
personal reflection   154
personal transformation   171, 172, 173–4, 181
personhood   54
persons   53–6, 69
   of great capacity   18–21, 24
   of medium capacity   18–20, 24
   of small capacity   18–20, 24
perspectival delimitation   7, 124–6, 128, 131, 134, 139
perspectival multiplicity/plurality   125, 126
perspective, linear   131–2
perspectivism   123–43
   ambivalence of Nietzsche's 124–6
   egocentric   124, 130, 131–2
   floating   124, 131–2
   nonegocentric   7, 123–43
   in Western art   131–2

phenomena 31, 35, 48–50
  higher order 48, 49, 51–2
  lower order 48–9, 51–2
  psychological 56–7
phenomenal consciousness 174–5, 178, 180–1
phenomenological naturalism 112
phenomenology 109, 117, 135
philosophy
  as therapeutic 13
  as training for death 14–15
  as way of life 11–27
"physical," definitions of 34
physical causality 56
physical parts (*rūpa*) 69, 171, 191–3
physical world 45
physicalism 33–7, 58, 93
  and ethics 46
  metaphysics 47
  Middle Way between dualism and physicalism 45–7
  and naturalism 48
  reductive nature 45–8, 54, 59
physico-chemical level 51, 54–5
physics 31, 34, 48, 156
physicSism 34
Pinker, S. 233
"placental economy" 200–1
Plato 4, 14, 24
Platonists 13
pleasure 15
pluralism, philosophical 3–5, 7
"pluralism by partition" 5
poiesis 136
political theory, Buddhist 210–11
poststructural relativism 33–4
pragmatic efficacy 112–16
pragmatic reasoning 115
pragmatism 93
Prajñākaragupta 35
Prāsaṅgika-Mādhyamika philosophy 17, 18, 22
prejudice 34

present moment
  focusing attention on the 15–16, 25, 167, 168
  infinite value of the 15
  location of happiness within the 15
Priest, G. 80, 96
principals 130
"principle of perspective" 134
Prinz, J. 171, 176
priority 75
process externalism 6, 119
Protagorian world-picture 132
Proust, M. 158
psycho-ethical therapy 59–60
psychological causality 56–7
psychological defilements 59, 60
psychological phenomena 56–7
psychological therapy 236
psychology
  clinical 168, 169, 180
  moral 59, 111, 208–9, 213–14
Pythagoras 24

q
qi 132
qualia 111
qualified argumentation 87–90, 94, 96–9
qualities 74
quantum mechanics 156
quasi-universals 92
quietism 94–9
Quine, W.V. 100
Quinean program 98, 99
Quinn, P.L. 3

r
radical nondualism 7
rational conduct 213
rational materialism 226
rationalism 205, 212, 217
rationalists 221, 222, 225, 226, 231
REAL 99–100

realism   135
reality   37–8, 87
  absolute   98
  Buddha on   47
  conventional   69, 70–2
  emergent levels of   49–51, 55
  hierarchical structuring of   73, 80
  as participatory affair   31
  relative   98
  self-awareness as   37
  ultimate   69, 70–1
  Western orthodoxy of   73
REALLY operator   88–90, 96, 98
reason   25
  and desire   216
  and the European
    Enlightenment   206, 212–13, 216, 217, 218
reasoning
  deductive   115
  inductive   113, 115
  inferential   116
  pragmatic   115
reasons   6
  and causes   109–20
rebirth   8, 18–20, 24, 205–7, 222–6, 228–31, 234–6
  awareness of   225, 236
  cessation   228
  as fiction   234
  and motherhood   197
  necessity of   235
  and suffering   224
reductionism   111–12
  see also Abhidharma
reflection   166, 180–1, 213
reincarnation   225
relation   114
  external   29
  internal   29, 36, 39
  and metaphysical dependence   63–83
relational structure of existence   29, 30, 31, 33, 36

relativity, special theory of   232
religious authority, rejection   205, 206, 212
religious freedom   212
religious meaning   58–60
religious tolerance   212
Renaissance Western artists   124, 131
responsibility   217
restraint   21
retreats   210, 223
revelation   158
rhetoric, of uncertainty   145–63
Rolls, E.   170
Roman philosophers   11, 12, 23, 24, 25
Rosch, E.   110
Rousseau, J.J.   212, 214
rūpa (form)   69, 171, 191–3
Russell, B.   73

s
"sage, the," state of the   12, 15, 25
Said, E.   156
Śākya Chokden   37
Sakyamuni   190
Salzberg, S.   179
saṁkhāra (volitional activities)   172–3
samsara   228
  liberation from   205, 223
  and motherhood   197
Samyé monastery   16
Sangha   207–8
sañña (cognizing)   171, 173–4
Sanskrit sources   89, 236
Śāntarakṣita   89
Śāntideva   18, 21, 213–15, 218, 230
Sariputra/Shariputra   192–3
satellites   130
sati   168–9, 170, 178, 180–1
satipaṭṭhāna (establishing *sati*)   170
satori   157, 159–60
Schaffer, J.   78, 80
Schouten, M.   119
Schubert, R.   170

Schulman, G.L.   178
science   45–6, 49, 50, 99, 221
Scottish Enlightenment   215–18
Scotus, J.D.   73
secular humanism   206
"seeing things as they are"   181
self   123, 130, 136, 191, 208
  absence of   35
  Buddhist theory of the (five
    skandhas)   191–2, 208, 208–9,
    210, 216, 217
  emptiness of the   7
  meditations on the   7, 15
  negation   131
  as not the center of the universe
    133–4
  as nothingness   136
  permanent   54
  rejection of the autonomous   215
  transcendence   131, 134
  transformative reorientation of
    the   215
  true   131, 209
  see also no-self
self-awareness   36–7, 154, 158
self-being (*svabhāva*)   69, 70, 72
self-confidence   130, 131
self-discovery   146
self-emptying   136
self-expression, imaginative/creative
  146, 155
self-knowledge   155
self-love   213, 215, 218
self-realization   146, 147, 155,
  156, 160
self-reflection   145
self-transcendence   131
  horizontal   134
  vertical   134
selfishness   131, 213, 218
selflessness   24–5
sensitive dependence on initial
  conditions   172
sensory processing   170

separation   75
Sera Chökyi gyaltsan   89
serenity meditation   6, 22–3, 25
serial killers   234
"seven cause-and-effect method"   21
Shakespeare, W.   135
shanshui paintings   132
Shell, R.   156
shishi wuai   72
Shizuteru, Ueda   131
Siddhārtha Gautama *see* Buddha
Siderits, M.   93, 96
Silk Route   68
Silverstein, R.G.   179
singularities, denial of   31
six perfections   21–3, 229
Skeptics   13
"skillful means"   138
Smith, J.E.H.   2–3, 5
Sober, E.   100
social engagement   8
social meaning   53
social/aesthetic level   51
society, socio-cultural
  transformation   214
Socrates   14
Socratic dialogue   13–14
solipsism   39
Song China   124, 131–2, 145–50,
  152–60, 195
  landscape painters   124, 131, 132
soteriological inclusiveness   192
soul, cures for   13
sound   115
speaking   116
special theory of relativity   232
Spinoza, B.   37
"spiritual exercises"   6, 11, 13–15, 17,
  19–20, 23–5
spiritual realization   146–7,
  155–6, 160
Sponberg, A.   190, 191, 192
Sprigge, Timothy   33
"stages of the path" literature   18

Stalin, J.   226
Steinkellner, E.   113–14
Stoicism   6, 15
Stoics   12–16, 24
Strawson, G.   32, 34
strong ontological emergence   49, 56, 57
Stuhr, J.J.   5
Su Shi   159
subject–object duality, primal confusion   208, 213
subjective idealism   6, 29, 30, 31, 35–9
subjectivity   34, 135, 196
subjects   37, 38
  and objects   135
  women as   196–7
substances   37
  individual (primary)   74–5
  simple   128–9
  unique suchness of   135
  universal (secondary)   74–5
Sudhana   129
suffering (*dukkha*)   17, 22–4, 50, 205, 223
  acceptance   22
  of change   223
  combating through philosophy   13, 18–19
  and desire   223–4
  and the Four Noble Truths   208
  liberation from   18, 24, 47, 138, 208, 223, 224, 229–36
  and motherhood   197, 229
  of pain   223
  pervasive   223
  primary causes   59
  and rebirth   20, 224
  reduction through mindfulness meditation   167
  and religious life   59
  universal nature   218, 228, 235
sufficient conditions   31
Sufficient Reason, Principle of   79
Sumeru, Mount   145, 151

Sun, the, Su Shi's parable of the   159
supermind   37
supernaturalism   59
Sutras   209
Svātantrikas   100
sympathetic joy   209–10

t

tabula rasa   136
Tahko, T.E.   78, 80
Taoist ethics   3
Tathāgatagarbha (Buddha womb teaching)   197–8
Team Buddha   230–5
temporality   114
"ten non-virtues"   21
Ten Oxherding Pictures   146–7
Tetsurō, W.   196
Thai Buddhism   207
thalamus   173, 174
"theory of everything"   92–4
Theravāda school (Way of the Elders)   68, 127
  and Buddhist Modernism   206
  and mindfulness meditation   166, 167, 168, 177
  and the path   225
things   49
thinking
  consistency in   218
  distortions of   181
  from the standpoint of others   218
  for oneself   211, 212–13, 217–18
Thompson, E.   110
three jewels   19, 236
threefold training   59–60
Tibet   16, 89
Tibetan Buddhism   6, 16–18, 166, 221, 225
  and Buddhist Modernism   207
  and concentration meditation   176–7
  philosophy   209
token-identity theories   111–12, 114
tokenism   3, 5

Touzi 150, 158
Tower of Maitreya 129
transcendence 15, 127, 131, 160, 214, 218, 224–5, 228
  see also awakening
transcendent reality 59
transcendental idealism 217
transformation 50, 171, 181, 214
  and art 58
  female to male 191, 195
  and meditative training 172, 173–4
  of moral orientation 213
  of motivational structure 213
  personal 23, 25, 228
  phenomenological 213, 215
  of society 214
  see also enlightenment
transformational experiences 149, 153
transformative reorientation of the self 215
transitivity (T) 64–7, 65, 75, 77–8, 81
  failures 79–80
Tripiṭaka 209
triple inferential method 113, 115
truth 114, 116
  customary 100
  modal 77
Tsongkhapa 11–27, 96–7, 99, 228–9, 232
  The Great Treatise on the Stages of the Path to Enlightenment 6, 11, 12, 13, 17, 18–23
Tsuchiya, N. 176
"twofold self-grasping" 213

u

Uddaka Rāmaputta 167
ultimately ungrounded (UG) 67
uncertainty 7, 145–63
  complexity 159–60
  first level of (negative meaning) 160
  as model of self-realization 145–8
  power of 156
  second level of (positive meaning) 160
  third level of (hermeneutic reflexivity) 160
uncertainty principle 156
unconscious error, theory of 93
universal attention 173, 175, 177–8
universal awareness 127–8
universal compassion 21, 22, 24, 25
universal substances 74–5
universals 88, 89, 91–3, 98–100
universe 31
  clockwork 156
  infinite 133, 137
  as multiverse 129, 133, 136–7
  and the Net of Indra 128–9
unqualified argumentation 87–90, 94

v

Vaerla, F.J. 110
vagina 198
Vaidya, P.L. 230
Vajrayāna 18
Van Norden, B.W. 4
Vasubandhu 35–6, 111
vedanā (affect valence) 171–2, 181
Vedic tradition 68
view, distortions of 181
Vinaya (Monastic Code of Discipline) 209
viññāṇa (consciousness) 171, 174, 175
virtue 21, 23, 209–10, 216, 232–3
visceral responses, awareness of 179
vision, normal 176
visual consciousness, disruptions to 176–9
visual cortex, damage 178
volitional activities 172–3

w

Warder, A.K. 50
Watson, B. 193
way, the 159

Way, dynamic   138–9
Weiskrantz, L.   178
welfare promotion   21
well-being   11, 12
   deficiencies in   12
   exercises for   12–15, 23
   highest form, nirvana   19
   and karma   19
   through enlightenment   17
Western Buddhism   206, 221–2
Western literary modernism   145–6, 154–9
Whitehead, A.N.   31
whole, the   15, 31
   focusing attention on the   15
   formation   48, 49, 51–2
will
   freedom of   57, 212
   heteronomy of the   213
"will to ignorance"   125
"will to power"   125, 126, 138
wisdom   22–3, 60, 213, 216, 218, 229, 230
Wittgenstein, L.   73, 99
womb *see* Buddha womb teaching
women
   emptiness   193
   inferiority   189, 192, 199
   objectification   194
   as subject   196–7
   as temptresses   191–2
women's bodies   7, 189–202
   as evil/impure   192, 193, 195–6, 197
   revalorization   192, 197–202

Woodhouse, R.   134
Woolf, V.   157
working memory   169, 170, 171, 175, 180–1
worldviews, Song   155

x
Xuedou   147, 149–50, 153–4, 158

y
Yogācāra ("the yogic practice school")   6, 29–30, 34, 35–9, 88–9, 94
   absolute idealism   29
   and metaphysics   36–7
   subjective idealism   29
yogic direct perception   225, 236
Young, Iris Marion   196–7
Yuanwu   147, 148, 149–54, 155, 158, 160
Yunmen   147, 158–9

z
Zen Buddhism   6, 123–43
   and mindfulness meditation   168
   nondualism of   7, 192, 196–7, 199–200
   nonegoistic perspectivism   7
   and uncertainty   145–63
   see also Chan Buddhism
"Zen malady"   152–3, 155
Zen masters   193–6, 207
Zhaozhou   150, 152, 153, 158
Zhou Chi   159
Zongchi   195–6